Cultures and Identities in Colonial British America

Anglo-America in the Transatlantic World
Jack P. Greene, *General Editor*

Cultures and Identities in Colonial British America

Edited by
Robert Olwell and Alan Tully

Johns Hopkins University Press
Baltimore

Printed in the United States of America on acid-free paper

Johns Hopkins Paperback edition, 2015
9 8 7 6 5 4 3 2 1

Johns Hopkins University Press
2715 North Charles Street
Baltimore, Maryland 21218-4363
www.press.jhu.edu

The Library of Congress has cataloged the hardcover edition of this book as follows:

Cultures and identities in colonial British America / edited by Robert Olwell and Alan Tully.
p. cm. — (Anglo-America in the transatlantic world)
Includes bibliographical references and index.
ISBN 0-8018-8251-6 (hardcover : alk. paper)
1. United States—History—Colonial period, ca. 1600–1775.
2. United States—Social conditions—18th century. I. Olwell, Robert, 1960– II. Tully, Alan. III. Anglo-America in the trans-Atlantic world.
E195.C85 2006
306'.0973'09033—dc22 2005010936

A catalog record for this book is available from the British Library.

ISBN-13: 978-1-4214-1846-9
ISBN-10: 1-4214-1846-0

Special discounts are available for bulk purchases of this book. For more information, please contact Special Sales at 410-516-6936 or specialsales@press.jhu.edu.

Johns Hopkins University Press uses environmentally friendly book materials, including recycled text paper that is composed of at least 30 percent post-consumer waste, whenever possible.

Contents

PART III: Politics and Identity

Cultures and Identities in Colonial British America

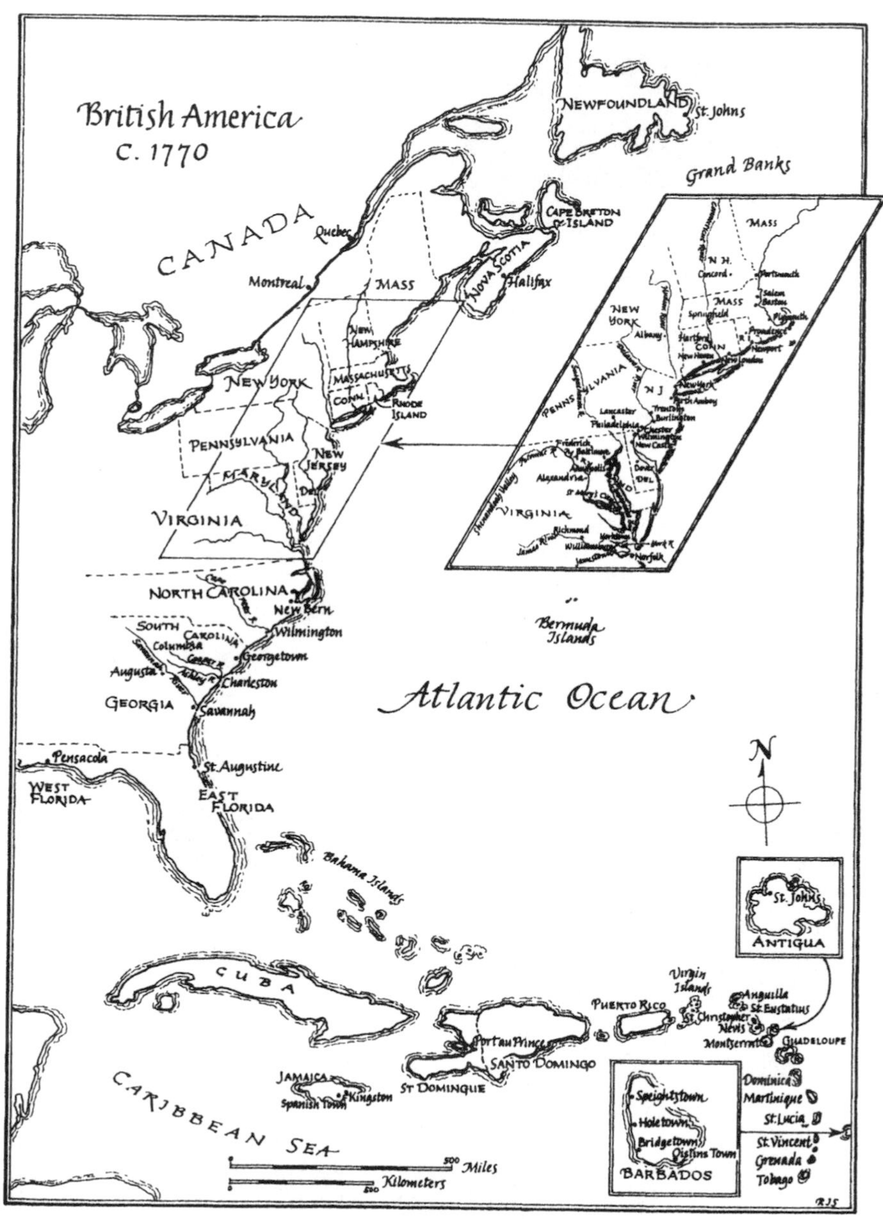

British America, c. 1770, drawn by Richard J. Stinely. From John J. McCusker and Russell R. Menard, *The Economy of British America, 1607–1789,* 2d ed., copyright ©1985, 1991 The University of North Carolina Press. Used by permission of the authors, publisher, and Omohundro Institute of Early American History and Culture.

Introduction

Colonial British America defines a large subject. By almost any historical standard, the 169 years between the establishment of Jamestown and the Declaration of Independence is a long time. For seventeen decades, or almost seven generations, the inhabitants of the North American Atlantic coast and British West Indies were all the colonial subjects of a distant monarch. In purely chronological terms, this broadly shared colonial period contains a good portion of Anglo-America's entire history. As many years lie between the beginning of the colonies and the Declaration of Independence as separate the latter event from the atomic bomb.

Naturally, such a long epoch saw great changes. By its end, British America spanned a vast territory. Between 1607 and 1775, the extent of Britain's American dominions grew from a tiny coastal outpost to a broad swath of settlements extending for fifteen hundred miles in an almost unbroken line along the Atlantic seaboard from Quebec to Florida and westward for 150 miles or more to the foothills of the Appalachians (in several places settlers had already passed through the mountains into the interior). At the end of the Seven Years' War, Britain's imperial map included all of North America east of the Mississippi River.

Simultaneously, in the Caribbean, British rule spread from Barbados, the first English foothold in the region, to encompass a dozen other islands (or island groups). By 1763, the British West Indian archipelago ran from the Bahamas down through the Lesser Antilles to Grenada and Tobago, almost from the coast of Florida to that of South America. North of this chain lay Bermuda, Britain's second oldest colony, founded by shipwrecked settlers bound for Virginia in 1612. South of it, among the Greater Antilles, was Jamaica, conquered from Spain in 1655. In terms of the value of their produce and the tax revenues that could be levied upon them, the Caribbean colonies were far more valuable to the British state than were the colonies on the mainland.

The enormous territorial expansion of Britain's empire in North America was more than matched by an increase in the colonial population. The growth of the colonies dramatically altered their relative importance within the larger British Atlantic world. In the seventeenth century, when the number of colonists was small (in 1660 for example, the total colonial population was only a third that of the city of London alone), the primitive, simplified, and subordinate nature of colonial society was self-evident. By 1710, however, the half-million inhabitants of British America were nearly equal that of the metropolis. By 1760, Britain's two million colonists formed a population treble London's and larger than that of Scotland. In 1775, British Americans accounted for nearly a fifth of all of George III's subjects.[1]

Nor, by the mid-eighteenth century, could British America any longer be considered to be culturally primitive. By 1750, the colonies included urban places such as Boston, New York, Philadelphia, Charlestown, and Bridgetown (Barbados) whose size and sophistication (if not age) equaled or exceeded Norwich, Nottingham, York, Worcester, and other English provincial towns. Likewise, in the fashion of their homes, furnishings, and clothes, as well as in their choice of reading matter (in fact, most of these things were either imported from England, or copied from English models), colonial elites in the third quarter of the eighteenth century lived in a style and manner very like that of the provincial gentry of England.[2]

In part, the astonishing growth of British America was the product of intercontinental migration on an unprecedented scale. Between 1607 and 1775, over two million people traveled from the Old World to begin new lives in British America. The volume of migration increased as the colonies grew. During the half-century of English colonization before 1660, approximately

250,000 people left Britain for America. To these, particularly in Barbados and the Leeward Islands after midcentury, were added fifty thousand African slaves. All told, the rate of debarkation in this first period was about six thousand per year. In the next century, a further one and a half million arrived, at an average of fifteen thousand a year. Finally, in the fifteen years before the outbreak of the Revolution, a half-million people came to British America, an annual average of more than thirty thousand newcomers.[3]

Among those who immigrated to the colonies from Europe before 1775, seven of eight originated in the British Isles (the remainder were largely Germans with a few thousand Swiss and French Huguenots). England alone was the birthplace of half of these; the remainder came from the "Celtic fringe" of Scotland, Wales, and Ireland. Whether they were drawn to the New World seeking freedom and opportunity, or were driven there by Old World economic and political pressures, most European immigrants arrived in British America as unfree laborers, who toiled at the command of another until they had served out their term.[4]

For a majority of all those who arrived in colonial British America, however, even such a hope of future freedom was denied. Enslaved Africans, who represented 60 percent of all the arrivals to British America before 1775, were the most involuntary of migrants. Dreams of New World property and prosperity also spawned nightmares of cruelty and cupidity. As the colonies expanded, so did colonists' appetite for human property. Both the numbers and proportion of African slaves among all migrants to the colonies increased over time, from one in six before 1660, to two in three through the seventeenth century and more afterwards. The cost of slavery and the slave trade in human terms can be seen in the fact that, while Africans may have accounted for six in ten of all migrants to colonial British America between 1607 and 1775, they or their descendants accounted for less than a third of the total colonial population by the end of the period.

Alongside immigration, an increasingly important factor in fueling colonial population growth was natural increase (the routine surplus of births over deaths among native inhabitants). By the mid-eighteenth century, the rate of natural increase among colonial inhabitants was sufficient by itself to double the population each generation. Thus, even with the dramatic upsurge in immigration in the previous fifteen years, the great majority of British colonial inhabitants in 1775 were American-born. The major exception to this rule were the slaves of the West Indies. Both the demographics of the slave trade and the high death rate on the sugar plantations meant that into the nineteenth century most West Indian slaves were African-born.[5]

By 1765, from Charlotteville on the island of Tobago to Charlottia on the banks of the St. Johns River in Florida, to Charlotte and Charlottesville in the Carolina and Virginia piedmont, to Charlottetown on St. Johns (now Prince Edward Island) in the Gulf of St. Lawrence, the British American empire extended for three thousand miles across a wide variety of climates, landscapes, and peoples. But, as this roster of newly founded towns all named for George III's new queen indicates, despite their diversity, the colonies also partook of a shared social, cultural, and political ideology and identity. Throughout this vast region, most literate colonial inhabitants sought to define themselves and their societies as, somehow, British.

But the meaning and character of Britain's empire was itself far from fixed in this period. The legitimacy of Britain's expansive post-1763 territorial claims may have been grudgingly acknowledged in the courts of Europe, but British authority had to be negotiated among the inhabitants of Quebec and with the indigenous inhabitants of the vast trans-Appalachian region. The outbreak of Pontiac's "rebellion" in 1763 demonstrated that Indians wanted a say in defining their own place in the empire. Over the course of the next decade, the imperial relationship and the nature of British sovereignty in America became a subject of heated debate throughout the entire English-speaking world.

For most of the eighteenth century, *Britain* and *empire* were novel and contentious concepts. The Kingdom of Great Britain was legally established only via the Act of Union that combined the Kingdoms of England and Scotland in 1707. One symbol of the newly invented national state was the "Union Jack," an amalgam of the ancient flags of England (the cross of St. George) and Scotland (the cross of St. Andrew). As a nation, Great Britain was in fact newer than all but a few of her American colonies. The contours of this emergent "British" identity were still being constructed. Most observers agreed that the English, Scottish ("North Britons"), and Welsh ("Ancient Britons") were included, but what of the Irish? Many colonial American elites assumed that they, mostly English in origin, Protestant in religion, and loyal to the king, had at least as good a claim to be "British" as the highland Scots, who had rebelled against the monarch in 1715 and 1745, or the Catholic Irish.[6]

The concept of "empire" was equally problematic. Before the 1760s, Britons had happily contrasted their own oceanic "dominions," based on migration and trade, with the territorial "empires" of antiquity or of contemporary

Spanish America that were founded on conquest and tribute. But the territorial acquisitions of the Seven Years' War, not only in North America but also in Africa and India, drastically changed this situation. For the first time, Britain sought to exercise authority over large territories inhabited by non-British peoples. The new British Empire included large numbers of "aliens": French Canadians, Native Americans, Africans, and Bengalis. Almost all Britons agreed that these "strangers" could not be granted traditionally English rights of self-government and would have to be ruled over with appointed and arbitrary power.[7]

To worried Englishmen, the very idea that England had become part of a larger "British empire" threatened traditional "English" liberties and identities. Those schooled in classical history quickly noted that Rome's attainment of empire was closely followed by the end of the Roman Republic. Thus, even while many Britons and British Americans celebrated the rise of the British Empire, others were already anticipating its fall, or at least were counting its costs. A year after the treaty of Paris, Edward Gibbon began to chronicle the decline and fall of the Roman Empire, a project he would complete in 1776.

Colonial British Americans took part in these debates on the meaning of Britain and of empire. Throughout much of the late seventeenth and early eighteenth centuries, colonists occasionally reflected in their public writings and private musings on their relationship to Britain and on the meaning of empire. In the mid-1760s, the Stamp Act crisis drew out the underlying questions into a much more heated and public forum. The ensuing discussion hinged on a historical question: How had the colonial experience shaped British New World societies? Were the inhabitants of colonial British America still culturally and politically British, and thus to be allowed a role in the governance of themselves and of the empire? Or, after the passage of 150 years, did British Americans more closely resemble other, non-British colonial peoples who must be governed?

Seen through English eyes, colonial societies had developed in ways that made them something less than truly British. As English visitors noted, the American colonies contained an exotic array of plants and peoples, customs and practices that could not be found in the old country.[8] But this was more than just a confusion of difference, a jumble of diverse voices, religions, and races. In the course of a century and a half, the cultures of the British colonies had each adapted to suit the limitations and possibilities of their own local situation. In terms of what they ate, and how they spoke, worshipped, and danced, eighteenth-century colonial cultures were indeed different. In the colonies, many European, Indian, and African practices had interacted with each other and with the American environment to produce a variety of cultural hybrids.

Perhaps the greatest of these colonial hybrids was African slavery. Although it had survived in the Mediterranean, and had been brought by the Spanish and Portuguese to the New World, slavery did not exist in England at the time that English colonization began. The first persons who were held as the absolute property of others within English territory were a small number of Africans brought to Virginia either in or before 1619. From this inauspicious beginning, slavery spread through British America and even to Britain itself. By the mid-eighteenth century, Africans could be found in all of the ports of the British Atlantic world; twenty thousand lived in London alone. But slavery remained almost entirely a colonial phenomenon. Most of the Blacks in Britain had arrived as the servants of American masters. Of the one million slaves in the British Empire in 1775, 95 percent lived in the American colonies.

All of these phenomena—the great expansion of settlements and population, the increasing size and sophistication of colonial cities and elites, and the adaptation of new practices such as slavery to local circumstances and opportunities—occurred across all of British America. But over such a great expanse of territory there were also wide regional variations. Older colonies or colonial regions, which had been the destination of immigrants in the early period, became, even by the late seventeenth century, exporters of surplus populations to newer colonies. By the mid-eighteenth century, such internal colonization, and intracolonial migration, was more important than transatlantic immigration in most of the established colonies. As settlement spread away from the coast and across yet ill-defined colonial boundaries, it produced its own domestic economic, social, and political tensions and ambiguities.

Once again, slavery can provide perhaps the best example of differences between and among the colonies. Although slaves were bought and sold throughout British America, and advertisements for slaves can be found in every colonial newspaper, the number of slaves in the local population varied widely across the continent. Those regions where labor demand was high, potential profits great, and the work regime intense imported thousands of slaves. Others areas, lacking one or more of these characteristics, imported fewer. The distribution of slaves across British America was a spectrum running from south to north. At one end were the West Indian colonies where 60 percent of the all slave imports were landed and where, in the eighteenth century, slaves constituted almost 90 percent of the inhabitants. In the mainland colonies nearest the Caribbean (the Floridas, Georgia, and the Carolinas), slaves were approximately half the population. Northward, in the Chesapeake colonies (Virginia, Maryland, and Delaware), about one third of the people were enslaved. In the colonies of the middle Atlantic (Pennsylvania, New Jersey, and New York) the situation was the reverse of the Caribbean; slaves were only 10 percent of the local population. Finally, in New England, the chains of slavery bound just 3 percent of the people.

With the exception of the West Indian islands in which the aboriginal populations were either quickly destroyed or marginalized, the offspring of European and African arrivals experienced an extensive and extended interaction with Native Americans. Despite the demographic disaster that Old World diseases wreaked upon native populations and cultures, the negotiations of trade and treaty, as well as casual social intermingling, were more characteristic of native-colonial relations than were implacable hostility or violent warfare. Through their engagement in commerce, Native Americans were also active participants in the creation of the new transatlantic and colonial worlds.[9]

As a consequence, eighteenth-century colonial British America contained remarkable contrasts. The societies of the Caribbean islands were centered upon the sugar plantations, forced labor camps in which a small number of white masters and overseers brutally exploited an enslaved black majority. In New England, the central institution was the town meeting, in which all freeholders ostensibly had a voice and a vote. Most of New England's inhabitants were native-born to the third or fourth generation, and the region's economy was based largely on small family farms. Even if one takes care to avoid stereotypes (there were after all, some family farms in the Caribbean, and a few thousand slaves in New England) it is remarkable how the same parent culture could have produced two such disparate societies.[10]

English settlement in the West Indies and New England had begun almost simultaneously in the 1620s. Over the course of the ensuing 150 years, the influences of climate, the forces of the market, and immigration or lack of it eroded almost all traces of their common origin. By 1775, the strongest ties between the Caribbean and New England colonies were those of trade rather than culture. Their strongest cultural connection ran not to each other but to their mutual dependence upon, and identification with, Britain.

To investigate the historical processes that could create such divergent colonial societies, one must first examine the dynamic at work within the colonies themselves. The cultures of the British American colonies were complex and fragile creations. The Janus-like predicament of colonists—looking across the Atlantic to Britain and also to their own immediate surroundings and circumstances—was a classic characteristic of the colonial condition. Like contesting magnets, these opposing poles of attraction produced a powerful clash of forces and tensions with colonial societies that gave rise to a multitude of cultural responses and results.

For most immigrants, the desire to return to their land of origin remains strong. When that proves impossible, the response is often to strive to reproduce or perpetuate the old ways in their new worlds. Scholars have long debated the degree to which immigrants to America could successfully transplant or "carryover" distinct cultural practices from the Old World to the New, and pass them from one generation to the next, from the immigrants to their American-born children. In the colonial era, continued immigration meant that Old World ideas and customs might constantly be reinforced by new arrivals, and need not be the fading memories of a founding generation. As shorthand, we might term this imperative for cultural transplantation and perpetuation "inheritance."

But no sooner did immigrants disembark in the New World than they also set in motion a process of ethnogenesis. Most concretely, sexual relations between Europeans, Africans, and Native Americans soon produced new peoples, cultures, and identities. Within a generation of Columbus's landfall, the Spanish had created an elaborate racial typology that differentiated by name and status the position of two dozen or so different categories of New World peoples. For example, a child born of mixed European and African parentage was a "mulatto," of European and Indian, a "mestizo," of Indian and African, a "mustee," and so on through many possible combinations and gradations. The Spanish also coined the term "creole" (criollo) to designate those persons born in the New World of Old World parentage who, although racially and culturally Spanish, were considered slightly inferior to those born in Spain.

Most colonial British Americans had little use for the myriad racial categories created by the Spanish (except for the terms *mulatto* and *mustee,* which they adopted to denote children of partial African parentage). British Americans divided their world into the starker dichotomies of white or black, free or unfree, Christian or heathen. Slave masters used the term "country born" to differentiate creole from African-born slaves. (The former were thought more valuable because they were less likely to die of New World diseases, and were also thought less apt to rebel or run away.) Although not yet seen as racially distinct, Native Americans in the colonial period were likewise usually described by creole authors as a separate people.

But, at least until the final years of the revolutionary crisis, most white colonists identified and differentiated themselves more by kinship, wealth, and religion than by their place of birth. To be sure, a gentleman fresh from England possessed a social asset that he could use to his advantage, but there was no lasting British American equivalent to the "peninsulars" of New Spain. Unless he could marry into the local elite, a newcomer would be left out of the tightly interwoven family ties that united the ruling class of each colony. If an Englishman remained aloof and apart from the wealthy creoles, admiration could quickly turn into resentment.

The concept of creole, however, offers historians a useful way to denote an important process at work within the colonies. The moment when the number of native-born inhabitants surpassed that of immigrants, that is, when a colony obtained a "creole majority," can be seen as a crucial developmental watershed. The experience of creoles is obviously quite unlike that of immigrants. A colony in which most people know the Old World only secondhand is quite different from one peopled largely with new arrivals.

But creoles, because of their Old World "inheritance" and two-sided identity, and their continued colonial relationship to the metropole, are also quite unlike indigenous peoples. Likewise, a creole society is one in which the prevailing culture is an intermixture of metropolitan traditions and colonial—that is, local—innovations and adaptations. Creole societies, like creoles themselves, felt the tug of both local and imperial identities and influences, between inheritance and experience. Historians have termed this process of colonial cultural development and adaptation "creolization."[11]

Because the historical preconditions, environmental parameters, and economic potentialities and limitations varied so hugely across the British Atlantic from Canada to the Caribbean, the process of creolization acted to accelerate cultural diversification and economic specialization among the British American colonies. As each group of colonists adapted to their own unique circumstances, their way of life drifted apart from that of the parent culture and other colonial regions that confronted quite different situations. The grandchildren of Englishmen who had all emigrated from London in 1640 lived very different lives (in terms of diet, clothing, language, and social practices) depending on whether their ancestor had traveled to New England, Virginia, or Barbados.

Creolization was a centrifugal force that worked to create cultures defined by their surroundings rather than by their origins. The outward pressures of creolization, if unchecked, might eventually have produced cultures so distinct that shared identities would have withered to irrelevance. Local, immediate experience would have gradually overwhelmed and eroded inherited traditions and memories of larger, older identities.

But in colonial British America, the effects of creolization, pushing colonial societies apart, were in part offset by countervailing, centripetal, forces that acted to pull colonial societies and cultures back toward each other and back toward the Old World center or metropole. Throughout the colonial period, there was a constant and ever-increasing flow of information, migration, and trade that linked British Americans to Britain (as well as Africa). New arrivals from across the Atlantic could invigorate and reinforce waning Old World customs. Early America was the western shore of a busy Atlantic world of ideas, peoples, and commodities. The ocean was less a moat than a highway.

Although its power waxed and waned according to time and place, the influence of the metropole was a constant presence in every colonial society. Metropolitan rule might be imposed directly, via governors, missionaries, and other royal officials appointed from London; through imperial trade regulations or colonial charters issued by monarchs or passed by Parliament; or even through imperial military forces and the demands and threats of imperial wars. But more commonly and far more importantly, the influence of the metropole was expressed more subtly and indirectly through economic or cultural ties.

Historians have begun to explore the contested meanings that Britain, British identity, and the British Empire had in those regions of the world that were under the control or influence of the merchants of London or the ministers of Westminster, and to demonstrate the powerful allure that Britain and Britishness had for colonial, or native, elites who sought membership in the imperial ruling class or who wanted merely to borrow the cultural authority of the Old World to help them govern the New.[12]

The desire of colonial British Americans to remake themselves and colonial society in British ways, and the resulting effects, have been termed "anglicization." Based neither upon inheritance nor experience, anglicization was largely a form of imitation and aspiration. The desire to "improve" their colonial world so that it might measure up to metropolitan standards was one of the most potent bonds of empire but it was also one of the most volatile. The chronic sense of inferiority that led colonials to admire and imitate British ways could easily become explosive if their aspirations and strivings to assimilate were met only with humiliating rebuff.[13]

From these two contrasting forces, creolization and anglicization, New World experience or possibilities and Old World inheritance or imitation, there emerged an ongoing dynamic that created colonial cultures. Taken together, their contrary influences frame colonial history and explain the creation and nature of colonial societies. When these two contesting forces interacted with other influential factors the creation of identities and cultures most clearly emerges as part of an ongoing historical process.

In chronological terms, the relative importance of New World experience and Old World inheritance changed as a given colony was transformed from an isolated outpost on the Atlantic coast into a populous, stable, and secure society. This developmental model of colonial change might be seen as occurring in three distinct phases.[14] In the first, or settlement phase, colonists were almost entirely immigrants with little firsthand experience of their new surroundings. Their initial plans and designs for agriculture, diet, and housing, as well as their models for social organizations, were necessarily those of the world they had left behind. But settlers soon discovered that many of these customary practices were unsuited to the new environment. In the colonies, some European crops and animals withered, while others thrived beyond expectation. Similarly, institutions that worked in established highly populated and differentiated Old World societies proved unfeasible or impractical on the isolated and sparsely populated colonial frontier.

The settlers' initial response was to adapt what they knew to the novel situation. Practices that could not be made to serve a practical purpose were discarded. The corruption of the Old World emphasis on indentured craft apprenticeship to the New World need for bound workers to hoe tobacco in Virginia or Barbados is an example of the first. The lack of towns in either colony is an instance of the latter. The result, in this first stage, was a dramatic "simplification" of society. Only the essentials needed for survival were retained. Those Old World ideas and practices that were abandoned in this process were the equivalent of the pianos that littered the route of the wagon trains across the American west in the nineteenth century.

Only after the problems of survival were solved could the colony progress toward the next phase of development. In this second period, the "settling down" phase, colonists were ready to learn and exploit what the New World and its inhabitants offered. First and foremost in this second phase was an eagerness to experiment with new plants and practices so as to maximize the economic potential of the colony, and the possibilities for individual wealth that it offered. The turn toward slavery, and toward the various regional "commodity cultures" in the late seventeenth century is one instance of this process. Having secured their collective and individual survival in the first period, colonists in the second sought to secure their collective and individual success.

Alongside such economically driven pursuits, colonists in the second era also acted collectively to improve their social environment and to make colonial cultural practices, such as kinship, more elaborate. Here too, however, the emphasis was on what works best rather than on preserving Old World traditions for their own sake. As the population grew and creoles became more numerous (although perhaps not yet a majority), colonial social organizations and institutions also became more complex, powerful, and active.[15]

The changes in economic development and social elaboration that colonies saw in the second phase were dictated by the nature of the colonial environment and local factors. It was during this period that the push of creolization was most powerful. Consequently, it was at the turn of the eighteenth century, when most parts of colonial British America were in this phase of their development, that their differences, both from each other and from Britain, were probably most pronounced.

In the third phase of colonial development, the inhabitants of British America sought to improve themselves and their societies and to "civilize" colonial society. The standard for comparison and model for replication was that of Britain itself. If the goals in the first two phases were survival and success respectively, in the third period the golden ring was status. Having made a success of America, wealthy colonists now increasingly sought to live, and be recognized as, gentlemen and attendant ladies. The very richest of the colonists, especially in the Caribbean, actually returned with their wealth to Britain.

But such a triumphant pilgrimage was beyond the resources of most colonial elites. (By the standards of the English aristocracy, most wealthy colonials were decidedly middle-class.) Instead, if they could not afford to live in Britain, colonists sought to make the colonies more British.

By the third phase of colonial development, generations of intermarriage and accumulated wealth had produced within many of the (increasingly creole) colonial populations a recognizable and functional elite. Among the elite the lure of anglicization was strongest, for it was they who stood most to benefit from it. The more that colonial society could be made to resemble Britain, the more the rulers of colonial society could claim membership in the British ruling class and the more they could (or so they hoped) command the respect and deference of their poorer neighbors.

The imperative to transform the New World into the Old was in part a political project implemented in large measure through a "civilizing process": consumption, refinement, and the emulation of institutional benchmarks and transatlantic discourses. Although colonial elites were a small minority of the population, their increasing control over the institutions of colonial society enabled them to bend colonial social practices and institutions toward British models.

In the third period of colonial development the pull of anglicization was greater than the push of creolization, and colonies became more alike as they all became more like England. But anglicization could never completely have its way. In order to buy the British goods they needed to reshape themselves into a landed "gentry," colonial elites could never completely abandon the colonial practices, especially plantation slavery, upon which their wealth and status depended. They could not halt the ongoing elaboration of provincial identities and cultures even if they had wanted to; for the process of creolization had its own momentum and logic.

It is possible to set any particular colony, at any particular time in its history, in one of the three parts of this developmental framework. Obviously, at the time of their foundation, all colonies are in phase one, but since the colonies were established at different times over the course of more than a century, two colonies might be at quite different stages simultaneously. For example, when Carolina was established in 1670, New England, Virginia, and Barbados had already progressed to phase two. In 1732, when Georgia was founded, these older regions were entering phase three, and South Carolina was in the second phase of its development.

Moreover, although all colonies proceeded through the same sequence, they did not necessarily do so at the same rate. Only when a colony had successfully mastered each phase could it proceed toward the next. Thus, New England solved its survival problem almost immediately and was in phase two within years of its founding, while Virginia was not safely out of the woods until almost fifty years after the establishment of Jamestown.

The shift from phase two to three, from the pursuit of success to the pursuit of status, was even more problematic. This transition was predicated upon the emergence of a coherent and confident creole elite within the colony. Colonies that were successful in economic terms might be less so as social organizations. The best example of such an "arrested development" were the smaller West Indian colonies. In the Leeward Islands, the wealthiest landowners were typically absentee planters who resided in Britain. Rather than try to transform their islands into miniature Englands (a difficult task in a society that was 90 percent African slaves) it was easier to simply return to Britain. Consequently, with the possible exception of Barbados (whose eighteenth-century nickname was indeed "Little England"), to the end of the colonial era all of the island colonies lacked a resident elite that was numerous and secure enough to take the anglicization project any further than personal consumption and exaggerated public claims.

Geography and landscape had a profound effect upon the creolization-anglicization dynamic. Within one colony, movement across space could function as the equivalent of the passage of time. A week's journey from the coast to the frontier might resemble travel backward across several generations, from a sophisticated, anglicized, port city (phase three), to the successful, but creole, agricultural interior (phase two), to the rude simplicity of the backcountry, where survival might still be precarious (phase one). Similarly, a fertile and navigable river valley might be culturally and economically more akin to the distant coast than to adjacent upland country.

Colonial cities were the parts of the colonial world that were closest to Britain in every sense. As ports, they were the threshold over which British goods, as well as news and people, crossed. As centers of colonial political, economic, and elite cultural life, cities felt the pull of anglicization most strongly and wealthy city residents were most able to realize their desire to "civilize" colonial society. In the backcountry, or in more isolated and less developed inland or tidewater regions, Britain both seemed (and was) much farther away, and the rawness and power of the New World environment could prove daunting.

Depending on their situation, different peoples reacted to the contrary push-pull of creolization and anglicization in different ways. For non-English colonists, the "empire of goods" and the cultural and political benefits of Britishness could act as a powerful agent of assimilation into a new "British" identity. All the inhabitants of the colonies could perceive the possibilities that British goods offered for improved status within both the larger colonial community and their own group. Even Native Americans and African slaves sought to acquire British manufactures and clothes, although they might blend them into various distinctive styles. Because the boundaries of Britishness were not yet determined, the idea could seem an inclusive and expansive one to many. To members of ethnic minorities, the process of anglicization was an invitation to their cultures and communities to partake in their own colonization and assimilation.

Because anglicization required a significant investment of both economic and political resources (although it also promised equally large returns), wealth was a powerful determinant of its effect. The richer colonists were, the more British goods they were likely to consume, the more likely they were to read British works, correspond with British merchants, family, or friends, and perhaps to even have traveled to Britain. Poverty, on the other hand, as much as geographic space, negated the pull of anglicization. Within the confines of a small colonial city like Boston, the degree of interaction with metropolitan culture could vary widely among different social classes living on the same street.

Cultural constructions of gender were also shaped by, or themselves may have shaped, the creolization-anglicization dynamic. Wealthy colonial wives consumed British goods as avidly as did their husbands. On the frontier they, like men, did without. But consumption, fashion, and luxury were seen by most eighteenth-century Anglo-Americans in highly gendered, and largely pejorative, terms. Political economists linked the rise in civility and commerce to a decline in manly and civic virtue. It is revealing that Benjamin Franklin blamed his own switch from a humble (and creole) "earthen Porringer with a Pewter Spoon" to imported china and silver on his wife's desire to keep up appearances with the neighbors.[16] It may also be the case that the arrival of British goods, such as tea sets and tea furniture, might have altered the organization of domestic space and redrawn the lines of gendered sociability within colonial homes.[17]

The essays that follow all focus upon some aspect of the complex dynamics between the imperatives of creolization and anglicization in early modern

British America. The contributors add new and specific perspectives to our general understanding of colonial development and its discontents. The tensions inherent in the colonial condition are sharply delineated in some cases and shrouded in others according to the complexities of local and transatlantic identities and contexts. Collectively, these essays illustrate the impulses of imitation, adaptation, and creativity that created numerous distinctive cultures, and yet also laid the foundations upon which an American identity could later emerge. This paradox is at the heart of the British American colonial experience.

The twelve essays in this volume are divided into three parts, each of which roughly correlates to one of the phases of colonial development described above. Part one, chapters one through four, focuses upon the challenges that nature and geography posed to European and African colonists. The sheer scale of the natural environment, and the vast contours of the Atlantic landscape, forcibly removed immigrants from the behaviors, contexts, and connections of their old lives and forced them to think and act in new ways. Colonists struggled to comprehend and give order to the strange and challenging new world that they found themselves in, and also to construct new identities that would enable them to dwell within it. Like Adam in paradise, early colonists had not only to number and name the beasts of the field but also to seek out fig leaves to cover their own cultural nakedness.

Part two, chapters five through eight, turns to the second phase of colonial development in which economic pursuits became of primary importance in shaping colonial societies. The authors in this section, while spanning the years from the mid-seventeenth to the late eighteenth centuries, and examining regions as diverse as the New England coast, Chesapeake, and Pennsylvania frontier, all attend to the power that the market had in driving colonists' actions and in shaping colonial culture. Although all the people whose lives are scrutinized in this section were interested in making a living, or making a profit, their very diverse local circumstances led them to take vastly different steps toward this goal, with equally divergent results. Colonial Americans may have all heard the same market-oriented drumbeat, but they had innumerable ways of dancing to the music.

Finally, the essays in the third section of the book, chapters nine through twelve, attend to the final phase of colonial development and to colonial politics and political aspirations. Political life and language was one of the most powerful ties of empire in the colonial period. In their speeches and resolutions in their provincial assemblies, and in their attitudes as expressed in their letters and newspapers, local elites sought to emulate and enact their notions of what it meant to be an independent British gentleman. At the same time, other groups within colonial society, from yeoman farmers and urban artisans to Native Americans, women, or even slaves could seek to assert their own influence and expectations. The boundaries between the imperial subject and individual subjectivity were being more clearly delineated, and questions about how particular provincialisms found expression in those discourses became especially germane during the decades immediately preceding the Revolution.

In the crisis of 1775–76, the disintegration of the first British Empire forced all of the inhabitants of British America to confront issues of identity. When colonial societies and individual colonists decided to support, either actively or passively, the colonial cause or the imperial status quo, they were choosing in essence between the forces of creolization or anglicization. Were they fundamentally American or British? But beneath that starkness of choice lay a formidable array of identity-related and culturally shaped complexities—a continuation of the often contradictory yet creative forces that constituted the colonial British American heritage.

Part I / Environment and Identity

CHAPTER ONE

The Nature of Slavery

Environmental Disorder and Slave Agency in Colonial South Carolina

S. Max Edelson

As he made his way on horseback across a South Carolina beach in the late 1770s, William Bartram reflected that it was "pleasant riding on this clean hard sand, paved with shells of various colours." A sighting on the horizon broke the naturalist's reverie with his surroundings. An approaching "party of Negroes" appeared to be a "predatory band" of the kind known to have "attacked, robbed, and sometimes murdered" those whites who ventured alone into the Lowcountry's many isolated tracts. Bartram had once before found himself surrounded by Africans in a "desolate place." On his short-lived East Florida plantation in 1766 with "no Wife, no Friend, no Companion, no Neighbour, no [white] Human inhabitant" nearby, Bartram's six slaves became "rather plagues than aids to him." His friends among South Carolina's planter elite warned that his "negros will run away or murder thee." One enslaved man proved "so insolent as to threaten his Life."[1] Bartram survived his brief career as a Florida planter only to face another group of potentially hostile slaves in another remote place. Without weapons or companions, he was "situated every way in their power."

Although "armed with clubs, axes and hoes," they let him "pass peaceably." Their "chief informed me whom they belonged to, and said they were going to man a new quarter at the West end of the bay." What he suspected were weapons turned out to be tools; this "predatory band" proved to be an orderly, almost deferential, detachment of workers assigned the task of clearing a new rice field. Bartram's inability to predict the intentions of slaves making their way across the sparsely settled Lowcountry gave rise to a momentary fear for his safety, a dark cloud of apprehension that dissipated quickly after they departed. The next day, and several miles farther into his journey, he returned to his characteristically romantic musings on the natural world as he rode "over expansive savannas, charmingly decorated with late autumnal flowers."[2]

South Carolina colonists understood slaves and nature together, as the sources of their prosperity and as sources of disorder that threatened their plantations, their society's future, and their lives. How did they come to terms with their dependence on a people and a place they saw as unpredictably wild? Those who lived every day outnumbered by slaves and surrounded by unsettled spaces could not resolve their predicament, as Bartram did, by simply exiting the scene. In a varied body of eighteenth-century poetry and prose, commentators placed the people planters enslaved and the subtropical landscape they settled in circulation with one another conceptually. Slaves appeared at times in these ruminations as extensions of the planter's will, agents deployed in transforming wilderness into ordered fields of maize, rice, and indigo; but they could also seem like wild beasts in human form, doppelgangers of the predators that lurked in the swamps and forests, ready to lay waste to plantations. Those who ridiculed South Carolina's culture as inherently uncivil joined together images of supposedly savage Africans with the swampy, stormy, superabundant Lowcountry as mutually reinforcing characteristics of an uncouth place. Slaves made an independent living on marginal and wild spaces but also demonstrated their capabilities as runaways who could live off the land. Despite the dangers planters courted by populating the plantation countryside with Africans, their belief that the region's climate enervated European bodies made their slaves indispensable mediators with the natural world. As they formulated equations that described their colony's prospects, slaves and nature were like dependent variables: a value for one was required to solve for the other.

Other Wild Beasts: Narratives of Disorder and Development

Writers who narrated the developmental progress of South Carolina's plantation society resorted, with uncanny repetition, to the same turn of phrase to convey their sense of a besieged world of agricultural order. They fixated on animals that emerged from the wilderness—wolves, bears, panthers, tigers, and other "wild beasts"—to threaten plantation society from the undeveloped interior. Colonial South Carolina was a hybrid society that possessed, like other mainland colonies, an exposed western border. The province's growing black majority also mirrored the unbalanced demography of the English Caribbean. When white South Carolinians invoked the figures of wild beasts stalking an unguarded internal frontier, allusions to this traditional embodiment of European fears of nature might have been penned in Boston or Philadelphia. What made such associations distinctive was the presence of black people in these wilderness encounters. Slaves appeared in reflections on colonial progress both as workers whose labor kept the wolves at bay and, because of their "barbarous, wild, savage natures,"[3] as predators that might bring plantation society to ruin.

Encamped with his party of explorers near the Santee River's swamps at the close of the seventeenth century, naturalist John Lawson was awakened by the "dismall'st and most hideous Noise that ever pierc'd my Ears." As his Native American guide informed him, "endless Numbers of Panthers, Tygers, Wolves, and other Beasts of Prey" emerged from the swamps every night in pursuit of deer.[4] Early modern naturalists categorized animals by their place along a continuum that stretched from the tamest domestic species to the most wild. The creatures that Lawson believed he heard howling in the Santee River swamps epitomized the most dangerously wild sort, those long used to give form to fears of the natural world.[5] By the late 1720s, when recently settled rice plantations along the Santee approached the site of Lawson's rude awakening, naturalist Mark Catesby echoed his predecessor's encounter with wildness to reflect on the colony's prospects for territorial expansion. The forces of "commerce, and luxury" had civilized the coastal plain, while the upper reaches of the province remained "unpeopled, and possessed by wolves, bear, panthers, and other beasts."[6] Catesby's use of the phrase resonated with biblical overtones. The idea that righteous communities earned seasons of plenty while "wild beasts" laid waste to errant backsliders helped strengthen the case for ongoing colonization. It also pointed to the vulnerability such endeavors faced by their proximity to wilderness.[7] As long as wild spaces harbored predatory animals within reach of settled plantation society, the virtuous work of enlarging an ordered domain must continue. The future of plantation society lay in displacing wild beasts with European colonists by transforming habitats into fields.

While Catesby envisioned the plantation landscape's future expansion, others looked back to the past to imagine the first tenuous moments when settlers had transformed wild spaces into ordered agricultural ones. In 1744 "Agricola" urged his fellow planters to grow and manufacture indigo, then an experimental commodity that promised to relieve their economy's dependence on rice as a staple crop. He asked them to emulate the pioneering behavior of the first rice planters. Their ancestors had ventured into "thick and deep Swamps" to cultivate rice. Without their willingness to live and work in a rank wilderness, he asked, "how many fine Estates would to this Day have remained ungotten; and how many valuable Tracts of Land would now have remain'd in the very Heart of our Settlements wast[e] and uncultivated, and Harbours only for Bears and Tygers and other Beasts of Prey?"[8] Vicious animals were figures that represented the dangers of venturing into places that lay beyond European control. Explicit fears of animal attacks masked deeper concerns in these reflections featuring "wild beasts." Imagining this settled landscape as a veneer imposed on a wasteland encouraged readers to see the establishment of plantations as, at best, a incomplete solution to the problem of securing spatial order. The mettle of the planter's own character—his virtue, competence, and expertise—was required to hold the line against a hostile natural world.

For these commentators on cultivation and nature, African and African-American slaves might stand on either side of this line separating environmental order from the prospect of disorder. When "cleared, opened, and sweetened by Culture," reasoned Governor James Glen, swamp wastes became remarkably fertile rice lands. Rice agriculture had "drained and cultivated" the Lowcountry's "otherwise useless" swamps, as Lieutenant Governor William Bull argued in a similar vein; if left in their natural state, these swamps would have served as "inaccessible shelter for deserting slaves and wild beasts."[9] As workers, slaves wielded the axes that turned swamps into fields, the hoes that beat back infestations of weeds, and the shovels and picks that excavated the ditches and drains required to control water on lowcountry rice plantations. Slaves redeemed wild spaces for agriculture. As runaways, rebels, and thieves who acted beyond planters' scrutiny, however, they might join the list of predators that wild spaces harbored. In these imaginative associations, Africans possessed dual personalities, one savage and the other civil, that specific environments brought to the surface of behavior or suppressed.

Charles Woodmason's 1757 Georgic poem "Indico" pitted slaves against wolves in lowcountry forests, locked in a battle to give South Carolina its second staple commodity. "Arm'd with destructive Steel thy Negroes bring," Woodmason writes, "With Blows repeated let the Woodlands ring." As they brought down trees with fire and ax, slaves initiated a "Sylvan War" that encircled plantations with defensive clearings safe from "midnight Wolves, impell'd by Hunger's Pow'r." An aggressive trade drawing slaves from "Angola's Coast, and savage Gambia's Shores" to "this new World" assured planters of a steady supply of workers "Whose Constitutions, temper'd to the Heat / By Situation of their native Soil, / Best bear the scorching Suns, and rustic Toil." Woodmason's vision of heroic planters as, in the words of David Shields, "*de novo* creators, witnessing the imposition of a design upon a seemingly chaotic natural profusion" featured slaves as the primary agents of agricultural expansion.[10]

Although South Carolina's plantation society enjoyed, at the close of the colonial era, the kind of territorial security and commercial prosperity that earlier writers could only wish for, another Georgic, "Carolina; or, the Planter" (1776), amplifies the adversarial confrontation between slaves, woods, and the wild beasts harbored within them with a heightened sense of peril. Planter-poet George Ogilvie surveyed "Nature's wild landscape" and found Europeans, in the figure of a hunter turning away from ominous woods, incapacitated by fear at the edge of the wilderness. A tangle of roots, thorns, and vines obstructs the "invader's way" but offers shelter to "countless serpents." Ogilvie's forests rang with paralyzing cries:

> And hark! from dark recesses of the wood,
> How fierce the language of the rav'nous brood!
> Loud screams the *Wild-cat, Wolves* yet louder howl,
> And shaggy *Bears* like distant thunder growl;
> Whilst *Cat-o-mountains*, with discordant roar,
> Join the harsh grunting of the tusked boar.
> Till circling danger ev'ry sense subdues
> But fear, which to bewilder'd thought renews
> The fabl'd phantoms of our childish age,
> And demons in the shape of monsters rage.

In "Carolina; or, the Planter" wild beasts along with insects, disease, and volatile weather, constituted a menacing natural front that slaves must erode through steady labor at clearing tree cover. The "gleaming ax your vig'rous lab'rers wield" opened secluded spaces to view, eliminated shelters for dangerous animals, and carved a clear border between field and forest.[11] While other commentators equated runaway slaves with wild beasts, these two poets imagined them as the indispensable motive force—"hands" in the planters' lexicon—that maintained and expanded the plantation landscape.

In 1671, when the year-old Ashley River settlement struggled to survive as a lone European outpost surrounded by Native Americans, a settler recorded that "we are something in feare of [th]e Wol[v]es, who are too plenty."[12] Colonists in the eighteenth-century Lowcountry, however, seldom came face to face with the "wild beasts" that loomed large in European consciousness as symbols of untamed wilderness and specters of social decline. Wolves, bears, and other large mammals, highly sensitive to habitat destruction and the human presence on the land, retreated deep into the Carolina interior in advance of plantation settlements. The colonial legislature passed several acts "to encourage destroying beasts of prey" before 1740 that rewarded Indian hunters for depopulating the colony of its larger carnivores. Early planters mentioned flooding, drought, and hurricanes as natural threats, but rarely the "red in tooth and claw" encounters between settlers and predators that these writers placed front and center in their meditations on slavery, agriculture, and nature. In fact, the most deadly creature in early Carolina was the malaria-bearing mosquito, but in this early era colonists considered the insect as an exotic pest rather than a vector for life-threatening infections. Alligators, a novel American menace for European colonists, similarly inspired little in the way of mortal fear and were regarded as posing a danger only to dogs and "other young creatures about a plantation."[13] Settlers encountered the wild beasts of the unsettled Lowcountry primarily in their imaginations, as figures that imbued spaces beyond the plantations with malevolence toward European enterprise.

Slaves as Environmental Agents within and beyond Plantations

As South Carolina legislators reflected on the meaning of a 1739 slave uprising at Stono River that left more than twenty whites dead, they attributed its root causes to the recent, robust expansion of plantation production. Because planters had forced thousands of slaves into the grueling labor of cultivating rice, it was, ironically, "our own Industry" that proved to "be the Means of taking from us all the Sweets of Life and of rendering us liable to the Loss of our Lives and Fortunes." The hurricane that devastated Charlestown and its surrounding countryside in 1752 likewise stirred colonists to acknowledge "a deep sense of their dependent condition," exposing a reliance on the natural world that was as great, and double-edged, as their dependence on African slavery. The Lowcountry's fertile freshwater swamps and its extended subtropical growing season made rice-planting fortunes possible, but at the cost of an annual "hurricane time" that in this calamitous year demolished buildings, carried off livestock, and leveled flourishing fields. For years afterwards travelers navigated around broken trees that the storm had uprooted and scattered across the roads.[14]

The rebellion and the hurricane, the two most memorable catastrophes of their kinds in the eighteenth century, became touchstone events in colonists' memories. The "great power and indiscriminate fury" of the attacking slaves and the "violent and terrible Hurricane" undermined a contented admiration for their "fine and flourishing Collony" and inspired dark visions of South Carolina's demise at the hands of uncontrollable forces. The disasters of 1739 and 1752 forced colonists to acknowledge that their New World province drew its economic vitality from two sources that, like a lowcountry river prone to overflowing its banks, could be channeled toward profitable production but were also capable of wreaking "sad havock" across the plantation landscape.[15]

Writers who described ax-wielding slaves doing battle against the woods and the dangers that lurked there saw Africans as extensions of their masters' agency. Their labor magnified the power of a single planter, enabling him to turn overgrown tracts into productive plantation land. The commonplace practices of slaves at work in and around plantations reveals that they were more than simply "hands" that South Carolina planters deployed to transform an unruly wilderness and hold the line against its encroachments. Attuned to the complexities of the natural world that surrounded lowcountry plantations and encouraged by necessity and desire to make extensive use of its resources, slaves came into engagement with both the wild and cultivated sides of this landscape. As small-scale producers who grew and gathered things to eat and goods to sell and as runaways who preyed on plantations like the wild beasts their masters feared, slaves acted as environmental agents in the spaces where plantations and wilderness met. Planters tried to impose a hard line of separation between plantations and wilderness, but slaves opened and inhabited the spaces in between.

Slaves served as South Carolina's navigators, transporting goods to market, carrying letters, and guiding European travelers. Black cowboys dispersed into unclaimed savannas to tend the cattle herds that supported the colony's livestock industry.[16] Those from rice-growing areas in West Africa came to the Lowcountry with a cultivated eye for discerning how the meandering watercourses and swamp systems next to which they lived and in which they worked might replenish field fertility, supply rice plants with water, and drown competing weeds.[17] By the middle decades of the eighteenth century, such pioneering encounters with the natural world grew more rare for most field laborers. As the regimen of rice, indigo, and provisions labor resolved into a year-round routine, slaves interacted with the altered world of the plantation more intensively. They attacked weeds with hoes throughout the growing season, repaired irrigation banks and ditches throughout the winter, and, armed with axes, turned woodlands and swamps into new fields before the next round of spring planting began.

At night, on Sunday, and in the late afternoon after they had completed their daily tasks, however, slaves ventured routinely into the swamps, forests, and other spaces that separated plantations from one another. Planters allocated slaves "as much land as they can handle," often on the unclaimed uplands, wetlands, and pastures just inside or beyond property boundary lines. Slaves used the region's abundant supply of open ranges to raise livestock, selling rendered tallow, meat, and live animals for cash. One of Richard Hutson's slaves pastured his mare "on the other side of the Cut." His master knew about the animal but had never seen it. Just beyond plantation fields, on plots that planters referred to as their "fields" and "gardens," slaves cultivated a wide range of European, American, and African produce, from commodities such as cotton and rice to food crops including turnips, maize, "Guinea rice," sweet potatoes, beans, peanuts, watermelons, squash, pumpkins, and sesame. They gathered and sold honey and myrtle wax to their masters.[18] Ex-slave Charles Ball recounted his experiences as an avid exploiter of such natural resources during the first decade of the nineteenth century. After a forced transportation from Maryland, Ball soon found his bearings in South Carolina, becoming "well acquainted with the woods and swamps for several miles round our plantation." He established his own "garden in the woods" from which he gathered "lettuce, and other salads." Venturing deep into the swamps, he set traps for raccoons, opossums, and rabbits. Putting a growing knowledge of the area's wildlife to use, he captured ten snapping turtles as they attempted to lay their eggs and dug a makeshift holding tank that preserved them.[19]

Knowledge of the woods made it possible for slaves to adapt an African pharmacopoeia and sustain spiritual practices with gathered plants. "Negroes are the only people," wrote lowcountry visitor Janet Schaw, "that seem to pay any attention to the various uses that the wild vegetables may be put to." Such work enhanced the role of doctors and conjurers as leaders within plantation communities and offered alternatives to planters' harsh medicinal regimens of purgatives and emetics.[20] Sampson, a "Negro who used frequently to go about with *Rattle-Snakes* in Calabashes," earned his freedom as well as a government annuity for perfecting a snakebite cure. He proved his treatment's efficacy by "suffering himself to be bitten by the most venomous Snakes" and then applying a healing salve concocted from heart snakeroot, spleenwort, club-moss, and creeping goldilocks to the mortified wound. Naturalist John Bartram's host showed him "several plants that [Europeans] made use of for to heal [the] different infirmities of th[ei]r family & neighbors." Just as they exploited African agricultural skills to master rice planting, colonists made use of their slaves' expertise with medicinal plants.[21]

Those who worked in these wild and semi-wild spaces as slaves exercised a de facto possession over the borderlands at the edges of plantation settlements. Alive with movement and work, this interstice between plantation fields was a space understood, used, and traversed primarily by Africans and African Americans. When activities on such marginal lands remained within the orbit of planters' influence, they seemed to bring out those characteristics that masters most desired in their slaves as agents. Planters tended to approve of slaves' work in their own fields, gardens, and hunting grounds. The task system, by which slaves claimed time to produce independently after they completed a daily work assignment, also extended a customary right to make use of uncultivated lands within and beyond the plantation. By making this extralegal, but nonetheless proprietary, stake in "all their Little Estates" secure, masters encouraged slaves to render up a measure of obedience and find more reasons to remain on plantations than to run away from them.[22]

Slaves' abilities to survive and navigate within such spaces, however, also threatened to turn these lands from a slave-controlled plantation hinterland into a staging ground for subversive actions. When they directed their environmental agency against their masters' authority, they extended the most dangerous kind of wilderness right to the planter's doorstep. For every slave like the praised and manumitted Sampson, colonists suspected, there were countless others who used their facility with wild plants to poison whites, the "most common single offense that brought slaves to the gallows."[23]

Colonial South Carolina runaways departed most frequently between June and September to avoid the most onerous phase of rice labor. Charles Ball's own August runaway attempts, separated by twenty years, also depended on available supplies of ripening corn, peaches, and sweet potatoes he could expect to pilfer along his escape route to the Chesapeake. Ball avoided roadways and retreated into the swamps during the daytime, navigating northward by the stars and telling time by the position of the rising sun. Runaway advertisements noted that escaped boatmen, itinerant craftsmen, and other skilled workers knew their way around the province and made frequent journeys to distant plantation districts to visit family and friends.[24]

Runaways sometimes joined together in gangs that preyed on plantation settlements. Colonists monitored with apprehension slaves who moved together through the unguarded spaces of the Lowcountry and "lurketh about in [the] swamps among [the] inhabitants." Several runaways joined the crew of a French privateer in 1758, intent on augmenting their numbers by piloting the vessel to the colony's southern coast and "plundering some Plantations . . . of their Negroes." After more than a hundred slaves fled into the interior in 1766, South Carolina officials suspected them of planning a "general insurrection." Acting governor William Bull proposed recruiting Catawba Indians, another group with extensive knowledge of the Lowcountry's unsettled places, to capture them.[25] By January 1774, a band of runaways had been thinning the ranks of George Austin's cattle for a year, killing them "while they feed in the Day-time about the Woods." Only in midsummer did a search party of overseers and "able Fellows" surprise these "Rogues" who had been encamped at a "pretty secure retreat at the head of a small Creek." Ensconced in the "thick woods" at an "extremity" of Austin's land, their camp contained a canoe and ample stockpiles of fish and grain. These gangs menaced the plantations their labor had once sustained from the cover of wilderness and during wartime crises that impaired colonists' ability to respond with force. Writing in the midst of the Seven Years' War, Governor James Glen viewed slaves as the colony's most "dangerous Enemies . . . ready to revolt on the first Opportunity, and are Eight Times as many in Number as there are white Men able to bear arms."[26] The demonstrated practice of runaway groups living off the land near plantation neighborhoods like guerrilla forces sparked fears of a Stono-like uprising in which slaves might emerge from the woods to kill colonists, rather than merely poach and slaughter their cows.

The typical lowcountry plantation centered on a village-like core of white residences, gardens, barns, and workshops from which masters and overseers directed slave work. Situated on high and dry pinelands, this "settlement" area alone was entirely cleared of trees and opened to unobstructed view. Surrounding this was a larger ring of rice, indigo, and corn fields, scattered and interspersed among uncleared wetlands and woodlands. Slaves lived in impermanent structures, called "huts" rather than houses, that often adjoined the fields where they completed their daily tasks or stood next to the barns where they pounded the rice they had harvested at the close of every growing season.[27] Between these fields and at their edges, slaves planted their own crops in tracts their masters recognized but did little to regulate. Under cover of darkness, slaves took to the wilderness to hunt, gather, and attempt to escape their enslavement. Planters commissioned estate maps that rendered these spaces from a bird's-eye perspective, as if legal title to the land also conferred an ability to open it to absolute scrutiny. Taking into account the wide ambit of slaves' activities throughout this landscape offers a view from ground level. Slaves exercised a practical command of liminal spaces in the Lowcountry in ways their masters could never match nor always control.

Slaves as Environmental Mediators in a Volatile Climate

Despite the dangers of extraordinary events such as slave uprisings and mass runaway attempts, planters depended on slaves as indispensable environmental mediators because they saw themselves as fundamentally unsuited to the climate. The region's turbulent weather, its life-threatening diseases, and its oppressive heat convinced Europeans that their bodies and their characters were in mortal jeopardy in a place buffeted by subtropical extremes. As planters sought refuge from this climate, they left Africans and African Americans to endure unmediated exposure to its enervating effects while at work in swamps, fields, and forests. Social critics, scientific observers, and economic commentators saw slaves as the colony's primary interlocutors with the natural world. They ventured where planters feared to go and survived where their masters died. Whether attempting to demean South Carolina society as crude or mounting a justification for African slavery as environmentally necessary, these observers envisioned a plantation landscape inhabited by slaves rather than mastered by planters.[28]

Detractors of this slave colony satirized planters' claims to civility, blending images of stagnant swamps and uncouth Africans to make the point that South Carolina was a place too savage to redeem. After experiencing the vast black majorities of the plantation districts in 1737, Swiss immigrant Samuel Dyssli declared: "Carolina looks more like a negro country than like a country settled by white people." With mortal diseases rampant across the countryside and forests teeming with "tigers, wolves, wildcats," his slight rested as much on the colony's natural environment as on its demography.[29] Persecuted loyalist Robert Wells sent a poem to his wife at their Johns Island plantation that feared for her safety, "sequestered in the Marshy Shade / Agues and Fevers lurking in each Glade." His idealized vision of rural England suggested a landscape of hills and dales and "gently purling Streams." Carolina offered neither daisies, green meadows, nor gentle fogs. Instead, "Here Afric's Squalid Sons and Daughters grim! / Rank Vegetation there, deep Mire and Mud / While yonder creeps the torpid, dingey flood." A visiting naval officer was more blunt in his association of enslaved Africans with a disordered environment. Captain Martin's 1769 poem depicts Charlestown as a city defined by mosquitoes, shark-filled waters, and barren land. Its "burning heat and chilling cold" and "Inconstant, strange, unhealthful weather" were matched by the racial confusion of "Black and white all mix'ed together."[30]

Planters spent wealth generated by slave labor in pursuit of more refined material lives, but these critiques called attention to the crude stock that sustained such gentility. Puncturing colonists' pretensions in this fashion forced them to acknowledge that Carolina was far from the environmental paradise promised its first settlers. Once touted as a western analogue to the exotic and productive Mediterranean, Levant, and Far East, colonists soon perceived the Lowcountry as a place in which remarkable fertility brought with it extremes of rankness and decay. By the mid-eighteenth century, first-hand experiences with sudden frosts, devastating hurricanes, weed-choked fields, and, above all, oppressive heat led seasoned veterans of the Lowcountry's climate to describe this corner of the New World on its own terms, as an exceptionally volatile natural place.

Long after the last uncritical paeans to the region's fruitful soil were published,[31] European nature observers lingered on the theme of rapid vegetative growth. This theme, first invoked to depict the place as new Eden, now drew attention to the Lowcountry's malignant bounty. All things degenerated in Carolina. Settlers risked early deaths here, and plants and animals introduced to domesticate the region into a recognizably English place seemed to suffer the same fate. Cheeses failed to keep, apples rotted as they ripened, and English gardens had to be replanted with new vegetable seed every year "to prevent degenerating." Because the Lowcountry produced in great quantities the supposedly crude crops of Native American agriculture, such as maize and pumpkins, but failed to yield good wheat and barley, one experienced settler described the land as "fertile" but not "productive."[32] Horses likewise "multiplied fast, but degenerated greatly." Despite the pride some took in their pigs and poultry as "a Kind superior to the rest of the World," sophisticated observers with a sense for advanced English livestock raising practices, with their emphasis on improving bloodlines through strategic breeding, knew better. The living things of the Lower South were, at best, degraded copies of their European progenitors.[33]

Like other living things in the Lowcountry, colonists were themselves subject to the degenerating effects of a superabundant climate. In a "climate so disorderly," European bodies contended with "excessive hot" summers, autumns that were "one Minute serene, the next cloudy and tempestuous," and winters featuring "piercing cold." The "boisterous" winds blew "changeable and erratic" from "different points of the compass without any regularity." The dangers of internalizing the effects of the weather that produced such "violent" and unexpected shifts was plain to observers who understood health as the product of a carefully maintained balance of bodily humors. "[O]verheating and getting cold" in a climate that was so "unsettled" combined with the poisonous "exhalations from stagnated waters and marshy swamps" to make living and working in this climate particularly threatening to European constitutions.[34]

Alexis de Tocqueville, eager to find fault with the pro-slavery arguments he heard while touring the United States in the early 1830s, dismissed the notion that agricultural labor in the most southern states was fatal to whites "whereas Negroes can work there without danger." In the mid-eighteenth century, decades before abolitionists launched a sustained crusade to end human bondage, colonial slave owners were seldom compelled to defend it with pat claims of environmental necessity. Defend slavery they did, however, precisely because Africans seemed as well suited to South Carolina's climate as Europeans seemed maladapted. Critics and defenders of plantation society alike worried less about the ethics of enslaving human beings than they did about the problem of making South Carolina a civil place for European life and work. Africans, although their presence compounded the already "savage" qualities of the plantation countryside, allowed Europeans to escape direct exposure to South Carolina's natural world. Planters had no recourse to modern explanations for the immunological advantages that some West Africans possessed in New World environments. Because tasks in the rice swamps differed so dramatically from English expectations for agricultural labor, however, and perhaps because they knew that some West Africans had experience with wetland rice growing, planters saw slaves as having as much affinity with work that they found harsh, alienating, and beyond the capacities of transplanted northwestern European bodies. Even Tocqueville saw the logic of African labor in the unforgiving Lowcountry, "where rice is cultivated . . . and especially so under a burning tropical sun."[35]

Colonists understood the transplantation of Africans to the South Carolina Lowcountry as a roughly lateral movement from one hot climate to another. English immigrants, by contrast, risked unbalancing bodily humors by moving from a temperate climate to one featuring climatic extremes in general and dangerously hot temperatures in particular. In 1735 Charlestown resident Samuel Eveleigh believed that only enslaved African laborers could cultivate rice swamps in Georgia, even as the new colony's trustees declared their intention to ban slavery there. He remained "positive that the Commodity can't . . . be produced by white people. Because the Work is too laborious, the heat very intent, and the Whit[es] can't work in the wett at that Season of the year as Neg[roes] do to weed the Rice."[36] By the end of the century, planters adhered to the principle that "climate, the nature of the soil, [and] ancient habits forbid the whites from performing this labor," and without slaves to battle the elements "all fertile rice and indigo swamps will be deserted, and become a wilderness."[37]

The vulnerabilities of white bodies to the extremes of the Lowcountry's climate placed slaves exclusively on the front lines in the struggle to contend with nature.[38] Late eighteenth-century historian Alexander Hewit wondered if South Carolina might have followed Virginia's example of foisting the labor of early plantation settlement on the backs of indentured servants. This problem of physiological commensurateness between peoples and places, he concluded, distinguished the rice-producing Lowcountry from the tobacco-producing Tidewater. Hewit speculated that "white servants would have exhausted their strength in clearing a spot of land for digging their own graves, and every rice plantation would have served no other purpose than a burying ground to its European cultivators." Imagining the impact of a seventeenth-century absence of slave labor on the region's eighteenth-century development, Hewit envisioned such a South Carolina as little more than a collection of marginally productive highland farms separated by intervening swamps. "The low lands of Carolina, which are unquestionably the richest grounds in the country, must long have remained a wilderness, had not Africans, whose natural constitutions were suited [to] the clime and work, been employed in cultivating this useful article of food and commerce." This imagined landscape, retrospectively deprived of its slave labor, was a place in which nature, not culture, held sway. As "the only cultivators of the soil in this low country," slaves stood between planters and wilderness.[39]

Slaves shielded settlers from direct exposure to a debilitating climate and did the work Europeans believed they themselves could not endure, but exposure to Africans posed its own risks of moral decay. Critics of plantation America charged that planters had been made temperamentally volatile by the violence, heat, and immorality common to warm-weather slave societies. Heedless, vain, and above all hotheaded, the characters of English planters had become debased by long exposure to a rank natural world and their interactions with so-called savage people. Particularly as slave masters, planters had earned a reputation for "high and haughty" demeanors that found frequent expressions in violent outbursts toward enslaved dependents.[40] Born and bred to "tyrannize from their infancy, they carry with them a disposition to treat all mankind in the same manner they have been used to treat their Negroes," reported visitor Ebenezer Hazard in 1766. Even preeminent slave owners who prided themselves as "able" planters, and thus self-possessed enough to bear the "Short Comings of Negros" without lashing out constantly against them, mused darkly on the "influence & effect of the Negro Slavery upon the morals & practices of young people." The "rough means" planters employed to discipline slaves redounded on the planters who meted out the beatings.[41] Just as plants and animals degenerated South Carolina, critics assailed planters' characters as debased versions of virtuous English originals.

Loath to accept the bleak future that this malicious strand of transatlantic criticism implied, the colony's most sophisticated weather observers extended the hope that South Carolina's slaves might yet redeem its climate. Air and water that stagnated under an oppressive canopy of dense foliage, early modern doctors believed, produced dank places more suitable for "reptiles and insects" than European bodies. By ridding an overgrown landscape of its trees, slave workers would open the miasmatic spaces that promoted degeneration, cleansing it of the "putrid autumnal Effluvial" thought responsible for seasonal outbreaks of "ague," or malarial fever. "[C]learing the land of its Woods," according to midcentury physician John Lining, promised to produce dramatic climatic improvement in the province by 1800. As slaves advanced on the wilderness with their "gleaming Axes" in the second half of the eighteenth century, however, the lands they cleared and embanked for rice production gave planters a "command of water" they used to initiate ambitious irrigation projects. Instead of transforming the Lowcountry into an increasingly dry, open, and habitable place, however, the expansion of plantation agriculture spread water "over the face of the country." Far from improving a notorious disease environment, this altered landscape of vast reservoirs and "stagnant waters" became a new source of dangerous "corrosive vapours."[42]

As the rice plantation economy accelerated in the early eighteenth century, the rapid "Africanization of the lowcountry labor force" placed slaves between Europeans and a volatile environment, insulating planters from the degenerating effects of a wild climate and securing for them the means to lead refined material lives.[43] Populating the plantation countryside with slaves also exposed colonists to metropolitan charges of cultural debasement. Seen as both the perpetrators and victims of a uniquely disordered American place, planters saw their colony, once promoted as "the most amiable Country of the Universe," relegated to the status of a crude dystopia.[44]

Knowing the Characters of Slaves

That slaves and nature were the key ingredients of the colony's prosperity and, at the same time, harbored its most dangerous disorders was a tension that shaped South Carolina's distinctive culture of slavery. The 1712 slave code expected Africans, because of their "barbarous, wild, savage natures," to commit "disorders, rapines, and inhumanity, to which they are naturally prone and inclined." This conception of slaves as innately wild, copied directly from Barbados's slave code, was the general view of early eighteenth-century whites who could not "be persuaded that Negroes and Indians are otherwise than Beasts, and use them like such."[45]

Such language was conspicuously absent from South Carolina's comprehensively revised Negro Act of 1740, even though this law was designed to monitor and discipline slaves following the Stono River uprising. Several of its provisions rested on the assumption that whites could judge the characters of blacks effectively. Colonists could allow their slaves to move about on their own and even carry guns, provided they carried a written ticket by which their masters vouched for their trustworthiness. Those caught without such passes could be "examined" by any white person, who was authorized by the statute to arrest and whip the offender, or, after reading reassuring signs of emotion and demeanor, let the slave go.[46] Barbados lacked the marchland that separated the Lowcountry's cultivated riversides from its expansive interior. The island's notoriously brutal labor regime combined with its densely concentrated slave majority made it hard for planters there to imagine that slaves left to their own devices might be anything other than wild beasts in human form.[47] Lowcountry slaves traveled between dispersed plantations, journeyed from countryside to Charlestown and back again, and made daily excursions into an unregulated terrain of forests, savannahs, and swamps surrounding every plantation. In place of racial generalizations about black savagery, South Carolina colonists initiated a search for the ways in which slave character was molded by experience. Identifying rogues within the colony's black majority made the danger of violent slave resistance seem both contained and identifiable. Believing that others became sensible dependents meant that they could be trusted, even when whites could not monitor their whereabouts and activities across so much space.

In the eyes of their masters, slaves might fall into one of three categories: "sensible," "new Negro," or "rogue." By revealing their social and economic abilities slaves appeared, in a term used more than any other to describe individuals with whom whites could communicate, as "sensible."[48] The word denoted qualities of awareness, capability, and rationality, and was thus frequently applied to describe those among the colony's rising contingent of skilled slave workers. Sensibility was a synonym for cultural fluency. Those born in South Carolina possessed the resources, not least of which was an ability to speak English that sounded right to European ears, that became hallmarks of the trustworthy slave. Sensible slaves seemed "reasonable creatures," "not given to any Vice," "honest," and "of a good temper & tractable." Because they were thought to be "pleased with their Masters, contented with their Condition, reconciled to Servitude, seasoned to the Country, and expert at the different kinds of Labour in which they are employed," they could be counted as "strong seasoned handy Slaves."[49] Those who attended a 1738 sale of a "choice parcel of sensible Slaves" preferred to buy creoles when they could. Other sellers touted "prime country born Negroes" and advertised slaves selected as much for their "characters, in point of honest and sobriety" as for "ability." Slaves distinguished only by the fact that they were "native or acclimatized" sold for more at auction than did recently imported Africans.[50]

Sensibility was a form of practical comprehension, a grasp of the subtle shadings of white expectation between slavery's formal rules and its shifting customary practice. Having this quality suggested that a slave would steer clear of thoughtless acts of resistance and take advantage of incentives for compliance: such choices reflected good sense. But the term said more about personality than it was meant to vouch for character. Masters described runaways as sensible to better identify them for recapture. For hundreds of skilled slaves whose runaway attempts were advertised in South Carolina newspapers, sensibility was indistinguishable from "cunning" and craft skills from craftiness.[51] Whites did not trust every sensible slave to be obedient, but they did expect them to know the stakes of resistance as well as the conditions under which independent behavior would be tolerated or repressed. Whites believed they could reason with sensible slaves.

In contrast to the cultural competence of the country-born, recently imported Africans appeared to whites as "weak Raw New Negroes." Planters saw the wildness of Africans in the same way that they viewed uncultivated nature. As with savage places, the inchoate disorder of savage peoples' characters could be improved by Europeans. Charlestown tradesmen purchased economically priced boys out of the slave trade and trained them in their crafts. These new Negro apprentices could quickly develop good English language skills, even if they also bore "country marks," the product of ritual scarification that concluded an African childhood.[52] For the most part, however, planters believed African-born slaves to be as dangerous to white security as they were necessary to bring new lands into cultivation. The fighters who took up arms at Stono River were mostly recent arrivals from Angola. Before the first Guineaman of the season anchored in Charlestown harbor with its human cargo, planters began the cultural work of prejudging the characters of the slaves they might buy. Although ethnic assumptions about docile Gambians and morose Ibos amounted to little more than "shallow stereotypes," their wide circulation among whites reveals a strong desire to fix the diverse Africans who came to South Carolina through the slave trade into stable categories of character.[53]

Africans who refused to be disciplined, improved, and acculturated, despite the clear threats they posed, did not seem as dangerous to colonists as did creoles who used their abilities for subversive ends. Those whose artfulness had crossed a line into rebellion could not be negotiated with. They became "rogues" who acted in antipathy to white society and with heedless disregard of the consequences. Given the "mischievous practices of ye negroes born in ye countrey & town," sometimes described "as if thay was all either murderers runaways or robbers," some whites preferred the uncertain dispositions of new Negroes to the demonstrated criminality of these predatory rogues.[54] Whites captured most of the slaves involved in "playing the rogue" after a "wicked and barbarous" 1720 plot to "destroy all the white people in the country and then to take the towne" was discovered. Some were "burnt some hang'd and some banishd."[55] Because country-born runaways, arsonists, and thieves grew up learning the rules that whites imposed, their crimes could not be fobbed off as the product of an African upbringing. Nor was roguery assumed to be a universal racial characteristic. Rather, repeated acts of disobedience revealed "evil minded" dispositions that inhered in the character of the individual as a permanent stain.[56]

With several thousand new Africans pouring into the colony each year, it became harder for whites to find a "Negro of a good Character" within South Carolina's rising black majority.[57] The "Act for the Better Ordering and Governing of Negroes and other Slaves in this Province," as the Negro Act of 1740 was officially known, increased official scrutiny over slaves and masters in the hopes of preventing another uprising. Its all but unenforceable provisions amounted to a prescriptive fantasy of immobilized slaves kept in check by the eternally vigilant colonists. The "Act for the Better Strengthening of this Province," also passed in the year after Stono, had more far-reaching consequences. Whereas the Negro Act sought to scrutinize and modify behavior, this Duty Act sought to reproduce sensibility within the African-American population by regulating the slave trade. Import duties on slave arrivals in Charlestown had long been tiered to make undesirable slaves more expensive.[58] The Duty Act of 1740 raised the rates on suspected rogues and new Negroes to effectively prohibit their importation. The law used a formula based on height to determine the tax, imposing a £100 rate on those four feet two inches and taller that more than doubled the price of an African adult at market. Lesser rates of £50 and £25 were reserved for shorter slaves. This made it less costly to buy young children; "sucking children" were exempted from any state-imposed charge. Only the very youngest Africans, who might be introduced into slave society as virtual creoles, were allowed to pass through the demographic net imposed by the Duty Act's tariffs. An additional £50 was added to the price of those slaves imported from another colony, a class of "Plantation Negroes" frequently sold for their crimes. Taken together, these restrictions sought to quarantine South Carolina from rogues bred elsewhere in colonial British America and slow the "great importation of negroes from the coast of Africa, who are generally of a barbarous and savage disposition."[59]

For the better part of the 1740s, the law effectively stopped the slave trade into South Carolina.[60] Instead of declining during the ban, South Carolina's slave population surprisingly "increased; so that in all Appearance the Negroes bred from our Stock will continually recruit and keep it up."[61] South Carolina's experiment with demographic engineering proved that insulating the province against barbarous Africans and cunning rogues could steer the black population toward sensibility without sacrificing economic growth. When the rapid expansion of the plantation economy in the early 1760s brought thousands of new African slaves to the Lowcountry, these duties were imposed again in hopes of creolizing the slave population.[62]

Because the worst rogues were made in the colony, not imported from Africa or the other plantations, the idea that an increasingly native-born black population made slavery safe for colonial growth was a fiction. So was the notion that colonists could read their slaves' personalities from the surface of behavior, especially when enslaved people did their best to shield their inner characters from white scrutiny. Masters conceded that reliable dependents might turn into unpredictable rogues, catching them unawares. In 1780, a year that brought invading British forces to the Lowcountry, James Thomason warned Isaac Harleston of a "nest of thieves & villains lurking about the plantations" that had become a "constant nuisance." Thomason sent word of this danger by a messenger who, if he did not return in a week's time, was likely to join these "runaways & rogues" who prayed on the plantations near Strawberry Ferry in the heart of the core plantation zone. Although this man was "one I can confide in as far as any," he admitted, "There is no knowing a Slave."[63]

Masters tried to convince themselves that they could sort reliable from threatening individuals with consistency and that changing the assessment of any slave from sensible to rogue (or, more rarely, in the other direction) followed changes in the individual's behavior. In fact this was a shifting standard that moved with the master's humor and suspicions, plaguing slave life with uncertainty. When masters held slaves up to the ideal put forward by the Negro Act, any unmonitored movement, material autonomy, or act of insolence might appear as a sign of the rogue revealing him- or herself. Most masters knew that slaves violated the provisions of the colony's slave code as a matter of course, a point that "The Stranger" made in 1772 when he reproached them for tolerating nighttime revels on the city's outskirts, illicit taverns, and many other departures from the spirit and letter of the law. What an enslaved person never knew was whether any action would be held to the formal, rigid standard of total subjugation or to the informal, looser standard of general latitude. Most South Carolina slaves lived in the ambiguous space between the extremes of abject meekness and outright rebellion, where the distance between appearing as a "sensible & good fellow" or a "great rogue" could be frighteningly narrow.[64] So arbitrary were the judgments that could deliver such punishing consequences that some simply resigned themselves to the possibility that no matter how unimpeachable their conduct, they might not escape the volatility of white opinion about black character.[65]

When colonists saw the region's black majority as a threatening Negro mass scattered across the landscape in such great numbers, their vulnerability could seem overwhelming. As they judged slave character and assessed those who emerged as individuals from this hostile population, they found a way to moderate the paralyzing prospects of impending rebellion. "Many people express great fears of an insurrection," reported visitor Josiah Quincy, Jr., in 1773 while "others treat the idea as chimerical." Sudden panics and harsh repressions against slaves alternated with "long periods of laxity," as Philip D. Morgan has observed, throughout the eighteenth century. Masters suspected their slaves of murderous impulses in one moment, and just as quickly believed that "there was not so much reason to be afraid of the Negroes, as was at first suspected."[66] During conspiracy scares, some colonists reverted to the racially homogeneous vision of slaves as ungovernably wild, but many others attempted to disarticulate the threat of slave violence, lodging it in the suspect hearts of rogues and Africans and freeing them to trust their own sensible slaves.

Every planter accomplishment in the transatlantic marketplace brought with it the financial resources to import new African captives, build new plantations, and deepen the bonds of servitude for those African Americans born in the colony. The growth of this labor force meant fortifying an internal enemy within plantation society and extending a strategic vulnerability over broader reaches of space. Born of a pressing desire to be able to gauge the loyalties and foretell the behaviors of those who worked in and around dispersed plantations, masters sought, without much consistency or success, the key to slave character in the influences of ethnicity, upbringing, and experience. Judging slave character involved thinking about the subjective perspectives of the enslaved, but this acknowledgement of distinctive personalities did not signal a humanitarian softening of racial thought or an easing of patriarchal rule. The sensible slave, the rebellious rogue, and the uncouth African were caricatures projected onto individuals for the purposes of enforcing a repressive racial order. Presuming to know the characters of slaves shielded the sensible from daily suspicion, but cleared a path to torture and kill those deemed rogues, whose subjectivity was thought to consist of little more than the predatory instincts of wild animals. Whites could regard the slaves who populated town and countryside as the "greatest curse that ever came to [A]merica," but because "there is no raiseing rice without them" planters never seriously envisioned building plantations without slaves.[67]

"Good unexpected, Evil unforeseen / Appear by turns, as Fortune shifts the Scene" begins an anonymously authored 1737 poem published in the *South-Carolina Gazette.* Readers throughout the British Atlantic world would have recognized this piece as a conventional Christian meditation on the futility of worldly accomplishment in the face of impending mortality. For colonists in the subtropical coastal plain, the poem's language resonated in more specific ways with their efforts to establish and maintain plantations at the Atlantic edge of a "savage" continent. By the mid-eighteenth century the ranks of the planter elite were filled by many who had been "rais'd a loft" from fairly humble social origins; others came "tumbling down" from lofty heights as bad seasons, weak markets, and ungovernable slaves dissipated plantation estates. Strong international demand for rice and indigo and relatively open access to cheap land and long credit created opportunities for those who had fallen to "bound, and rise again."[68] For those whose slaves cultivated the tidal floodplains, the "Ebb and Flow" of happiness was an apt metaphor for the particular "Viccissitudes" encountered by lowcountry colonists. Embodying volatile change in the figure of "Fortune" asked readers steeped in the Atlantic republican tradition to understand the need for a corresponding stance of "virtue" required to counter Fortune's challenges.[69]

John Drayton, surveying South Carolina's plantation landscape at the turn of the nineteenth century, saw planters in command of an army of slave workers who forced an agricultural order upon a rank natural world. "So woods may be cut down, and the lands on which they grew may be made to produce grains, which nature never planted there," he observed. "But, withhold the hand of cultivation" by granting slaves their freedom, Drayton prophesied, "and nature immediately causes weeds and plants to spring up again; and, in the course of time, covers them with her dark retreats, and stately forests." In a South Carolina without slavery "the extensive rice fields which are covered with grain, would present nothing but deep swamps, and dreary forests; inhabited by panthers, bears, wolves, and other wild beasts."[70]

By 1800, planters had recovered from the disorders of the War for Independence to rebuild vast rice plantations in the Lowcountry and transform the Backcountry interior into the first cotton belt. From this stance of agricultural confidence, Drayton nevertheless persisted in the tradition of fearing "wild beasts" as a menacing threat to South Carolina's survival as a slave and plantation society. As harbingers of disorder, these imagined animals continued to exert a pull on the sensibilities of South Carolina elites who redoubled their dependence on slavery to keep the wolves at bay. Even as the imagined countryside turned more bucolic than threatening for whites later in the nineteenth and twentieth centuries, the figure of the "black beast rapist" captured an echo of long-standing associations between African Americans and predatory animals in plantation America.[71]

Slaves struggled with their masters over the exercise of power in the colonial Lowcountry by challenging legal authority with customary rights and undermining ideals of absolute mastery with resistance. This leading historiographical vision of negotiated authority has placed masters' search for social order against slaves' pursuit of autonomy as the central dynamic of the slave societies of British plantation America. In the Chesapeake, Caribbean, and Lower South planters found that the disorders of slavery permeated every sphere of activity they undertook, from the business of producing transatlantic staples to the quest to emulate metropolitan standards for civility. To explain how tense standoffs between masters and slaves shaped distinctive regional plantation societies, historians have begun to trace variations in terms of the specific influences of producing tobacco, sugar, and rice on labor systems and the demographic profiles of plantation communities.[72] Slaves and masters faced off against (and came to terms with) one another within the context of a pervasive material world. Their struggles for power did not take place on an abstract stage or at the metaphorical negotiating table, but within the very real spaces of colonial landscapes. In the South Carolina Low-country, each plantation was encircled by unsettled, uncultivated spaces that slaves used, knew, and traversed, but which planters understood, in both practical and intellectual terms, as a dangerous frontier.

CHAPTER TWO

"For Want of a Social Set"

Networks and Social Interaction in the Lower Cape Fear Region of North Carolina, 1725–1775

Bradford J. Wood

Peter Dubois spent the late winter and early spring of 1757 in the port town of Wilmington, North Carolina. Evidently, Dubois was visiting this region of North Carolina for the first time, but he had acquaintances elsewhere in the colony, and he wrote several detailed letters about his visit to his friend Samuel Johnston, a prominent lawyer and political leader in the older settlements near Albemarle Sound. Dubois's letters to Johnston record various reactions to Wilmington and its inhabitants. Initially at least, Dubois expressed pleasant surprise. He told Johnston that "my Entertainment at this Place Exceeds my Expectations," and that "from what I Have yet Seen it has greatly the preference in My Esteem to New Bern." From Dubois's perspective, which had undoubtedly been influenced by his own travels and by the normative assumptions of eighteenth-century Anglo-America, in Wilmington "the Regularity of the Streets" "Equal[led] to those of Philadelphia and the Buildings in General [were] very Good." He found that "Many [of the buildings were] of Brick two & three Stores High with double Piazzas w[hi]ch Make a good appearance."

Still, while Dubois remained in Wilmington at least another few months and continued to acknowledge the ways in which the town's inhabitants upheld eighteenth-century Anglo-American standards of civility, he remained dissatisfied with his visit. As a newcomer to Wilmington, he lacked a network of social connections to make his stay more enjoyable, and as a consequence he expressed his discontent to Johnston in no uncertain terms. In February, after praising Wilmington's streets and buildings, he told Johnston somewhat playfully that "I Cannot yet find a Social Co. who will Drink Claret & Smoke Tobacco till four in the Morning. I Hope However to Make Some proselytes Soon . . . In which I don['[]t doubt but [that I] Shall have the Best wishes of All Lovers of Society." Less than a month later, he expressed himself more bluntly: "I Live Very Much Retired for want of a Social Set." Dubois recognized that Wilmington presented some social opportunities, admitting that the gentlemen of the town might provide him with the "Social Set" he desired, but he found them "Intollerable" because "Gaming Prevails in all Companies." Dubois considered gaming "the Bane of Society." Instead of making connections with "the Devotees of Cards," he decided to "Pass My hours Chiefly at Home with my Pipe and Some agreeable Author." But Dubois clearly did not relish this solitude, and he admitted to Johnston that "I have often'd Longed for ye Co." He felt isolated from Johnston and other familiar acquaintances while he was on the banks of the Cape Fear, and he "Wish'd the distance to Edenton Might be Rode in an hour or two." Because he knew that he could not readily travel from Wilmington to Edenton, he hoped that Johnston would make him feel better by writing as frequently as possible.[1]

Dubois' letters to Samuel Johnston illustrate the importance of social networks in colonial British America. Few early Americans would have been content to do without either a "Social Set" or the other forms of satisfaction and support that colonists derived from kinship, local networks, and other common bonds. As Dubois's letters also reveal, social interaction often depended on complicated considerations. Dubois's assessment of the gentlemen of Wilmington and their proclivity toward gambling depended heavily on his own assumptions about acceptable and enjoyable companionship. Many other early Americans might have been more tolerant of gambling, but powerful and broader cultural constructions related to concepts such as civility, status, race, ethnicity, gender, and religion played a large role in determining patterns of interaction everywhere in colonial British America. Similarly, many early Americans maintained meaningful relationships over considerable distances, just as Dubois relied on his friendship with Samuel Johnston. Correspondence undoubtedly offered the most frequent and practical opportunity for long-distance communication, though the possibility of riding "an hour or two" or even farther might have been a tempting way to overcome shorter but still significant distances.

Still, Dubois often "Longed" for Johnston's company, and anyone reading his letters is left with a sense of his isolation. Travel to Wilmington proved to be a significant social obstacle for Dubois, and few factors played as important a role in the construction of early American social networks as distance. In this sense, Dubois's experience seems atypical. As an elite white male, Dubois was far more likely to travel longer distances and exceed the geographic limitations of his regular social networks than were poorer whites, bound laborers, and women. But geographic circumstances influenced patterns of interaction for everyone in early America. As Darret Rutman and others have powerfully reminded us, social interaction in early America usually meant face-to-face interaction.[2]

Historians have not yet fully explored the implications of geographic constraints on social interaction in eighteenth-century America. Instead scholars in recent decades have devoted much more attention to the ways that Anglo-American settlers transcended geographic barriers to participate in a much broader Atlantic world. The experience of migration tied many settlers to friends and relatives in more distant locales. Increasingly elaborate networks of trade and commercial activity extended contacts both through ocean ports and overland to other regions. Finally, by the mid-eighteenth-century awareness of and concern relating to the British Empire intensified. As many scholars have correctly pointed out, these opportunities for transatlantic interaction had powerful influences on life and society in colonial British America.

Moreover, local patterns of social interaction and broader cultural influences from other parts of the Atlantic world were neither mutually exclusive nor in tension. Indeed, the two tendencies could reinforce each other. Neighborhoods and local experiences gave individuals a social language of responses and understandings that could be applied to interactions in a transatlantic context. Extralocal interactions enabled individuals to refine their conceptions of themselves and their neighbors by contrasting them with others and framing them within broader conceptualizations. But, given the obstacles imposed by early modern life, these external contacts and associations could never fully transcend the continuing, concrete, and far more frequent experiences of social interaction within more confined geographic parameters.

The basic conditions of social life in colonial British America therefore provided a powerful impetus to the formation of provincial cultures and identities. By the eighteenth century, settlers found their lives closely rooted in social worlds that were different from and distant from metropolitan models. Given the importance and relatively rapid development of these new social worlds, it is not surprising that in some ways settlers began to identify as strongly, or perhaps even more strongly, with their homes on the periphery than with the metropolitan center. Anglo-American settlers created new and relatively self-contained societies, even while they envisioned those new societies as British.

Consequently, geographic considerations still tied the social development of Anglo-American societies tightly to local and regional cultures. But geographic constraints did not lead to simple patterns of geographic determinism or persistent localism. Different opportunities for interaction were integrated into a sophisticated array of choices influenced by geography, individual interests, and cultural preferences. Anglo-Americans also chose from an increasingly broad range of social interactions over time. As colonists expanded geographically, they also expanded their social horizons and opportunities, and, by the eighteenth century, more elaborate social networks within the colonies encouraged the development of a different, more provincial, form of Anglo-American identity.

Historians of the seventeenth-century Chesapeake have demonstrated the early importance of relatively small and geographically confined neighborhoods. As one leading authority has discovered for St. Clement's manor in Charles County, Maryland, "All the repeated and ordinary contacts of male residents involved other households lying within an approximate five-mile radius of the home, a journey of an hour or two."[3] Such confined social networks must have made it difficult indeed for early settlers to find a satisfactory social set. Initially, colonists had two potential worlds of social interaction. First, they had the relatively simplified, still somewhat unfamiliar, and small-scale social world of their new neighborhoods. Second, they had the social world that they had left behind when they crossed the Atlantic. Transatlantic social ties had a powerful allure, but they were extremely difficult to participate in or maintain. In other words, the processes of social simplification necessitated by settlement across the Atlantic prevented a more elaborate set of social opportunities in the colonies and heightened the importance of distant British bonds. Under these conditions, the development of any kind of colonial identity remained constrained by the intensely felt desire to maintain the metropolitan ties that provided settlers with more fully satisfying social interactions.

By the mid-eighteenth century, however, this situation had changed dramatically. The incredible internal growth and external expansion of the British colonies had contributed to the rapid development of increasingly elaborate and widespread social networks. Different kinds of social networks and different possibilities for social interaction transformed the experience of Anglo-American colonists. Colonists could now choose their social interactions more selectively, and they understood social interaction in geographic terms that were determined by far more than just the Atlantic Ocean. Peter Dubois, for example, chose between social opportunities that were far more characteristic of the eighteenth century than they were of the seventeenth century. Wilmington with its piazzas and regular streets, the taverns of gamblers that Dubois spurned, and the regular mail service that delivered letters to Samuel Johnston in Edenton all marked the dynamic and increasingly complex social world of eighteenth-century America.

This essay examines the dynamics of social interaction in early to mid-eighteenth-century America in order to elucidate the relationship between developing patterns of social interaction and the powerful emergence of a provincial identity in Anglo-American societies. It does so with a case study, focused on the Lower Cape Fear region of North Carolina, where Peter Dubois wrote his letters to Samuel Johnston in 1757.[4] As this essay will demonstrate, in the Lower Cape Fear colonists continued to experience important interactions in neighborhoods, but they also moved beyond neighborhoods, participating in much more complicated networks and patterns of behavior that encouraged an emphasis on extralocal identities. Rather than relying on a clearly defined hierarchy of social relations based on proximity or some other single criteria, colonists chose between different relationships as circumstances dictated, alternating between neighbors, household members, extended kin, nearby town dwellers, business partners, and others. They made their choices based on various considerations, just as Peter Dubois weighed the distance to alternative locales such as Edenton, the consolation derived from distant correspondents, the regular streets and piazzas of a more urban setting, and the "Intollerable" company of gamblers. While social networks became more complex and settlers chose from a broad array of possible connections in the eighteenth century, for most colonists regional networks such as those that developed in the

Lower Cape Fear proved to be at least as important as neighborhood bonds, province-wide ties, or transatlantic connections. In the decades before the American Revolution, a patchwork of regional networks and cultures provided the basis for early American societies that had moved beyond the local communities of the seventeenth century but had not yet fully embraced the "imagined communities" of the modern nation-state.

Colonial American historians have paid considerable attention to local interaction since the late 1960s, when a handful of scholars began to publish methodologically sophisticated studies of New England town life. Long before the mainstream of the American historical profession embraced the idea of an interconnected early modern Atlantic world, scholars such as Kenneth Lockridge, Philip Greven, John Demos, and Michael Zuckerman focused on the importance of local interactions in town settings.[5] The influence of the *Annales* school of historians in France, the Cambridge Group in England, and other pioneering social historians enabled New England town studies to raise provocative new questions using creative research techniques. These works treated places such as Dedham, Massachusetts, as relatively tightly knit, homogenous, stable, and orderly seventeenth-century communities. Moreover, their work spawned a whole genre of early American community studies, and made local communities central to debates about the early history of New England. New England community studies often conveyed the notion that the characteristics of New England towns enabled an unusual and idealized kind of social interaction that has largely been lost in the modern world.

Within a decade, the New England town studies began to receive criticism from a number of perspectives. Some critics wondered whether individual town studies painted an accurate picture of colonial New England, while others questioned the relevance of New England towns for the rest of early America.[6] Other scholars called for a more careful interrogation of the concept of community or for a more explicit rationale for the use of local case studies. By this time historians had begun to engage more fully with scholars working with local studies in other disciplines, especially sociology and anthropology.[7]

The strongest challenges came from historians of the seventeenth-century Chesapeake Bay area. While New England towns seemed peaceful, unified, secure, healthy, and idyllic, settlements along the Chesapeake appeared to be contentious, divided, spread out, fragile, unhealthy, competitive, and brutal. More limited and less descriptive sources also made local studies' methodologies far more difficult to utilize for places south of New England. Still, Chesapeake scholars refused to accept the assumption that these settlements lacked the kinds of positive social interaction associated with communities. As the work on the early Chesapeake burgeoned and many scholars focused on different localities, it became clear that the terms of the debate would have to be recast. Strong neighborhood and network bonds did develop in Virginia and Maryland, but they developed in ways that contrasted sharply with those in the scholarship on New England towns. Darret and Anita Rutman's masterly research project, *A Place in Time, Middlesex County Virginia, 1650–1750,* marked the most complete study of colonial American social interaction to date. In addition to his work on *A Place in Time,* Darret Rutman also penned a number of perceptive essays that analyzed the meaning and characteristics of communities and social networks in early America. Rutman redefined community as any field of human social interaction and then argued that, as a consequence, communities clearly existed in Middlesex County and elsewhere in the Chesapeake. Even more significantly, Rutman drew heavily on the work of sociologists and geographers, using an approach known as network analysis to shed light on early American social interactions.[8] By the early 1990s, when James R. Perry published an impressive monograph about the strength of social bonds on Virginia's Eastern Shore in the first half of the seventeenth century, most scholars were willing to concede Rutman's point that some form of broadly defined community existed in the early Chesapeake.[9]

In recent years, many scholars have admired the work of the Rutmans, but for a variety of reasons few have followed their example.[10] The basic conditions of social interaction in the New England and Chesapeake colonies had received substantial attention for about two decades by the 1990s, and not many historians can marshal the enormous resources the Rutmans put into *A Place in Time.* The term "community" itself may also confuse more than it clarifies at this point in the discussion. Moreover, recent historiographic trends have emphasized cultural processes, such as the construction of race, instead of seemingly more localized social developments and circumstances. But in order to understand broader processes in the early modern world, historians must also understand local details, and these approaches are by no means in tension. Scholars who study local social interaction also face greater challenges if they try to place their work in the eighteenth-century contexts of colonial expansion and the integration of the Atlantic world. Partly for these reasons, a burgeoning and newer body of scholarship on the colonial Lower South—consisting of South Carolina, North Carolina, and Georgia—has given little consideration to local social networks or interactions.[11] Yet the Lower South is a fitting place to explore the development of social networks and interactions, because these settlements may have been even more competitive, diverse, spread out, fluid, unhealthy, and disorderly than the early Chesapeake, and must have presented a challenging social environment for colonists. With this in mind, the rest of this essay turns its attention to one region in the eighteenth-century Lower South, the Lower Cape Fear region visited by Peter Dubois in 1757.

The early history of the Lower Cape Fear sheds light on many of the most important forces that shaped eighteenth-century provincial America. As in most places in eighteenth-century America, inhabitation of the Lower Cape Fear did not result from transatlantic settlement schemes. The Lower Cape Fear region began as "the colony of a colony." Permanent settlement in the area did not begin until the 1720s, making the Lower Cape Fear one of the last significant coastal enclaves to be settled by British colonists in America. Indeed, late settlement not only contributed to a more distant and provincial attitude toward the metropolis, but also meant that the Lower Cape Fear functioned in some senses as a "coastal backcountry," distinct in a variety of ways from other parts of the North Carolina Tidewater. Still, despite a relatively small and sparse Anglo-American population of a few thousand, by 1775 the Lower Cape Fear had emerged not only as a distinct region, but also as the wealthiest and arguably most important region in North Carolina. Settlers in the Lower Cape Fear discovered that neither considerable separation from the metropolis, differences with other parts of North Carolina, nor late settlement prevented growth, prosperity, or self-definition.

The increasingly connected eighteenth-century Atlantic world did play a role in the settlement of the Lower Cape Fear. Merchants and entrepreneurs from England, Scotland, Ireland, the West Indies, and from other mainland colonies migrated to the region in order to take advantage of the economic opportunities associated with the Lower Cape Fear port towns of Wilmington and Brunswick. Because port facilities in other parts of North Carolina had been so limited, the Lower Cape Fear ports promised unprecedented transatlantic profits and interactions for the colony. Still, these transatlantic opportunists discovered that the Lower Cape Fear remained a deeply provincial and American locale. Despite a heterogeneous merchant elite, the Lower Cape Fear's settler population remained dominated by immigrants from South Carolina or from other parts of North Carolina. Enslaved people of African descent made up the largest portion of the Lower Cape Fear's population throughout the colonial period, indicating the interconnectedness of very different cultures throughout the Atlantic world. But ties between the Lower Cape Fear and Africa remained distant; North Carolina engaged in no direct trade with Africa, and almost all of the region's slaves had been introduced to other colonies and other experiences with Anglo-American slavery before they ever set foot in the region. Thus, in a variety of ways, the people of the Lower Cape Fear remained colonists tied to the larger British Atlantic, but they also lived in a provincial world that was increasingly different from the metropolis or even from the colonial worlds of the seventeenth century.

Growth provided the driving force behind the construction of distance between the metropolis and provincial regions like the Lower Cape Fear. In Richard Hofstadter's apt phrasing, "It was growth—growth consistently sustained and eagerly welcomed, growth as a source of grand imperial hopes and calculating private speculation—which was the outstandingly visible fact of mid-eighteenth-century life in the American colonies."[12] North Carolina itself went from a scorned, small, poor, and notoriously disorderly settlement clinging to the coastline around Albemarle Sound in 1700 to the fifth most populous colony in mainland British America by 1775. The history of the Lower Cape Fear and other regions like it demonstrates the important implications of this growth because new settlements did not develop formlessly. As colonists settled new areas, they simultaneously attempted to impose their own cultural standards on the new societies they created, and continually reassessed those standards in accordance with their own experiences. Both of these processes required settlers to consider the character of the new places they occupied and to develop a new understanding of their own relationship to geographic spaces. For many people, regions became the most important functional geographic unit of social interaction, and the importance of regions made a powerful contribution to the development of provincial identities.

By the mid-eighteenth century, metropolitan ties remained important to the people of the Lower Cape Fear, but they begin to seem less obvious and visible when compared to the importance of another more meaningful set of interactions—those defined by experiences within the Lower Cape Fear region itself. The rest of this essay will give a more detailed description of land acquisition, kinship, and centralization, three key aspects of social interaction in the Lower Cape Fear that demonstrate the growth of a social world that functioned on a regional and provincial level.

Identifying the Land

The acquisition, clearing, and use of land made it possible for Lower Cape Fear settlers to construct a provincial British world of their own. While conceptualizing and developing the natural environment of the Lower Cape Fear, settlers recognized regional characteristics and ultimately came to identify those characteristics with their way of life. At the same time, the acquisition of land contributed to the growth and elaboration of Lower Cape Fear society, because land ownership played a central role in social and economic relationships. In southeastern North Carolina and everywhere in early America, the creation of networks, neighborhoods, communities, regions, and colonies depended on the organization of geographic space.

Settlement in the Lower Cape Fear began late, but land acquisition proceeded quickly. The initial impetus for settlement came from a small group of South Carolina planters, led by Maurice and Roger Moore, who were participating in the expansion that spread out geographically from a small settlement around Charleston and rapidly made South Carolina the wealthiest, most slave-labor-oriented, and most politically assertive British colony outside of the West Indies. Despite the fact that the Lower Cape Fear region emerged as the consequence of a distinct and separate settlement with important leadership from South Carolina, various factors led to its incorporation within the political boundaries of North Carolina, a colony that may have been as poor and fractious as any in British America. Lower Cape Fear lands offered benefits to a variety of interests; North Carolina elites could distance themselves from the economic and political problems that had plagued the colony since its inception, South Carolinians could attempt to recreate the prosperous circumstances of the area around Charleston, and other transatlantic merchants could utilize the region's port towns. Perhaps because of this common desire for land ownership, tensions related to land and property ran high as soon as settlement began.

From the arrival of the Moores and their allies in 1725 until about 1740, settlers in the Lower Cape Fear laid claim to as much territory as possible in a competitive, disorganized, and largely illegal rush to acquire land. The Moores and some other elites patented massive amounts of land that led to a long-term pattern of stratified property-holdings in the region. Two of North Carolina's governors, George Burrington and Richard Everard, exacerbated these difficulties by violating their instructions, grasping at land for themselves, and participating in a variety of violent, illegal, and controversial activities. Speculative ventures, the improper issuance of patents, a political struggle over the collection of quitrents, and a switch from proprietary to royal government added further complications to the land situation in the region. Matters began to improve, however, around 1740 because Governor Gabriel Johnston reached an accommodation with Lower Cape Fear leaders regarding the payment of quitrents and some other issues related to property ownership.

The enormous contention and confusion about land ownership during the early years of settlement obscures an important development in the region's early history. In a mere fifteen years a preponderance of the Lower Cape Fear region's best lands not only had been acquired, but in many areas had also been partly cleared and put in use. No matter how much settlers fretted about their title to lands, they quickly shaped the land to their own purposes. And after 1740, when arguments over land ownership began to subside, the region's land use and development continued. The rapid acquisition of land before 1740 merely marked the first stage in a process of infusing the land of the Lower Cape Fear with a distinct and provincial British identity that continued throughout the colonial period. Lower Cape Fear settlers interacted with the region's land in at least three crucial ways: by developing an economy focused on the exploitation of pine forests, by assessing the health conditions of different geographic spaces, and by constructing geographically defined neighborhoods or locales. Each of these patterns of behavior encouraged a sense of identity within the Lower Cape Fear itself and distant from metropolitan identities and places.

By the end of the colonial period the Lower Cape Fear had the most fully developed and profitable naval stores industry in colonial British America, and this had important implications for the relationship between settlers and the land. Large-scale producers of naval stores needed access to comparatively large amounts of land, but they had little commitment to the long-term improvement of much of this land. Lower Cape Fear residents repeatedly emphasized this difference to metropolitan authorities, who insisted that land should be cleared and distributed for more familiar agricultural purposes. Because of the better opportunities for profit in the naval stores industry, producers showed few scruples in fulfilling their insatiable need for land. In some cases individuals simply used trees on lands that belonged to neighbors.

Lower Cape Fear residents adapted to the characteristics of the land in other ways. The same swampy, well-watered lands that proved useful for the region's rice planters also turned out to be ideal breeding areas for malaria-carrying mosquitoes. Because mosquitoes were seasonal, one more effective response to this situation was to move away from swampy lands during the worst months of the summer and early autumn. Residents of the Lower Cape Fear found that drier lands along the coast provided a refuge from mosquito-borne diseases even though they misunderstood the source of their illness, and the area around New Topsail Sound became a popular summer vacationing spot for wealthier inhabitants fleeing disease.[13]

Settlers also made the lands of the Lower Cape Fear their own by assigning new names and interpretations to the landscape. They did this most personally by naming their own plantations and estates. Early maps and other sources reveal a proliferation of identifiable family estates in the Lower Cape Fear region during the colonial period.[14] Some plantations simply applied family names to the land, as in Howe's Point, Halton Lodge, and Castle Haynes. Some estate names offered their own descriptions of the physical features of the land, as in Pleasant Oaks, The Forks, and Green Hill. One plantation name, Lilliput, evoked the imaginative and literary interests of its owner, Eleazer Allen, who owned an extensive library. Peter Mallet's plantation name, Negro Head Point, served as a grisly reminder of the region's brutal devotion to slavery. The incongruously named Buchoi plantation, owned by Alfred Moore, sounded like a Huguenot estate, but actually conveyed the family experience and kinship-related identity of the Moore family, which owned another plantation that had been given a similar name by Native Americans on Goose Creek in the South Carolina Lowcountry. Despite the variations, all of these estate names demonstrated the imaginative power of Lower Cape Fear settlers to redefine the land they used and occupied.

Equally important, settlers also identified commonly recognized sites that served as focal points for discussions of the landscape and the construction of "neighborhoods." A closer look at three of these geographically defined neighborhoods reveals a relationship between location and social interaction that bears important implications for the development of a provincial identity. Moreover, attention to social interaction in neighborhoods reveals that within decades of initial settlement, Lower Cape Fear residents had successfully articulated local social networks. Throughout the rest of the colonial period, the population of the Lower Cape Fear remained relatively sparse and dispersed, but these factors did not prevent settlers from creating geographically based patterns of social interaction.

Perhaps no part of the Lower Cape Fear region attracted as much attention from early settlers as the first neighborhood, Rocky Point, on the Northeast Branch of the Lower Cape Fear River.[15] The area received its name from early explorers who noticed an uncharacteristic collection of rocks and stones along the banks of the river. A 1734 visitor described Rocky Point as "the finest place in all Cape Fear."[16] Maurice Moore, the founder of the Lower Cape Fear settlement, as well as many of the Lower Cape Fear's wealthiest men, lived in the vicinity of Rocky Point. A total of sixty-two different landowners and residents of the Rocky Point neighborhood can be identified from various records; all but nine of these individuals owned land near Rocky Point, and the rest appear to have been heads of households.[17] Tax lists attest to the wealth of these Rocky Point residents.[18] Of the thirty-four who appeared in tax lists, thirty-three owned slaves, with an average of over twenty slaves each. At first glance the largest plantations near Rocky Point appear to be a northern extension of the profitable South Carolina lowcountry plantation society that exploited large numbers of slaves to produce rice, indigo, and other export staples. This impression is somewhat misleading because, while Rocky Point had about a dozen men of extraordinary wealth, most of the landowners in the area exhibited holdings that were modest by South Carolina standards and more typical for the Lower Cape Fear. Still, by 1773, an advertiser in the *Cape Fear Mercury* could expect his audience to be familiar with "The well known valuable LANDS of Rockey Point."[19]

In contrast to the famous prosperity and status of Rocky Point, the second neighborhood, which surrounded Lockwoods Folly River and Inlet, became a home for somewhat humbler people. The origins of the name "Lockwoods Folly" cannot be reliably traced, but two different interpretations suggest the dual identity of the neighborhood. On the one hand, several contemporaries tell the story of a Barbadian settler named Lockwood, who tried to settle there in the seventeenth century but who made some foolish blunders that led to the place's temporary abandonment.[20] This interpretation of the name probably would have suited those who emphasized the neighborhood's shortcomings compared to Rocky Point and other places. This ill-fated attempt at settlement also reinforces the perceptions of the Lower Cape Fear that emphasize its similarity to the rest of North Carolina as a comparatively poorer and more marginal part of the Lower South. Planters in this region could not produce large crops of rice and indigo as others did in South Carolina and Georgia, and they depended on less profitable exports like naval stores, lumber, and provisions. Anglican missionary John MacDowell conveyed this impression of Lockwoods Folly when he described families of poor dissenting fishermen who lived there.[21] Compared to Rocky Point, at least, the area did seem poor. Virtually no contemporary maps show important plantations near Lockwoods Folly, whereas some show as many as a dozen near Rocky Point.[22] Fewer individuals owned slaves, and the neighborhood's slave owners averaged only slightly more than a third as many slaves as their counterparts at Rocky Point.[23]

On the other hand, another interpretation of the name Lockwoods Folly emphasizes the place's positive aspects. In the seventeenth century, English-speaking people sometimes used the French word "folie" to describe a pleasant place or favorite residence.[24] In this sense, Lockwoods Folly could be seen as a pleasant location where newcomers obtained land and bettered their prospects, though not as much as others did at Rocky Point. Landed wealth, at least, was noticeably less stratified at Lockwoods Folly, and this neighborhood might have offered better opportunities for settlers with more modest resources. Perhaps these facts explain why one visitor to North Carolina commented that Brunswick County, which included Lockwoods Folly, lacked poor residents, especially near the sea.[25] During the colonial period Lockwoods Folly had several ferries in operation, a site for holding Anglican religious services, at least one grist mill, and a road commission.[26] Shortly after the Revolution, when the town of Brunswick remained practically abandoned due to a fire and other problems, Lockwoods Folly became the county seat of Brunswick County. Thus, the advantages of Rocky Point and the misfortunes of Lockwoods Folly could easily be overstated.

A third Lower Cape Fear locale, Old Town Creek, or simply "Town Creek," combined characteristics of both Rocky Point and Lockwoods Folly. Some of the wealthiest and most important men in the Lower Cape Fear also made their home along Old Town Creek, which enters the Cape Fear just south of Wilmington and just below the shallow "Flats" that make the Cape Fear impassable for large oceangoing vessels. Slave ownership was significant and widespread along Town Creek, but the neighborhood never approached the status of Rocky Point. As the Lower Cape Fear marked a midpoint between the wealthy rice planters of South Carolina and the small farmers of northern and western North Carolina, Town Creek marked a midpoint between the powerful, affluent Moore family at Rocky Point and poor fishermen at Lockwoods Folly.

The varied characteristics and reputations of these three locales not only show that settlers had begun to articulate their own interpretations of Lower Cape Fear geographies, but also enable an analysis of the relationship between recorded interactions and distance within the region.[27] Contemporaries were most likely to record interactions that affected property ownership. Not surprisingly, then, the surviving sample of interactions favors those who owned substantial amounts of property. Still, it seems likely that basic patterns of interaction often transcended differences of wealth.[28] Evidence from all three of these neighborhoods powerfully demonstrates that distance played an important role in the development of Lower Cape Fear social networks. Settlers linked to any of the three neighborhoods were far more likely to interact with those in their own neighborhoods than in neighborhoods elsewhere.

Indeed, distances proved to be a determinative factor in the development of social networks. Statistical analysis confirms that, when both participants can be traced to one of the three neighborhoods, a strong negative correlation exists between distance and interaction.[29] Thus, Lower Cape Fear residents participated in social worlds that they themselves had shaped through the construction of perceptual environments, landed estates, and neighborhood social networks, but they also responded to characteristic eighteenth-century geographic constraints. Ultimately, land use and acquisition in the Lower Cape Fear occurred in a regional context that resulted from the interplay of geographic factors and increasingly extralocal but still provincial concerns.

Family and Kinship

Kinship provided one of the most powerful organizing principles for Anglo-American cultures. In the Carolina colonies, and virtually everywhere else in colonial British America, settlers placed a premium on family and kinship networks. For a variety of reasons, migrants to any region of colonial America also found it difficult to recreate these networks. In the Lower Cape Fear, as in a number of other southern settlements, demographic disruption combined with distance to hinder the formation of elaborate kinship ties and normative family structures. Still, given these obstacles the development of family and kinship ties in the Lower Cape Fear progressed at an impressive rate, and by the end of the colonial period families played a crucial role in social interaction within the region.

"The Family" dominated the Lower Cape Fear during the first decades after settlement in more than one sense. Lower Cape Fear residents gave the nickname "The Family" to the many allies of the settlement's founder, Maurice Moore, who relied on his brothers and on many other elaborate kinship ties to enhance his influence in the region. The name may have originated as a term of derision by Moore's enemies, but in any case it underscores the significance of Lower Cape Fear kinship networks. The Moores provide an instructive if exceptional example. As the most powerful family in the region, they articulated an elite model of behavior that many other families no doubt emulated. A close look at the Moores' family relationships also illustrates that contemporaries were correct about them in at least one respect.[30] They clearly developed impressive and complex kinship ties in the Lower Cape Fear.

South Carolina Governor James Moore and his wife Margaret Berringer Moore had ten children, including Maurice and Roger. Despite the Moores' prominence in South Carolina, almost one whole generation of Moores participated in the migration to the Lower Cape Fear. Four of the ten children never moved to the Lower Cape Fear, but three of these, Jehu, Anne, and Margaret, died before settlement in the region was fully underway. Only James Moore, Jr., lived in South Carolina for many years after Maurice founded Brunswick, probably because, as the eldest male heir, he could expect to inherit more land in South Carolina than any of his siblings. Perhaps not surprisingly, brothers Maurice, Roger, Nathaniel, and John all moved north together. More striking, however, sisters Mary and Rebecca and their husbands did the same. Mary, in fact, married into two of the region's most prominent immigrant families, the Howes and the Cliffords, before dying in 1735. Rebecca Moore married wealthy South Carolina merchant William Dry, and they both moved to the Cape Fear in the 1730s, where William became one of the most powerful merchants in North Carolina. Also, Rebecca's story may reflect a more personal aspect of family relations. Moore family records claim that Rebecca and Roger Moore were twins, perhaps explaining some of the motivation for the Drys' migration. In any case, kinship played an undeniably powerful role in this generation of the Moores' movement to the Lower Cape Fear.

Once families had relocated to the Lower Cape Fear, they began to identify with their new homes and to develop new networks of interaction, and the Moores were no exception. Marriage provided the most important means of cementing intraregional ties. Even though the Moores had much stronger ties to South Carolina than did more typical immigrant families, from the first generation they intermarried more with Lower Cape Fear residents than with outsiders. South Carolina Governor James Moore had eighteen grandchildren who probably reached marriageable age after their parents moved to the Lower Cape Fear, and at least ten of them married other Lower Cape Fear residents. Four others appear to have died unmarried, and only four married South Carolinians, even though they were all born in South Carolina, and most had two parents from South Carolina. Not only did this pattern assure that later generations of Moores would be even more deeply rooted in the new region, it also tied the Moores to numerous other prominent Lower Cape Fear families.

Unfortunately, existing records make it impossible to speak precisely about marriage tendencies among all the residents of the Lower Cape Fear, but among elite families clear patterns can be discerned. Land patents are a good guide to the wealthiest individuals who arrived during the region's land rush between 1725 and 1740. The ten individuals who patented the most acres in the Lower Cape Fear included Roger and Maurice Moore, and they both had already chosen spouses when they brought their families to the Cape Fear.[31] Of the remaining eight, six married into other prominent Lower Cape Fear families. One, George Burrington, did not have a wife while in the Lower Cape Fear. Robert Halton, the remaining exception, proves the rule, because he had a wife in England when he arrived in North Carolina, never remarried, but had an openly avowed illegitimate son by a woman from the Lower Cape Fear. With or without a formally acknowledged marriage ceremony in the Lower Cape Fear, most of these men had developed strong emotional ties to the region from an early date.

Slave ownership rankings, derived from tax lists generated between 1755 and 1773, reveal more about the elite's matrimonial entanglements during the last decades before the American Revolution. By this time, the process of kinship network formation had progressed considerably in the Lower Cape Fear. Among the top ten slave owners in the Lower Cape Fear, eight married into other elite Lower Cape Fear families, and one remained unmarried.[32] The one leading slave owner who did not take a Lower Cape Fear bride, the younger William Dry, married Mary Jane Rhett of South Carolina, partly because of his Moore family ties as the son of Rebecca Moore. Evidently, by this time, the rest of the Lower Cape Fear elite intermarried with one another as much and probably more than with the Moores. Also, the region's elite had entered into another generation by the late colonial period, and a number of the largest property owners in these years had been born in the Lower Cape Fear, reinforcing regional identities even more.

By the late colonial period, marriage also served to integrate wealthy individuals into the Lower Cape Fear elite. While six of the top ten slave owners had some kind of kin relationship to the Moores, the remaining four indicated a complementary trend. All four of them apparently came from families who did not participate in the original migration from South Carolina and Albemarle and who drew on transatlantic sources of wealth and influence. Frederick Gregg came from Ireland, and the Quinces and Eagles both came from England, though Richard Eagles, Sr., had lived in South Carolina for a time. William Ross, Sr., is of unknown origin, though his name strongly suggests Scottish origins. Ross not only married into the Lower Cape Fear elite but probably acquired most of his slaves and other property by doing so, having married the widow of Edward Moseley and John Sampson. Thus marriage simultaneously enabled the elaboration of kinship networks, integrated newcomers into preformed networks, and opened another avenue for economic mobility to males.

Lower Cape Fear wills provide additional evidence about family and kinship in the region. Indeed, because testators normally made reference to all of their immediate family members in their wills, an analysis of 278 extant wills for New Hanover and Brunswick counties before 1776 provides by far the best evidence about Euro-American colonial Lower Cape Fear families. Lower Cape Fear wills leave no doubt that the nuclear family gave Lower Cape Fear residents their strongest ties.[33] The will of Lower Cape Fear planter Benjamin Heron illustrates a typical testator's perspective. When Heron composed his will before departing on a journey to England in 1770, he expressed considerable concern for his children and placed much of his trust in his wife Alice because of his "great affection and esteem" for her and because he had "the greatest confidence and faith [in her] . . . from the long experience . . . of her good heart and mind." For Heron, like many others, those outside of the nuclear family took only secondary importance. Almost 60 percent of all individuals mentioned in wills were members of the testator's immediate family.[34] The percentage of nuclear family members among those mentioned in wills would no doubt be even higher if Lower Cape Fear families did not experience a pattern of demographic disruption that made it more difficult for Lower

Cape Fear residents to establish the normative nuclear family pattern central to Anglo-American cultural expectations. Well over half of all testators did not have a nuclear family when they wrote their wills.[35]

The frequent disruption of nuclear families placed additional pressure on local extended kinship relations. When a spouse or a sibling died, relatives might seek emotional support or assistance from other kin. The will of Lower Cape Fear widow Sarah Allen shows how one Lower Cape Fear resident adapted to the consequences of high mortality rates. Sarah immigrated to the region from South Carolina with her wealthy husband, planter Eleazer Allen. Eleazer passed away before the couple had any children, but Sarah's will indicates that she found support with an extensive network of extended kin. Sarah mentioned nineteen different individuals in her will, including a number of nieces and grandnieces. One niece was even bequeathed Sarah's wedding ring "as a memento of my Conjugal happiness, not doubting hers is equal, and may it be as lasting," and the husband of another favorite niece also figured prominently in Sarah Allen's will by being named an executor and receiving "a mourning Ring in Testimony of my Sense of his invarrying goodness to me." At the same time, other factors made it difficult for Lower Cape Fear residents to rely extensively on extended kinship networks. For one thing, extended kin networks could also be affected by high mortality. Perhaps even more important, because settlement in the Lower Cape Fear did not begin until relatively late in the colonial period, a high percentage of the region's residents were immigrants who were far removed from many of their relatives. Consequently, extended kin may have been important, but they were often too far away to be of much help. Assistance had to come from individuals who were relatively nearby or at least within the Lower Cape Fear region.

The choices of Lower Cape Fear testators demonstrated these limitations on extended kin networks. Testators were far more likely than not to choose non-kin as the executors of their estates. Executors were of paramount importance for those writing wills because executors bore the important burden of protecting the family's interests and insuring that the testator's wishes were respected. Ideally, most testators would have chosen widows or adult sons to be executors, but this was not always an option. The high frequency of non-kin executors suggests that many Lower Cape Fear residents could not rely on extended kin to provide this very important service. At the same time, it should not be assumed that extended kinship relationships were unimportant for settlers in the Lower Cape Fear. Indeed, except for the selection of executors, testators seem to have placed greater emphasis on extended kin relationships than on non-kin relationships. More wills mentioned extended kin, and in greater total numbers.

Lower Cape Fear residents alternated in their emphasis on extended kin and non-kin for several reasons. First of all, many Lower Cape Fear residents could not rely on extended kin in the region because none lived nearby. Over half of all Lower Cape Fear testators made no reference at all in their will to extended kin. Most Cape Fear residents left their extended kin behind when they migrated to the region, and even extended kin in the Lower Cape Fear might succumb to the region's deadly diseases. Benjamin Heron made his wife an executor of his estate, but he also included "my esteemed friends" Lewis Henry DeRosset, Frederick Jones, and Samuel Swann, Jr., as executors. Executors had to be nearby and actively involved in the handling of an estate, so if kin were far away or in poor health, testators wisely chose trustworthy friends, neighbors, or other non-kin. Benjamin Heron, for example, might have preferred to make his brother Charles Heron an executor of his estate, but Charles's residence in England made this choice impractical.

Yet, extended kin ties probably remained important to Lower Cape Fear residents regardless of distance. Indeed, the absence of extended kin in the Lower Cape Fear may have made settlers fonder of relatives in their old homes. They indicated as much by referring to extended kin in their wills and often by making them bequests of at least symbolic value. Charles Heron was mentioned in Benjamin Heron's will, and received bequests for both himself and his son, but DeRosset, Jones, and Swann received no bequests. Settlement in a new region simply required that new networks be formed within the region, whether based on kinship or other criteria, to complement more distant sources of support and assistance networks. The construction of wills, then, reflected competing tensions between geographic limitations that prevented reliance on kin from outside the region and a provincial awareness of kinship ties that sometimes crossed regional boundaries.

A more focused examination of Lower Cape Fear wills uncovers somewhat less emphasis on neighborhood connections. In the three neighborhoods of Rocky Point, Lockwoods Folly, and Old Town Creek, the wills of forty-one colonial residents have survived. Of the 313 names mentioned in the wills from these three neighborhoods, however, only fifty-seven can be identified as neighbors. These numbers can be misleading, of course, because most of those mentioned in all wills were nuclear family members who would not have been identified as separate heads of households or residents in any of the three neighborhoods. Still, neighbors made up less than a third of the individuals mentioned who were not part of the testators' immediate families. On the other hand, of the relatively small minority of people who were mentioned in wills but who had no identifiable kinship relation to the testator, most can be identified as neighbors. These findings show that neighborhood connections probably did have considerable significance, but, for the purposes of inheritance at least, those connections were still much less important than kinship connections. Ideally, testators probably preferred to leave bequests to individuals who participated in both kinship and neighborhood networks. Of the fifty-seven neighbors who rated mention in these wills, thirty-six, a significant majority, were also somehow related to the testator. Failing this congruence of kin and neighbor, testators most often overlooked distance and turned to relatives, but distance still proved to be a delimiting factor. It was highly unusual for Lower Cape Fear testators to mention anyone who resided beyond the Lower Cape Fear region in their wills.

A close examination of family and kinship in the Lower Cape Fear thus reveals important regional boundaries to kinship networks and, by extension, circumstances that encouraged an increasingly provincial perspective on family interactions. Surviving letters from Lower Cape Fear residents indicate a strong attachment to distant kin, and it is likely that settlers worked hard to maintain often far-flung family relationships. But whatever psychological importance distant kinship connections had, the day-to-day experience of family life, rooted in matters such as marriage, birth, death, and inheritance, transcended neighborhoods but still usually took place within the confines of the Lower Cape Fear region. By the mid-eighteenth century settlers had developed powerful family allegiances that tied them to their own region in ways that were neither entirely transatlantic nor local but were provincial in scope.

Regional Centralization

Whether rooted in the settlement process or linked to cultural assumptions about kinship, social interaction in colonial British America did not occur in an arbitrary and entirely unpredictable way. Even in highly dispersed populations like those in newly settled regions like the Lower Cape Fear, people quickly established common meeting places to serve various institutional, cultural, and social functions. Most notably, while the southern colonies were famous for their lack of urbanization, the Lower Cape Fear had two important towns: Wilmington and Brunswick. Any systematic look at social interaction in the Lower Cape Fear must consider the activities in these towns as a necessary complement to other interactions. Indeed, if these towns appear small when compared to colonial Charleston or Philadelphia, it would be difficult to exaggerate their importance for social interaction in the Lower Cape Fear. These towns not only provided locations for social interaction, they also provided regional centers to reinforce provincial identities, simultaneously offering competition to and imitation of metropolitan models.

In the Lower Cape Fear region, unlike in some other parts of the southern colonies, centralized meetings or interactions did not occur separately but overlapped and reinforced each other in the region's two towns. Virtually all public or private functions requiring interaction and travel in the Lower Cape Fear took place in either Wilmington or Brunswick. The New Hanover and Brunswick county courts were located in the towns. The region's two Anglican parishes were roughly conterminous with the two counties, and the churches were also located in Wilmington and Brunswick. Lower Cape Fear economic exchanges normally took place in the stores of the two port towns, making it easier for merchants to import and export goods across the Atlantic and up and down the Cape Fear River. Official warehouse sites were also set up in the towns, where laws required the inspection of all major export commodities.[36] In addition, both Brunswick and Wilmington served as locations for specifically social gatherings, which often took place in coffee houses, ordinaries, and similar sites. Thus, English cultural norms related to law, religion, and civility could all be reconstructed through the Wilmington- and Brunswick-centered provincial experiences and perceptions of Lower Cape Fear residents.

A whole variety of important matters encouraged Lower Cape Fear residents to take part in county court proceedings. Quantitative records of settlers' participation in county legal actions in Lockwoods Folly, Rocky Point, and Town Creek clearly demonstrate that. No strong correlation connected distance between neighborhoods and litigation in legal actions that appeared in the New Hanover county court minutes and dockets.[37] There does appear to have been a comparatively large amount of litigation involving residents in Rocky Point, but this finding is most likely a consequence of the neighborhood's considerable and interrelated property interests rather than that of simple proximity. Indeed, the large number of the county court actions, which were so frequently related to debt and other property matters, suggests that business networks also transcended neighborhoods. After all, a litigant had both to attend the county court and to have behaved in some context that caused a grievance against the defendant to bring suit against someone outside the neighborhood.

Thus, neighborhood networks played an important role in the Lower Cape Fear, but social networks also extended well beyond these neighborhoods and were ultimately also shaped by interactions in the Lower Cape Fear's towns. Quantitative evaluation of interactions indicates that residents were far more likely to have connections with those who either owned land or lived in Wilmington than even with other members of their own neighborhoods. Brunswick never achieved the size of Wilmington, but it also helped to shape social connections. Furthermore, the number of ties to the two towns showed no significant relationship to distance. Discussion of the importance of towns in economic and political development is a commonplace among historians, but my data strongly suggests that urban areas powerfully influenced the formation of social networks as well. Wilmington and Brunswick were, as many scholars have reminded us, not especially large urban centers. Yet, even in this relatively rural and sparsely populated region, the presence of towns did much to shape the way settlers experienced interactions with one another. Thus, town and neighborhood networks combined to give spatial structure to the bulk of social interactions in the Lower Cape Fear.

The centralization of social networks in the Lower Cape Fear region coincided with the growth and definition of the region itself. By the 1770s the region was the most important functional geographic entity for the people of the Lower Cape Fear. Many settlers had moved beyond the highly localistic neighborhoods that characterized the first settlements in the seventeenth century but had not yet become participants in larger arenas such as the North Carolina Assembly or the Continental Congress. For the vast majority of colonists and slaves in the Lower Cape Fear, social interaction and experiences were overwhelmingly likely to take place with other residents of the Lower Cape Fear region itself. Neighborhoods and local contacts tell only part of the story, but there is little evidence that many inhabitants of the Lower Cape Fear participated in social networks that crossed into other regions of Anglo-America. Thus, in 1770, John Barnett could write from Northampton County in the Albemarle area of North Carolina that "in this part of the Province we have hardly any communication with Cape Fear."[38]

In the three neighborhoods of Rocky Point, Lockwoods Folly, and Town Creek, settlers seldom recorded interactions with people from beyond the Lower Cape Fear. County recording procedures may have been somewhat biased toward local transactions, but conveyances, wills, powers of attorney, and other documents usually identified individuals from distant locations. This data does not, however, suggest that the Lower Cape Fear was isolated from the outside world. On the contrary, many Lower Cape Fear inhabitants had important and meaningful social relationships with those in other regions or across the Atlantic. Such relationships could only be expected because many, if not most, of the residents of the colonial Lower Cape Fear had immigrated from other locales. High levels of physical mobility in the early modern Atlantic world acted against isolation and localism, even in the most peripheral locales. Even more important, all of the early and mid-eighteenth-century Anglo-American colonies experienced rapid integration into Atlantic markets and economic networks. The growth of print culture also gave some individuals ways of identifying and communicating with those in distant places. Finally, the British Empire provided colonists with still another set of broader identifications and concerns.

None of these external influences, however, changed the far more regional character of society in the colonial Lower Cape Fear. Indeed, limited exposure to outsiders may have strengthened ties within the region because it made regionally distinctive characteristics and experiences more evident. Furthermore, all of these forces remained distant to most people in the Lower Cape Fear. Most people did not constantly migrate, engage in transatlantic trade, read voluminously, or attend the Continental Congress. Those who did may have been harbingers of important changes, but, during the colonial period, they remained atypical, and their influence did not immediately overwhelm older and dominant patterns of social interaction.

In sum, distance continued to limit social interaction for most colonists in eighteenth-century British America, but the constraints of distance could be considerably mitigated by regional growth and development. For several decades after 1725, settlers took up land in the Lower Cape Fear region and organized their social world to enable social connections between neighborhoods. Between 1725 and 1775, Lower Cape Fear colonists used nuclear families, extended kinship relationships, and non-kin ties for some basic forms of support that transcended neighborly relations. Also, during the colonial period the Lower Cape Fear region's two port towns provided a centralized structure for social interaction. Finally, by the time of the American Revolution, the Lower Cape Fear had emerged as a distinct and separate region that delineated the limits and possibilities of social interaction for its inhabitants. Because of the widespread growth, rapid development, and important regional divisions throughout the Lower South colonies, the Lower Cape Fear was also probably far from unique. Eighteenth-century Anglo-American settlers, both within and beyond the Lower Cape Fear, participated in the gradual emergence of a provincial pattern of social interaction, as increasingly complex and extensive regional networks offered an alternative to the transatlantic or localized networks that were more important in the seventeenth century.

CHAPTER THREE

"Almost an Englishman"

Eighteenth-Century Anglo-African Identities

Daniel C. Littlefield

"Striving to be both European and black," Paul Gilroy argues, "requires some specific forms of double consciousness . . . [W]here racist, nationalist, or ethnically absolutist discourses orchestrate political relationships so that these identities appear to be mutually exclusive, occupying the space between them or trying to demonstrate their continuity has been viewed as a provocative and even oppositional act of political insubordination."[1] The "double self" of blacks in the West engaged the particular attention of black intellectuals in the twentieth century. But for Anglo-Africans, the dilemma of divided identity dates back to the very origins of the early modern Atlantic world. One might expect this duality to be the predicament of creole Anglo-Africans who were born in the West and educated according to western norms, but who lived in societies that regarded them with a profound racial bias. But what about native Africans who came into contact with Europeans during the era of the slave trade? To what extent might they, familiar with their natal cultures and subject to the worst of western excesses, also develop a double consciousness? If they continued to regard themselves as Africans, was this feeling entirely unmodified by their western experience? If they adapted themselves to their new situation, how

African did they remain? Or, rejecting essentialist notions of African or Anglo, we might ask how such people defined or redefined themselves in the crucible of the Atlantic world at the height of the slave trade.

Many historians have written about the maintenance of an African consciousness among North America's enslaved population.[2] These studies of early African-American life demonstrate cultural persistence among enslaved or newly freed peoples on the continent.[3] While these scholars by no means impart a static quality to America's black community or minimize its vitality, most do suggest a single trajectory toward identity formation. They presume a journey from Africa to America wherein, depending on one's perspective, Africans would have traveled from "backwardness" or bewilderment to "enlightenment" or acculturation, while simultaneously struggling to maintain their personal integrity and sense of self—what Sterling Stuckey, perhaps, would call their "Africanity"—against a preponderance of forces that pulled them toward assimilation and deracination.

More recently, Ira Berlin has modified the argument and reversed the process. His vision of "Atlantic creoles" posits an incoming "charter generation" of sophisticated and culturally mixed peoples in early America who had already diverged from the Africans among whom they may have been born.[4] These people approached the developing Atlantic community, even in America, with familiarity and confidence. Berlin conceptualizes a movement from creole toward African through the eighteenth century as the plantation regime solidified, planters consolidated their authority over the places and people they claimed to own (absorbing much of the knowledge that Africans initially brought to America), and increasingly imported large numbers of relatively unskilled and unsophisticated Africans to labor in the plantation fields. By the nineteenth century, southern slaveholders would contend, and maybe even believe, that the situation had never been otherwise. Proslavery writers would have scoffed at the notion that their ancestors had regarded Africans, in some areas of their mutual involvement, as their equals in wisdom, skill, and capacity. The story of Africans in America, therefore, is not a simple journey from either unspoiled simplicity or ancient sophistication to unending struggle and cultural contestation, but is a winding path, marked by twists and turns.

Berlin's "Atlantic creoles" were not unique. African cultures were transformed upon contact with Europeans, and the extent to which Atlantic creoles, or what John Thornton calls "Afro-Atlantic culture," differed from other African cultures is largely a matter of focus or perspective. Thornton has been particularly effective in showing change and continuity within an African context and connecting African societies with those elsewhere. However, even when Africans adopted western ideas or practices, scholars have diverged over the extent or seriousness of the adoption and the depth of their comprehension.[5] Arguments also occur on the question of what should be considered as "African." Sidney Mintz and Richard Price, in a seminal essay, suggested that the roots of African-American culture lay in Africa when people from different cultures were thrown together in the coffles that brought them to the coast, and in the ships that carried them to America.[6] As enslaved Africans began to interact and form new methods of communication and ways of interpreting their lives, their beliefs, and their fate, so began a new culture. Africa survived in the New World not so much via "carry-overs" (specific objects, beliefs, or practices that can be traced directly to particular African locales), but through deeper "cultural grammars" (modes of perception and expression), particularly in art and social relations, that were shared in many parts of sub-Saharan Africa.[7]

Yet, despite Africans' resilience and creativity, the context of their central contribution to the creation of the culture, economy, and society of the larger Atlantic world exacted a psychic cost. The contact between Africans and the West may have forged an African-American culture, but the contest of cultures had destructive as well as constructive consequences for the identities of enslaved migrants to America and their descendants. Since most blacks who had contact with Europeans were slaves, such common forms of slave resistance as maroonage or rebellion reveal something about Africans' reaction to slavery but relatively little about Africans' response to European culture per se. Since most blacks were not permitted the luxury of a formal education, let alone access to pen and paper, few written accounts of eighteenth-century black attitudes survive. But those that exist suggest that while Africans hated slavery, their response to western civilization as a whole was more ambivalent. Most of these Anglo-African authors were willing to accommodate themselves to western life and thought at least to the extent that western life and thought were able to accommodate themselves to them.

Regarding Africa

Principles of cultural relativity inevitably influenced newly enslaved Africans' encounter with Britons. If the first aspect of Africans that Englishmen remarked upon was their color, the reverse was also the case. Olaudah Equiano, an Ibo man, kidnapped from southeastern Nigeria in the middle of the eighteenth century when he was about ten years old, was convinced when he first met Europeans that he was to be eaten by these "white men with horrible looks, red faces and loose hair."[8]

If Europeans regarded Africans as savages, Africans returned the compliment. Again Equiano: "The white people looked and acted, as I thought, in so savage a manner; for I had never seen among any people such instances of brutal cruelty; and this not only shewn towards us blacks, but also to some of the whites themselves. One white man in particular I saw, when we were permitted to be on deck, flogged so unmercifully with a large rope near the foremast, that he died in consequence of it and they tossed him over the side as they would have done a brute."[9]

Still, novelty induced wonderment, and European skills captured the imagination. Although Africans were adept at negotiating the Niger Delta and other African locales in sometimes sizeable canoes, Europeans' oceangoing sailing ships appeared to be magical. Mechanical navigation devices were also objects of curiosity and amazement. Most slaves, especially the men who were often kept chained and confined in the hold, had little occasion to observe such things during the middle passage. Yet enslaved women and children were occasionally allowed to remain on deck. To Equiano, what he saw, amid his fear and distress, led him to respect the strangers who had abducted him. "What struck me first," Equiano later remembered of his arrival in Barbados, "was that the houses were built with stories, and in every other respect different from those in Africa: but I was still more astonished on seeing people on horseback. I did not know what this could mean; and indeed I thought these people were full of nothing but magical arts."[10]

American slavery, however, was racial slavery, and enslaved Africans soon learned that in their new world whites were on top and blacks were on the bottom. An association of their color with inferiority developed quickly. James Albert Ukawsaw Gronniosaw, from Bornu in northern Nigeria, recalled his introduction to the power of print this way:

> when first I saw him read, I was never so surprized in my life, as when I saw the book talk to my master, for I thought it did, as I observed him to look upon it; and move his lips.—I wished it would do so to me. As soon as my master had done reading, I followed him to the place where he put the book, being mightily delighted with it, and when nobody saw me, I opened it and put my ear down

> close upon it, in great hopes that it would say something to me; but was very sorry, and greatly disappointed when I found it would not speak, this thought immediately presented itself to me, that every body and every thing despised me because I was black.[11]

If Gronniosaw's account of his childhood feelings is accurate, he internalized his racial inferiority with astonishing rapidity as he could not have been aboard ship for more than a week before he first observed his master read. But as with all ex-slave narratives, Gronniosaw's words must be very carefully sifted.[12] Eighteenth-century Anglo-Africans were addressing a western audience with its own preconceived assumptions about, and expectations of, Africans. Nevertheless, Gronniosaw's story may be said to mark, unintentionally perhaps, a new cultural moment, the beginning of a new literary tradition, and a distinctive cultural ethos. It represents a critical moment in acculturation, in identity formation, in self-presentation, and in self-deprecation. It is at once an expression of pride in accomplishment (the author's subsequent attainment of literacy) alloyed with a measure of self-doubt or self-abnegation. This portrait was not necessarily a true reflection of the author's self-perception, rather it evinced a fretful concern about how one would be perceived by others. Even if Gronniosaw's account of the "talking book" was not literally true, it still had powerful symbolic value. The story assumed a life of its own and was repeated in several other African narratives between 1785 and the second decade of the nineteenth century. These other renderings implied ignorance and distress, misplaced arrogance, and a yearning for enlightenment, but none repeated the recognition of racial inferiority indicated by Gronniosaw.[13]

However, Gronniosaw had always had a sense of alienation, even before his enslavement, and his family considered him unstable. He took to his white master with an unseemly alacrity. His "beloved" sister, one of the few members of his family with whom he got on well, was apparently an albino ("quite white, and fair, with fine light hair") and perhaps he was consequently predisposed, in the words of Henry Louis Gates, to privilege "whiteness . . . at the expense of his blackness."[14] Unlike other eighteenth-century Anglo-Africans who wrote or had their reflections recorded, he failed to condemn slavery or the slave trade. He did not even condemn English racism, although he certainly experienced it. More often than not, he seemed to interpret his hardships in class rather than racial terms. He was, after all, married to an English woman, who, with their children (one of whom from her previous marriage was white rather than mulatto), suffered as he did. Moreover, he was aware that his skin color may have attracted some of the help as well as some of the trouble that came his way.[15] Gronniosaw emphasized his African identity in his story, but whatever ambivalence he suggested about English life was personal rather than cultural or ideological and, for him, the good, on the whole, outweighed the bad.

Equiano's reaction to Europeans was vastly dissimilar from Gronniosaw's but it also indicated an attitude that facilitated acculturation: "I now not only felt myself quite easy with these new countrymen, but relished their society and manners. I no longer looked upon them as spirits, but as men superior to us; and therefore I had the stronger desire to resemble them; to imbibe their spirit and imitate their manners."[16]

Eighteenth-century Anglo-African writers were unusual people. Their lives were vastly different from that of most blacks in the British Atlantic world. Not only were they literate, and had had far greater contact with whites than was customary, but they had gained their freedom and had usually spent a significant part of their lives in England rather than in the slave colonies of British America. It would be difficult and unwise to expect that every African shared the feelings of this most fortunate few. In this regard, the relative mildness of the writings of the Anglo-Africans is their most striking quality. Perhaps their own fortuitous circumstances predisposed them to forgive Europeans for their wrongs. In fact, those Anglo-Africans who accepted Christianity often excused their captivity as providential. "One great duty I own to Almighty God," Ottobah Cugoano, a Fante from the eighteenth-century Gold Coast, wrote,

> [is] that, although I have been brought away from my native country, in that torrent of robbery and wickedness [the slave trade], thanks be to God . . . I have both obtained liberty, and acquired the great advantages of some learning, . . . and, what is still infinitely of greater advantage, I trust, [is] to know something of HIM *who is that God whose providence rules over all* . . . And in some manner, I may say with Joseph, as he did with respect to the evil intention of his brethren, when they sold him into Egypt, that whatever evil intentions and bad motives those insidious robbers had in carrying me away from my native country and friends, I trust, was what the Lord intended for my good.[17]

Cugoano's comments are all the more significant because he alone among eighteenth-century Anglo-African writers composed an extended polemical critique of western hypocrisy and the exploitative nature of European overseas expansion. He even criticized the religious component of this venture, displacing his ire, however, on Spanish Catholicism. He excoriated "the fanatic monk" Vincent Valverde, for example, who accompanied Francisco Pizarro on the conquest of Peru. Although he condemned Pizarro as a "treacherous bastard" in contrast to the noble Inca emperor Atahualpa, and likewise discredited Cortes to the advantage of Montezuma, Cugoano's sternest attack was on the religious justification of conquest as enunciated by the priest. Of course, this attack on Spanish missionary activity was easy for an Anglo-African to make, for it tied him to a vaunted English tradition of anti-Catholicism. But Cugoano's argument was with Spanish methods and not with their Christian message. In fact, he still desired that Africa be Christianized. Cugoano did not appreciate and may not have cared that even a peaceful conversion might be subversive to Africans' culture.

Cugoano was more hard-headed (meaning willful, realistic, and perceptive) than some, for it may be, as Keith Sandiford argues, that his "solid sense of native African values" prevented him from entirely succumbing to the "powerful inducements to self-negation that encompassed" blacks in the West.[18] But this was only relatively true. For inherent, and sometimes explicit, in Cugoano's statements of his religious commitment was an ambivalence about his own African background and identity. To the extent that most eighteenth-century Anglo-African writers were religious, they tended to interpret everything as a part of a divine plan, and however fondly they remembered their homeland and wanted to return there (and some did return), non-Christian Africa was viewed as somewhat deficient. Thus, an African woman enslaved in Massachusetts, Phillis Wheatley, wrote:

> 'Twas mercy brought me from my Pagan land,
> Taught my benighted soul to understand
>
> That there's a God, that there's a *Saviour* too
> Once I redemption neither sought nor knew.
>
> Some view our sable race with scornful eye,
> "Their colour is a diabolic die."
>
> Remember, *Christians, Negroes,* black as *Cain,*
> May be refin'd and join th' angelic train.[19]

Despite her critique of western racism, Wheatley still considered her capture and enslavement as providential and her African birthplace as "benighted."

Philip Quaque or Kweku also demonstrates this perspective.[20] Sent by a local ruler from the Akan region of modern Ghana for education in England in 1754, Quaque was the first African to be ordained in the Church of England. He was thirteen years old when he left home, and by the time he returned as a missionary for the Society for the Propagation of the Gospel (SPG) eleven years later, he was unable to speak his native language, or in any case to speak it well. He performed his religious duties through an interpreter. It may be true that a language long unused—even a natal one—can virtually evaporate. Moreover, the English placed a strong emphasis on extirpating the indigenous languages of those they sought to "civilize," including the Scots, the Irish, and the Welsh. It is unlikely that Quaque's teachers encouraged him to maintain his native tongue, or indeed that they expressed much interest in it.[21] In England, Quaque absorbed lessons and attitudes that placed little value on the language and culture of the people from whom he came and whom he returned to serve (and save). Moreover, he came back with an English wife, whose education and outlook probably reinforced his sense of separation. He lived and worked in Cape Coast Castle, away from the local community, and often dined at the governor's table. His letters to the SPG in London read very much like those of white missionaries at the same time.[22]

Other Africans-in-exile occasionally tried to retain their native tongue, and under more difficult conditions than Quaque's, and the difference between his attitude and theirs is worth exploring. Newport Gardner, taken from Africa in 1760 at about the same age as Quaque and enslaved in New England, made a conscious effort to remember his language, and for the same reason that ought to have motivated Quaque: "so that in case Providence should open a way, he might return to Africa, and find a people with whom he might converse intelligibly, and to whom he might communicate the great truths of the gospel." Years after his uprooting, he was able to address two Africans he encountered in a slave cargo in their local language and remind them that he had once met them in Africa.[23]

Of course, Quaque left willingly, or at least as a result of a community decision, while Gardner was an involuntary emigrant. Quaque, a free person and a student, sought deliberately to acquire another culture if not to lose his own. Gardner, enslaved, had less access to the host culture. However, he was also a member of a world apart, a black community where variant cultural developments validated various African values and practices. Gardner also became literate in English, though, unlike Quaque, he acquired this through his own efforts rather than via formal education, and he did not lose his regard for at least the linguistic portion of his African heritage. Quaque, by contrast, absorbed his lessons with alacrity and embraced English culture to the detriment of his own.

The difference in context was crucial. Most masters did not care what their slaves did outside the bounds of duties and the household so long as some semblance of the masters' version of good social order prevailed. Indeed, in a racial caste system some divergence might be preferred, a consideration that underlay the whites' amused toleration, for example, of "Negro Election Day" a New England ritual that had African content and analogues.[24] Most whites who viewed (and often enjoyed) these celebrations did not appreciate the significance of the African components. They interpreted the rituals as imperfect representations of white New England practices and saw in them an ultimate sanctioning of the established order. But Quaque's teachers had other expectations that Quaque may have absorbed almost too well. Three years after his return to Africa, for example, he was directed by the SPG "to endeavour to recover his own language." Yet, even this admonition from those with whom he so closely identified himself could not compel Quaque to lose an aversion he had so deeply imbibed. He complained of the "vile jargon" spoken on the coast, and described it as "the only obstacles [*sic*] of learning in these parts." He sent several of his children to England to avoid their learning it as well as other "vile customs and practices" of the region.[25]

Quaque's abnegating attitudes were such that when he began a school, he proudly wrote the Society that only mulattoes were admitted. Reading his letters to the SPG, it is difficult to tell that they were written by an African, much less one native to the region in which he was posted. To some degree, Quaque's profoundly English prejudices may have been a simple matter of self-presentation. He obviously desired to please his Anglican mentors and patrons; to demonstrate how well he learned his lessons; how finely attuned he was to English norms and prejudices; and also to excuse himself for any possible failure. Shortly after his return to Africa, for example, he alerted the SPG that he did not expect to get much assistance from the local British officials "they being all Scotch and Irish People, rank Presbyterians."[26]

In other instances, it appears that Quaque had so thoroughly elided his origins that he had come to see himself as an Englishman in fact, as well as in cultural terms. As a postscript to one letter to the SPG he described "the jubilee or the first fruits offering with the natives of Africa, which they generally term blacks' Christmas. This custom, I learn, is a traditional institution handed down to them time immemorial by the ancients, the performance of which is held sacred by them annually."[27] He writes of "them" as if he were a stranger to the region rather than a person born there. Even if he were ritually reenacting the religious concept of having been "born again," that concept did not require amnesia. Quaque's posture was in striking contrast to that of Equiano who reminisced fondly about his people. "We are almost a nation of dancers, musicians, and poets," Equiano wrote, using a more inclusive pronoun.[28] It may be that writing from England, forty years after the fact, Equiano was engaged in a nostalgic attempt to recapture a romantic past while Quaque was dealing with a very stressful present. Quaque may also have deliberately patterned the tone and perspective of his reports to the SPG after others he had seen. In any case, he certainly evidenced a remarkable ability to distance himself from his origins, itself an extraordinary exercise of self-will and self-denial.

Given his position as the resident missionary at a slaving factory, it is perhaps too much to expect Quaque to condemn the slave trade outright. Unlike most other Anglo-African writers, he had never been a slave himself. Quaque's personal knowledge of slaving was confined to his observations on the coast, and through employment in the castle he was an indirect participant in the business. Both the Africans and the Europeans with whom he associated were involved in the slave trade and it would have required greater perception, sensitivity, and commitment than he apparently possessed to have adopted an oppositional stance. Quaque did venture an occasional criticism of slavery as practiced elsewhere, however. He wondered, for example, about "the true picture of inhumanity those unhappy creatures suffer in their miserable state of bondage, under the different degrees of austere masters they unfortunately fall in with in the West Indies?"[29]

Like some of the Anglo-African writers who had been enslaved, Quaque probably extenuated the trade, when he thought about it at all, in terms of its religious and civilizing mission. Yet, he was also quick to perceive cant. He responded to a complaint about British tyranny in a Massachusetts sermon during the revolutionary crisis by questioning the minister's claim that Americans had God on their side. "Good God can this be possible," Quaque replied, "when I behold with Sorrowful sighing, my poor abject Countrymen over whom You without the Bowels of Christian Love and Pity, hold in Cruel Bondage. This Iniquitous Practice methinks seems to set Religion aside and only making Room for the height of Ambition and Grandeur."[30] Such observations of American hypocrisy were commonplace in Britain also, so even in this regard, Quaque's words were calculated to please his British patrons. But he also accepted his personal relationship to the enslaved ("my poor abject Countrymen").

Whatever his personal rectitude, and it appears to have been unobjectionable, Quaque's example did not inspire emulation. He had difficulty getting the Europeans, nominally Christians already, to pay the minimal ritual obeisance to Christian duties signaled by attendance at Sunday services, and his obligation to engage in the daily hurly-burly of trade hardly added to his distinction as a priest. What, if anything, about his life there was to inspire African admiration may have been little different from whatever it was that attracted them to Europeans, and that was seldom Europeans' religion. After eight years on the coast, Quaque had baptized barely fifty people, mostly whites and mulattoes, only a few blacks. One of these was a sixty-year-old repatriate from Rhode Island, whose forty-eight years in servitude evidently had not soured him on Christianity.[31] Or if it had, he was one of the few people Quaque's example may have claimed. Even Caboceer Cudjo, the man who sent Quaque away for schooling, could not be convinced. He pleaded that he was too old to convert: "I immediately made a reply, that he was not, and that a voluntary Act was more acceptable in the sight of God, than those of a forced Nature." But the old man would not be moved.[32]

Toward the end of his life, Quaque complained bitterly about the "avaricious disposition of the blacks" and described himself as a "prophet . . . [with] no honour in his own country."[33] Unfortunately, he had become so culturally estranged from "his own country" that neither local marriages, the outrageous neglect of his mission by those who had sent him, a compulsory involvement in local business in order to survive, or occasional discrimination by whites on the coast, caused Quaque to renounce his faith or identification with the West. He must have suffered some disillusionment and a gradual loosening of his ties to Europe, however, for when he died he left five years salary uncollected. His ties to his SPG sponsors had loosened to such an extent that he would not even claim their lucre.[34]

None of this is to imply that Quaque accepted everything European entirely unthinkingly. Even he blamed the deterioration of the quality of life in his region on the presence of European settlers. (The Africans "preferred the white man's vices to his religion," an early chronicler of Quaque's mission commented.)[35] For a major problem with Christianity was that it contrasted enormously with the way Europeans actually lived. First, it was often difficult for Africans, including Quaque, to reconcile slavery with Christianity. Secondly, the higher morality that Europeans said they had over that found in pagan Africa proved too often to be lacking in common decency. This was true even among the most religious of white people. Olaudah Equiano was permitted to buy his freedom in 1766 from Robert King, who, as a Quaker, probably at the time should not have owned him in the first place; or, in any case, was likely already under pressure to manumit him. But King did not part with him willingly. Despite the promise that he could buy himself after he had acquired £40 sterling, when Equiano came up with the money, King wavered. Indeed, if Equiano had not taken the precaution of having with him a friend who knew about the deal, his master may not have honored his promise: "'What,' said he, 'give you your freedom? Why, where did you get the money? Have you got forty pounds sterling?' 'Yes, sir,' I answered. 'How did you get it?' replied he. I told him very honestly. The captain then said he knew I got the money very honestly and with much industry, and that I was particularly careful. On which my master replied I got money much faster then he did, and said he would not have made the promise he did if he had thought I should have got money so soon."[36] Equiano's fear that he might not get his freedom was well-founded. A previous master had already broken a promise to that effect. Such experiences as these among Christians were disheartening to new converts who took the religion seriously. Especially since in traditional Africa religion is such an important aspect of everyday existence.[37]

Gronniosaw thought that the discrepancy was a result of the fact that he lived in a slave society, and that if he got to England things would be different. But no such luck. "I was astonished when we landed [in Portsmouth] to hear the inhabitants of that place curse and swear and otherwise profane. I expected to find nothing but goodness, gentleness and meekness in this Christian land, I then suffered great perplexities of mind. I inquired if any serious Christian people resided there, the woman I made this inquiry of, answered me in the affirmative; and added that she was one of them. I was heartily glad to hear her say so."[38] However, when he entrusted her with all his money, she refused to give it back to him, and denied that he had ever given her any. Incidents such as these made blacks dubious about Western values. Clearly they did not put Gronniosaw off, and Cugoano and Equiano used Western ideals to critique Western realities. Even when Equiano contrasted the simple virtues of his homeland to the European-sponsored corruption wrought by the Atlantic trade in humankind, that rhetorical strategy gained force from its appeal to current European notions about noble simplicity.

While some Africans remembered their African background positively in contrast to what they saw in Europe and America, their Western education prevented a wholehearted acceptance of the cultures from which they came. The ambivalence remained. It should not be strange, then, that some of their descendants, born in America, should also have mixed feelings. This is so even though they faced different stresses than an earlier generation.

Phillis Wheatley, brought to America from the Senegambia region at a young age and given a classical education, talked more about race and slavery than scholars once thought, but what she had to say was ambivalent. Thus, in her poem to the Earl of Dartmouth during America's revolutionary crisis she said:

> Should you, my lord, while you peruse my song,
> Wonder from whence *my love of Freedom sprung,*
> Whence flow these wishes for the common good,
> By *feeling* hearts alone best understood,
> I, young in life, by *seeming cruel fate*
> Was snatched from *Afric's fancied happy seat;*
> What pangs excruciating must molest,
> What sorrows labor in my parent's breast! . . .
> Such, such my case. And can I then but pray
> Others may never feel *tyrannic sway?*

The ambivalence comes from her Christianity. Like many eighteenth-century Anglo-Africans she took the religion seriously. Consequently, although she spoke disparagingly about her "cruel fate," she could not help but suggest that Africa was lacking—"Afric's fancied happy seat." Her twin concerns about Africa and Christianity are contained in her first published work "On the Death of the Rev. Mr. George Whitefield":

> Take him, ye *Africans,* he longs for you,
> Impartial Saviour is his Title due.
> If you will walk in Grace's heavenly Road,
> He'll make you free, and Kings, and Priests to God.

Significantly, in the American editions of 1770 and 1773 the word "free" was omitted, though it appeared in the London edition of 1771. Clearly, "free" could have a temporal as well as religious significance, and perhaps Wheatley meant both, for imbibing Western prejudices against Africa clearly did not include accepting that Africans were uniquely suited to servitude, even if slavery were part of God's plan for civilizing or Christianizing the continent. She made this clear in a letter to Samsom Occum in which she wrote: "I have this Day received your obliging kind Epistle, and am greatly satisfied with your Reasons respecting the Negroes, and think highly reasonable what you offer in Vindication of their Natural Rights: Those that invade them cannot be insensible that the divine Light is chasing away the thick Darkness which broods over the Land of Africa." Wheatley took advantage of America's revolutionary ferment to add: "How well the Cry for Liberty and the reverse Disposition for the exercise of oppressive power over others agree I humbly think it does not require the penetration of a Philosopher to determine."[39]

Although she did not know Quaque personally, Wheatley supported his African mission, and expressed disappointment that it had not been more successful. Admitting that she had no knowledge to the contrary, she nevertheless hoped that "if Philip would introduce himself properly to them" by "setting a good example," he might yet wean them away from error.[40]

Regarding Britain

Africans may have been attracted by European literacy and learning more than anything else, for Quaque was not the only African sent to Europe for education. We have indicated that Africans were full participants in a developing Atlantic world whose economy was largely powered by African labor. This trade called into being along the coast an "urban culture of . . . *nshonamandshi*" or "sea-towns" that, as Ray Kea has argued, were themselves "commercial centers . . . [and] sites of theoretical and practical activities. The sea-towns were heteroglossic speech communities in which 'borrowing, lending, panyaring, or selling' ordered social relations." They supported an African social and cultural elite whose interest in the West extended beyond the pecuniary. By the end of the eighteenth century there were various reports of Africans and Afro-Europeans (those of mixed blood) traveling to Europe for enlightenment and entertainment. One Liverpool resident wrote in 1788: "Exclusive of those who are sent here for education, many adults visit this country from motives of curiosity, and parents send their children occasionally from all parts of that [African] coast, to receive some advantage and improvement, by observing the manners and customs of civilized society, (or as they phrase it, 'to learn sense and get a good head')."[41] The comment simultaneously suggests wealth, sophistication, and an acknowledgment that the West has something valuable and distinctive to offer. It suggests pride and self-confidence as well as recognition of something yet to be learned. Nevertheless, within an African context (as the case of Caboceer Cudjo shows), Africans could choose the rate or measure at which they were prepared to learn or accept it. Those submerged in Western society, even as free people rather than slaves, had fewer choices or sources of pride.

This point can best be made through Ignatius Sancho. He was not born in Africa but rather on a slave ship in transit. He was therefore raised entirely in the West and but for the racial nature of English culture had little reason to identify with Africans or other people of color at all. He can never have had a memory of Africa. The fact that he developed such an identity, the fact that he had to do so, has everything to do with the crisis of blacks in the West. Sancho's sentiments are expressed in letters published after his death, and were important, as was Wheatley's literary production, as evidence that blacks could inscribe rational thoughts on paper and were therefore worthy of the regard due other members of the human family. His letters suggest that he never quite achieved his goal of being accepted as a member of the English middle class.[42] His failure to gain complete acceptance prevented his total identification with English society; that is to say, it assured his "double-consciousness." He could glory in English valor ("We fought like Englishmen," he crowed in 1779), shudder at England's dismal wartime prospects ("The British empire mouldering away in the West—annihilated in the North—Gibraltar going—and England fast asleep"), and then divorce himself from the situation entirely: "I am only a lodger—and hardly that."[43] Recognizing that fact did not permit him to adopt the radical stance of Cugoano for, as Keith Sandiford indicates, Sancho wrote before the full flowering of abolitionist sentiment in Britain and could not afford to alienate those people whose attentions and forbearance conceded him what little comfort and distinction he achieved.[44] He turned the knife subtly. Having lived nearly all his life in England, and never even visiting another country, he could hardly be assimilated to other than English norms.

Blacks did have a noticeable presence throughout the British Isles in the eighteenth century and perhaps in some locales they developed their own cultural peculiarities and Sancho absorbed these. Estimates of the black population in Britain have ranged as high as twenty thousand or more in the eighteenth century. David Northrup argues that probably more blacks lived in Britain by the end of the period than in all the rest of Europe combined.[45] These facts seem to suggest at least the possibility of a variant culture. But the blacks were "atomized in separate households, cut off from the cultural nourishment and reinforcement made possible by even the most inhumane plantation system," conditions that militated against significant cultural distinctiveness. This is not to say they never got together. They did have occasion to meet, sometimes by chance, where they could air common grievances, make common cause, and share common experiences. At the end of the century, a critical mass allowed them to develop community gathering places, frequent black pubs, and form community churches. One or more all-black brothels had been established, though their customers, presumably, would not have been. This situation most likely developed after significant numbers arrived following the American Revolution, and much of this was toward the end of Sancho's life or after his death. Throughout the period, the population was largely male and unlikely for that reason alone to have segregated itself willingly from the rest of society. They influenced English popular culture (and high culture as well) in music especially, and by the end of the 1780s "white Londoners as well as black were dancing to black music at what a contemporary account describes as 'an innocent amusement, vulgarly called *black hops.*'"[46]

Yet Sancho, like many notable blacks of the period, was raised in white households and spent most of his adult life among white people. Indeed, that was part of the problem. African-born Equiano talks about an aspect of his own developing self-awareness: "I had often observed, that when her mother washed her face [he said of a white playmate] it looked very rosy; but when she washed mine it did not look so; I therefore tried oftentimes myself if I could not by washing make my face the same colour as my little play-mate . . . , but it was all in vain; and I now began to be mortified at the difference in our complexions."[47] How much more formative was Sancho's experience, having been raised in England and mistreated at an early age because of his complexion. His first English owners, for example, deliberately denied the obviously intelligent youngster the least chance of mental improvement in order to keep him subservient, and finally drove him to run away. While their reasoning may not have been entirely racial, it had evident racial implications, and the advice of the nearby Duke of Montagu that he be permitted an education had a definite racial basis. This enforced consciousness of racial difference, and the pain surrounding it, may help explain why Sancho, virtually alone among prominent blacks in eighteenth-century England, married another black.[48] Sancho's absorption of a racial antagonism inherent in English culture was one index of his acculturation; and he recognized himself as a standing rebuke to the norm.

The unfortunate reality of quotidian existence reinforced the schismatic personality these circumstances produced. Thus he tells one friend, "We went by water—had a coach home—were gazed at—followed, &c. &c.—but not much abused." Even if the abuse was not entirely racial, in a racially-based society it was bound to take on racial overtones.[49] So much more for another incident: "I shall take no notice of the tricking fraudulent behaviour of the driver of the stage—*as how* he wanted to palm a bad shilling upon us—and *as how* they stopped us in the town and most generously insulted us."[50] The "dreadful objectivity" (to use Richard Wright's terminology) that comes with this internal conflict also creates self-doubt—great or slight, depending on one's success in combating it. Sancho's self-parody is constant and somewhat painful to read. When he refers to his "convexity of belly exceeding Falstaff—and a black face into the bargain" one might dismiss that as witty self-deprecation, especially in context, for he continues "waddling in the van of poor thieves and pennyless prostitutes—with all the supercilious mock dignity of little office," to complete a droll scene.[51] But when he habitually describes himself using such terms as "a coal-black, jolly African" and "a poor, thick-lipped son of Afric," even in a humorous mode, one suspects a serious insecurity is involved.[52] He apologizes for a mistake by exclaiming "why he must think me blacker than I am," refers to the anti-Catholic Gordon rioters as committing "worst than Negro barbarity," and calls West India-born Julius Soubise, who lived a scandalous life of gambling and womanizing, "a little Blacky."[53] Nevertheless, he offers Soubise friendly advice based on their common complexion and his own sense of racial responsibility: "Look around upon the miserable fate of almost all of our unfortunate colour—superadded to ignorance,—see slavery, and the contempt of those very wretches who roll in affluence from our labours. Superadded to this woeful catalogue—hear the ill-bred and heart-racking abuse of the foolish vulgar.—You, S[oubis]e, tread as cautiously as the strictest rectitude can guide ye."[54]

This racial burden is well-nigh constant, so when he recommends another black man ("white tooth'd—clean—tight—and light little fellow;—with a woolly pate—and a face as dark as your humble") he is careful to add "I like the rogue's looks, or a similarity of colour should not have induced me to recommend him."[55] He had connections to other blacks in London as well as to elite whites and was highly conscious of his and their relative social positions. He was also aware that he was more fortunate than many.

Yet, his identity was such that he could say inaccurately "I am not sorry I was born in Afric."[56] Ogude views this positively as a measure of his attachment to Africa. I view it negatively as an index of his alienation from the country where he was bred and for which he expressed affection. His disaffection resulted not only from a dislike of his nation's relationship to slavery, nor alone from a disgust with its racial prejudice, but also from an imbibing of its racial norm. I do not mean to suggest self-hatred on his part, for self-doubt need not become pathological. Had that been the case he would not likely have married another black.

By Sancho's standards Wheatley, whom he admired, comes off rather well. Of course, some version of the argument about Sancho might also be made about Wheatley, for she was only seven or eight years old when she left the continent and offered little remembrance of it. Yet she did refer to her African background when she adduced or implied various criticisms of western practices and once, only once, she wrote playful poetry about Africa as if she might recall it:

In fair description are thy powers display'd
In artless grottos, and the sylvan shade;
Charm'd with thy painting, how my bosom burns!
And pleasing Gambia on my soul returns.[57]

Among other things, the last line reinforces the notion that she was from somewhere in the Senegambia region, which scholars debate. Ogude argues that what she wrote about the newly forming American nation provided a vehicle for her "sublimated consciousness." It was her "puritanical education," Ogude thinks, that suppressed her feelings and rendered her incapable of speaking about slavery or other facets of her personal travail with the same emotion she displaced in American nationalism.[58] But this still points toward her acculturation.

She could be equally humble or satirical in her regular assumption, like Sancho, of the role of the "poor African," particularly in correspondence with people of note, but she does not engage in self-ridicule. She is self-effacing in her concessions to American racial prejudice by, for example, politely refusing ritual offers for her to eat with white guests, and normally taking her meals instead at a table aside. This was a common experience for prominent black American personalities and one generally spared Sancho because, for all its racism, he lived in a society that was not quite so racially obsessed. Yet some might prefer his keen awareness to her occasional seeming obliviousness. So while she could praise her friend and supporter John Thornton for championing the cause of "Humble Africans and Indians" who were "dispis'd on earth on account of our colour" she seemed surprised when that spite was manifested toward her.[59] She admitted meekly to Thornton later that "The world is a severe Schoolmaster, for its frowns are far less dang'rous than its smiles and flatteries, and it is a difficult task to keep in the path of Wisdom. I attended, and find exactly true your thoughts on the behaviour of those who seem'd to respect me while [I was] under my mistresses patronage: you said right, for some of those have already put on a reserve."[60] But she had a memory of Africa that Sancho did not and therefore she had, at least in theory, a choice that he did not.

This "choice" may have been more apparent than real, for Wheatley was quite young when she left Africa, younger than either Equiano or Gronniosaw, and offered little remembrance of it. Yet she retained sufficient memory of Africa to allow one scholar plausibly to argue that she might have been born among the Fula. But her mistress was determined to limit her contact with other Africans, even those in the household, and reprimanded a black coachman, and by implication Wheatley herself, when they sat together as he drove her home from an engagement in Boston. The significance of such an incident was bound to create internal conflict and some measure of alienation because on other occasions she was reminded that she was just like other blacks. For example, when she joined Boston's Old South Church in August 1771 she was confined to the "Negro Pews." The decision to sit with the coachman may have been her own, motivated by a desire for human contact, and a closeness the coachman welcomed. But this recognition of kinship, whether of race or condition, or perhaps just of special circumstance, was to be denied her.[61] The strictures on Wheatley in the New World were somewhat greater than those on Sancho (and others) in the Old, and the conflicting nature of her designation was characteristic of Africans in her situation. It may be that she did not fully appreciate the significance of the disassociation imposed upon her while she was under her mistress's keeping, thus her hurt confession to Thornton. Moreover, her death at age thirty-one, alone and impoverished while her husband was in jail for debt, accurately captured the meaning of the "reserve" of her patrons when she sought to follow her own path.[62]

Sancho and Wheatley had the "double-consciousness" of life in a racially based society, even if Wheatley had occasional glimpses of an earlier existence. Philip Quaque had the "double-consciousness" of liminality, though he came pretty close to identifying totally with the English; yet, that impression is deceptive. Even after he expressed the wish for his children to lose "their Mother's vile Jargon," he went on to desire that they be provided for after he was "annihilated and intered [*sic*] in the Sepulchre of " his "Ancestors."[63] This casual reference to the manner of his burial is inconsistent with his adverse opinion of traditional customs and reveals internal tensions that are not always otherwise in evidence. If one were to argue that there is no tension here at all, that his apparent inconsistency is no more than a feature of a bicultural man who could shed one identity or another at will, that identity, as James Clifford has argued, is not "a boundary to be maintained but a nexus of relations and transactions" to be engaged, others still did not express the same kind of distaste for the mother tongue, even to white people, so Quaque practiced a psychic sleight of hand.[64] The others we have discussed were both liminal *and* lived in racially restrictive societies. Equiano claimed, or assented to claims, on two occasions, though not in his formal narrative, that he was born in South Carolina—a situation at odds with his generally accurate descriptions of Africa, not all of which could be easily obtained in extant eighteenth-century sources. These claims could also be viewed as part of an identity determined by circumstance. If the suggestion that he was born in America rather than Africa can be sustained, part of the argument made here would need to be modified but perhaps only in the direction of emphasizing the African nature of early South Carolina.[65]

Another important contrast between Sancho and African-born Anglo-Africans, is the prominence of some kind of religious experience or commitment. Extended passages of their works sound very much like religious tracts. This may be partly strategic: Christian humanists of one sort or another were at the forefront of the struggle against slaving and, eventually, racism. Besides, lacking modern scientific evidence for racial equality, their prime defense derived from the Bible. Therefore Africans emphasized both their literacy and their Christianity as essential features of their claim to humanity. They then used the religion to spotlight western practices that were so often and so strikingly at odds with Western beliefs. Their ability to see so sharply the disjunctions in Western life derived partly from their position as relative novices. Sancho, having known nothing else, felt no need for a public profession of faith, though he, too, stressed the inconsistency of Christian doctrines with slavery and racism. As Edwards indicates, his resentment is palpable when he writes about "the most unchristian and diabolical usage of my brother Negroes," when he conveys his good wishes "to all those who have charity enough to admit dark faces into the fellowship of Christians," and when he employs a secular variant "Pray be so kind to make our best respects to Miss A——s, and to every one who delighteth in Blackamoor greetings."[66] He occasionally gives religious advice, as in that to Soubise: "the more you study the word of God, your peace and happiness will increase . . . use your every endeavour to be a good man—and leave the rest to God"; or records a religious reflection, as when he rejects the idea of "eternal Damnation" as "derogatory to the fullness, glory, and benefit of the blessed expiation of the Son of the Most High God—who died for the sins of all—all—Jew, Turk, Infidel, and Heretic;—fair—sallow—brown—tawny—black—and you and I—and every son and daughter of Adam."[67] But this was a Christianity assumed rather than proclaimed.

Whether Sancho felt his singularity more deeply than those born in Africa, whether his "specific form of double consciousness," was more painful is debatable, though one suspects it might have been. And yet, Ogude thinks not. "[T]he worst effects of slavery and all its concomitants," he writes, "is best illustrated in the near-castration of the African psyche and the destruction of his intellectual integrity," and he includes Sancho in this category. Moreover, he applies that edict across the ages of European contact with Africans. These early African writers established what he argues has "recognizably become the contemporary African world view," and that view has not much changed since the sixteenth century.[68]

Notwithstanding individual exceptions to the contrary, the racial nature of Western culture has affected Africans similarly throughout the ages regarding the issues of identity it raised. Still, one can nevertheless distinguish certain factors for evaluation. Leaving aside emotional distress caused by physical displacement, one could argue, for example, that the most significant moment of the meeting for Africans with an experience of traditional society was the introduction of a new way of viewing the world, meaning the recognition of a need to reorder the senses to privilege sight rather than sound. (Limitations of space do not permit a full development of this argument, which would apply particularly to the era before the European penetration of Africa.) But it was a moment that could engender a sense of inferiority as well as wonder. Another moment, a step toward an erasure of the insecurity and inequality possibly engendered by the first and by subsequent social drawbacks, was the acceptance of Christianity. The African novice greeted this discovery also with wonder, and those who mastered literacy felt a call to proclaim in print both their new belief and new community. This new community was religious, western, and literate, with all the significance that Gates endows these terms. But Sancho, as native to all three (he was born into a western, Christian society, including literacy and all it entailed) felt no need to proclaim himself to the same extent, even if the act of writing, in his assumed role as African, carried some of the same qualities for him as for the others. Christianity counteracted but did not overcome western racism.

For some Africans, the threat to psychic health produced by the obvious conflict between Christian ideal and earthly reality, between European assertions and European actions, proved unbearable. John Henry Naimbanna was the twenty-four-year-old son of a local ruler in the region of Sierra Leone.[69] A free black settler in the region encouraged him to acquire an English education, which illustrates one effect of the presence of westernized Africans on the coast. The fact that Naimbanna agreed illustrates another effect. He obviously thought the mastery of western knowledge was important, and when he arrived in England in 1791 he applied himself assiduously. He was sensitive about the need for such learning, however, and about the state of his society that compelled him to travel abroad. Zachary Macaulay, a resident of Sierra Leone at the time, described him as "uncommonly pleasing in his behaviour, shewing much natural courtesy, and even delicacy of manners [and] . . . of a kind and affectionate disposition. He was quick in all his feelings, and his temper was occasionally warm."

Among the things that his hosts were anxious to teach him was the meaning of Christianity, "to convince him that the Bible was the word of God," and he received that doctrine "with great reverence and simplicity." He took to studying the Bible for hours alone and was much affected by its teachings. He learned that he should dispense with his traditional African sense of pride, that he should forego revenge, and that he should cultivate humility. He determined to carry missionaries to his own country and wean his people away from their local beliefs. But one day in the House of Commons, he took great offense at a proslavery member's negative characterization of Africans and threatened to kill him if ever he got the chance. His friends reminded him of the Christian obligation to forgive one's enemies. He replied that he could forgive everything but an injury to his people's character:

> If a man should try to kill me, or should sell my family for slaves, he would do an injury to as many as he might kill or sell, but if any one takes away the character of black people, that man injures black people all over the world; and when he has once taken away their character, there is nothing which he may not do to black people ever after. That man, for instance, will beat black men, and say, "O, it is only a black man, why should I not beat him?" That man will make slaves of black people; for when he has taken away their character, he will say, "O, they are only black people, why should not I make them slaves?" That man will take away all the people of Africa, if he can catch them, and if you ask him "Why do you take away all those people," he will say, "O, they are only black people, they are not like white people, why should I not take them?" That is the reason why I cannot forgive the man who takes away the character of the people of my country.

He was told that even this he had to forgive. He acquiesced and was silent. But this was a message he took to his people with evident difficulty, and as he approached the African coast on his return trip he began to sicken and after he landed he died. Thus, concludes Macaulay, expired an "enlightened African, from whose exertions, had he lived, not only the [Sierra Leone] Company might have derived important services, but under his government, Christianity might have found a fostering friend."

The story is emblematical of the burden placed by Europeans and their religion on Africans who must have shuddered, as Naimbanna surely did, at the task of reformation before them, particularly in view of the inconsistencies in the lessons they had to convey. Macaulay interprets Naimbanna's death as partly the result of his qualms about his ability to rehabilitate so backward a people. I see it otherwise. He clearly was wracked by doubt but not by self-doubt; he was dubious, rather, about the value of the message. He was taught to give way before his despoiler and to swallow his pride in the face of insult. He was asked to conspire in his own enslavement, to cooperate in his personal deracination, to agree, in Ogude words, to psychic castration. For, in the context of eighteenth-century society, that, more often than not, is what Africans were asked to do. And the order in which Macauley expresses his regrets, first about the loss to the company, then about the loss to religion, is an accurate reflection of the connection between religion and imperialism that might, for Naimbanna, have proven difficult to miss. He had already widened his allegiance, like all blacks in the West, beyond the confines of his own homeland to include Africans everywhere, and the situation he observed did not bode well for his people unless, as many black Christians were forced to conclude, it was all part of God's inscrutable plan. For some people, this may have been more difficult to accept than for others.

Divided Identities

Looking at the writings and reflections of these eighteenth-century Anglo-Africans, one can well understand how and why black radicals in the 1960s sometimes rejected Christianity as an opiate and unsuitable to a revolutionary generation. They charged that Christianity was a tool of imperialism and used to sap revolutionary potential. In some cases this may have been true. But, on the other hand, Christianity was a two-edged sword, and people like Nat Turner and Denmark Vesey in nineteenth-century America envisioned rebellion based at least partly upon a Christian vision.

For our purposes, the important thing about these eighteenth-century African writings is that they reveal the thought processes of cultural hybrids. Although they came from an African background, they accepted values that conditioned them to think very much like members of the western cultural elite, even though their views were modified by the experience of racism and slavery. They accepted the religious reward as largely worth the cost. Unless we trace culture to the genes, however, Ignatius Sancho should properly be separated from the others. But he himself and everybody else considered him to be an African and he did have close ties to the black community in London. These facts say less about him than about the shortcomings of the West and about the ethnically absolutist discourses adduced by Gilroy. They explain why many of the African-American descendants of these eighteenth-century progenitors rejected their attitudes.

The majority of Africans, bound to work in the fields, may never have experienced the same kind of ambivalence. Maroons throughout the Americas left the plantations and recreated African societies in the wilderness in an attempt to replicate the societies they had left; and yet they were changed. And where they did not change enough, they proved a hindrance or an embarrassment to their progress-minded brethren—the ones who stayed on the plantations and (or, in Africa) took to western learning and succeeded to political authority in the wake of European expulsion. For the preservation of African values alone was no guarantee of success, however that might be measured, in a world dominated by the West. These early African, Afro-European, and African-American writers grappled with issues of identity that still haunt their modern counterparts.

CHAPTER FOUR

Conservation, Class, and Controversy in Early America

Robert M. Weir

"Cape Cod was like to be a place of good fishing, for we saw daily great whales of the best kind for oil and bone." At times, one of the first Pilgrims wrote, they even "swim and play about us." Once, when one floated for some time "within half a musket shot of the ship," two men tried to shoot it, but "he that gave fire first, his musket flew in pieces, both stock and barrel." The would-be marksman escaped injury, but the whale "gave a snuff, and away."[1] As a harbinger of how many colonists would treat the flora and fauna of the New World, this incident seems sadly portentous. Certainly, the initial reaction of many Englishmen upon encountering the abundant wildlife of the western hemisphere was to kill it. Felling trees required more work and therefore reasons better than whim and impulse, but the need for wood and cleared land usually proved more than sufficient. In many ways, "The people of plenty" were indeed, as William Cronon has noted, "a people of waste."[2]

As Jack P. Greene has observed, "persisting tension between . . . experience and inheritance" characterized colonists' social and cultural development. The one drove them toward accommodations with changing circumstances; the other pulled them toward Old World models. One led to creolization, the other toward anglicization. That such powerful and pervasive forces would have influenced the colonists' encounters with the natural environment seems highly probable, but few scholars have given the resulting interplay much attention. Fortunately, sophisticated recent studies by William Cronon and other environmental historians have vastly increased our understanding of ecological changes during the colonial period. Specialists in the history of conservation have also been aware for some time that many of the colonies enacted at least a smattering of statutes designed to protect timber and wildlife.[3] Yet the context of this legislation often remains obscure and, as discussants in a roundtable sponsored by the *Journal of American History* noted a few years ago, the "greatest weakness of environmental history as it has developed thus far" is "its failure . . . to explore the implications of social divisions for environmental change." This omission, one might add, is particularly striking in the light of illuminating findings by E. P. Thompson and others regarding the game laws and social conflict in Britain during the eighteenth century.[4]

These considerations suggest that examining some of the social dimensions of environmental attitudes and legislation in America from the early seventeenth to the late eighteenth centuries might be useful. To make the project feasible, I restricted the scope of the investigation—at the expense of some regional variation—to the indigenous biota and the European inhabitants of selected English settlements in North America, especially Pennsylvania. The present discussion also generally omits the commercial trades in deerskins, beaver pelts, and pelagic fish, which have been the subject of considerable scholarship.[5] My initial hypothesis was that because the evident depletion of natural resources in Europe had already produced some attempts at conservation, American colonists would initially try to reproduce these practices in much the same manner that they sought to perpetuate many other cultural patterns. The working assumption was that the settlers would have taken some time to realize that they were in the midst of plenty, that learning how to waste would have consequently been a gradual process, and that the conservation legislation of the late eighteenth century would have represented a belated recognition that they had assimilated that lesson all too well. Although this scenario has borne some (remote) relationship to the discernable facts, reality is not so tidily packaged. The early colonists were neither oblivious in regard to their immediate environment nor puppets of their past. Equally important, broader social concerns clearly affected their attitudes and access to fish, game, and timber. How this happened is a question to which this essay seeks some preliminary answers.

European Background

The colonists' European origins provided their initial frame of reference for understanding their relationship to the environment of the New World. The whale that escaped the Pilgrims off Cape Cod would have been royal property had it been captured in English coastal waters. Whales, sturgeons, and other "royal fish" belonged to the Crown; in fact, according to some legal authorities—including Sir William Blackstone—all game did. Some other writers disagreed and maintained that wild animals belonged to no one. In practice, however, William the Conqueror and his successors construed the prerogative broadly, setting aside large tracts as royal forests in which only the king and those to whom he granted permission could hunt, fish, or cut timber;[6] interlopers risked draconian penalties, including death, but in 1217 the barons of England forced King Henry III to accept the Forest Charter. This counterpart of the Magna Charta restricted the severity and scope of the forest laws; further erosion weakened these laws to the point where they were little more than dead letters by the end of the sixteenth century, though the Tudor and Stuart monarchs continued to enjoy their special hunting prerogatives. The Crown also favored certain individuals with special privileges in the form of rights to free warren, chase, and park. All were exclusive franchises to hunt deer and game within designated areas. Elsewhere, various qualification acts restricted the right of the less privileged to hunt even on their own property. Most "gentlemen" however met these qualifications.[7]

In 1670–71, Parliament imposed more stringent restrictions that were to remain the foundation of the game laws until their repeal in the nineteenth century. This statute barred most people from hunting animals defined as game. Persons who possessed a landed estate worth £100 per year, those with a lease on land for ninety-nine years or longer worth at least £150 per year, and holders of one of the hunting franchises described above, as well as the sons and heirs of an esquire or someone of "higher degree," were the favored exceptions. Those who met these qualifications (accounting for less than one percent of the rural population) were not confined to their own land; they could hunt anywhere not otherwise restricted.[8]

Numerous other statutes supplemented the basic game act during the long eighteenth century. Thus, one passed in 1692 imposed penalties on "inferior tradesmen, apprentices, and other dissolute persons neglecting their trades and employments, who follow hunting, fishing, and other game, to the ruin of themselves, and damage of their neighbours." None of these laws, however, stopped poaching. In fact, attempts to enforce them led poachers to blacken their faces to disguise themselves and to operate in gangs, some of them mounted. Parliament responded in 1723 with the Waltham Black Act (9 George I c. 22), which enumerated some 250 offenses, more than fifty of which were capital crimes subject to the death penalty or transportation to the colonies. Further attempts to strengthen the system failed, and Parliament, finally recognizing that its efforts were counterproductive, repealed the property qualification in 1831.[9]

Complex regulations also governed fishing, which was—as one of the leading early writers on the subject observed—of such "great national importance" that "we find numerous statutes for the regulation and preservation" of fisheries. Despite a welter of private privileges of various kinds, these laws generally recognized the right of all subjects to fish in the open ocean and navigable rivers, while the owners of the adjacent soil usually possessed exclusive rights to fish in non-navigable bodies of water.[10]

Multiple acts spelled out how those who enjoyed fishing rights were to conduct themselves. "An Act for the Increase and Better Preservation of Salmon and Other Fish" in the rivers of Southampton and Wiltshire counties passed in 1705 provides a typical example of these regulations. The preamble noted that "the owners and occupiers of the salmon fisheries within the said counties, regarding only their private and greedy profit," destroyed the "stock of the said fisheries, by preventing the breed of good fish to pass in season through their fishing wyres . . . from the sea into the said rivers to spawn, and by killing such as are under size, and by fishing continually out of season." The statute therefore not only forbade fishing in local waters at certain times but also mandated that salmon under eighteen inches were to be thrown back.[11]

Despite many exceptions to the broad principles outlined above, fishing laws were inherently less convoluted than the game acts. Conserving fish entailed regulating the behavior of those who enjoyed exclusive or nonexclusive rights in particular bodies of water. The game laws, on the other hand, had more complicated ulterior purposes. These, as Sir William Blackstone observed in 1765, included not only the "preservation of the several species of these animals, which would soon be extirpated by a general liberty [to hunt]," but also the "prevention of idleness and dissipation in husbandmen, artificers, and others of lower rank." In addition, these laws were supposed to head off "popular insurrections and resistance to the government, by disarming the bulk of the people: which last," Blackstone remarked, "is a reason oftener meant, than avowed, by the makers of forest or game laws." How successful the system was in achieving any of these purposes is debatable, but it clearly failed in the last. Although the 1670–71 act expressly authorized game keepers to search the houses of persons not meeting the property qualifications for guns and other prohibited devices, "no vigorous attempt to completely disarm the parish population" followed, according to the scholar who has most closely studied the subject. In the 1680s, however, King James II did try to confiscate the weapons of his opponents, but the Glorious Revolution put a stop to that; and the Bill of Rights expressly included the right to "have arms."[12]

Another, ultimately self-defeating, purpose of the game laws was to assuage the egos of the landed gentry who had suffered from the devaluation of rank during the Civil War and Interregnum, for which they blamed the urban bourgeoisie. The game laws forced their nemesis, "the moneyed interest," to "concede the superiority of land over other forms of wealth." There was the satisfaction and the rub. Symbolism as well as substance accounted for the game acts; in a sense, they were less about the conservation of particular species of wildlife than the conservation of a distinctive social status. As one nobleman observed as late as 1827, to legalize the sale of game "would deprive the sportsman of his highest gratification . . . the pleasure of furnishing his friends with presents of game: nobody would care for a present which everybody could give."[13]

Whether the legal codification of such snobbery promoted conservation is questionable, but it certainly produced resentment, considerable criticism, and some spiteful poaching. Even Blackstone considered the game laws to be "confused," a "bastard slip" of the old forest laws, "productive of the same tyranny" to the common people. Many individuals chafed under the inability to kill game on their own lands and the trampling of their crops by hunters, but the legal restrictions were probably most galling to men whose holdings fell just short of the qualification to hunt. A retired army officer, who had assumed that he could hunt on his own land, spoke for them in 1770 after he encountered "a little creature of fortune, my neighbour, who meeting me in the fields, with an haughty air, informed me, that I had no right even to carry a gun, much less to kill game." Convinced that he "lived in a state of slavery" on his own estates, "by means of the fish and game acts," the officer announced that he planned to move to Nova Scotia.[14]

Because the need for conservation was more obvious, and the accompanying social distinctions were not as blatant, less controversy surrounded the laws governing timber. Huge forests covered much of England during Roman times; by the end of the seventeenth century probably less than one eighth was wooded, and only three royal forests had substantial stands of trees suitable for ship timber, let alone masts, most of which had to be imported from the Baltic countries and the colonies. Other uses of timber were less exacting but frequently demanding enough to create local shortages, but the critical needs of the navy clearly created the most concern.[15] Nor was England alone in this. Authorities in other European countries, including France, believed that they faced similar scarcities.

Recognition of the problem produced two remarkable documents during the 1660s. In England, John Evelyn, who was a founder of the Royal Society, issued a wake-up call in *Silva; or A Discourse of Forest Trees* (1664), which quickly became influential. Viewing the depletion of the forests as a result of the increase in shipping, glass works, iron furnaces, and plowed fields, Evelyn denounced the current selfish desire to "extirpate, demolish, and raze" all the "goodly woods and forests" left by our "prudent ancestors" and called for both conservation and reforestation. The other, equally famous document was the French Forest Ordinance of 1669, Louis XIV's codification of much previous legislation on the subject. Conservation practices—including the preservation of "stallion" trees to reseed cut-over areas—were to prevail widely in private as well as public lands. How effective this edict was is debatable, but it influenced forestry in other European countries and helped to make French naval administrators the envy of their English counterparts.[16] More important in the long run, the Forest Ordinance and Evelyn's work signaled an increasing realization in the Old World, where the evidence had been accumulating for centuries, that man could destroy as well as improve his environment. Stewardship required foresight.

Forests and Timber

Like other Englishmen, American colonists in the early seventeenth century assumed that man was God's vice-regent on earth. The garden of Eden, in which there were no weeds, brought forth fruit without labor on Adam's part, and the lion and the lamb lay down peaceably together. Adam's fall, however, not only brought sin into the world but also disrupted the harmony of nature. Man, whose lot thereby became one of toil, bore a heavy responsibility for making restitution. His job was to improve the earth, to complete the job of creation that his sin had interrupted. Thus God gave him dominion over all living things, and bade him go about the work.[17]

Armed with this authority, the early explorers and settlers encountered a new world that revealed few signs of human "improvement." Many Native Americans who practiced cultivation were also migratory, and even the sedentary groups frequently left large tracts of uninhabited territory between themselves and others as buffer zones or game preserves. Land-hungry Europeans rationalized that, not having improved their surroundings as they should have, Native Americans lost title to it; those who would presumably do a better job therefore had a right to take over.[18]

What they were taking over was intimidating as well as inviting. The term *wilderness* after all signified wild, out of control, ferocious, beyond the pale of civilization. Accordingly the wilderness was that portion of creation where humans had not yet fulfilled their God-given assignment of subduing and improving the earth. *Desert* and *forest* were interchangeable terms that connoted unproductive areas largely devoid of human inhabitants. William Bradford, whose Pilgrims were on a spiritual journey, was not particularly interested in the surrounding natural environment. No cornucopia to him, it was a "hidious and desolate wilderness," threatening rather than inviting. Others, more secularly oriented, took a more sanguine view. Early South Carolinians, their descendants observed, encountered "a dreary wilderness," but they "improved and cultivated the colony to so great maturity, that it is become the land of plenty." But without slaves to work the rice swamps, they believed, it would quickly revert to "a desert waste." The Pilgrims perceived physical and spiritual peril in the wilderness; South Carolinians saw economic possibilities and future productivity. But neither of them would have subscribed in any literal sense to Thoreau's later claim that "in Wilderness is the preservation of the World."[19] Most early Americans preferred nature tamed.

But early arrivals encountered nature in the raw where it was largely unknown and unpredictable. Ecologists once thought that different plant and animal species regularly succeeded each other until an ecosystem eventually reached a mature, stable equilibrium. Now, however, many scientists believe that constant change is the norm and that ecosystems are considerably more dynamic than they had assumed. No doubt many of their early counterparts like Peter Kalm, the Swedish botanist who traveled through the northern colonies in the 1740s, suspected as much, for he remarked about large trees falling in a forest during an otherwise calm night. Moreover, storms and fires often accelerated such natural changes. Numerous Europeans were surprised to find that fire had cleared the underbrush in many forests so that they resembled European parks. Yet the grass that sprouted after these fires could be lush in places and thin in others. Knowing what to expect over the next hill took experience.[20]

In the face of their new environment the earliest settlers fell back on practices that they had known in England. Doubtless, they wished to perpetuate familiar cultural patterns in an alien environment, but they were also inclined to prudence in the face of a wilderness whose dimensions and resources were still undetermined. Because town land was finite and heavy timber was difficult to transport, local governments quickly took care to conserve accessible supplies, and these conservation measures usually antedated provincial statutes. The first town meeting on record at Hingham, Massachusetts, in 1635, stipulated, for example, that "all Cedar and Pine Swamps be in common and preserved for the Towne's use." During the next twenty-five years, the town passed nearly as many regulations governing timber, most of which restricted cutting and transporting it outside of the community. Newbury and Sudbury, Massachusetts, Newtown and Oyster Bay, New York, and in fact many other northern villages, quickly adopted similar measures.[21]

Furthermore, the preservation of timber continued to command widespread attention throughout the colonial period. William Penn's land conveyances stipulated that settlers were to leave one acre in trees for every five acres cleared. Farther south, where longleaf and loblolly pine forests stretched to the horizons, interest in preserving them developed more slowly. But even there concerned residents condemned firing the woods at inappropriate times when excessively high temperatures damaged soil and timber while the resulting smog obscured harbor entrances; and consequently legislatures tried to curb wasteful burning. They also routinely protected trees along roadsides where shade was essential for man and beast. All in all, knowledgeable scholars have estimated, colonial and state governments enacted "hundreds" of forestry laws during the seventeenth and eighteenth centuries.[22]

The shortage of timber for masts in England also prompted imperial authorities to become directly involved. Thus, the Massachusetts Bay charter of 1691 protected all trees above a specified size on public lands. Further restrictions followed so that after 1722 cutting any white pine on Crown lands from Nova Scotia to New Jersey without special license from the navy was illegal. As a result, one royal official noted, "it became almost a general interest of the country to frustrate the laws."[23] In short, excessively broad and rigid regulations undermined the policy.

Capitalizing on American resources for ship construction made sense, however, and by the eve of the Revolution colonial shipbuilders were constructing approximately £300,000 sterling worth of ships annually. Although most of this building occurred in the north, southern live oak made for particularly good ship timbers. Accordingly, a knowledgeable South Carolina merchant, Henry Laurens, believed that if the United States failed to limit exports and conserve its live oaks after the Revolution, "Europeans will laugh at us, [and] our Children will rue the folly of their Fathers." Plant "ten young trees" for "every Live Oak you cut down" was his prescient maxim; and by the 1860s the U.S. government would establish live oak reservations in the southeast that totaled over a quarter of a million acres.[24]

Rivers and Fish

The realization that fish as well as timber needed protection developed more slowly. With the exception of a Massachusetts law passed in 1668, most of the statutes that attempted to provide it date from the 1680s or later. At first, the enormous spring runs from the Atlantic Ocean doubtless made the supply of fish seem inexhaustible, for as an observer at Plymouth noted, "the greate smelts passe up [the rivers] to spawne . . . in troupes innumberable." Yet by the 1740s long-time residents around Philadelphia told Peter Kalm that "in their youth, the bays, rivers and brooks, had such quantities of fish that at one draught in the morning they caught as many as a horse was able to carry home." Now, though, they might fish all night and catch nothing. Dams, other obstructions in the rivers, and over-fishing in all seasons, contemporaries believed, caused the decline in the fish population.[25]

Although legislatures in most of the colonies had begun to address the problem by the 1730s, authorities in Pennsylvania were particularly alert to it, because Philadelphia grew rapidly, and fishing in the adjacent Delaware and

Schuylkill rivers quickly became an important activity for many people. Having received fishing rights with the title to the soil and rivers of his colony in 1681, William Penn apparently first planned to give purchasers of riparian tracts exclusive fishing privileges in adjacent waters. But settlers demanded wider access, and his second Frame of Government (approved by the assembly in 1683) opened fishing rights in navigable streams to everyone. Shortly thereafter, Penn also approved a law prohibiting racks and weirs (fish traps and dams) in the rivers. A governor of the colony would later observe that he thereby "copied from the Example of our Mother Country, where, by the Wisdom of the Legislature, many wholesome & effectual Provisions have been divers times made for the free & open Navigation of the Rivers, & preserving the Breed of Fish." Despite this and subsequent regulations, obstructions remained a recurring problem. Attempting to circumvent it, a concerned citizen in 1732 advocated building fish ladders and ponds at dam sites, apparently to no avail.[26]

Two years later the legislature passed still another act to "more effectually" prevent erecting "Wears, Damms, &c." in the Schuylkill River. This law remained in force for nearly thirty years, but it quickly became the subject of heated controversy. Petitioners called for an amendment that would permit weirs during April and May, while the fish were running. The house was receptive to the idea, but "a great Number of inhabitants," especially along the upper reaches of the river, objected to relaxing the rules, and Lieutenant Governor Patrick Gordon sided with them. "Divine Providence," he observed, provided "for the support of the Inhabitants of the Earth" by giving the "Fish of the Sea" an instinct that annually impelled them to "crow'd up even to the highest parts" of rivers "to lay their Spawn, on which their Breed & further Increase is said wholly to depend." Consequently, "in all well regulated Governments, particularly in England, the utmost Care is taken for Preservation of the Fishery to prohibit whatever" might interfere with fish reproduction. In his estimation, however, local fishing techniques were pernicious. "Great Numbers of People mostly on Horseback, for a Mile or two or more, with large Bushes, Stakes, or other Instruments" wade in the shallow water, beating "with great Noise" and raking "the Bottom of the River" to drive fish into the traps. If such practices were not restricted, he predicted, fish would eventually "desert" the river. Furthermore, he added, "tumultuous Meetings, riotous Behaviour, Quarrels, Contentions, & even Outrages amongst the young People and others who assemble as to a Merry-making or a publick Diversion" characterized this fishing, and no encouragement should be given to "anything that is generally attended with such Consequences, as are a Reproach to any Government, whose Business it is to preserve Peace, Tranquility, & good Order." Accordingly, he refused to approve any relaxation of the current restrictions.[27]

Not everyone, however, concurred with Lieutenant Governor Gordon's sound but rather patronizing observations, and traps continued to appear in the Schuylkill. Receiving a complaint about them in 1738, a justice of the peace for Philadelphia ordered their removal. But when constables attempted to enforce the law, they "were violently sett upon & assaulted by a great Number of Men riotously and tumultuously assembled armed with Clubs, Staves, and other Weapons." The fate of the culprits and the identity of the complainants remains hidden, but some educated guessing is possible. The elite as well as the common people liked to fish, and in 1732 some of the former founded what is now one of the oldest sporting clubs in the English-speaking world, "The Schuylkill Fishing Company of the Colony in Schuylkill," later called the "State in Schuylkill." They set up a mock state, elected a governor, and built a clubhouse at a picturesque site on the river from which they sallied forth to hunt and fish, using—among other tackle—the predecessors of modern fly rods. That persons so equipped would have frowned on large fish traps and boisterous crowds muddying the river seems highly probable.[28]

Fishing was also serious business for those whose livelihoods depended on it, and skullduggery sometimes accompanied the resulting competition. Someone once dropped a large boulder in the Delaware where Edward Broadfield drew his nets, which was "no Man's particular Property (being almost in the Middle of the River, and free for any Person)," apparently because Broadfield "catched so many Fish as spoiled his [competitor's] Trolling." Abuses were also rampant in the Philadelphia oyster trade. Noting that "large Quantities of Oysters" from Delaware Bay and elsewhere had been "sold in this Province, at moderate Prices, to the Benefit of the Public, and great Relief of the Poor" and that gathering "Oysters in the Summer Season will tend to prevent their future Increase," the legislature forbade their sale in Pennsylvania between 10 May and 1 September. It soon appeared, however, that "some Persons, who carry about Oysters for Sale" covered the contraband shellfish with clams and went on their merry way. The legislature countered by imposing fines and confiscation of the illegal catches for the use of the poor.[29]

Meanwhile, commerce increasingly conflicted with the preservation of natural resources. "G. J.," writing in the *Pennsylvania Gazette* in 1760, noted that improved navigation would benefit everyone living along the Schuylkill and its tributaries; he therefore advocated public and private efforts to promote the removal of obstructions. The result was an act of the assembly passed in March 1761 "for making the River Schuylkill navigable, and for the Preservation of the Fish in the said River." Its title not withstanding, boats took precedence over fish. The act appointed commissioners empowered to "cut, blow up, remove . . . all Trees, Rocks, Beds of Gravel, Sand, Mud, Wears, Fishing dams, Baskets, Pounds, Stones," and other impediments. They also had a free hand to erect dams, locks, or whatever else they believed would aid navigation.[30]

Amid all of this activity, fishing in the Schuylkill continued to stir controversy. Attempting to prevent overfishing, the assembly stipulated in 1767 that one large net could be used at a particular location only once in a twenty-four hour period; those who had piers or fishing rights on opposite sides of the river were limited to alternate days. Renewal of the law in 1771 prompted some downstream fishermen to declare that they would not obey it; others—probably from upriver—countered with a public notice implying that violators would be prosecuted. But the escalating pre-Revolutionary controversy soon gave Philadelphians more pressing matters to think about. After the war, the legislature, amid a flurry of petitions and a roll-call vote, again limited the use of seines on the Schuylkill.[31]

Problems involving other major rivers in eastern and central Pennsylvania prompted less noticeable contention but more significant solutions, when the assembly in 1761 enacted a statute for "the Preservation of Fish in the River Delaware, Sasquehannah, and the Lehigh." In response to the "much diminished . . . great Quantities of Fish, which were formerly to be found" in these rivers, the legislature prohibited the use of various traps and large shore-to-shore nets. Suspending clauses postponed the effective date of the act until neighboring colonies had passed similar legislation. New Jersey complied quickly, but seven years elapsed before Maryland concurred.[32] Though later modified, this act set a precedent for intercolonial cooperation, and especially along the Delaware River residents attempted to keep each other informed about relevant changes in their practices. Still, violations of existing regulations continued, and by 1781 burned hulks sunk during the Revolution obstructed fishing near shore. These and other problems prompted the appointment of commissioners empowered to settle questions of jurisdiction over the Delaware River. An act of the Pennsylvania assembly passed in 1783 then ratified the resulting agreement that declared the river to be a common highway, equally free and open to residents of New Jersey and Pennsylvania. Each state had the right to regulate and protect the fisheries adjacent to its shore.[33]

Nevertheless, despite this milestone legislation, the Delaware and other waterways remained the subject of numerous petitions, public debate, and extended discussion in the legislature.[34] In late 1786 a member of the house, D. Clymer, moved for a more comprehensive solution that would regularize the laws governing navigation and fisheries on the larger rivers of eastern and central Pennsylvania. Individuals published detailed accounts of these streams, public meetings in central Pennsylvania pronounced improved navigation of the "utmost importance," and a "Society for promoting Improvement in Roads, and Inland Navigation" gathered information and memorialized the legislature. After a general survey of the situation, a committee of the house recommended that £10,310 be appropriated for river improvements and supporting roads. And by 14 April 1791, the secretary of the commonwealth was advertising for bids to undertake an ambitious program of public works.[35]

Although the enthusiasm for improved transportation overwhelmed the concern for preserving fishes, the colonial and state legislatures—as even this limited survey of major statutory milestones demonstrates—had spent a great deal of time on the intractable problem of reconciling conflicting claims involving freshwater fisheries. That fish were confined to particular bodies of water both exacerbated and simplified problems concerning them.

Hunting and Game

Game that ranged freely over the countryside presented related but fundamentally different issues. Once again, Pennsylvania provides an illuminating case study, in part because material from Maryland and New Jersey appeared in its newspapers and, more important, because Pennsylvanians discussed the game laws over a long period of time. In 1681 Penn received implicit hunting rights in the royal charter to Pennsylvania. Although his "Conditions or Concessions to the First Purchasers" suggested that he planned to convey to these fortunate individuals property rights to the game as well as to the soil on which it roamed, he implicitly extended hunting and fowling as well as fishing privileges to all inhabitants by offering them as inducements in his promotional literature. Then, in response to local demands (as in the case of fish), the second Frame of Government (1683) explicitly confirmed these rights: "And that the inhabitants of this province and territories thereof may be accommodated with such food and sustenance, as God, in His providence, hath freely afforded, I do also further grant to the inhabitants . . . liberty to fowl and hunt upon the lands they hold, and all other lands therein not inclosed" except manors. This same provision would also appear in the Frame of Government of 1696.[36]

Pennsylvania offered bounties on predators during the first decade of settlement but imposed few if any restrictions on hunting for the first forty years. In 1721, however, the legislature passed "An Act to prevent the Killing of Deer out of Season, and against carrying of Guns and Hunting by Persons not qualified." This statute stipulated that no one, except "Free Native *Indians*," who were exempt from its provisions, was permitted to kill deer from the first of January through the end of June. Furthermore, because trespassing hunters caused problems, those who hunted on enclosed or improved lands without the owner's permission were subject to a fine of ten shillings. Anyone "who is not Owner of Fifty Acres of Land, and otherwise qualified in the same Manner as Persons are, or ought to be by the Laws of this Province, for electing of Members to serve in Assembly," who carried a gun or hunted "in the Woods or uninclosed Lands, without License or Permission" from the owner or owners, was subjected to a five-shilling fine. These provisions fortified an owner's position regarding improved land but compromised it vis-à-vis unenclosed tracts. Gauging how much effect the changes had is difficult. Presumably, they did not affect most of the large holdings of the Penn family to which William Penn had given access under the Frame of Government. Moreover, the curious wording regarding voting qualifications—Pennsylvania imposed an unusually long two-year residency requirement—suggests that the property qualifications may have been primarily intended to discourage nonresident hunters.[37]

Apparently, this restriction did not become much of an issue until later, and it remained part of Pennsylvania law for the next forty years. In contrast, Virginians' experiment with a similar property qualification was short-lived. In 1705 the legislature there also penalized hunting, fishing, or fowling on another's land without his permission, but allowed anyone who owned six slaves to pursue wounded game onto "other lands where he hath not leave to hunt." Five years later, the Burgesses wanted to rescind this last provision, but Governor Alexander Spotswood, who believed that other sections of the act encroached upon the royal prerogative, prevailed upon them to repeal the entire law.[38]

Explanations for the difference between Virginia and Pennsylvania practice must rest largely on inference. In the early eighteenth century, hunting had not yet become fashionable among the gentry, and Virginia landholders may well have been as unhappy about the infringement of their property rights as those without slaves were at being the victims of an invidious distinction. Certainly, men like William Byrd of Westover were careful about granting permission to hunt on their lands. Byrd (who had trouble killing a partridge for his wife) allowed one individual to "shoot in the marsh provided he brings me the meat and keeps the feathers for himself." As commander of the local militia, he also ordered his troops to disarm Indians who ranged over patented lands. And many years later, George Washington politely but firmly refused a neighbor's request for permission to hunt on his land, noting that it was a privilege that he wished to reserve for himself and his guests.[39]

Doubtless Pennsylvanians were as interested in protecting their property rights as Virginians, but at least those living in the densely populated vicinity of Philadelphia may have been more concerned about hunting accidents. The property qualification section of the Pennsylvania act began by noting that "diverse Abuses, Damages, and Inconveniencies have arose by Persons carrying Guns." Given the blunt language common in the eighteenth century, these words should probably be taken at face value rather than as code aimed specifically at wandering hunters. Certainly a number of accident reports appeared in the *Pennsylvania Gazette* after it began publication a few years later. "One James Henricks riding in the Wood, near Susquehanah with his two Sons, in pursuit of Game," for example, snagged the trigger of his gun on a bush and shot "his Son James in the Back. . . . He liv'd scare a Minute" before dying in the arms of his brother who, the newspaper reported, had accidentally killed his own cousin three years earlier while hunting. A few years later, a hunter, mistaking a child for a deer, shot and killed him. "Scarce a Year passes," the printer added, "without one or more of these unhappy Accidents."[40]

Whatever the reason, Pennsylvania's property qualification survived acts passed in 1730–31 and 1749–50. But in 1760, the assembly enacted an important statute "to prevent the Hunting of Deer, and other wild Beasts, beyond the Limits of the Lands purchased of the Indians by the Proprietaries of this Province; and against killing Deer out of Season." This act, which again exempted

Native Americans from its provisions, designated 1 August to 1 January as the hunting season for deer, and strictly prohibited white settlers from hunting on Indian land. Firing guns in Philadelphia or near public highways was also forbidden, as were hunting on Sunday or on improved or enclosed land without the owner's permission. Significantly, however, the law made no mention of the fifty-acre qualification for hunting on open land, and it specifically repealed statutes that had contained this provision.[41]

This action occurred at a time when, as the preamble to the bill explained, "many disorderly People have made it a Practice of Hunting on the Lands not yet purchased of the Indians, to their great Damage and Dissatisfaction, which may be attended with fatal Consequences to the Peace and Welfare of this Province." Better and safer, the assembly reasoned, to have "disorderly" persons hunting on white settlers' lands than Indians.' At the time, British authorities were also planning a major expedition against French Canada, and they had just asked the Pennsylvania legislature to raise troops.[42] Having excluded men who could be recruits from hunting in accustomed areas on Indian land, legislators probably thought it politic to mollify them by a concession with symbolic as well as substantive import. Moreover, the change in policy endured. In 1770, after some Cumberland County men calling themselves Black Boys waylaid a trader taking weapons to the Indians, the legislature quickly passed an "Act for punishing wicked and evil disposed Persons going armed in Disguise." Much of this statute followed the British Waltham Black Act verbatim, but it omitted the clauses concerning game. Prohibited behavior involved injuring persons and property, not hunting.[43]

The Pennsylvania Constitution of 1776, commonly considered to have been one of the most radically democratic state constitutions of the revolutionary era, also affirmed the value that frontiersmen—and others—placed on hunting rights. Both the draft printed for public consideration and the final version stipulated that "the inhabitants of this State shall have liberty to fowl and hunt, in seasonable times, on the lands they hold, and on all other lands therein not inclosed; and in like manner to fish in all boatable waters, and others not private property." Once adopted, the constitution of 1776 prompted considerable opposition and a long, ultimately successful campaign to replace it. Early on, "a Meeting of a large and respectable Number of the Citizens of Philadelphia" maintained that much extraneous matter cluttered the constitution, which was "confused, inconsistent, and dangerous." Among the supposedly irrelevant provisions were those relating to fishing, fowling, and hunting; and the streamlined conservative constitution of 1790 dropped these sections.[44]

In other contexts, many people continued to regard these provisions as significant. Replicating parts of Pennsylvania's first constitution, Vermont's constitutions of 1777, 1786, and 1793 included the liberty to hunt, fish, and fowl. More significantly, during the debate in 1787 over ratification of the U.S. Constitution, the omission of such clauses figured prominently among the concerns of those who thought the Constitution should have a Bill of Rights. Noting that the Constitution contained nothing about hunting and fishing, which were "unalienable rights," Anti-Federalists feared the imminent adoption of game laws. Writing in the *Pennsylvania Gazette*, "One of the People" tried to counter these reservations with a short but illuminating homily: "What should we think of a gentlemen, who, upon hiring a waiting-man," told him that "I shall always claim the liberty of eating when and what I please, [and] of fishing and hunting upon my own ground?" The master was free to do as he pleased; the servant's duty was obedience, and if he failed in it, he could be discharged. Liberty would never be safe, nor governments reformed in America, the writer maintained, "till we banish European, and in particular British, ideas of the nature of the one and of the origin of the other" that tended to make us "Look upon our rulers as our masters,—whereas they are nothing but our servants."[45]

But these deeply ingrained ideas about government persisted and eventually produced the federal Bill of Rights. Among the additions proposed in the Pennsylvania ratifying convention of 1787 was a stipulation "That the people have a right to bear arms for the defense of themselves and their own state, or the United States, or for the purpose of killing game; and no law shall be passed for disarming the people or any of them, unless for crimes committed, or real danger of public injury from individuals." Other proposed amendments to safeguard fishing and hunting rights echoed Penn's Frame of Government and the Pennsylvania Constitution of 1776. Failure to include such guarantees, Anti-Federalists continued to believe, were significant reasons for opposing the Constitution.[46]

At least on the narrowest grounds, the Anti-Federalists were unduly concerned. The states would consider game laws within their own purview, and subsequent judicial interpretation forbade territorial legislatures from enacting them. But the broader question has become extraordinarily controversial. When James Madison reduced the welter of suggested amendments to manageable proportions, he omitted any mention of game laws. But the right to bear arms became enshrined in the Second Amendment. Whether its wording converted an individual right as expressed by the Pennsylvania Anti-Federalists into a collective one has long been a question of controversy.[47]

Nevertheless, a closer look at why many early Americans found game laws so objectionable is in order. The conservation features were not the primary issue, for petitioners sought only the "liberty to fowl and hunt in seasonable times," not perpetual open seasons. Rather, their main fear was that game laws would be a prelude to a disarmed populace, vulnerable to tyranny. "Pompilius," writing "On the mischievous Effects of Militia Laws," which he considered to be a waste of time, revealed some of their key assumptions in constructing his argument. "There is no danger of our citizens forgetting the use of arms, while we are strangers to *game-laws,*" he maintained. "A youth of 16 years of age, who has been trained by necessity or choice to the amusement of hunting in our American woods has a better foundation for his becoming an effective soldier, than a whole nation of farmers who have been educated (from the operation of game laws) in an ignorance of fire arms." Instead of applying European principles to the United States, we should recall that "our origin—local circumstances—principles and manners have no parallel in the history of mankind. Let us first discover *who*—and *what*—and *where* we are, and we shall soon be able to discover how to govern ourselves."[48]

Even as they celebrated their uniqueness, colonists continued to reveal considerable interest in the English game laws, perhaps partly because they remained collectively somewhat ambivalent about them. Negative views, as we have seen, had long been common, and an item from Britain was doubtless reprinted in a *Virginia Gazette* of 1766 because it reflected tensions in the English system. "Last week," according to the account, "an officer of the Guards went to poach, with two favourite dogs, upon a Gentlemen's estate in Surry," when the owner's servant rode up and shot one of the dogs. Killing the servant's horse in return, the poacher announced "that that was horse for dog, but the next should be man for dog; upon which the servant thought proper to walk home to his master." Whether many emigrants left Britain to escape the game laws is unknowable, but some Americans clearly believed that was often the case; and many immigrants obviously reveled in their new freedoms. Thus, while describing conditions on the Pennsylvania frontier, a recent settler pointedly observed that he felt safe because local residents were armed. "Besides a well-trained militia we have all guns in our hands. For there is no disarming or game act as with you [in Scotland]."[49]

Some historians might question his assessment of the militia and gun-ownership but not the legal situation. English law did not automatically follow the settlers to America, and none of the British North American colonies adopted the English game laws. For, as the South Carolina legislature observed in 1712 when it made several British acts subject to local enforcement, different circumstances rendered many other English statutes "altogether useless" or "impracticable here." Americans could therefore congratulate themselves that they had long since done what the British were only beginning to consider seriously during the 1790s, when the *Pennsylvania Gazette* reported supposedly imminent changes in the game acts among other reforms designed to prevent a British upheaval comparable to the French Revolution.[50]

Yet, as is well known, some colonists assiduously attempted to model themselves on the English gentry. Colonel Benjamin Tasker of Maryland even went so far as to establish an enclosed deer park of nearly one hundred acres, which he stocked with English deer. The increasing popularity of fox hunting in England also made it correspondingly fashionable in the colonies, and by 1770 "A JERSEY FARMER" observed that it had recently grown to "a surprizing Head." George Washington, among others, was a devotee of the sport, for which he ordered an expensive hat, a scarlet waistcoat, and a monogrammed whip from England. Others in his circle thought releasing a bagged fox in front of the ladies for their "diversion" was capital sport.[51]

The women may or may not have been amused, but some individuals were obviously displeased at the behavior of their neighbors. Landon Carter recorded in December 1774 that "Yesterday . . . my low grounds were alive with fox hunters [whom he named]; my fences all pulled down, Cattle drove out of their Wits and the wenches obliged to Climb the trees." He accordingly wrote "sharply" to the gentlemen, but apparently took no other action. No doubt, he wished to avoid serious trouble with men of his own social status, but custom, sanctioned by judicial interpretation, restrained other southerners from curbing even the common people. William Elliott of South Carolina, who regretted the situation, later transcribed what he observed in a local court where counsel interrogated a witness: "Would you pursue a deer if he entered your neighbor's inclosure?" Answer, "certainly." Even if you destroyed his crops and fences? Yes. You would thereby "commit a trespass. . . . There is no law . . . [to sanction] such an act." Answer, "It is hunters' law, however!" And, Elliott added, "hunters' law is likely somewhat longer to be the governing law of the case in this section of country; for the prejudices of the people are strong against any exclusive property in game, as everyone feels who attempts to keep it to himself."[52] In short, Elliott feared retaliation.

Such acquiescence invited abuses, according to the "JERSEY FARMER." Indeed, he believed, it had become "dangerous, in some Places, for a Man to think himself so much Master of his own Land, as to attempt to hinder those Freebooters [fox hunters] from ravaging every Part of it at their pleasure." Unless steps were taken to prevent it, such practices would soon "become as rampant here as in England, where a Man shall see a Score of Horsemen with Hounds, driving over his Improvements, laying open his Enclosures, tearing up his Grain and Pasture, and dare not ask them why they do so?—For why? They are called Gentlemen." Many small landholders might erroneously believe that they were powerless to stop these depredations because the law sanctioned them, but nothing, he observed, was "more easy, especially in the Jerseys, where it is as unlawful to hunt on my Ground" without my written permission "as to rob my House." If a "few substantial Men in a Neighbourhood" joined together "with a becoming Resolution to see themselves regarded, they would soon see those haughty Gentry, that now think it beneath them to ask Leave," become "very careful to keep off their Land." He then quoted the relevant portions of the New Jersey hunting statutes and concluded that landholders had only their own "Supineness" to blame for having the laws "trampled upon" and themselves "treated like Vassals." This prompted a response from "A FOX HUNTER" who sought to defend his "Brethren" with some queries that he snidely hoped the farmer would consider "if he is not too busy cutting his Firewood."[53]

These interchanges prompt several reflections. The Jersey Farmer was most familiar with the laws of his own province, but many—if not all—the colonies offered the same theoretical protection to landholders, large and small. Thus, during the Revolution a French army officer, the Baron de Viomenil, was astonished to find himself unceremoniously evicted while hunting on the property of a Rhode Island farmer who threatened him with a stick.[54] And in America property holding was widespread. As a result, despite a few exceptions like the abortive experiments with property qualifications in Pennsylvania and Virginia, the game laws in the colonies generally inverted the pattern of their European counterparts. There, the system privileged rank at the expense of the small property holder; in America, the laws privileged all property holders at the expense of (nebulous) rank, while custom favored the common people in the large open spaces of the south. Thus we find small freeholders who could invoke the law against rich neighbors and wealthy men, who were reluctant to use it against anyone.

No wonder that Americans congratulated themselves on their "happy mediocrity" in contrast to Europe with its "few rich and haughty landlords" and "the multitude of poor, abject, rack-rented, tythe-paying tenants."[55] Such observations suggest an obvious but easily overlooked point: long before the Revolution, the colonial elite sought to emulate the English gentry; but the common man often had reason to consider the British model less appropriate. And lest he forget that fact, the well-known contrast between the American and British game laws served as an emphatic reminder. The natural environment of the New World and the social structure of colonial societies had combined to weight the adaptation and replication of English environmental law toward creolization rather than anglicization.

None of this is meant to suggest that the colonial fish and game laws always worked to the advantage of the small property holder—or always preserved wildlife, for that matter. Particularly in the late eighteenth century, when economic development and internal improvements became all the rage, the interests of large mill owners and of river navigation took precedence. Thus, the act to clear the Schuylkill River foreshadowed future developments; it not only authorized the commissioners to promote navigation at the expense of the fish, it also gave them leeway to allow a large mill dam to remain while they demolished structures belonging to small mill owners and poor fishermen, or so some individuals claimed. Similar developments, Gary Kulik has found, occurred in Rhode Island, and no doubt elsewhere.[56] "Improvement" was the name of the game.

Yet improvement could foster as well as hamper conservation efforts as it became apparent that changes in the environment endangered some flora and fauna. Thus familiarity with the European situation, where centuries of concentrated human habitation had depleted some natural resources, made even the earliest colonists aware that the seemingly boundless forests and game might in fact be limited. But as knowledge of their surroundings increased, they relied less on English precedent and more on practical experience to shape environmental legislation. As a result, the statutes of the late colonial period reflect what Peter Kalm repeatedly found—namely, evidence of declining natural abundance. Among those who recognized that "progress" had a price, the novelist James Fenimore Cooper was one of the more eloquent and observant. He had grown up on the New York frontier, and his most realistic fictional work, *The Pioneers* (1823), was almost a conservationist tract. But the words of one of its central characters reflected contemporary priorities. "It is not as ornaments that I value the noble trees of this country; it is for their usefulness."[57]

Flora and fauna were good or bad insofar as they served the needs of humankind. Thus snakes, other predators, and "vermin" fared poorly. Killing poisonous snakes is perhaps understandable—though the naturalists John and William Bartram tried to avoid it—but what should one make of the following incident? According to Kalm, an old Swede and a Native American once encountered a snake while walking together. "The Indian begged him not to touch it, because it was sacred to him." The Swede, who might otherwise have let the snake go, then killed it, "saying: 'Because thou believest in it, I think myself obliged to kill it.'" Although the effect of such behavior on Indian-white relations is perhaps all too obvious, his rationale prompts a collateral question: If spiritual concerns made Native Americans "keepers of the game," as some historians believe, to what extent might other religious beliefs have made white settlers killers of the game in defense of their faith?[58]

Whatever the answer, there is no doubt that one of the first acts in many towns and counties was to establish bounties on wolves and foxes, and virtually all of the colonies eventually did the same. Men also waged war on squirrels. When the rodents became too numerous, according to one contemporary, Hector St. John de Crevecoeur, "the county assembles and forms itself into companies to which a captain is appointed. . . . They march, and that company which kills the most is treated by the rest." The result could be an astonishing slaughter. In Rhode Island one such campaign, whose quarry included birds as well as squirrels, bagged 5,878 creatures in three days of hunting. Crevecoeur, who was sufficiently observant to note that "the wolves, finding the deer becoming scare, have learned how to feed on our sheep, [and] the fox, for want of pheasants and partridges, lives on our poultry," thought that "we should be a little more generous than we are to the brute creation."[59]

Crevecoeur and some others were approaching the concept of a balance of nature, but humans were still God's vice-regents. Just as the solar system had once been thought to revolve around the earth, humankind remained the center of the universe throughout the seventeenth and eighteenth centuries. Even Tom Paine, who could imagine a "*plurality* of worlds" peopled by other inhabitants, believed that "as . . . the Creator made nothing in vain, so also must it be believed that He organized the structure of the universe in the most advantageous manner for the benefit of man." Americans, who had had less time to recognize the results of their mistakes, could therefore manipulate the checks and balances of nature with fewer misgivings than some Europeans. Thomas Jefferson brought in turkeys to eat the worms that fed on his tobacco plants, but when he considered making his garden a refuge for all species, he pointedly exempted predators.[60] Meanwhile, the Swedish taxonomist Linnaeus noted that after Americans slaughtered the birds that ate their corn, worms destroyed their meadows. Still, no one seems to have had many second thoughts about the fact that wolves were extinct in England by the sixteenth century. Even if these beasts had disappeared there, they still abounded in America. "Such is the economy of nature," Jefferson believed, "that no instance can be produced of her having permitted any one race of her animals to become extinct; or her having formed any link in her great work so weak as to be broken."[61]

Such assumptions help to explain why, despite a far greater concern for the environment than has been commonly recognized, many colonial conservation efforts failed. And so it was when a flock of unknown birds "not So large as a Parot but of a most beautiful yellow from an orange to a lemon" appeared at Landon Carter's plantation in Virginia, an overseer "shot at them and killed two," which Carter had stuffed for his mantlepiece.[62] Though he thought them too big, his description suggests that they may have been Carolina parakeets, which are now extinct.

Part II / Exchange and Identity

CHAPTER FIVE

Beyond Declension

Economic Adaptation and the Pursuit of Export Markets in the Massachusetts Bay Region, 1630–1700

James E. McWilliams

Historians of colonial New England have traditionally portrayed the seventeenth century as a time when cultural and commercial interests clashed. According to this interpretation, New England began in the 1630s as an experimental community of reformers who based their lives on covenant theology, subsistence farming, and small, tightly knit towns. These "peaceable kingdoms" thrived through the interdependency of civil and ecclesiastical tenets, a patriarchal authority that preserved each family as a "little commonwealth," and a preindustrial mentalité that curbed potentially destructive acquisitive instincts. Around 1660, however, this situation changed. Commerce emerged to wreak havoc on the social harmony that had long buttressed New England's position as "a city on a hill." "The market" came along and dispersed towns, distracted settlers from their tormented search for grace, imposed a greedy impulse on a once-communal people, and generally undermined the Puritan rigor that had characterized life for the region's first two generations. Bernard Bailyn conveyed this cultural declension in the following terms: "Stronger forces were at work, and the faithful witnessed a continuing alienation from ancient ideals and social forms."[1]

More recently historians have started to complicate this older narrative. Conceptualizing commerce and culture not as mutually exclusive social forces, with one disrupting the other, but rather as coexisting and supportive developments, they have relied primarily on Max Weber's formulation that Puritan values nurtured commercial behavior and thereby took the edge off commerce's destructive tendencies. Whereas an older generation of historians once argued that commercial endeavors compromised New England's pietistic ideals, this more recent group claims that profit and piety existed in a sort of symbiotic embrace. Settlers' zealous efforts to build gristmills, farms, counting houses, ships, and fishing flakes, according to this critique, nurtured the Puritan effort to succeed financially while at the same time deepening their relationship with God. As one historian has recently summarized it, Puritans "developed a culture that was both the most entrepreneurial and the most vociferously pious in Anglo-America." Within a Weberian framework, historians have answered the question of how, as Joyce Appleby puts it, "an economic system, destructive of customary ways, had been able to penetrate the walls of habit that immured men and women living in traditional societies."[2]

But were customary ways really destroyed? While the Weberian critique of seventeenth-century New England effectively opposes the timeworn declension narrative, it avoids a significant, extremely basic, economic question. *Economically speaking,* what were New England's "customary ways"? A reliance on Weber allows historians to blend profit and piety, but only *after the quest for profit is seen to emerge.* The Weberian critique continues to assume, much like the declension narrative it purportedly challenges, that the pursuit of profit was still a behavior that appeared as an exogenous force, out of nowhere, and with abrupt, ahistorical immediacy.[3] The failure to examine the deepest origins of New England's economic habits, and to trace how those habits evolved throughout the century, thus leaves economic historians under the dubious impression that New England settlers, as the declension narrative has always claimed, lived and worked in a kind of preindustrial utopia of bartered exchange and communal harmony.

Migrants to every region of British America, whatever their demographic characteristics or driving theological imperatives, had to build an infrastructure capable of supporting a viable local economy. Historians of colonial New England commonly note the relative ease with which Bay Colony settlers organized stable communities around the imperatives of covenant theology. Their overwhelming attention to communal stability, however, slights the more improvisational strategies through which towns and individuals worked to establish the economic basis for that stability. Studies of the seventeenth-century New England economy, in other words, have generally failed to historicize market development. As a step in this direction, this essay removes New England from its traditional declension and Weberian frameworks and places it within the developmental framework that has been applied so successfully to the broad experiences of the southern colonies.[4] It does so by working within a current historiographical trend that implicitly challenges the rigid exceptionalism that these more established interpretations have promoted.[5] This newer scholarship exhorts historians to consider the region's settlers not so much as loyal denizens of a Bible Commonwealth, but rather as economic actors struggling to adopt inherited metropolitan norms to the shifting limits and freedoms of the colonial periphery. Such a consideration has almost exclusively framed analyses of other colonial British American colonies. This essay thus makes it a premise for historical change in seventeenth-century New England as well.

A focus on internal economic development especially illuminates the adaptations required of Massachusetts Bay settlers hoping to accomplish the economic goal that burdened every colony in British America: securing leverage in the transatlantic market.[6] By the eighteenth century, coherent societies based on remarkably distinct economic characteristics—societies tied into different regions of the transatlantic world through different staple commodities—had emerged to distinguish New England and the southern colonies. The overwhelming scholarly attention to these differences, however, has obscured the underlying internal economic developments that established the preconditions for these regional distinctions in the first place. In light of this problem, an emphasis on the mechanics of internal economic change during the Massachusetts Bay region's first seventy years encourages an investigation of economic adaptation during a period when the most obvious qualities of these two regional economies—their respective labor systems and export commodities—had yet to develop. Every seventeenth-century colony, whatever its religious orientation, faced the daunting task of integrating its peripheral local economies into the transatlantic market. With respect to this important quest, New England should not be labeled exceptional. Culture, in the end, did not accommodate a newly emerging commercial attitude. It evolved with it.

Improvising an Infrastructure

The Massachusetts Bay Colony's initial investors articulated their goals without ambiguity. In no uncertain terms, they expressed a desire to export fish and timber to generate handsome returns on their investments. Francis Higginson, an early settler, fueled enthusiasm for potential cod exports when he reported that "the abundance of sea fish are almost beyond believing." In 1635 the General Court, the Bay Colony's leading authority, convened a committee to "consult, advise, and take order for the setting forwards and managing of a fishing trade." Towns including Marblehead were quick to grant potential fishermen "ground as they stand in need of." Similar expectations and policies structured the earliest timber trade. Matthew Craddock, an absentee investor, demanded of Samuel Endicott that the colony "provide us some staves, and other timber of all sorts." Investors offered lucrative incentives for "experienced men in the ordering and taking of clap board and pipestaves" to migrate to the Massachusetts Bay Colony. The General Court supported investor intentions when it regulated timber clearing to ensure that "good timber for more necessary usages" always remained available for merchants to export. In these ways and others, the colony's organizers sized up the region's rich natural resources and established what they considered to be the necessary preconditions for their exploitation.[7]

These preconditions, however, turned out to be far more extensive than the "settlement undertakers" had ever imagined. Their despondent correspondence confirms the extent of their miscalculation. John Tinker, a founding investor, noted, "It is a very greate grievanc and generall complainte among all the Merchants and dealers to New England that they can have noe returnes . . . insomuch that if there be not some course taken for beter payments of our Creditors our tradeing will utterly cease." Another investor, Thomas Dudley, complained that "the estates of the undertakers, who were 3 or 4000 pounds engaged in the joint stock . . . was now not above so many hundreds." John Davenport and Theophilus Eaton insisted that their desire "of staying within this patent was real and strong." However, they continued, "to our great charge and hindrence, our almost nine months patient wayting in expectation of some opportunity to be offerred us" dampened their enthusiasm. Winthrop was forced to admit to Simon D'Ewes that, "There come no benefit of your money but losse."[8]

On paper, the loss made no sense. A joint-stock company had raised the funds, English settlers with pockets stuffed with hard cash were pouring into the colony, men experienced in international finance controlled the venture, overseas demand flourished, and New England abounded with exportable resources. Where, then, were the returns? The investors, half of whom remained in England, had overlooked the complete absence of a regional infrastructure necessary to execute even the most rudimentary tasks necessary for systematic exportation.[9] Economic development in the 1630s singularly hinged on this basic prerequisite of economic growth. Migrants from England had abandoned one of the most sophisticated regional economies in the western world. New England, by contrast, was an environment completely lacking in the most basic components of infrastructure. Families engaged in the daily struggle to build farms, roads, boats, and bridges suffered the consequences of infrastructural inadequacy with disturbing regularity. To them, export failure made tremendous sense. Exporting staple products to satisfy their colony's investors was the last thing they had on their minds.

A few illustrations capture the depth of their predicament. During the first decade of settlement, travel over even the shortest of overland distances frequently turned into a life-threatening ordeal. "One Scott and Eliot of Ipswich," Winthrop recorded in his journal, "were lost in their ways homewards [after picking up timber] and wandered up and down 6 dayes and eate nothing . . . they were found by an Indian, beinge almost senselesse for wants of rest." He later reported "a mayd servant of Mr. Skelton of Salem" who, on a trip to Saugus, "was lost 7 dayes and at length come home to Salem." During this time, Winthrop elaborated, "she was in the woods, havinge no kinde of food, the snow being very deep and cold." A fifty-year-old man "lost his waye between Dorcester and Winaguscus," during which time he "wandered in the woods and swamps 3 dayes and 2 nights with out takinge any food." Being "neare spent," according to Winthrop, "God brought him back to Scituate, but he had torne his leggs much." These incidents reflected more than typical traveling hazards. Instead, they confirmed the impact of the Massachusetts Bay Colony's initially primitive infrastructure on a people accustomed to a far more advanced economic foundation.[10]

Transportation by water was equally treacherous. Unfamiliar swells and eddies, unpredictable weather trends, ambiguous points of disembarkation, and new, quickly assembled sailing vessels all wreaked havoc with settlers who attempted river and coastal trade. One Salemite, for example, "carrying wood in a cannoe in the South River was overturned and drowned." Mishaps like his occurred routinely during the first decade of settlement, and much more than they would later in the century. When six Salem men went "fowling in a canoe," a strong current overturned them near Kettle Island, drowning five of them. Winthrop recalled an incident where "a man almost drowned here in the narrow river in a canoe" after having "laden his canoe so deepe with dung that she sunk under him, scarce anything surviving." Two men and two boys, maneuvering a "small boat" that they had "overladen with wood" between the coast and Noddles Island, "were cast away in a great tempest . . . in the night." A man working with his servant and brother "putt much goodes in a small boat in [the] Charles River" and proceeded to "oversett the boat, with the weight of some h[ogs]h[ead]s, so as they were all 3 drowned." Such mishaps, rather than reflecting events endemic to any actively commercial society, more likely reveal the settlers' basic lack of familiarity with water routes, new vessels, and proper weight thresholds.[11] They reflected, in other words, the region's infrastructural inadequacy.[12]

So while the Massachusetts Bay Colony's investors demanded ample returns of fish and timber, the settlers who were supposed to be harvesting those exports were busy confronting a region marred by a rudimentary economic foundation. Migrants hardly ignored the problem. The realization that they could not travel a mile or two without facing serious danger naturally motivated common settlers to adapt the familiar elements of local economic stability to the shifting vagaries of a strange wilderness. This extensive undertaking meant organizing the landscape into defined, recognizable, and replicable zones of productivity. Town selectmen tempered the general decentralization of economic and political authority in the Bay colony with explicit legislative efforts to structure precisely where and when settlers pursued particular economic endeavors. Historians of seventeenth-century New England have lavished generous attention on topics such as land distribution, subdivision, and fee-simple ownership—not to mention congregational organization—as developments central to town stability. We know next to nothing, however, about the processes through which towns accomplished the fundamental task of ordering their generous grants into arenas of economic activity. How, we should ask, did they build an infrastructure?

They began with farm animals. As the decade progressed, Bay colonists adapted inherited habits regarding the separation of domestic animals and crops to their new landscape as they worked to maximize the production of commodities essential not to the prerequisites of an export trade, but rather to their immediate survival on the colonial periphery. Massachusetts Bay residents devised sophisticated organizational plans to execute this adaptation. As towns became more densely settled, the obvious problems associated with trying to plant and tend crops, catch and dry fish, and transport timber while maneuvering around haphazardly penned cattle became increasingly evident. Not only did cattle occupy potentially tillable plots of land but they overpacked otherwise healthy soil, eluded shoddily constructed fences to rummage through planted grain or stakes of fish, and demanded precious family labor for their daily upkeep.

In response to these everyday problems, towns licensed "cowherds," or cowkeepers, to provide what immediately became a valuable service. These men collected a yearly fee of £20 to remove scores of cattle from the towns' agricultural areas during daylight hours between April and November. A typical keeper's contract included a signed promise to leave the town common with the cows "by six of the clock in the morning" and to return them a half an hour before sundown. Cattle owners were expected to deliver their cows to the common before the keeper left, but the keeper, under penalty of three pence per cow, had to make sure that no cow remained stranded there overnight, and that all of them wound up back in their respective houselots. Some cowkeepers offered specialized services such as milking milch cows in the morning and evening, taking along bulls for reproductive purposes (impregnation fee: ten pence), and arranging for branders to mark cows. We do not normally count such men as pivotal economic players, but they quickly became crucial actors in the fledgling economy.[13]

Cowkeepers and towns adjusted their policies according to the types of cows present in a particular town. Many keepers accepted any cow, often signing up as many as one hundred for a single season. Others specialized, taking only milch, draught, "dry" cattle, or calves. Towns, moreover, often demanded that certain cows graze certain areas. For example, a town might decree that "there shalbee noe Dry Cattle kept up[on] this side the river" with the exception of those kept on private lots or those "Cows neer calvinge." Draught cattle, according to Newtown records, were to be kept "beyond Bar[rett] Lampsons Planting field between the cow comon Ray[le] [and the] Charlestown Rayle." Matthew Hitchcock appointed his son "for the summer for to helpe keepe the drie heard over the water till the calves should be sent over which was the xxth of May." Newtown further designated space "for the milch Cowes to lyein on nights," requiring that "noe other cattell whatsoever to go there." Boston undertakers declared that "all barren cattle (except such as are constantly imployed in draughte), and weaned calves 20 weekes and weaned mayle kidds shalbe kept abroad from off the neck." Dorchester went so far as to designate the ratios of different types of cattle permitted on its grazing lots: "10 kidds to one Cow; two yearlings to one Cow . . . one working ox to a Cow, one mare and a colt to two Cowes, 4 calves for one Cow," and so on. These carefully calculated arrangements helped colonists squeeze as much milk, beef, leather, and corn as they possibly could from rugged frontier conditions.[14]

As with cows, towns directly understood how swine interfered with local efforts to build an economic infrastructure. Settlers thus furthered the process of organizing the economic landscape by designating hogreeves to control swine. Salem ordered that "all swine shall goe under keeper: or be kept up, and that all swine taken abroad without a keeper it shall be lawful for any man to pounde them and to have for every swine 2s 6d before they be taken out of the pound." Two years later the town raised the fine to ten shillings, if a hog "is found without a keeper." Newtown coordinated the strategies of ringing and pounding with the oversight of the hogreeve. After ordering that "every one shall Ringe ther hoggs before the 20th of this month," the town required that "all hogges in the towne shall be ringed by Wm Wilcok," and then appointed John Clarke as the hogreeve, "to discharge that office to the order of the Court." This measure displaced some responsibility from pig owners, as they could now blame escaped swine on insufficient ringing, a fault that cost the ringer sixpence per pig. Anyone choosing not to ring their swine had to pay a fine "as often as [their swine] be found doing damage." Dorchester constructed a public pound, ordered private pig sties demolished, hired keepers, and ordered that "none shall keepe any swine to let them runne in the Commons without sufficient yokes and rings within one miles of any corne field." Boston enacted a policy whereby anyone who found a pig rooting through their crops could avoid the hassle of locating the offending animal's owner and simply "send a note of them to the foldkeeper" by placing notice on the whipping post. Swine would always roam, root, and destroy, but settlers quickly established reasonable measures to minimize crop destruction and maximize their invaluable pork supply.[15]

Building cartways and roads was an equally pressing order of business. Moving cows daily from commons to outer pastures, transporting hogs to public pounds or to islands, and hauling timber for fences, houses, and fuel necessitated adequate footpaths and cartways. Town leaders focused mainly on road building and maintenance within their own boundaries, rather than between towns, and the impetus to construct these roads—as with the impetus to organize livestock—invariably arose from local demands, rather than from export-related concerns. Newtown (early Cambridge), for example, granted Andrew Warner a license to "fetch home ayl[wives] from the weir," as long as he oversaw the construction of a cartway to that weir. It similarly allowed John Benjaman to farm a particular plot of land under the agreement that "the windmill hill shall be reserved for the towns use and a cartway of two rods wide the same." It granted land to Simon Bradstreet under the stipulation that he "make a sufficient cartway along by his pales and keep it in repair 7 years."[16]

Salem similarly linked land grants to road building and maintenance requirements. The town requested that Richard Ingersoll and Lawrence Leach, while building their farms, "be sure to leave roome for high ways for cartes to bring home wood," adding that "they doe promise to make a sufficient cart way." After determining where "to feed the cattle on the Lord's Days," the Salem townsmen built a highway "beyond the swamp on the Nor[th] side of Mr. Johnson's lott" to enable keepers to move the cattle to this newly designated location. Granting Israel Stroughton rights to build a watermill, the Dorchester townsmen ordered that "there shall be a sufficient cartway . . . made to the mill at the common charge." In such ways, the first pathways closely adhered to local economic needs.[17]

Towns further improved local roads by linking requests for land extensions and alterations to local road development while keeping a relatively vigilant watch on road conditions. Part of the privilege of owning land in most towns included maintaining "a sufficient way unto his allotment of ground," but when landholders applied to the town for permission to expand, enclose, or alter property, the town frequently linked the grant to a requirement that the grantee set aside space for a new path or cartway. Dorchester's George Hull thus received "the meadow that lyes before his doore where he now dwells" as long as he agreed to make "a sufficient way for passidge." When a Mr. Holland applied to enclose a marsh adjacent to his property, Dorchester granted him clearance to do so under the requirement that he leave "a little part of marsh which is without the inclosure" in order to clear space for the building of "a sufficient high way." Jonathan Gellet's grant to fence a plot of common land required his building "a sufficent cartway." When four adjacent Boston landowners went to build fences around their property, the town intervened and requested that, in enclosing their boundaries, they "preserve a path way, of a rod breadth, between payle and payle." In these small but nonetheless significant ways, town leaders strategically and incrementally connected English settlers' quest for a viable local infrastructure to the towns' broader, long-term transportation needs.[18]

Fences were the final order of infrastructural business. Town governments approached the issue of secure fencing from three directions. First, they required all settlers to fence their home fields and common grounds. "For as much as divers of our towne are resolved to some English grain this spring," Salem announced in a typical missive, "it is therefore ordered that all comon and particular home fences about the town shall be sufficientlie made up." Those who refused the order "shall forfeit his sayd lot." Whereas rules governing the movement of swine generally assumed that the beasts' owners held sole responsibility for their peregrinations, several towns enacted fence regulations that placed equal burden on fence builders whose corn required protection. "Every man shall make his fences sufficient for all his planting ground," Boston townsmen declared, "upon paine that if any losse doe come for defect therein, that damage shall be satisfyed by such upon whose fence the breach shalbe." Dorchester similarly decreed that "if any hoggs commit any trespasse in any of the corne fields within the plantation . . . the owner of the Pall where they breake in shall pay the on[e] halfe of the trespasse."[19]

Colonists immediately exploited the region's rich store of timber not for exportation, but for the more modest goals of fencing off their gardens, cornfields, and cattle lots.[20] Conceptions of what actually constituted an acceptable fence varied tremendously. The second component in the process of ordering the economic landscape with fences thus required settlers to meet a series of increasingly rigid specifications. Newtown, for example, initially demanded only that fences be of a post-and-rail design rather than the less secure crotched model. Boston similarly started with a basic requirement that fences be "a doble rayle with mortesses in the posts, of 10 foot distance from each other." By the end of the decade, however, these requirements had become significantly more stringent. Boston sought to "see to the makeing of such styles and gates as may bee needfull for every field," and Newtown demanded that a fence be set in a ditch at least two feet deep, and reach at least four feet in height, and issued a 3s. 6d. fine for "every rodd of fence that is faieling." Dorchester followed suit, judging fences insufficient unless "they be well set and bound at least 4 foot above ground." For fences built around larger plots of corn, rather than around house lots, Dorchester demanded that settlers construct a fence with at least five rails. Towns vigilantly enforced these requirements.[21]

These specifications, finally, demanded the appointment of fence viewers—the third and final stage in the process of zoning off economic activity. Fence viewers took responsibility for fences in a specific section of town. When they found a fence defective, they could either employ their own resources to repair it, demanding payment from the fence's owner, or they could publicly report the defect at the town meeting, where the owner of the degenerate fence received the censure of his righteous, well-fenced brethren and a fine. Most fence viewers earned about three shillings a day for their services and, like hogreeves and cowkeepers, came to play a pivotal role in establishing the Bay Colony's earliest infrastructure.[22]

Settlers may have failed to export fish, fur, and timber during these settlement years. They may have floundered on unfamiliar rivers and coastal passageways. They may have lost their way between bordering towns. Nevertheless, settlers and settlement undertakers had not only bought, divided, granted, and brought the land along the coast of the Massachusetts Bay under cultivation, but, in just a few years, they had organized what had once seemed an unfamiliar and uncivilized landscape into recognizable and replicable zones of economic activity. This accomplishment might very well have been the settlers' greatest achievement during their first decade. To be sure, the specialization of space and labor through the strategic arrangement of cows and hogs, the construction and maintenance of cartways and fences, and the provision of services such as cowkeepers, hogreeves, and fence viewers did not contribute to the primary economic goal of producing exportable commodities in a direct or measurable way. Nevertheless, these crucial initiatives, mundane as they seem, proved essential to the more immediate demands of achieving a competence in a settlement economy. They were the vital economic prerequisites for eventual participation in the regional and Atlantic economies.

Developing Local Exchange

Building on local infrastructure foundations, the Bay Colony quickly developed strong patterns of commercial exchange that supported the growing demands of a nascent economy on the colonial periphery. It was an element of development, moreover, that scholars of New England have also generally overlooked. In accordance with the staples model, historians conventionally claim that Barbadian and Iberian demand for cod and timber in the 1640s sparked the export trade that lured New England into the powerful orbit of the transatlantic economy that, in turn, dominated local commerce. From the perspective of the local economy, however, it appears that internal demand drove local economic development as much as export demand. Local economic patterns arose not only in response to the "linkage effects" of an early export orientation, but also to the strong local demand generated by the ongoing efforts of common settlers working to capitalize on their new infrastructure and approximate recognizable patterns of commercial exchange. This development requires us to examine in some detail the daily trading habits of Bay Colony farmers.

Traditionally historians have portrayed New England's commercial farmers as pious, industrious men who, after meeting subsistence needs, rushed their excess apples, corn, and beef to Salem and Boston for export. This trajectory of trade, however, had an important middle stage. Three commercial farmers whose account books survive—John Pickering, John Burnham, and John Barnard—provide representative evidence that the Massachusetts Bay region's development primarily followed an internal logic very much distinct from the colony's emerging export concerns. These farmers' accounts reveal the workings of an internal economy that responded to, and developed around, constantly shifting supplies and demands of basic, locally available, commodities and services. Their activity thus not only suggests the need for a broader conceptualization of seventeenth-century trade, but collectively reveals a second internal adaptation in New England's early development. The patterns of local exchange developed by New England's seventeenth-century commercial farmers complemented the infrastructural improvements carried out during the first three decades and, in so doing, moved the region closer to full integration into export markets.[23]

For commercial farmers, occupational flexibility and regular access to a range of products that could be sold locally were the most basic requirements for active participation in the local economy. Throughout the seventeenth century and well into the eighteenth, the Massachusetts Bay region's nascent economy demanded that its participants maintain close ties to several commodities and that they remain capable of performing several basic services on demand. While most colonists labeled themselves with specific occupational designations, the increasingly complex task of doing business in the Bay Colony more often than

Table 5.1. Goods Exchanged by John Pickering, John Burnham, and John Barnard
(in percent)

	Pickering (Salem)	Burnham (Ipswich)	Barnard (Andover)
Meat	18	5	5
Grain	14	38	20
Wood	8	7	.6
Textile	8	7	12
Manufactures	6	2	6
Service/Labor	25	18	39
Money	8	4	9
Dairy	3	1	.2
Miscellaneous	10	18	8.2

Note: Miscellaneous items included for Pickering: oil, lime, molasses, tobacco, land, powder, bricks, hay, and salt; for Burnham: molasses, sugar, rum, tobacco, fish, turnips, apples, rosin, a dog, lime, oil, mustard seed, salt, beans, flax seed, and vinegar; and for Barnard: salt, turnips, cider, apples, tallow, tobacco, butter, powder, bricks, wine, onions, peas, sugar, oil, and hay.

Sources: John Pickering Account Book, 1684–1716, F.M. fp1; John Burnham Account Book, 1698–1700, F. Ms. B9963; and John Barnard Account Book, 1688–1700, F. Ms. B259 and private microfilm. All account books at the Phillips Library, Peabody Essex Museum.

not required proficiency in a range of seasonal by-employments. This young economy rewarded broad diversification for commercial farmers intent on developing trading relationships with neighbors whose particular set of supplies and demands complemented their own (see table 5.1).

Commercial farmers not only embraced a wide range of goods and services, but they consistently participated in a diversity of markets—domestic, local, and export. In the course of a single day, for example, a commercial farmer might sell Indian corn to a neighboring town, provide his family with a barrel of cider, and unload a cartful of staves on a Salem or Boston ship bound for Barbados. Viewed through the scope of the staples model, the shipment of staves would stand out as the most significant, growth-oriented, economic transaction. Seen from the perspective of the commercial farmer's accounts, however, a fuller sense of market interdependency emerges, and the significance of the internal economy in directing the flow of goods stands out as especially vital to that connection. In analyzing farmers' production of different goods for different clients in a local setting, we begin to understand the underlying mechanics of regional economic adaptation as a crucial step toward full integration into export markets.

Hundreds of specific accounts uncover the economic diversification practiced by individual traders engaged in constant internal exchange. John Pickering, a Salem farmer, possessed a substantial amount of land with several barns, an extensive garden, an orchard with a cider mill, a pasture in the South field, advanced husbandry instruments, and land bordering a sawmill.[24] His farm epitomized the seventeenth-century quest to establish a domestic competence. The range of his and his family's productive operations is reflected in the list of goods he sold to John Hovey between 1686 and 1689. During this time, he was able to offer Hovey lamb, mutton, pork, timber, corn, money, butter, cheese, sweet oil, and a 150-pound hog—all from his own farm.[25] His access to a variety of domestically produced goods and natural resources enabled him to acquire products locally that he would otherwise have had to do without or import at a higher cost, and it permitted him to hire skilled labor for tasks that he had neither the time nor equipment to perform on his own. He sold Eleazer Keefer, a Salem neighbor, cow hides, beef, corn, and lime in return for shoes that Keefer made and pieces of leather that he tanned.[26] He provided John Harvey, a carpenter, with wood supplies, beef, and money in exchange for Harvey's work in framing his house, building a barn, and hauling the timber required for these projects. Over a four-year period, he sold Manassas Marsten bricks, hay, lamb, wood, and mutton in exchange for Marsten's making "shoes for my horse," "mending a hook and putting a link into a chaine," "mending one plow halter," and for "one plowshare and bolter for horse plow." John Neale cobbled eight pairs of shoes for Pickering between 1686 and 1688, for which Pickering returned money, pork, mutton, and cheese.[27]

Pickering's local exchanges with a single client usually occurred over the course of several years, but they could also be fleeting and comparatively isolated in nature, executed only to fulfill an immediate and short-term need. On 4 May 1690, for example, he sold Samuel Ingersoll three shillings in wood, a peck of salt, and seven pounds of pork. A few days later, Ingersoll paid Pickering in five full days of work, which was carried out by a servant. Their account then closed. During the same year, George Ingersoll bought wood, money, and veal from Pickering in exchange for eight and a half days of work. During the summer of 1684, Pickering purchased five days of labor and about two pounds in money from Salem's John Marsten. In January and February, he paid Marsten with ten shipments of Indian corn. These accounts did not drag on for years, as many did, and such relatively quick exchanges became the bread and butter of a developing internal economy.[28]

The coexistence of distinct internal needs and access to a diversity of locally demanded commodities similarly underscored John Barnard's trading routine.

His account with the couple Francis and Alice Faulkner lasted over five years and included hundreds of transactions—almost all of them goods and services that were locally produced and consumed. Barnard provided the Faulkners with goods including Indian corn, wheat, rye, malt, "wool from Ipswich," hay, sheepskins, apples, dung, and a variety of farming and transportation services. Alice Faulkner, in turn, met the bulk of Barnard's textile needs by "making John's coat," "by my Jackit and britches," "by making three kersey jackits," "by making John's waist coat," and many other textile-related services.[29]

This particular account especially highlights how directly reciprocal internal transactions could actually be. Barnard, for example, hired Francis Faulkner's labor for clearing and sowing fields, and then sold him milled corn and rye. Faulkner, who owned a press, sold Barnard cider for the apples that Barnard had grown in his own orchard. Barnard would sell Faulkner wool that he either sheared from his own sheep or bought in Ipswich and, in return, would buy shirts, pants, and jackets, from him. Faulkner would also do the dirty work of slaughtering Barnard's livestock, only then to turn around and purchase his veal, mutton, pork, lamb, and beef. This tight reciprocity appears in other accounts as well. Barnard, to cite just a single example, unloaded several bushels of barley to a trading partner who lived one town over, in Bradford, and in return collected four bushels of malt.[30]

Other transactions were less reciprocal and extensive, but they still revolved around the ongoing effort to merge local supply and demand. For five bushels of corn, Job Tyler sold Barnard seventy-five pounds of beef, wove thirty yards of cloth, and paid twelve shillings in money. This exchange was their only recorded transaction. Internal trade depended not only on the presence of internal demand, but on the timing of that demand as well. In 1699, Barnard credited Joseph Lovejoy for "mending one day and making hay, by carting 2 loads of hay, by one day of his man," and "by fencing at meadow."[31] Later that year, Barnard paid Lovejoy by "mowing," and "by fencing at the meadow." Why didn't these men simply fence their own fields? Or, for that matter, why did Barnard both sell and buy beef? The answer involves timing. When the precise demand arose—when the fence crumbled or when the beef supply diminished—Barnard had already invested his labor, goods, and time in other endeavors. In an economic environment lacking extensive slave or servant labor, independent farmers often found themselves fixing each other's fences and selling each other beef in the same month, or even in the same week. As the local economy developed, domestic networks of exchange attained a level of reliability and flexibility that would take the export market many years to achieve.

Barnard's economic activity thus covered a gamut of goods, services, and markets, but the bulk of his activity mainly focused on selling small amounts of grain locally in exchange for services that both improved his Andover farm and processed its diverse products for sale in local markets. He cultivated wheat, Indian corn, rye, hops, and barley, and sold these goods for services including carting posts for fences, making plow yokes, carting loads of hay, having hundreds of bricks made, repairing barns, drawing timber, dressing flax, malting barley, carting apples, and even, somewhat unexpectedly, "making the tobacco garden." He often relied on partnerships in order to improve his access to requisite farm improvements. With three of his clients, for example, he paid "for quarter part of an ox," which they shared for plowing usage. When the ox had run out of steam, they then divided the hide. Barnard noted in a margin, "due to me a quarter of the hide."[32]

John Burnham's transactions further confirm the influence of mutually co-existing local demands and the importance of access to a diversity of goods on regional productive trends and trading patterns. Burnham, like his contemporaries, wore many hats. Surviving records refer to him as a carpenter and a husbandman, deeds confirm his ownership of a gristmill on the Chebacco River, his uncle had an interest in a sawmill, and his will lists marsh and meadow ground, several houses and barns, carpentry tools, utensils, husbandry tools, extensive livestock holdings, and horses.[33] Burnham regularly tapped his diverse resources to acquire necessary household goods and to improve the productive capability of his farm. Selling primarily grain, timber, and processed wood, he obtained shoes, cotton, wool, fish, cider, clothes, hides, iron, and all sorts of farm labor. Transactions remained gauged to the demands of neighbors who concentrated resources in specific economic activities that generated specific needs. Over a four-year period, Burnham sold Nathanial Perkins, an Ipswich weaver, 15.5 bushels and three pecks of corn, 6.5 bushels of barley, ten sheep, nine lambs, a pair of oxen, hay, a pound of wood, and a pound of tobacco. He also provided several services, including "tending the cows two days at Ipswich," "a horse for two days," and "shoes mended." Burnham sold the Ipswich yeoman John Smith hay, corn, wood, and a cow, in addition to providing services such as "fetching hay" and "cutting and drawing wood." To another yeoman, Isaac Perkins, he sold turnips and barley.[34]

Burnham also provided both raw timber and processed wood for local consumption. Exploiting his access to a sawmill, he sold hundreds of boards, shingles, and raw wood to several small farmers and artisans in Ipswich and neighboring towns. To John Whipple, an Ipswich joiner, he provided 198 feet of "sawen boards" in November 1697 and 398 feet more in June 1698. Nathanial Rust, also of Ipswich, purchased small parcels of wood from Burnham on twenty-two occasions between April 1703 and October 1705. Burnham's accounts mention Thomas Perrin, a Rowley farmer, as owing him for "logs sawn at my mill," as well as "1000 foot pine boards, 1438 hemlock boards, 608 pine boards sawen," and "1319 pine boards sawen." Ipswich's blacksmith, Isaac Littlehale, made three visits to Burnham between 1692 and 1694 for "407 foot boards, 304 boards and 9 slabs, and 308 foot boards."[35]

While wood processing remained vital to Burnham's economic activity, grain accounted for the majority of his trades. In this endeavor, as in his others, Burnham seems to have oriented his transactions around patterns of local demand. Growing his own grain and acquiring it from other commercial farmers, Burnham maintained inventories throughout the year and unloaded it during times of heightened demand. Although the evidence is often murky, it generally appears that Burnham sold timber, labor, domestic goods, transportation services, and processed wood in order to obtain not only household necessities, but also hundreds of bushels of recently reaped grain. He would then hold the grain until the spring and early summer, when most farmers had run low and were initiating new planting, to sell his inventory. Forty-five percent of his grain transactions occurred over four months, between March and June. This was a time when internal demand would have peaked. On the other end of the agricultural year, 36 percent of his grain transactions occurred between November and February, when he purchased excess corn from local farmers, or even from Virginia. The summer months, however, accounted for only 13 percent of his corn transactions. A similar trend occurred with Indian corn. Forty-seven percent of his Indian corn transactions took place between March and June, when he sold scores of bushels locally. Another 36 percent of his Indian corn trades transpired between November and February, when Burnham bought it from a relatively well-supplied market. Only 14 percent of his Indian corn transactions occurred between July and October. His strategy seemed clear enough: to profit in the local economy.[36]

Burnham, finally, did not record prices with enough consistency for us to construct a comprehensive price list, but a scattering of corn prices supports the economic logic underlying his grain transactions. Between December 1704 and May 1705 (with March being the start of a new calendar year), Burnham recorded enough prices to reveal his strategy for buying and selling corn. In December and February 1704, he bought corn for 2s. 6d. per bushel. The next month, March 1705, he turned around and sold corn at 2s. 8d. per bushel. The rate rose until the fall harvest, when Burnham started to buy again. In May 1705, Burnham was selling at 3s. per bushel; in June sales dropped slightly to 2s. 9d. per bushel; but by September 1705, the price had risen back to 3s. per bushel.[37] While this evidence is limited in quantity, it does suggest that Burnham traded corn as a local commodity while paying very close attention to levels of local supply and demand.

Like settlers throughout British America, Pickering, Barnard, and Burnham worked within a local economic context supported by a viable infrastructure and driven by the demands of rural families trying to further their estates on the periphery of colonial British America. While overseas demand in places like the West Indies and the Iberian peninsula certainly helped along economic development throughout New England, commercial farmers engaged in the daily routines of local exchange provided the real foundation for economic stability and, in so doing, enhanced the region's eventual ability to embrace overseas opportunities with systematic trade. As settlers carried out local exchanges of local commodities, they improved transportation facilities, opened stores and warehouses, established solid trading partners and firms, and pioneered financial arrangements conducive to local needs. These developments, which are too often labeled "linkages" to export concerns, were generated from within, and provided a solid foundation from which New Englanders could push themselves into the transatlantic market.

Negotiating Internal and External Markets

The final element supporting a region's full integration into the transatlantic market concerned the ability of merchants to balance the local exchanges described above with rising export demands. These men have been traditionally portrayed as Typhoid Marys disrupting the relatively harmonious patterns of exchange described above. And indeed, their explicitly profit-oriented endeavors appear to stand in sharp contrast to the more immediate, subsistence-oriented goals of small farmers like Burnham, Pickering, and Barnard. Rarely, however, have historians explored the symbiotic and fluid relationship that often prevailed between commercial farmers and merchants. The lack of attention to this relationship is unfortunate because merchants—in order to integrate their regional economy into the transatlantic market—had to negotiate the internal and external economies with judicious aplomb. As a result of this negotiation, Massachusetts merchants—much like their Chesapeake counterparts—had achieved significant leverage within the transatlantic economy by the late seventeenth century. This final section contextualizes this leverage in the region's ongoing internal development. Conventional interpretations of increasing merchant activity in New England, rooted primarily in the declension model, have highlighted the disruptive impact that the rise of commercial activity had on the region's increasingly besieged communal ethos. From the perspective of a developing internal economy, however, merchant strategies suggest not so much the decline of "peaceable kingdoms," but rather the shrewd manipulation of economic processes that had been evolving for several decades. Much as the Chesapeake had forged its own economic adaptations on the periphery of the colonial empire, so had New England. Their outward manifestations might have diverged, even radically so, but their underlying economic adjustments to different environments provided the essential common denominator for future regional convergence.

George Corwin, a man who would become one of the Bay Colony's most powerful merchants, provides a concrete example of a merchant's early negotiation between the developing internal and external economies.[38] He accumulated extraordinary wealth through the exportation of what would become the region's staple products: fish and timber. However, Corwin's accounts from his early years as a trader, from 1653 and 1657, capture him before his rise to prominence. Historians have overlooked his activity as an emerging merchant, in part, because of the common perspective through which colonial merchants are often examined. Consistent with the staples approach, economic historians of colonial British America have traditionally charted the meteoric rise of Britain's commercial status from the unwavering perspective of the metropolis. Commercial and financial revolutions, according to this dominant viewpoint, developed in the context of a set of Navigation Acts that aimed to establish mercantile control over British America in the wake of the Civil War. More recently, however, historians including David Hancock have explored a perspective more commensurate with the economically decentralized nature of the British economy in the colonial American world. This angle, which aims to "stress the interplay between metropolitan and colonial forces," highlights the economic bonds linking colonial commercial planters (or merchants) and their London and Bristol agents. This final section thus extends this perspective even further into the decentralized colonial setting by examining the relationship between George Corwin and the Bay Colony economy with which he regularly dealt in his quest to become a member of the growing transatlantic community.[39]

Historians who have studied merchant activity within the New England colony have situated the merchants' emergence primarily within a declension narrative. Bernard Bailyn portrayed the first New England merchants as men who "represented the spirit of a new age," whose "guiding principles were not social stability, order, and the discipline of the senses, but mobility, growth, and the enjoyment of life." As a group that was "economically oriented toward England," and experiencing a "growing sense of distinctiveness," the merchants had "shifted from the parochialism of rural and Puritan New England to the cosmopolitanism of commercial Britain." These merchants are the pivotal actors behind what Jack P. Greene has called a "behavioral revolution" that "provided identity models and standards of personal conduct . . . that stood at marked variance with the original values of the leaders of the founding generation."[40] They were, in this interpretation, the wedge that separated the Bay Colony from its communal origins and ideals.

To an extent, such a characterization remains accurate, and George Corwin would eventually fit neatly into it. During his initial years as a young merchant, however, between 1650 and 1656, he could hardly afford to stay aloof from the "parochialism" of local economic affairs. To the contrary, he relied on the local economy as both the market for his imports and the source of his exports. Whatever his place vis-à-vis the religious ideals of Puritan New England, and whatever the nature of his relationships with London or West Indian agents, he maintained intricate ties to local residents and the local economy that they had created throughout the colony's first two decades of development.

Table 5.2 summarizes the extent and nature of Corwin's involvement. Between 1650 and 1656, he established accounts with at least 132 residents, eighty-seven of whom have been linked to a specific town in Essex County, Massachusetts. Of these men, a majority (51 percent) lived in Corwin's home town of Salem. Others, however, resided throughout the Bay Colony, from Lynn to Newbury. Later in the century, Corwin's accounts would stress his relationship with a select group of elite suppliers who provided Corwin with

Table 5.2. Overview of George Corwin Account Sample

Town	Avg. Acct. Debt	Avg. Acct. Length	No./% of Sample
Ipswich/Gloucester	£6 8s. 4d.	16.7 months	17/20%
Wenham/Beverly	£4 7s. 4d.	25.3 months	11/13%
Salem	£5 9s. 8d.	13 months	45/51%
Lynn/Marblehead	£2 11s. 6d.	17 months	9/10%
Rowley/Newbury	£3 3s. 9d.	20 months	5/6%

Sources: The identity of 87 out of the 132 residents in the account sample could be positively linked to a specific town. Verifications relied on George F. Dow, ed., *The Records and Files of the Quarterly Courts of Essex County*, vols. 2–8; *The New England Historical and Genealogical Records* index; and several "marginal secondary sources," particularly town histories. The remaining data all came from George Corwin Account Sample Data Base, created from the George Corwin Account Book, located in George Corwin's Letters, Bills, Ledgers and Day Books, 1651–84 [(12 scrapbooks) mss, The Phillips Library, Peabody Essex Museum].

thousands of pounds worth of fish and timber for export. In the early 1650s, however, with the fishing and timber industries still in their infancy, Corwin's accounts instead reveal the highly decentralized nature of merchant activity, as well as its complete dependence on the workings of the local economy. He traded with residents in every Essex County town, and his accounts with them look quite different than they would once he became an established transatlantic trader.

Several aspects of his accounts are worth mentioning. Most notably, they deal in relatively small values, with the average account balance coming to about four and a half pounds, a figure that stands in stark contrast to the thousands of pounds with which he would later deal and more consistent with that of common farmers with whom he dealt. He also kept his accounts open for a relatively long period of time. With so little cash moving through the local economy, Corwin—like most commercial farmers—received the vast majority of payments for imported goods in farm produce. The nature of this kind of payment required that Corwin keep his accounts open, often without a single balance payment, much longer than would later be customary—an average of about eighteen months. Benjamin Balch's account was typical. Balch purchased a range of imports from Corwin, including powder, cloth, soap, wine, and matches, on the following dates: February 25, 1652, April 13, 1653, May 2, 1653, and June 8, 1653. He did not balance his account until January 14, 1655, when he paid Corwin in "work," Indian corn, and wheat.[41] At other times, payment could come within a couple of months. William Langley purchased lace, buttons, and silk from Corwin on November 15, 1656, paying him with £73 and 114 pounds of pork on December 18 of the same year. But, more often than not, payment within a few months was rare. In a typical set of transactions, "Mr. Norrice" bought a variety of sundry consumer imports on fourteen occasions between June 1653 and September 1654. Norrice made one return—a "cart"—in October 1653, and then never paid Corwin anything until December of the next year, when he made returns in wheat. His final payment on goods that he stopped purchasing from Corwin in September 1654, came in March 1655.[42] As these reflective transactions indicate, Corwin found it more useful to conform to the limits and opportunities within the local economy rather than to shape those limits and opportunities to the demands of the export economy. The delayed payments evident in the Balch and Norrice accounts, which were not even paid in full, were typical of the ways in which commercial farmers worked locally, and reflected standard procedure at this stage in the region's economic development.

As these examples also suggest, Corwin not only spread his business over several towns and among scores of residents, but—again like the local commercial farmers—he dealt with them on a consistent basis. To note only a few examples, John Leach purchased tobacco from Corwin on six separate occasions between March and November 1653; Richard Leach made thirteen such purchases during the same year; Thomas Gordon bought goods including pots, vinegar, lace, and cotton nine times that year; and John Beckett made twenty-four appearances in Corwin's accounts for everything from butter to smoking pipes in 1655.[43] Very rarely did Corwin execute a discrete trade for a large sum of goods, as would later become customary. Instead, he calibrated his trading patterns to the preexisting trading habits of a local economy, wherein most farmers and artisans found it more beneficial to purchase imports conservatively and often, rather than liberally and all at once. Nor did he sell large batches of imports to shop owners or re-exporters, as both had yet to become popular retail outlets for imported inventories. Whatever the nature of Corwin's relationship with overseas agents, the families spread throughout the Bay Colony working on small farms to achieve a basic competency were the ones who ultimately sustained his initial foray into the transatlantic world.

And not just as reliable consumers. Given our knowledge of New England's exports, perhaps the most revealing aspect of Corwin's early accounts is the nature of the returns he accepted in exchange for imported goods. Once again, the conventional wisdom with respect to New England merchants leads

Table 5.3. Returns among and within Account Sample

Product	% of Accts.	Mean % within Accts.
Dairy	28	49
Brewing	19	50
Grain	47	50
Livestock	42	50
Fish	1	15
Wood	3	42

Source: George Corwin Account Sample, 1653–56; from George Corwin Account Books, 1651–56.

us to expect that Corwin would have been collecting large parcels of fish and timber products from concentrated suppliers for bulk shipment to overseas venues. According to the logic of the local economy, however, it would seem equally likely that he would collect the same sort of goods that Bay residents like Pickering, Barnard, and Burnham had been trading with each other for many years. And indeed, between 1653 and 1656, it is this latter option that prevails in Corwin's records. Moreover, not only does Corwin rely almost exclusively on farm produce for his returns, but he often recycled these returns into the local economy, thereby blending the import and export markets in ways previously unappreciated by historians.

An overview of 132 accounts supports these claims. The same goods that Bay colonists traded amongst themselves within the confines of the local economy appear in overwhelming quantities in the returns of Corwin's clients. As table 5.3 documents, 42 percent of Corwin's clients between 1653 and 1656 made returns in some form of livestock, be it beef, pork, bacon, cows, or hogs. Even more clients, 47 percent, made returns in some kind of grain product—Indian corn, wheat, rye, or oats. Dairy and brewing products were also common, with 28 percent making returns in eggs and butter, and 19 percent paying Corwin with beer, barley, or malt. Six percent of returns came through peas. Somewhat astonishingly, given the common claim that fish and timber formed the basis of the export transition, only 1 percent of returns were in fish, while just 3 percent came through wood products.[44] When returns were made in the form of these products, their percentage within the overall account was substantial. Dairy returns averaged 45 percent of each account in which it appeared; beer products averaged 50 percent, as did grain returns; and livestock, finally, made up 48 percent of the accounts in which it was traded as a

Table 5.4. Selected Purchases Made in the George Corwin Account Sample, 1652–1657

Patron	Total Items	Textiles	Manufactures	Groceries
Thomas Cromwell	29	16	9	4
John Herbert	8	4	3	1
Ezekial Rogers	4	3	1	0
Mr. Hubert	3	2	1	0
Francis Lawes	8	2	6	0
John White	14	2	8	4
John Barton	5	3	1	1
Daniel Epps	6	2	3	1
Henry Cook	5	1	2	2
Mr. Earos	4	3	0	1
Rich. Johnson	4	3	0	1
Joseph Jencks	26	8	13	5
Joseph Rowell	3	1	0	2
John Barton	3	1	1	1
Zack. Harrick	3	1	2	0
Thomas Putnam	39	18	11	10
Isaac Cummings	2	1	1	0
Neal Jewells	11	3	6	2
Sam Shattock	3	0	3	0
Nath. Pickman	31	8	11	12
William Langley	3	1	2	0
John Beckett	34	12	10	12
Bray Williams	26	9	11	6
John Proctor	32	17	11	4
Mr. Perkins	12	1	9	2

Source: George Corwin Account Sample, 1653–56; from George Corwin Account Books, 1651–56.

return. These products were not only traded often for imported goods, they were traded as large proportions of accounts.

Corwin sent most of these returns to the West Indies, but he occasionally recycled these goods back into the local economy. A sample of twenty-five of the 132 clients illuminates this tendency. As table 5.4 shows, Corwin's clients primarily purchased textiles and manufactured goods, but, occasionally—18.8 percent of the time—they relied on him for provisions produced within the region. Thus we find Nathaniel Putnam buying not only soap, buckram, lockram, and hooks from Corwin, but local products like malt and pork as well. For these goods, he traded "work at Rittings," "carting of peas from Jeggles," and "work at house." Joseph Jencks, a local blacksmith and iron worker with little time to grow his own grain, bought "corn at Goodman Potter's" from Corwin, as well as canvas, shot, and tobacco. He paid for these items with

Table 5.5. Prices and Interest Charged on Selected Goods

Commodity	Price/date in Acct.	Price/date in Probate	% Markup
Indian corn	3s./bushel (Dec. 1655)	2.2s./bushel (Nov. 1654)	27%
Wheat	5s. 6d./bushel (Dec. 1655)	4s./bushel (Nov. 1654)	27%
Malt	5s. 2d./bushel (Apr. 1656)	4.5s./bushel (July 1656)	10%
Brandy	2s. 6d./quart (Nov. 1655)	2s./quart (July 1661)	20%
Cotton	3s. 9d./yard (June 1654)	2s. 6d./yard (Oct. 1654)	33%
Stockings	2s. 6d./pair (Feb. 1654)	2s. 1d./pair (June 1654)	17%
Lockram	2s. 3d./yard (Mar. 1654)	1s. 6d./yard (June 1655)	33%
Canvas	2s. 3d./yard (Sept. 1655)	1s. 10d./yard (Mar. 1655)	19%
Gloves	2s. 4d./pair (May 1654)	1.3s./pair (Oct. 1654)	43%
Serge	5s. 8d./yard (Mar. 1654)	3s. 8d./yard (Mar. 1654)	35%
Holland	4s. 4d./yard (Nov. 1653)	4s./yard (Oct. 1651)	8%
Linseywoolsey	4s./yard (Feb. 1653)	3s. 5d./yard (Oct. 1654)	15%
Kersey	5s. 6d./yard (Jan. 1653)	3s. 8d./yard (Mar. 1654)	37%

Source: George Corwin Account Sample, 1653–56; *The Probate Records of Essex County*, vol. 1.

twenty-four hoes. Elias Stileman, to cite a final example, took liquor, silk, nails, canvas, and a saw from Corwin, in addition to Indian corn and pork.[45] To a modest extent, Corwin's duties involved not just importing goods, but taking a page from the commercial farmer's book and distributing them within and throughout the local economy.

We really have no way to investigate how Corwin got along personally with the residents he traded with, but the question should not be how peaceable his relations were but, for our purposes, how profitable. A roughly cobbled-together price list indicates that Corwin's reliance on a wide scope of clients as consumers and producers of a wide range of goods was likely a useful early strategy to ease one's way into the export market. Corwin charged substantial interest on his imports, anywhere from 8 percent to 43 percent (see table 5.5).

Almost forty years ago, Darrett B. Rutman highlighted a paradox that historians have yet to resolve. On the one hand, he explained, New England's notoriously rocky soil and unexpectedly frigid climate made the region seem like a place where agriculture "was not an encouraging business." The "trades of the sea," historians had reasoned, would provide for Bay Colony migrants. On the other hand, Rutman wrote, "there is the unavoidable fact that the land dominates both town and commonwealth records." Settlers obviously placed great stock in the value of a balanced and healthy farm. Rutman continued, "The interaction of commerce and agriculture—the fact that neither could have existed without the other, that New England itself probably could not have persisted without both—has been left unexamined."[46]

An examination of George Corwin's accounts in the years before his emergence as a prominent fish and timber trader catches him at a pivotal moment in his career. It is a moment that provides an underappreciated perspective on the internal economy's role in the Bay Colony's evolution toward the Atlantic market. Here we find a trader flush with imported goods, eager to unload them, and fully reliant on the settlers and products that had been sustaining the local economy for over two decades. As a merchant trying to build a transatlantic trade before the emergence of fishing and timber companies, Corwin's activity takes us beyond Rutman's correct claim that "commerce and agriculture" could not "have existed without the other" and forces us to confront how commerce not only coexisted with agricultural activity but, more directly, how it could not have developed at all without the maturation of an agriculturally based infrastructure, networks of local exchange, and the acceptable adaptation of trading habits to a peripheral economy. Corwin could think globally only by acting locally.

Situating the internal economic development of colonial New England in the larger context of British America allows us to reconsider Jack P. Greene's oft-quoted comparison of the early New England and the Chesapeake regions. He writes, "it would be difficult to imagine how any two fragments from the same metropolitan culture could have been any more different . . . they seem to have been diametric opposites."[47] The creation of a reliable and flexible infrastructure, the emergence of internal commercial trade patterns, and the merchant negotiations forged to secure power in the transatlantic market reflected not so much a basic difference as parallel regional attempts to adapt inherited metropolitan expectations to New World realities. The particular regional methods and manifestations might have been notably distinct, but the dogged pursuit of export markets provided seventeenth-century British American colonies with an overarching, even unifying, common pursuit. Even in New England.

CHAPTER SIX

Paternalism and Profits

Planters and Overseers in Piedmont Virginia, 1750–1825

James M. Baird

The degree to which slave masters were also capitalists continues to animate debates about the nature of slave society in North America. Although the controversy originated as an argument over the nature of the antebellum South, the tendrils of this debate are discernable in recent interpretations of colonial slave societies. Some historians highlight colonial planters' embrace of modernity, while others stress their social traditionalism. In interpreting eighteenth-century Virginia, for example, one can focus upon planters' adaptability and innovation as managers of complex economic concerns who sought to maximize the production of crops for international markets. Alternatively, one might devote attention to the essential conservatism of planters in their quest to exercise authority over a gradation of legal dependents—relationships characterized by extensive reciprocal duties and obligations. At the root of both dynamics lay slavery, an institution that was itself Janus-faced. Slavery was an integral component of a dynamic, market-driven Atlantic economy; at the same time, and especially in its North American form, the social relations between master and slave were fundamentally contrary to market principles.[1]

For historians adhering to a strict definition of capitalism, capitalist society is characterized by a free market in labor. Thus, the South's continued reliance on enslaved workers increasingly separated it from the capitalist social and economic development underway in England and, after the American Revolution, in the northern states. In the North, some have argued, the American Revolution triggered a second, market revolution, which ushered in a capitalist transformation that deposed the household as the main locus of production and replaced the familial relationship between householder and dependent with the impersonal relation of employer and wage laborer. By the mid-nineteenth century, "only a wage, not household discipline, connected farm laborers and city workers to their masters" in the northern states. While southern slaveholders continued to rely upon physical coercion, or its threat, to extract labor from their bondsmen, northern employers could use financial incentives and compulsions to maximize the efficiency of their free workforce.[2]

In an argument that continues to be influential, Eugene Genovese asserted that, in contrast to the weakening of household modes of authority elsewhere, southern planters reinforced the household model by suffusing relations between slaves and masters with the legitimating discourse of paternalism. From the vantage point of the paternalist paradigm, slaves were conceived, first and foremost, as members of the plantation family. Viewing their bondsmen as more than simply laborers, paternalistic masters interjected themselves in the medical, familial, and religious lives of their slave "dependents." Taking advantage of the opportunities that existed within the guise of paternalistic rule, slaves strove to gain a small measure of control over their own lives, claiming as rights concessions that paternalists conceived as privileges. As it affected the arena of production, it is argued, this paternalistic bargaining process hampered planters' attempts to enhance plantation efficiency and trapped the slave South in a cycle of underdevelopment and economic colonialism.[3]

Genovese's assertion of the centrality of the paternalistic master-slave relationship was predicated upon a claim that has elicited surprisingly little attention from subsequent historians. In Genovese's depiction of "the world the slaves made," white overseers were only of marginal importance in the ideological, or even practical, maintenance of slavery in North America. Genovese claimed that only one-third to one-quarter of slaves worked under the authority of men who were not their masters in the antebellum South. While the large size of slaveholdings and the prevalence of absenteeism rendered slavery in the Caribbean impersonal and exploitative, Genovese argued that the smaller scale of plantations in North America contributed to master-slave relationships characterized by an intimacy and mutuality that often impeded the pursuit of profit.[4]

Even when they were employed, Genovese argued, white overseers often reinforced the tenets of the master-slave relationship. Overseers exhibited high rates of turnover. In their dealings with slaves, overseers often encountered established work routines and a farrago of customary privileges accumulated over years, often with the sanction of owners who considered such bondsmen as family members as well as property and workers. Should an overseer transgress these privileges or otherwise breach the norms of good management, slaves ran to their masters for redress. In this manner, overseers served as lightning rods for plantation conflicts. They carried out disagreeable but necessary oversight and discipline and in doing so deflected slaves' ire away from their masters. When such conflicts resulted in a slave seeking aid from the master, the ritualistic exchange that followed—with the aggrieved slave's assumption of a deferential posture eliciting a master's paternal magnanimity—bound together slave and master yet further.[5]

Genovese located the emergence of paternalism in the third quarter of the eighteenth century.[6] Given the particular characteristics of the Chesapeake, it is not surprising that historians have found the earliest expressions of the paternal ethos in the region.[7] In the Chesapeake, as recent studies have confirmed, small slaveholders predominated and seasonal, long-distance absenteeism, of the kind prevalent in the Caribbean and the other major mainland slaveholding colony, South Carolina, was rare. Moreover, a combination of demographic, environmental, and social conditions allowed the Chesapeake's slave populations to become self-reproducing as early as the second decade of the eighteenth century. By 1780, 95 percent of Chesapeake slaves were American-born. This demographic fact promoted closer relationships between master and slave in the Chesapeake than was the case in the lower South where, to the end of the colonial period, Africans remained a significant proportion of the enslaved. As a recent comparative study puts it, "close and regular contact between masters and slaves was a fact of life in the Chesapeake." No longer "strangers," slaves in the late eighteenth-century Chesapeake were seen as a familiar part of the plantation household.[8]

This essay reexamines the centrality of the paternalist imperative in master-slave relationships by focusing on planters' relations with, and employment of, white overseers in the late colonial and early national Virginia Piedmont. Certainly, there is much evidence that many planters did conceive of themselves as paternalists, and that slaveholder paternalism in practice damaged overseers' authority over the slaves. Other conflicting imperatives, however, also shaped planters' relationships with overseers, and through them, with slaves. The most important of these was the pursuit of profit.

In promising overseers a share of the crop and in discharging those overseers whom they found unproductive, planter-employers structured the contractual relationship with their overseer-employee so as to provide incentives for maximum productivity. Moreover, contrary to Genovese's assumptions, the employment of overseers was actually quite widespread. Indeed, the proportion of slaves working under overseers expanded sharply in the very period that Genovese and others have argued witnessed the emergence of paternalism. Moreover, absenteeism was in fact quite common in the newly settled Virginia Piedmont and many overseers were untroubled by a watchful resident employer. By the end of the colonial period, over one-half of Virginia's working slaves lived and labored not under the paternal eye of a master, but under the direction of a hired overseer, an intermediary largely excluded from the web of mutuality that operated within the plantation household, and one compensated chiefly by a share of the crop that those under his power cultivated.

Planters' self-conception as paternalists emerged in a period marked by significant increases in the production of market crops and the intensification of labor regimens. In long-settled tidewater counties where Virginia's planters faced declining yields, they attempted to sustain output by exploiting their slaves more effectively. Their efforts were successful. In the half century before the American Revolution, the colony's tobacco output grew at a rate of 2 percent each year. In the evaluation of one historian, "the behavior of some late eighteenth-century tobacco planters even calls to mind the frenetic, single-minded preoccupation with the crop that characterized their predecessors a century and a half earlier—when Virginia was North America's first boom country."[9] By 1775, a good proportion of Virginia's tobacco crop was made in the Piedmont, where fresher land allowed higher yields, and overseers often worked slaves free from the daily intervention of prying employers.[10]

Taking advantage of southern Europe's subsistence crisis, many planters after midcentury turned to wheat cultivation to supplement and occasionally to replace their concentration on tobacco alone. This decision greatly increased the demands on slave labor as employers now found ways to work their bondsmen year round and often into the night. From a longer perspective, Virginian planters' attempts to take advantage of new market opportunities, maximize productivity, and intensify their demands upon their labor forces were part of longstanding pattern. Planters in the late colonial period were acting upon imperatives that their forefathers would have recognized readily.[11]

Taken together, these developments suggest a new context for understanding paternalism's emergence in late eighteenth-century Virginia. The adoption of a paternalistic ethos by colonial planters was in part, as others have noted, an attempt to suffuse their relationships with dependents with a legitimacy gained from the adoption of contemporary, metropolitan norms. In addition, I suggest that the language of paternalism served to screen planters from the exploitative, and increasingly distant, nature of plantation slavery in the third quarter of the eighteenth century that they themselves played the formative role in establishing. By the occasional, almost ritualistic, expression of the paternal impulse, planters could hide both from their slaves and themselves the fact that, outside of these performative moments, they chose to manage their bondsmen through other men. These men, provided as they were with the incentive to produce the largest crop, and who were only short-term overseers of a specific quarter and its slaves, had little reason to employ a similarly paternalistic authority. The paternal ethos was, I suggest, born of a desire to distance masters from the reality of the exploitation that they otherwise encouraged and in which they were complicit. Rather than provide the foundation of an alternate social ethos, eighteenth-century paternalism demonstrates the extent to which Virginian slaveholders were at the forefront of the increasing Anglo-American commitment to market practices if not market principles.[12]

Familial Ties

The evidence for slaveholder paternalism in late colonial and early national Virginia is rich and varied. Significantly, it was often most clearly manifest in dealings with overseers. Trusting in their masters' paternalistic self-conception, slaves ran, on occasion, to their figurative fathers to complain of overseer mistreatment. Moreover, the concessions that slaves claimed from paternal masters—gains that they considered rights, though their owners more often considered them privileges—were, on many occasions, deployed against overseers. Overseers, often temporarily employed and rarely considered a part of the employer's household, could find themselves frustrated by "customary" understandings between a master and his slaves that stemmed from their longstanding familial relationship.[13]

Slaves routinely challenged overseers by absconding after being punished. Some preempted overseers by running to their masters when the threat of punishment had been raised, while others used the threat of flight to discourage an overseer from even considering using force. Planters recognized that audience-seeking slaves were often involved in a tactical duel with an overseer. Moreover, planters harbored doubts about slaves' capacity for truthfulness. Despite these reservations, and despite the recognition that according an audience on such occasions compromised the authority of overseers, planters often rationalized giving truant slaves a hearing. For many planters, their investment in a paternal self-conception obliged them, sometimes against their better judgment, to play the role of benevolent father to the supplicant slave. Philip Vickers Fithian, tutor at Robert Carter's Nomini Hall plantation, documented just such an interaction: "an old Negro Man came with a complaint to Mr. Carter of the Overseer . . . The humble posture in which the old Fellow placed himself before he began moved me . . . he sat himself down on the Floor clasp'd his Hands together, with his face directly to Mr. Carter, & then began his Narration."[14] Playing the role of submissive child, a slave could be confident that a paternalist would fulfill his obligation as protector of his dependents.

Of course, planters listened to their slaves' complaints out of self-interest. Their investment in slaves was long-term, while overseers came and went. Transient overseers often lacked local attachments in a world and a time in which credibility was closely associated with an intimate knowledge of an individual's reputation and place in the community. In this context, permanent residents, including masters, viewed overseers with skepticism at best. To the suspicion accorded outsiders, employers appended a disdain for those who were willing, or financially compelled, to work for others. In masters' letters and diaries, overseers were routinely depicted as drunken, lazy, cruel, and, not least, deceitful.[15]

In view of their dubious regard for overseers, many paternalist planters, encouraged slaves to inform them not just of an overseer's ill use, but of other examples of mismanagement. The slaves belonging to Robert Carter of Nomini Hall were particularly forthcoming on these matters. In 1774, five men appealed to Carter at his Billingsgate quarter in Richmond with complaints about their overseer John Crab. Crab, they reported, had badly mistreated Carter's stock. Moreover, he had retained much of the brandy and cotton produced at the quarter for his own use. Finally, the slaves attested, the overseer entertained his own extended family regularly, generously allowing them to feed their horses with his employer's fodder.[16]

Other employers likewise depended on the intelligence of their slaves in monitoring the performance of their overseers. "There is nothing like having a proper Check on such kind of People," J. H. Norton wrote his agent, in defending his use of slaves' information in superintending a distant overseer. Admitting that "it [was] not altogether proper to attend to the Tales of Negroes," Norton distinguished a master's permitting the unsolicited complaints of his slaves from his own active inquiries of them on matters in which they had no direct interest.[17]

John Mercer applied a similar logic. "I now have enquired of the Negroes as to his Conduct & tho[ugh] they are not legal Evidences yet I have allmost constantly found Negroes tell Truth enough of distant . . . villainous . . . overseers."[18] Finding himself under attack from his agent for such views, Mercer made the same distinction that Norton had applied. Mercer was confident that James, whom Battaile Muse, his agent, accused of lying, had told the truth. "I asked him certain questions he did not know which way I wished him to answer," Mercer explained.[19] To indulge a slave's tales was indeed inappropriate, these paternalists agreed, but to rely on their responses to questions broached by their master was a different matter.

Paternalists looked upon slaves as part of their plantation family, who in exchange for food, lodging, and paternal care owed their master not only the benefits of their labor but also fidelity and submission. From this perspective, Mercer insisted, a slave's duty was to "answer any questions his Master puts to him."[20] J. H. Norton's conviction that, where he had "inquired [into] it [was his slaves'] business to give [him] a true Ac[coun]t," echoed Mercer's view.[21] While not altogether immune to the suspicion that blacks were innately untrustworthy, many paternalists nonetheless believed that in situations where slaves seemingly had nothing to gain from dishonesty, their sense of duty to their master would ensure their honest response to his inquiries.[22]

Slaveholder paternalism also diminished the authority of overseers in other ways. Planters, who adopted a paternal self-definition to legitimate their authority, gave slaves the opportunity to accrue and then defend privileges as they played upon paternalists' very concern with exercising authority legitimately. As a consequence, when overseers encountered slaves, they confronted people who were not simply the mere extensions of a master's will, as the theoretical underpinnings of slavery might have suggested. Rather, many slaves in Virginia succeeded in carving out areas of social and cultural life that were protected not by law but by the authority of custom. When such practices had the support of their masters, that authority was substantial.

Slaves' accrual of customary privileges in a number of different realms diminished overseer authority. Paternalist planters' defense of the integrity of slave families, for example, challenged the authority of overseers in a number of ways. Families provided an arena of slave autonomy beyond an overseer's jurisdiction and constituted important resources with which to protest an overseer's transgressions. Furthermore, overseers whose own authority was confined to an individual quarter, the productivity of which they themselves depended on for recompense, were often confronted by slaves whose family members lived "abroad," and who took advantage of the limited rights of visitation that paternalist planters routinely extended to them. On other occasions overseers were frustrated by slaves' absenting their quarter to attend religious meetings, often with the permission of their owners.

Slaves on large estates often claimed a range of individual and collective rights in their work lives. Although overseers attempted to impose more efficient work habits on their charges, many of the labor privileges claimed by slaves, overseers complained, had been established with either the knowledge or the explicit support of their charges' owners. Robert Carter's Sukey claimed, for example, that "She [had] Lease of" Carter to "Stay at home & wash her Cloaths at Any time when She please[d];" that it was his "ord[er]s & She would Do it in Defiance" of her overseer.[23] While overseers often held only a brief tenure of one or two years, the objects of their authority enjoyed the advantage of having life-long relationships with the master that would likely continue far beyond the termination of that same overseer's incumbency.[24]

When exercised over time, slaves defended their privileges as rights enjoying the authority of custom. In the Burwell household in Mecklenburg County, "Aunt Christian" clearly articulated the basis in custom of the claim that many slaves made to exercise some control over the work regimen. "Aint I bin—long fo' dis yer little master . . . was born," she argued, "bakin' de bes' bread, an' bes' beat biscuit and rice waffles, all de time in my ole marster time?" "An' I bin manage my own affa'rs, an I gwine manage my own affa'rs long is I got breff," she insisted.[25]

Overseers were often confronted by slaves' collective defense of their customary work routines. Battaile Muse wrote despairingly to his employer, George William Fairfax, of the resistance he encountered from Fairfax's slaves. Their defense of their customary work regimen, secured with the collusion of their owner, he reported, had left the overseer's task impossible:

> the Negroes Very dificult to mannage Owing to the Great Indulgences they have had I am Convinced that the old ones will never be Broke to Labour—the number of young negroes & number of old ones and the Middle age that can Labour partly free in their dispositions renders your . . . Estate unprofitable and Very dificult and Troublesome to mannage all the Porke I raise is given to the negroes they are high fed and well clothed and they worke at their own discretion—they are given to complaints which they are too much Indulged in to make them Either happy to themselves or serv[icea]ble to their master.[26]

Simon Sallard had reported the same pattern some fifty years earlier. The slaves at the Rickneck quarter of the then-minor Robert Carter had, he reported, "Lived For So Long That They would not work but as they Pleas[e]d."[27] Upon being corrected, several of the slaves had run to the estate's administrator who ordered the overseer's immediate dismissal. As the case of Aunt Christian likewise suggests, conflicts over the control of work regimens were doubtlessly accentuated at such times. In a transitional period, before falling under the authority of a new master, slaves exerted themselves to protect their hard-won gains.[28]

Their defense of customary patterns of labor, practiced with the knowledge of their owners, left slaves with some power in their relationships with overseers. Many overseers in the employ of paternalist planters learned that only by compromising with their slave charges could they enjoy any success. Failure to do so could lead to the kind of stalemate that Landon Carter reported between his overseer Watts and his gang. "His hands and he are so dissatisfyed with each other," Carter recorded, "that neither do anything."[29]

Paternalism, as a set of social practices, contributed in substantive ways to the triangular relationship between masters, slaves, and overseers. Paternalist planters, invested in their self-conception as benevolent fathers, granted credence to their bondsmens' entreaties. Some, moreover, relied upon their slaves' information as a guide to the performance of a particular overseer. Meanwhile, the enslaved took advantage of the paternalistic self-conception of some owners to establish social institutions and practices that, in turn, limited an overseer from enjoying unencumbered dominion over them. Indeed, some overseers found that to perform their occupation successfully they needed to win their charges' approval. "I think there are few greater curses in life," one overseer, faced with such contradictions, reflected, "than to be tyed to a parcel of Negroes to make them do their duty." "Pray if there is a young man your way worth the name of an overseer," he pleaded with his employer, "send Him here [to replace me]."[30]

Overseers and Absentees

There is a danger, however, in exaggerating the reach of slaveholder paternalism. It appears in historical records in the form of momentary interventions rather than as the consistent application of a principle. Though slaveholder paternalism impinged upon overseer authority in a range of ways, its implementation was sporadic and uneven. In its eighteenth-century form, slaveholder paternalism served as a check on the overriding imperative of maximizing production, rather than as the dominant social ethos.

Virginia's planters used overseers not stingily but readily. Moreover, many overseers operated without the hindrance of a resident employer. In short, planters, paternalists included, readily turned over their quarters to the supervision of third parties who had no long-term interest in the well-being of their charges. Given these realities, it is unlikely that more than a smattering of slave complaints ever found their way to benevolent masters; their occurrence in the historical record highlights aberrations at the expense of the quotidian experience of exploitation that took place beyond the master's eyes and, therefore, was seldom reported.[31]

Longstanding, contradictory imperatives limited the influence of slaveholder paternalism. By compensating overseers with a share of the crop made under their management, employers knowingly gave overseers incentive to overwork their charges in an attempt to maximize the quarter's production. And, by discharging overseers when they failed to produce enough either at year's end, or even before harvest, employers reinforced their commitment to profit maximization, while betraying an altogether less paternalistic conception of social relationships as far as they extended to overseers.

Tobacco was a difficult crop, the successful cultivation of which required close supervision. Reinforcing the constraints posed by the need for vigilant superintendence, the fact that the best tobacco soils occurred in small, dispersed plots, likewise, placed limits on the optimal size of a planter's labor force. Unlike the rice fields of South Carolina or the sugar plantations of the Caribbean, work units in the Chesapeake remained relatively small.[32]

While Virginia's planters adhered to the logic of small work units and close supervision, many planters, including those with modest slaveholdings, were content to leave that supervision to hired overseers rather than perform that duty themselves. Quantitative sources allow us to substantiate these points with some precision. An admittedly small sample drawn from share payments appearing in court records, for example, indicates that the average labor force under overseers was but five hands.[33] A more comprehensive approach, utilizing tax records, suggests that resident planters in tidewater Virginia were as likely as not to employ a free dependent—most likely an overseer—when they owned seven slaves.[34] Resident planters in the Piedmont were likely to deploy a free dependent, in all likelihood an overseer, when they had just four to six taxable slaves.[35]

The observations of contemporaries lend support to these conclusions. Many planters, travelers noted, were only too willing to turn over the task of management to unrelated employees. The anonymous author of *American Husbandry,* for example, caustically commented that "the planters, who have the power of being good cultivators of their fields, abandon them to the overseers of their Negroes, and pursue only their own pleasures."[36] Thomas Anburey, who sojourned in Virginia during early 1779, confirmed that insight, noting that "most of the planters consign the care of their plantations and Negroes to an overseer, even the man whose house we rent, has his overseer, though he could with ease superintend it himself; but if they possess a few negroes, they think it beneath their dignity."[37] Moreover, the trend over the third quarter of the eighteenth century was in the direction of a sharply increased reliance upon slave overseers.

For Virginia's commitment to slavery both intensified and broadened in the quarter century preceding Independence. Within tidewater Virginia the utilization of slave labor surged dramatically. For example, in tidewater Lancaster County, measured crudely, slaves increased from about one-half to almost two-thirds of the total population between 1746 and 1775.[38] Two related processes contributed to this development. First, nonslaveholding households diminished both in number and in relation to slaveholding families. Second, the proportion of large slaveholders in the county's population—those owning ten or more taxable slaves—increased rapidly, almost doubling over the same thirty years. As a result, the proportion of slaves owned by large planters increased from 37 percent in 1746 to almost 57 percent in 1775. In sum, by the end of the colonial period there were fewer white households in the county than had been there at midcentury, and those households that did remain tended to own more slaves than had their midcentury counterparts.[39]

The expansion of slavery into the Piedmont is more fully established in the historical literature. Driven by their desire for profits, Virginian planters transported slaves above the fall line onto more fertile lands. In doing so, they relied not only on importation but also on the native slave population's natural growth. As Henry Fitzhugh noted, "my Negroes increase yearly by which I am enabled to settle new quarters and consequently my exports must increase."[40] By 1780, more slaves lived in the Piedmont than in the Tidewater. Data gathered from surviving tithe lists allows us to describe this transition with some precision.[41]

Goochland County, abutting the James River west of Richmond, was the terminus for many planters in search of new land for their tobacco crops. Founded in 1728, by the time of Independence the county housed close to twenty-five hundred tithables, considerably more than most tidewater counties, and almost double Goochland's own population twenty-five years earlier. As the county's total population grew, its slave population increased disproportionately. Thus, while slaves represented about 47 percent of the total population in 1754, just sixteen years later in 1770 they made up 53 percent of the population. Increasingly, too, slaves found themselves housed on larger plantations—while two-fifths of taxable slaves lived in units of seven or more in 1754, by 1770 three-fifths of taxable slaves did. In Loudon County, nestled below the Appalachian Mountains in Virginia's Northern Neck, the same process, though more muted, was evident. There, migrants from the Middle Colonies—German, Scots-Irish, and Quaker—directed most of their energies to the cultivation of grains with family labor. Slaveholders were a distinct minority. However, Virginians moving westward also settled in the county, and they utilized slave labor in the production of tobacco. By 1780 slaves accounted for about one-third of Loudon's population, up from under one-fifth just fifteen years earlier.[42]

Absentee proprietors were responsible for a significant part of slavery's expansion into the Piedmont. The involvement of absentees was particularly marked in Loudoun County where, though they were just 3 percent of the county's households in 1765, absentees owned over two-fifths of the county's slaves. While by 1780 this imbalance had diminished somewhat, absentee proprietors still held 30 percent of the county's slaves in that year. Absentee slaveholders played a significant role in the settlement of Goochland County also, although because slaveholding was much more common among the resident population than was the case in Loudoun County, their contribution was less patent. Yet, as in Loudoun County, Goochland's absentees tended to own significantly larger holdings than their resident counterparts, resulting in their ownership of a disproportionate share of the county's slaves. Nor was absenteeism a transitory phase: in Goochland absentee households continued to represent 13 percent of the county's total households into the 1770s, as they had in the 1750s. If anything the importance of absentees increased over time; by 1770 almost one-third of the county's slaves were owned by nonresidents, a slightly larger share than in 1755.[43]

As a consequence of the continued vigor of absenteeism on the one hand and the increased concentration of slavery in larger units on the other, Virginian planters placed mounting reliance on slave overseers to work their bondsmen. By these estimates, over one-half of Lancaster County's 1775 slave population worked under an overseer. In Goochland County, two-thirds of the county's taxable slaves were lodged under overseers in 1770. In both counties, the vast majority of these overseers were not family members, but hired labor. While planters with overseer sons might have some confidence that their offspring would follow their fathers' long-term management priorities—upkeep of the general plantation, solicitousness toward the well-being of their slaves—as well as replicate efforts to produce a bountiful tobacco crop, they could have less assurance in the conscientiousness of men bound only by an employment contract to their employers' interests.[44]

Indeed, despite their protestations, employers gave overseers very little reason to cleave to their long-term interests. By compensating them with a share of the tobacco, and often wheat crops, that they raised, planter-employers gave their overseers an incentive to concentrate their efforts on the production of market crops alone at the expense of general plantation duties, and to overwork the slaves in pursuit of the largest possible crop. By calibrating their outlay on their overseers with the size of crops made under their direction, employers contained the risks associated with bad years.[45]

As a consequence, during poor years an overseer could expect little by way of compensation. In the terrible year of 1758, for example, the unfortunate Thomas Mason, overseer for Edward Ambler, received just over ten shillings for his share of the crop. Henry Gray, overseer for William Dabney, made just over £3 current money for his share, while Henry Richardson, an overseer for George Washington, received but one pound and fifteen shillings for his tobacco crop that year. During more propitious times, however, the share system rewarded men for their relative productivity. For example, Daniel Campbell, an overseer for Randolph Tucker in 1790, produced 1,698 pounds per share, valued at just over £15 current money. John Jenkins, however, outdid him. Also employed as an overseer for Tucker in the same year, he produced an impressive 4,917 pounds per share, worth over £49 current money. With such rewards awaiting the productive overseer, the opportunity for gain often encouraged him to overwork his enslaved charges and to concentrate on the raising of market crops alone, at the expense of other plantation tasks.[46]

Of course, the incentives proffered by the payment of a share did not uniformly produce rapacious overseers. Besides a share of the crop, overseers received provisions and lodging, perks that Landon Carter for one thought counterbalanced rather too effectively the lure of the reward that a large crop promised. "He [the overseer working for a share] is commonly contented with a house and Provisions," the skeptical diarist noted baldly, "cares little about what he makes; and generally makes up a Short share, by what he can steal privately from his imployer; when with a little more care in this point he might do very well in most years and with a clear conscience."[47]

Yet Carter's was the minority opinion, outnumbered by those observers struck by the deleterious effects of the system. Critics noticed the disastrous consequences that an overseer's payment by crop share had upon the treatment of slaves. Thomas Anburey, for one, spelled out the logic of the system: "thus the whole management of the plantation is left to the overseer, who as an encouragement to make the most of the crops, has a certain portion as his wages, but not having any interest in the Negroes, any further than their labour, he drives and whips them about, and works them beyond their strength and sometimes till they expire; he feels no loss in their death, he knows the plantation must be supplied, and his humanity is estimated by his interest, which rises always above freezing point."[48] The French traveler,

Moreau de St. Mery, made much the same point, noticing that "the white overseers overwork them [slaves] detestably, because they get a percentage of the produce."[49]

If the share system encouraged overseers to overwork their slave charges, it also gave them an incentive to work on those crops for which they were paid a share at the expense of general plantation duties. Though John Mercer looked "to have the plantation properly conducted as well to Stock Pasture Ground as to the Care making of Tob[bac]o," he lamented that "it is too true that the best of Overseers have little Regard for any thing but the Crop of which they get a share."[50] Likewise, Thomas Fairfax complained that while his overseer, Russel, "set the people to gathering Corn" in his presence, when "we came away he renewed the treading [of the wheat]." Russel, Fairfax complained, would rather "thresh rye or tread out wheat" for that was more "conducive to his particular Interest than fallow ground or gather Corn or turn hogs out of the meadow [or] haul wood," none of which he was directly compensated for.[51]

Free Laborers on the Plantation

By providing overseers with an incentive to accentuate productivity, many employers divulged their overriding interest in maximizing the return from their plantations. This same concern governed other aspects of their relationships with their overseers. Planter-employers structured their relationship with overseers to maximize their own flexibility as plantation managers. Above all, employers of overseers insisted on their freedom to terminate ineffective employees midterm.

Virginia's large planters viewed relationships with other dependents—apprentices, servants, slaves, children, and wives, for example—in familial terms, with an emphasis upon extensive, reciprocal obligations. Planters viewed the household expansively to include all bound dependents, and thought of it organically as a corporate structure in which each member had a place. Yet for the most part, they conceived of their association with overseers in a far more limited way, as an employment relationship in which each party pursued his own interest. In short, in their dealings with overseers, planters shed the encumbrances associated with a master's responsibilities to his dependents, embracing instead the new and flexible relationship of employer of free labor. Acknowledging that they were instrumental to the productivity of their quarters, planters terminated overseers when they were unproductive or when a planter's labor needs changed over the course of a year. While many of Virginia's largest slaveholders emphasized the mutual obligations that tied together master and slave, these same men, as employers of overseers, were quick to end their contracts with, and their obligations to, the men who occupied these positions when circumstances so necessitated. Even where terms were in fact served out, employers often replaced overseers at the year's end, believing that men serving for longer terms became inured to the exhortations of their employers or worn down by the resistance of slaves. Rapid turnover left the overseer-employer relationship characterized as much by mutual antagonism as by a sense of mutual obligation.[52]

While most of this mobility consisted of overseers leaving an employer at the end of their annual terms, surviving evidence speaks more often to those occasions when disputes led to the thrusting out of overseers before their contracts had expired. Though this did not, in all likelihood, occur frequently, we can learn something of the more general motivations of both overseers and employers from such instances.

Edward Pridham deposed that despite eight months of "doing his duty as an Overseer . . . in taking due Care of every thing on the . . . Plantation under his Care," his employer, Robert Armistead, "did without any manner of Cause Quarrel with the . . . Pl[ainti]f[f] and refuse to permit him to Remain longer on the . . . plantation." The jury, hearing how his family had since been "destitute of House or Home . . . and driven to the Greatest Extremity of Want and poverty" found for him for the amount of nearly £20.[53] The same year John Ross, six months into a two-year position as overseer for a Cumberland County planter, William Mathews, was "dismissed, expelled, & removed from the Plantation." The early dismissal resulted in his losing the "great Benefit & Advantage Which would have arisen to him from his Share of the Crops . . . which would have been made & raised on the Plantation." Since his dismissal he had "been at great Labor & Expence to support & maintain himself & his Family . . . & also to provide for their Dwelling." As with Pridham, the jury found for the discharged overseer, not for the full extent of the requested damages but seemingly to compensate the overseer for the time worked.[54] Clearly some employers claimed the right to dismiss their overseers at will, without specific cause.

Planter-employers exploited the flexibility that such a privilege allowed them. It freed them, for example, from the obligation to look after overseers who had become incapacitated while in their employ. While masters of servants, for example, were legally bound to maintain such dependents even during times of sickness, employers of overseers viewed ill health as a cause for termination. When his overseer, John King, injured himself while lifting tobacco hogsheads, Landon Carter was confident "that if he should be a Cripple I will not be obliged to pay his wages."[55] Likewise, John Lumpkin and his employer, Philip Lightfoot, agreed, as a result of his indisposition, to "relinquish mutually any agreement for the present year."[56] Privileging their own interests, employers felt free to turn out overseers without concerning themselves with the fate of the overseer or his family.

Some employers terminated contracts after an initial agreement had been made merely because their plans for the deployment of their labor forces apparently changed. Hence, Constantine Rock complained that, although Jesse Carter had agreed to employ him as overseer for 1760, when he came to take his position on the plantation he had been refused access. The prospective overseer who had "dispose[d] of his former place ab[r]oad together with Many other things in Readiness to go to the plantation" found himself, then, in a precarious situation.[57] Some years later Stephen Burdett confronted a similar situation. Though he had verbally agreed to serve John Pierce as overseer, when he appeared to take his position Pierce was "not at home & [had] left word with his Son to Nail Up the Overseers house & not let me in."[58]

While planter-employers terminated overseers for a variety of reasons, underlying many such firings was the belief that the overseer had failed to promote the economic interests of his employer effectively. William Cabell, for example, turned away his overseer Hughes Bowles "for Neglect of every duty."[59] John Tayloe gave a certain Mr. Cannady one day's notice after castigating him for "absenting [himself], particularly in the midst of harvest." Not wanting a "misunderstanding," Tayloe agreed to pay him for services already rendered.[60]

Many employers were less willing than Tayloe to compensate those overseers let go for such infractions. Such cases entered the courts when, after having been dismissed, overseers sought to recover back wages for the work completed before their termination. For example, William Rutherford sued Richard Ball for nonpayment of wages when discharged as overseer in 1758. In response Ball countersued, claiming that Rutherford had been "so negligent in looking after the said Negroes and Plantation" that the corn and tobacco crops were pathetically meager.[61] Likewise, when Caleb Hynds brought an action against his employer John Bostick for back wages, Bostick countersued, claiming damages for the overseer's mistreatment of his slaves and the nonperformance of his contract.[62]

Seeking to avoid litigation, employers in the late eighteenth century increasingly inserted their right to terminate their overseers' employment into the articles of agreement. John Martin agreed to terms with William Smith, for example, "under the penalty of being turned off at Any Period."[63] Similarly, William Allason's agreement with Laurence Tompkins stated "that if he shou[l]d through carelessness or Neglect of . . . Business as Overseer, allow the . . . Business to suffer, He the said William shall be at liberty to turn him of[f] from . . . Business at pleasure, and submit to the Loss of his then past Labour in . . . Business as Overseer."[64] Over time, contracts became increasingly detailed and formal, and employers extended the range of offenses for which termination was an option. Alongside the cultivation of a market crop, articles of agreement now routinely mentioned the care of the quarter's slaves, stock, and tools as well as the upkeep of the plantation's fences as duties integral to the position, the nonperformance of which could lead to an overseer's dismissal. In addition, the terms of any prospective termination became increasingly specific in early nineteenth-century contracts. Robert Wormeley Carter, for example, in his agreement with Hudson Lyle, dictated "that should the said Lyles conduct prove exceptionable the said Carter is at liberty to discharge him at a days notice, allowing him Ten dollars per Month, with a due proportion of the provisions aforesaid, for his services during the time of his employment with the said Carter."[65] By expanding the range of offenses for which an overseer might be dismissed, and in detailing the process by which such a termination would be effected, employers augmented their maneuverability as market producers, enabling them to act quickly when they felt the economic interests of the plantation were being threatened.

In doing so, planter-employers forsook the patriarchal role of presiding over customary relationships with dependents with each party bound by extensive, reciprocal obligations and duties. Rather, many employers of overseers eagerly embraced a different kind of relationship, one that was, in essence, an employment relationship rather than an inclusive social relationship. The obligations of both parties in the overseer-employer relationship were specific and, increasingly, reduced to a written contract. Unlike other dependents, overseers were only considered members of their employers' households in superficial ways; indeed, unlike other white dependents such as servants or apprentices, overseers were often themselves married, and so exercised authority over their own households.[66] Planter-employers energetically upheld their right to dismiss overseers midterm. Even when overseers managed to survive their terms, it was not unusual for their employer to hire someone else for the following year. Scarcely, then, was the relationship between overseer and employer an expression of paternalism. Rather, the demands of market production played a formative role in shaping planters' approach to the relationship. Planter-employers structured their relationship with overseers to maximize their flexibility as plantation managers, freeing themselves from the constraints of paternal obligation.

While an employer's ability to terminate overseers with cause occasionally left the overseer the victim, sometimes overseers themselves were the beneficiaries of this newer conception of labor. Overseers who were unhappy in their positions could quit with limited legal consequences. Though masters claimed a property right to the labor of their bound workers—a right enforced with criminal sanctions against those who absconded—they enjoyed no such right with departing overseers, against whom they could only bring a civil suit for damages.[67]

While the remaining court records are fragmentary, it appears that employers seldom adopted this recourse.[68] Just one case of an employer suing an overseer for breach of contract appears in the loose suit papers of three counties. The case involved Gideon Marr, a planter in Cumberland County, whose overseer, Zachariah Davis, having agreed to serve him for the year left a short while into the term "under a pretense of going to finish his Former Crop," never to return.

Several details of the case are worth noting. First, Marr felt it necessary not only to document the breach of covenant, but also to demonstrate that the overseer's action had left him with no other alternatives. Having already agreed with Davis, Marr "refused Several Men that did offer to undertake the . . . place." Then Davis, having given him "no notice of the . . . Disappointment," absconded too late "to get Another Overseer most men being before that Time provided with plows." Moreover, Marr claimed that he had not only been damaged by Davis's breach of the agreement, but by his "pretend[ing] and giv[ing] out in Speeches that the . . . plantation is so much out of Repair & the slaves . . . so Mean & Useless that no Man Can Make a Crop with them." Whether these additional circumstances were necessary to bring suit or were simply included to win extra damages is not clear. However, they do suggest that by the mid-eighteenth century, the flight of unbound labor by itself may not have been enough for a damaged employer to bring suit.[69]

Though seldom appearing in court records, instances of overseers leaving their posts midway through their annual terms are interspersed throughout surviving plantation papers. Robert Wormeley Carter, for example, noted matter-of-factly in his diary, during the summer of 1783, that "this day my Overseer Morgan came to me and desired to be discharged he says he has been here 8 months, wages due him." The very next month Carter divulged that John Gordon "left me to go to live at Corotoman."[70] Just as employers withheld their paternal magnanimity if an overseer was indisposed or ineffective, so did many overseers exhibit little of the fidelity that was expected from dependents. Indeed, overseers embraced the relative freedom of an escape route, using it to exercise some control over their employment relationship. As the overseer Anthony Frazier put it, "if he was affronted he cou'd move at pleasure."[71] At a time when most dependent labor in British North America was carried out by family members, servants, or slaves, bound to their fathers or masters for extensive terms, overseers were free laborers, able to move on with limited legal consequences midterm, or with no legal repercussions at the end of the year. The evidence of extensive turnover suggests that overseers took advantage of these distinctions.[72]

Paternalism and Profits

By the end of the colonial period, more than half of Virginia's slaves worked under a resident overseer, a hired employee, rather than directly under the eye of a paternal master. Planter-employers terminated overseers considered unproductive and provided overseers with an incentive to maximize the production of market crops. In so doing they almost guaranteed that overseers would attempt to overwork their slave charges. All of this suggests that central to the motivations of planters in late colonial Virginia was return on capital investment. Slaveholder paternalism, such as it was, with an emphasis upon mutuality as opposed to exploitation, foundered upon this prior and continuing attachment to profitability.

While it is arguable that the maturation of slaveholder paternalism along the eastern seaboard in the nineteenth century, reinforced by a sluggish economy and a self-reproducing slave population, displaced other imperatives as an organizing principle of social relationships, that was surely not the case in the second half of the eighteenth century. During that period, the huge surge in agricultural production and the rapid expansion of settlement into the Piedmont were the key social facts, and they betrayed the expansive, dynamic, and developmental imperatives that shaped the social arrangements favored by Virginian planters. In this earlier period, paternalism served a compensatory function, shielding Virginia's large planters from the exploitation that surging agricultural production and the westward spread of slavery entailed. The examples of slaveholder paternalism with which this paper began, for example, drew almost exclusively from quarters in which the paternal planter was absent.[73]

This was but one of several strategies that planters pursued to distance themselves from their complicity in undisguised exploitation. It became increasingly common, for example, in the third quarter of the eighteenth century for large planters to center their most exploitative activities, the cultivation of market crops, on outlying quarters, often at some distance from the home house. At the same time paternalists peopled their home quarter with skilled workers, arrayed in workshops, away from the rigors of field labor and the routine disciplinary interventions needed to make field labor effective. One-fifth of the men and two-thirds of the female labor force on William Byrd III's Westover estate were domestics in 1769. George Mason recalled his father's home plantation as containing "carpenters, coopers, sawyers, blacksmiths, tanners, curriers, shoemakers, spinners, weavers and knitters, and even a distiller."[74]

Those disciplinary interventions were, for the most part, carried out by overseers, though the authority by which they did so stemmed from their employers. Moreover, the incentive to sustain productivity that often underlay individual acts of corporal discipline was likewise extended by the employers of overseers. Paternalists distanced themselves from these unpleasant facts by contributing to a discourse of overseer incorrigibility. Planters routinely referred to overseers as a collectivity with shared predilections. Thomas Jefferson, for example, referred to overseers as a "race"; James Barbour, an agricultural improver, described them as a "class."[75] The attributes that these men were said to share were uniformly negative: drunkenness, dishonesty, lustfulness, and brutality. "Of all the Sober honest Overseers I ever had or heard of," John Mercer wrote on one occasion, following the convention, "the one I have is the wors[t]."[76] In the same trope, Hugh Washington observed that "very few of the common Overseers . . . have the least feeling or humanity for Slaves."[77] Frances Tucker thought overseers "the worst part of mankind."[78] If overseers were, indeed, an innately brutal class of people, then surely it was they, and not those who employed them, who were to blame for the severity of plantation slavery, planters seemed to claim. Viewed in this light, overseers did serve as lightning rods on eighteenth-century plantations, though not merely as convenient focal points for slaves' resentments about unjust punishment. Overseers served useful ideological purposes for their employers too. By attributing the harshness of plantation slavery to innately incorrigible overseers, their employers removed from their sights their own complicity in the aggressively commercial nature of eighteenth-century cultivation that made such severity necessary.[79]

Throughout the eighteenth-century Anglo-American world, men wrestled with the contradictions wrought by the jostling imperatives of market production and household order. Central to this development was the emergence of a market for wage labor. Increasingly, masters no longer incorporated dependents within their own familial realm for the purpose of household order. Rather, as employers of wage labor they disclaimed their traditional obligations, preferring a far more limited relationship. They proceeded to bewail the decline in household order that followed from these decisions. Many landlords also withdrew from the time-honored reciprocities that marked relationships with tenants, retreating from the business of running their estates. In addition, absentee landownership became increasingly common. In response to the demise of recurrent customary exchanges with tenants and other dependents, landlords now participated in a "theatre of the great," relying on the occasional, ritualistic performance to convey their commitment to paternal obligation.[80]

Similar dynamics were evident in Virginia. Though paternalistic planters attempted to imagine their relationship with slave dependents as familial, the conceit was strained. Rather, at some distance from the exigencies of day-to-day labor relationships, many such planters, like their British counterparts, employed a distanced paternalism, often confined to ritualistic interventions, to conceal their commitment otherwise to the relationships of the market. The forms of labor evident upon Virginia's plantations represented two faces of that commitment: slaves, harnessed to commercial agricultural production, and overseers, in many ways the apotheosis of free labor.[81] Mobile, outside the reach of corporal punishment, and often beyond the supervisory purview of their employers, overseers were driven by individual financial incentives rather than by traditional, paternalistic, forms of labor discipline. Their extensive deployment by Virginia's planters was a powerful indication of planters' abiding commitment to the social relations of the market.

CHAPTER SEVEN

"The Fewnesse of Handicraftsmen"

Artisan Adaptation and Innovation in the Colonial Chesapeake

Jean B. Russo

The Reverend Hugh Jones, writing in 1699, expressed a contemporary view when commenting on Maryland's lack of towns: "We have not yet found the way of associating ourselves into towns and corporations, by reason of the fewnesse of handicraftsmen. . . . There are indeed severall places allotted for towns, but hitherto they are only titular ones, except Annapolis, where the Governour resides."[1] Jones, who correctly observed the legislature's lack of success in creating towns by fiat, recognized that the landscape he surveyed in Maryland bore little relationship to the English countryside where, in the flat lowlands, villages occurred at intervals of about one mile.[2] Writing nearly a century later, Thomas Jefferson reached similar conclusions about Virginia: "Our country being much intersected with navigable waters, and trade brought generally to our doors . . . has probably been one of the causes why we have no towns of any consequence. . . . There are other places [besides the few hamlets he identified] at which . . . the *laws* have said there shall be towns; but *Nature* has said there shall not."[3] Nature, having endowed Chesapeake colonists with a system of navigable waterways for transporting goods and a staple crop that encouraged dispersed settlement, shaped an economy in which "no advantage accrued to having a single port or a limited number of ports around which, in other circumstances, towns might have been expected to develop."[4]

The legislatures of Maryland and Virginia, as both Jones and Jefferson noted, endeavored on numerous occasions to create towns by statute. Maryland's General Assembly, in three separate series of acts passed between the 1660s and the early 1700s, enumerated "severall places allotted for towns."[5] The delegates passed their legislation under the rubric "An act for Advancement of trade," designating the new towns as the only entrepots where vessels trading in the province could unload and sell their cargoes and collect tobacco for return voyages.[6] Realization of the ostensible motivation, the centralization of trade, would have facilitated proprietary supervision and regulation of provincial commerce. But other, less explicit factors also influenced the recurrent passage of town acts. Had the efforts of the designated commissioners to lay out lots and persuade settlers to buy and build upon them succeeded, the Chesapeake landscape would have begun to look less like a wilderness and more like the English countryside. And had enough colonists flocked to the nascent towns, they might have provided a market sufficient to support the handicraftsmen whose "fewnesse" Jones lamented, further moving the province along the spectrum "from rudeness to refinement, from barbarism to civility." Establishing a landscape of settled villages whose residents included an array of artisans would be an important step in "transforming the uncultivated wilderness spaces in America into civilized social landscapes of the kind that existed in Europe."[7]

Although the legislative acts failed to achieve their goal of creating towns, the Chesapeake colonies realized the larger goal sought by the assemblies, of progressing from wilderness to civilized social landscapes, albeit in unanticipated forms. Village functions, such as governance, religious worship, commerce, and the like, scattered across the landscape rather than clustering together in recognizable settlements. Similarly, Jones's handicraftsmen situated themselves in the countryside among the tobacco planters whose custom they sought. During the century and a half between initial settlement and the apogee of colonial culture in the decade before the Revolution, the tidewater region experienced the transformation colonists sought, but not by replicating the metropolitan culture. Rather, settlers adapted that ideal to the realities of their own environment and economy, creating an amalgam of British practices and creole adaptations that reflected the opportunities offered and the constraints imposed by their New World experience.

The Rural Experience: Talbot County

Talbot County, an area of some three hundred square miles, lies between the Wye and Choptank Rivers in the middle portion of Maryland's Eastern Shore. Settlement began in the 1650s, when the area was still part of Kent County; sufficient growth by 1662 resulted in its creation as a new county in that year. As the region's population continued to expand, the legislature combined Talbot's northern portion with southern Kent to form Queen Anne's County in 1706, thereby giving Talbot its boundaries for the remainder of the colonial period. At the time of the division, the county had a population of about 1,400 taxables and a total population of perhaps 3,100.[8] By midcentury, residents numbered about 8,800 and by the end of the colonial period reached over 11,200.[9] The increase in population did not result, however, in any measurable urban presence in the county. Its nominal towns—Yorke, Doncaster, Dover, Kingstown, and even Oxford—never established themselves as viable urban centers.

The original county seat, the town of Yorke on Skipton Creek, apparently consisted only of the courthouse building (which also housed an ordinary), a prison, perhaps a second ordinary, and maybe one or two homes. The 1707 plan of Doncaster, designated as a town in three statutes, depicted four streets (a "main" street crossed by three shorter streets), forty-nine lots, and a market place, but identified only six lots by their owners' names. The surveyor marked five of the six as "improved formerly." The lot marked "RB" was likely the site of Richard Bruff's ordinary, but he relocated to the St. Michael's River ferry crossing in 1722. The county court recorded land transactions at Dover intermittently, but few traces survive of any other activity occurring there. Lots at Kingstown on Tuckahoe Creek occasionally changed hands either by inheritance or sale, but the town appears to have been the site of only one commercial venture, James Wilson's tannery. In 1712, the county court designated a site near Pitt's Bridge as the new county seat but the area, known only as "Talbot Court House," contained just the court building and a few houses well into the second half of the century. Oxford perhaps came closest to an urban place, according to ship captain Jeremiah Banning, whose memoirs described a midcentury town "whose strands and streets . . . were covered with busy, noisy crowds ushering in commerce from almost every quarter of the globe."[10] But Banning, writing from the perspective of nearly a half-century later, may have been moved by nostalgia for the town then being eclipsed by Easton (as Talbot Court House was renamed in 1788) to have exaggerated its earlier importance. Although a maritime center and port of entry, Oxford lacked both courthouse and church, and without them had no magnets to draw a broad cross-section of the county to its streets. The small number of people ever identified as "of Oxford" (particularly in contrast with the many "of Annapolis") suggests its relative unimportance as an urban place.

Settlement, then, adapted itself to the region's economic opportunities by following the decentralized Chesapeake pattern rather than the village-dominated model of the English countryside. Dispersal did not mean abandonment, however, of traditional institutions and services. A network of roads, developed and maintained by the inhabitants, provided access to courts, mills, churches and meeting houses, stores, ferries, ordinaries, lawyers and doctors, and craftsmen's shops. No one village or hamlet offered access to all, but if one considers the landscape not as an environment of scattered plantations and inchoate villages but as a dispersed village, in which village functions assumed a decentralized form, then a truer picture of Chesapeake settlement emerges, revealing it not as primitive and incomplete but as more subtle and complex than contemporaries perceived.

Just as towns took on a new form, so too did Jones's handicraftsmen adapt to the Chesapeake environment. Jones and others had expected artisans to serve as the stimulus to town development, but a region that had no economic need for towns offered no incentive for craftsmen to congregate together. Instead artisans followed the same adaptive pattern of dispersal as did tobacco planters and village institutions, a choice made even more rational by their own involvement in the tobacco economy. The region's artisans settled on plantations they owned or rented, scattered among the colonists who supplied many of their raw materials and who employed their skills.

As rural craftsmen, Talbot's artisans concentrated in the trades most useful to an agricultural community. Although the preindustrial urban world discriminated among nearly two hundred trades in classifying and describing its inhabitants, only a small fraction of these appeared in colonial Talbot County.[11] Craftsmen settled, trained, and persisted within a framework of opportunity shaped by the region's tobacco economy and its place within the broader Atlantic economy. Artisans could not establish themselves in the rural Chesapeake marketplace in defiance of that framework. A glover, for example, who wished to make and sell gloves, could find ready customers but could not sell his product at prices competitive with imported goods and still do as well as he could by planting tobacco. A coachmaker, on the other hand, skilled in making handsome carriages and desirous of serving the elite who purchased such items, would have to wait until the end of the eighteenth century to find enough customers who could afford his wares. For most of the colonial period, the relatively small number of Talbot residents with both the means and the desire to own a carriage imported one directly from England or, after midcentury, patronized an Annapolis coachmaker when in the capital for business or pleasure.

The array of *potential* crafts, then, can be divided into two broad groups. The first and larger group consisted of the crafts that never played a sustained role within the county during the colonial period. A diverse group, this segment can be divided further into three components, distinguished either by total absence or the timing of their appearance. The largest of the three subgroups consisted of highly specialized luxury trades, always restricted to urban centers with a wealthy clientele. Not surprisingly, craftsmen seeking employment in these trades never looked for work in Talbot: the county's planters did not need the services of gem cutters, bugle makers, or crafters of mathematical instruments. A smaller subgroup consisted of trades practiced by artisans who made an early appearance but who could not compete in a market so easily supplied from overseas; of these, glovers and hatters provide the clearest examples. The remainder, also a small group, included the crafts, such as cabinetmaking and coach making, that required a more concentrated market of prosperous customers than the county could offer until late in the century.

The skilled trades that generally enjoyed a presence in the county throughout the colonial period made up the balance of the potential crafts. Uniformly, men working in them offered products or services that needed to be supplied locally or that could utilize locally produced and abundant raw materials. The various processors of wood encompassed the largest group of rural craftsmen throughout the colonial period, with carpenters always the largest segment among the woodworkers. The second largest group consisted of the producers and processors of fabric, while leatherworkers made up the next largest group. Metalworkers, almost all of whom identified themselves as blacksmiths, contributed the fourth-highest number of craftsmen. The final category of any appreciable size consisted of the ancillary building trades. A scattering of others, such as barbers, bakers, butchers, and a few shipyard crafts completed the profile (see table 7.1).

Table 7.1. Talbot County Artisans, 1660–1760

Craft Group	1660–1689 No.	%	1690–1719 No.	%	1720–1739 No.	%	1740–1759 No.	%	Total No.	%
Carpenters	45		127		74		82		264	
Coopers	19		39		24		12		74	
Sawyers	5		25		16		15		58	
Wheelwrights	0		10		6		8		19	
Cabinetmakers	0		0		0		7		7	
Joiners	4		8		18		25		43	
Turners	0		1		2		0		3	
Coachmakers	0		0		0		1		1	
Millwrights	1		3		2		3		7	
House Carpenters	0		0		0		3		3	
Total Woodworkers	74	60	213	54	142	54	156	49	479	52
Shoemakers	7		33		29		26		79	
Tanners	3		10		6		6		19	
Saddlers	1		3		1		4		8	
Glovers	0		4		0		0		4	
Total Leatherworkers	11	9	50	13	36	14	36	11	110	12
Blacksmiths	5		18		22		27		57	
Braziers	0		1		0		0		1	
Silversmiths	0		0		2		2		3	
Total Metalworkers	5	4	19	5	24	9	29	9	61	7
Tailors	19		34		17		26		92	
Weavers	0		27		18		26		57	
Hatters	0		1		0		0		1	
Fullers	0		0		0		1		1	
Total Cloth Trades	19	15	62	16	35	13	53	17	151	17
Bricklayers	3		9		9		14		26	
Plasterers	3		4		2		7		16	
Brickmakers	2		2		1		1		6	
Glaziers	0		2		0		0		2	
Total Building Trades	8	6	17	4	12	5	22	7	50	5
Ship Carpenters	7		22		12		19		48	
Caulkers	0		4		0		0		4	
Sail Makers	0		0		1		1		2	
Blockmakers	0		1		0		1		2	
Total Ship Building	7	6	27	7	13	5	21	7	56	6
Barbers	0		4		0		0		4	
Total Service Workers	0	0	4	1	0	0	0	0	4	0
Butchers	0		1		1		0		1	
Bakers	0		2		0		0		2	
Total Food Trades	0	0	3	1	1	0	0	0	3	0
All Crafts	124	100	395	101	263	100	317	100	914	99

Note: For each row, the number of artisans in the four time periods does not equal the total number because some individuals' careers spanned more than one time period. Although many artisans appear in the records with more than one designation (e.g. tanner and currier or carpenter and joiner), no individual was counted in more than one craft.

Source: Adapted from Jean B. Russo, *Free Workers in a Plantation Economy: Talbot County, Maryland, 1690–1759* (New York, 1989), table 3.1, 139–140.

The distribution of artisans among the woodworking trades changed over the course of the colonial period, responding to growing density of settlement, diversification of the economy, increasing mean household wealth, and the incorporation of some skills into individual plantation workplaces. The number of coopers, for example, declined as planters trained workers of their own to satisfy the steady demand for hogsheads in which to ship tobacco.[12] A parallel decline took place among those identified as carpenters, but for a different reason. In the seventeenth and early eighteenth centuries, "carpenter" encompassed a range of woodworking skills, from building houses to fabricating hogsheads to making furniture. By the mid-eighteenth century, a greater degree of specialization began to occur. The number of joiners increased while the first cabinetmakers and house carpenters appeared in the area, indicative of an emerging distinction between men primarily engaged in building houses and those who focused on furnishing their interiors, a process fueled by a genteel clientele investing more resources both in constructing their homes and in filling them with the appropriate props.

Relatively little change took place in trades such as blacksmithing and tanning that required large capital expenditures. A tanyard or a smith's shop represented too large an investment to let sit idle, but also one that precluded casual entry into the field. The silversmith, the blacksmith's counterpart in fine workmanship, began to find steady employment in the area at the end of the colonial period and particularly after the Revolution, again responding to the emergence of Easton as an urban center. The number of weavers, on the other hand, declined dramatically by the end of the colonial period, undoubtedly reflecting the enhanced ability of consumers at all levels of society to purchase imported cloth. The binding out in the 1790s of Fanny Pasterfield as a weaver, the first female apprentice in any trade, symbolizes the craft's marginalization.

In all, over nine hundred craftsmen worked in Talbot County during the colonial period, seemingly a large enough number to belie Jones's reference to their "fewnesse." But these men were not and are not easy to find. Jones could not walk along the streets of a town or village, identifying the watchmaker at the Sign of the Crown and Dial or the hatter at the Sign of the Beaver and Lac'd

Hat. Nor could he scan the pages of the local newspaper to read notices placed by local tradesmen. The *Maryland Gazette,* which did not begin continuous publication until 1745, mostly drew the advertising shillings of Annapolis-based craftsmen; Talbot itself had no newspaper of its own until the 1790s. Anyone looking to purchase barrels, get a tool mended, or order a suit of clothes would have to rely on word-of-mouth referrals from kin or neighbors if he did not personally know the appropriate workman. A casual visitor like Jones would not be aware of blacksmith Thomas Bartlett working on his plantation along the Tred Avon, or of carpenter Peter Harwood on the Miles River, or weaver Stephen Wilson living at the head of the Wye River.

The county's residents, however, could find their way around their dispersed village, as can be seen by looking more closely at the working world of one Talbot artisan, blacksmith William Dobson. Dobson, who owned 585 acres of land, lived in Tuckahoe Hundred near the head of a branch of King's Creek, a site that placed him close to the geographic center of the county. Dobson does not appear to have been native-born, but he lived in Talbot for nearly twenty-five years before his death in 1733. By his own testimony, he was born about 1682, making him in his early fifties when he died. The St. Peter's Parish register noted the births of seven children born to Dobson and his wife Anne (possibly two wives of the same name) between 1710 and 1731, but not that of Isaac, his oldest son and also a blacksmith. The administration of Dobson's estate (appraised at £347 current money) included a list of debts outstanding at the time of his death. The London merchant house of John Hanbury owed Dobson £16, presumably a credit balance for tobacco marketed through the firm. Eighty-seven individuals accounted for the remaining debtors, with current money or tobacco balances ranging from two shillings to three pounds. Seven of the debtors probably lived across Tuckahoe Creek in nearby Queen Anne's County, but all seven had strong family ties to Talbot and may have lived in the county when they incurred their debts. The location of Dobson's shop placed him on the western perimeter of the hundred, within a few miles of four of the five remaining hundreds. From his central location, Dobson drew customers who resided in every one of the county's political subdivisions: twenty-five in Tuckahoe; fifteen in Bullenbrook to the south; sixteen in Island and eight in Mill, both lying to the northwest of Dobson's shop; twelve in Third Haven, to the southwest; and one in Bay Hundred, the most distant. The "village" in which Dobson worked extended out over a large part of the county.[13]

Dobson's neighbors knew their way to his shop, but the historians seeking Dobson and the county's other craftsmen face a challenge similar to Jones's. No census bureau kept track of household members, noting occupation among its categories of data. No city directories provided lists of residents, with special sections detailing all practitioners of various trades and businesses. Each constable did submit yearly to the county court a list of taxables in his hundred for use in determining the annual levy, but complete lists for Talbot survive only for the year 1733.[14] In that year, the six constables enumerated nearly nine hundred households containing about 2,300 taxable residents, but identified only three artisans, all members of the extensive Bartlett family living in Mill Hundred: John, a blacksmith, and James and another John, both carpenters. We don't know why the constable who compiled the list for Mill Hundred decided to list an occupation for the Bartletts, but we do know that he failed to do so for twenty-six other craftsmen, and his counterparts omitted occupational designations for an additional 110 men. Finding Jones's missing handicraftsmen thus requires the archival equivalent of riding up and down the county's roads: a sifting through court, probate, and land records to locate the will written by "William Dobson, blacksmith" or the land purchased by "Peter Harwood, carpenter" or the suit initiated against "James Acers, tanner."

This process of reconstruction undoubtedly underestimates the number of men who earned some portion of their livelihood from craft work but most likely comes close to capturing those who defined themselves as artisans. The distinction between casual by-employment and self-definition as a craftsman points to another aspect of rural Chesapeake adaptation, one that the constables' lists also suggest. The small size of the local market prevented rural artisans from supporting themselves solely through their craft work. Like their neighbors and customers, Talbot's artisans worked the land as well as their forges, looms, pit saws, and planes. The constables making up their lists of taxables generally saw no need to distinguish such men by their occupations, for the artisan households they visited on their rounds looked much like those of any other planter. The householder who occasionally did some carpentry or made a few pairs of shoes but who focused his efforts to earn his livelihood on cultivating tobacco defined himself as a planter. The artisan who supplemented his craft work by the crops and livestock he raised nonetheless considered himself a craftsman, not a planter, and defined himself in public documents by the skill that he practiced. Through the combination of craft work and planting, the rural artisan could maintain his craft identity in the absence of enough customers to provide a livelihood solely from his trade.

At the same time, assembling the artisan population in this manner reveals another facet of the adaptive process that occurred as successive generations peopled the Chesapeake. Just as the craft community as a whole exhibited a marked contraction of specialization, so too did the individual artisan find himself working as a generalist, rather than a specialist, particularly if the raw materials with which he worked were shared by a range of specialized crafts. Blacksmiths might also appear in the records identified as whitesmiths, tinsmiths, braziers, and coppersmiths. James Acers was not unusual among leather workers in being identified variously as a currier, tanner, and shoemaker, and inventories of such men often included hides and skins, shoemaking tools and lasts, and currier's knives. Court records labeled John Price and James Raglass as brickmakers in one instance and bricklayers in another. The same man might be described in one record as a carpenter, in another as a joiner, in a third as a cooper, and in a fourth as a shipwright; many more exhibited that diversity in practice even if they always carried the same craft designation in the records. The account books of planter Robert Goldsborough, for example, document the generalist nature of the work done for him in the early 1700s by two local carpenters, William Register and Peter Harwood.[15] Both constructed buildings, ranging from small henhouses to forty-foot tobacco barns and a forty-five-foot house with a shed. Both men did the work of coopers, fabricating tobacco hogsheads, cider casks, powdering tubs, and pails. One made a chair, which might have required joinery or turner's work to fashion the chair back or the legs. Each performed the work of a ship carpenter, making a mast, working on Goldsborough's boat, and constructing a canoe. General carpentry work included making gates, plows, a cider-press sword, a harrow, a sled, sheepfolds, and fencing. An urban craftsman might serve a market large enough to permit a specialist's role, but rural Chesapeake artisans had to be able to meet the varied needs generated by a much smaller clientele.

Talbot's craftsmen adjusted to their circumstances—a dispersed, limited market for their services or products—in one additional way, by shaping the size of their operations accordingly. No documentation points to the presence in Talbot of a workshop run by a master craftsman with the assistance of journeymen and apprentices. The only suggestion of a large-scale operation occurs in the inventory of planter Thomas Robins. The son of a merchant,

Thomas was born in 1672, the year after his father arrived in Talbot to represent a mercantile firm consisting of himself and two cousins. Over the course of fifty years, Thomas Robins amassed an estate of £1,430, whose assets included four skilled indentured shoemakers (one of them designated as the foreman); a well-equipped shop with four sets of shoemaker's tools, a set of currying and tanning tools, eighteen new lasts, and a parcel of old ones; finished products in the form of eight dozen heels and almost two hundred pairs of shoes (one hundred of them "Negro plain shoes"); and raw materials, skins, hides, and leather worth £165. Robins's household also included at least one apprentice, an orphan bound to him in 1718 to learn the shoemaking trade. Robins himself was not a shoemaker or a tanner, but an early entrepreneur with a modest shoemaking factory that must have served a local market (neither Robins's own workforce of twenty-three nor his entire household of about thirty would have warranted production on that scale). Robins's son George inherited the bulk of his father's estate. George maintained the shoemaking establishment, but on a reduced scale, and diversified his craft production into tailoring and woodworking as well.[16] The "factory" to make shoes existed as a brief anomaly only during the second decade of the century, perhaps brought into existence by the trade disruptions and stagnation of the tobacco economy that accompanied Queen Anne's War.

Most of the artisans tallied in table 7.1 operated as masters of their workshops but may have worked independently for a large portion of their careers. Many clearly trained their own children, just as William Dobson undoubtedly trained his son Isaac, or benefited from the labor of other family members. Weaver William Sinclair, for example, willed to his sister-in-law, Ruth Wilson, "the loom that she works with and a shuttle but no gear."[17] A small percentage may have purchased skilled indentured servants as assistants, but there is no evidence that any owned a skilled slave.[18] Some, particularly in the woodworking trades, worked in partnership. Richard Ratcliff and John Nuttall, for example, were sawyers employed by ship carpenter Robert Grayson for nearly a year, supplying 10,500 feet of plank, wood for making a coble (a short, flat-bottomed rowboat or fishing boat), and assistance with the main beams of a boat.[19] Henry Pratt and Aaron Parrott may have worked together for at least a decade, being employed to perform joiner's and carpenter's work for the addition to the St. Peter's Parish church between 1746 and 1753, but perhaps continuing in partnership until Martin's death in 1756.[20] For most craftsmen, however, the only well-documented source of assistance consisted of orphans or other children supervised by the county court, which frequently specified that boys be trained in the "art and mystery" of a particular craft.

Had Jones been correct in his association of crafts with towns, in his expectation that the presence of the former depended on the existence of the latter, colonists in the rural Chesapeake would have lived in communities bereft of the services of skilled artisans. Like the first settlers who arrived on the *Ark* and *Dove,* what they could not import they would have had to do without or improvise using their own rough-hewn abilities. Within the first generation of settlement, however, colonists began to adapt familiar English patterns to the realities of their new environment. Over the course of the colonial period, they fashioned a new network of craftsmanship that combined local production of basic necessities and some amenities with importation, whether from England or from Annapolis, of luxuries. Artisans, who could not have supported themselves by craft work alone, combined handicrafts with planting. Craftsmen located their workshops largely in the countryside, among their customers, rather than languishing for lack of towns. Rural artisans worked consistently within the disciplines of a specific raw material, such as wood or iron and other metals, but broadly among the various trades employing that resource. Workers in wood, for example, acted as carpenters, joiners, coopers, and shipwrights; blacksmiths hammered and shaped iron, steel, silver, copper, brass, and tin. Despite the range of artifacts fabricated in them, the workplaces themselves were small, generally needing only to house the craftsman and perhaps an apprentice or two. Within the contours of the network shaped by the region's settlement pattern, local economy, and place within the British Empire, rural artisans hewed wood, built houses, wove cloth, stitched clothing, and crafted furniture. English visitors might have been hard-pressed to find a familiar landscape, but rural colonists could rest assured that they had recreated the substance, if not the form, of the English model to which they aspired.

The Urban Experience: Annapolis

Annapolis, lying directly across the Chesapeake Bay from Talbot County, received its first settlers in the early 1650s. Despite the site's designation as Anne Arundel's county seat and a series of acts establishing it as a port of entry, little urban growth took place for most of the seventeenth century. In the winter of 1694–95, however, the legislature moved Maryland's capital from St. Mary's City to Annapolis, thereby laying the foundation for the latter's development into an urban center, although the process would prove to be a lengthy one. The initial shift of government brought an influx of population, as placemen and those with businesses catering to the government shifted their locus to the new capital. But the proprietary establishment was too small and the meetings of the legislature too infrequent to create a self-sustaining local economy. With good reason, Edward Papenfuse characterized the period from 1684 (the year of the town's first survey) to 1715 as "the uncertain years."[21] Nothing in its early history suggested that Annapolis would be any more successful as an urban place than the ephemeral towns of Talbot County.[22] When Ebenezer Cooke first visited Annapolis in the early 1700s, he found

> A City situate on a Plain,
> Where scarce a house will keep out Rain:
> The Buildings fram'd with Cyprus rare
> Resemble much our Southwark Fair.[23]

Papenfuse labeled the half-century from the restoration of proprietary authority in 1715 to end of the French and Indian War in 1763 as the era of "industrial expansion and bureaucratic growth."[24] Industrial expansion consisted of tanyards and shipyards, activities that could as easily be found in the rural Chesapeake. The maritime trades, in particular, did add an important economic element, but the workings of government played the stronger, long-term role in stimulating Annapolis's development as a colonial metropolis of wealth and sophistication. With reestablishment of the proprietary government in 1715, Lord Baltimore and his agents began a concerted program of extracting revenue from the colony.[25] The colonial bureaucracy gradually expanded to handle collection of hogshead duties and (eventually) quitrents, to grant land patents, and to oversee other administrative chores. The need to transact business with proprietary agents, to appear in provincial courts, or to attend General Assembly sessions brought visitors from all parts of the colony. Others arrived on ships engaged in overseas and coastal trade. These individuals needed lodging, food, and drink while in town and used their visits as an opportunity to purchase imported goods that might not have already made their way to landings along the rivers and creeks on which they lived. Cook, when writing the "Sotweed Redivivus" in 1730, could now say that he was

Bound up to Port Annapolis,
The famous Beau Metropolis
Of Maryland, of small Renown
When Anna first wore England's Crown
Is now Grown Rich and Opulent
The awful Seat of Government.[26]

Cook exaggerated somewhat, as the town's greatest era of richness and opulence still lay several decades in the future, but the interplay of imperial standards and provincial imitation had begun to reshape the city's physical and cultural landscape.

When Benjamin Mifflin visited from Philadelphia in 1762, he could still write that "the houses are generally Old, Ill Built, but 2 new ones I could See now Building . . . although there are several Large Buildings with capacious Gardens, I did not see One with Any Degree of Elegance or Taste."[27] But the two new buildings under construction symbolized the remarkable change in the town's character and appearance that had started in the previous decade, as wealth generated by several decades of tobacco trade prosperity and the growing market for Maryland wheat began to be spent in the city. By the 1750s, Annapolis had developed a lively social life, with theatrical performances, horse racing for stakes, and balls during the winter social season when delegates to the assembly were joined by their fellow gentry from around the colony. A dozen or more of these men began to build the large Georgian town houses that fostered a self-reinforcing process of development, as each new home made the capital city a more desirable place to be. At the same time, the increased construction activity drew more workers in the building trades and stimulated markets for the wares of craftsmen who could make the furniture to fill the houses, or for merchants whose cargoes included European furniture and decorative arts for those who coveted the highest quality and latest fashion.

By the 1770s, Annapolitans had done the impossible: they had created an urban Chesapeake society whose physical and social environments achieved a measure of success in emulating the standards of the metropolis. Visitors no longer disparaged the houses or the public buildings, but instead observed that "Annapolis . . . is a beautiful town . . . [and] contains a number of exceedingly good buildings."[28] More than one echoed the assessment of Dr. Robert Honyman: "[Annapolis] is larger than Williamsburg & has many fine houses in it. The new State-House . . . is a noble spacious pile of building &

I think in a very good taste."[29] The Reverend Jonathan Boucher, rector of St. Anne's from 1770 to 1772, wrote of Annapolis: "It was then the genteelest town in North America, and many of its inhabitants were highly respectable as to station, fortune and education. I hardly know a town in England so desirable to live in as Annapolis was then."[30]

Most Annapolitans must have regarded the new homes that so impressed the visitors with a mixture of awe, envy, and pride in the progress and refinement of their town. For craftsmen like clockmaker William Faris or silversmith John Inch or saddler Charles Willson Peale or cabinetmaker John Shaw, the new wealth also carried the possibility of increased business for their shops. Even if the wealthiest Annapolitans called upon local silversmiths mostly for repair work, ordered their carriages from England, and continued to import much of their most fashionable furniture, they still spent considerable sums in town that put cash in the pockets of local shopkeepers, tavern owners, artisans, and others who in turn spent that income in one another's businesses.[31] The size of the urban population, numbering from one thousand to thirteen hundred between 1760 and the Revolution; the corresponding density of the local market, enlarged seasonally by legislative and provincial court sessions; and the resulting concentration of purchasing power together succeeded in inverting the Reverend Jones's causal relationship: because the town developed, handicraftsmen settled there.[32]

Over the period between 1655 and 1777, just over four hundred artisans worked in Annapolis (see table 7.2). At first glance, as a group they appear similar to the craftsmen who located both in Talbot and in rural Anne Arundel: they can be assigned to the same broad categories of workers, with woodworkers constituting the largest category in each area. But urban craftsmen differed from rural workers in a number of significant ways, as a comparison between the men *and women* working in Annapolis and in rural Anne Arundel can begin to illuminate (see table 7.3). Rural colonists in Anne Arundel, as in Talbot and other Chesapeake counties, tended largely to be planters, 80 percent of whom earned their living almost exclusively from the land. Perhaps 15 percent followed a profession, kept a tavern, operated a store, worked as laborers, or pursued one of a miscellany of occupations. Approximately 10 percent worked as craftsmen in trades that served the needs of an agricultural community. From the earliest years of settlement, however, the Annapolis occupational structure took a very different shape, with both a greater diversity of occupations and a denser concentration of practitioners within specific

Table 7.2. Living Population of Annapolis Artisans, 1655–1777

Craft Group	1690–1719 No.	1690–1719 %	1720–1739 No.	1720–1739 %	1740–1759 No.	1740–1759 %	1760–1777 No.	1760–1777 %	Total No.	Total %
Carpenters & Joiners	20		25		18		28		68	
Coopers	0		0		2		3		5	
Sawyers	1		1		0		1		2	
Wheelwrights	0		1		2		2		4	
Cabinetmakers	0		0		4		8		12	
Turners	0		0		0		2		2	
Coachmakers	0		0		0		6		6	
Millwrights	0		0		1		1		2	
Instrument Makers	0		0		0		2		2	
Carvers	0		0		0		1		1	
Total Woodworkers	21	47	27	32	27	21	54	26	104	26
Shoemakers	2		7		10		10		26	
Tanners & Curriers	2		3		1		2		8	
Saddlers	2		3		6		8		14	
Glovers	0		1		0		0		1	
Harnessmakers	0		0		0		1		1	
Whipmakers	0		0		1		0		1	
Total Leatherworkers	6	13	14	16	18	14	21	10	51	13
Blacksmiths	1		3		3		9		15	
Brass Founders	0		0		1		2		2	
Silver/goldsmiths	0		7		5		6		16	
Watchmakers	0		1		5		6		11	
Pewterers	0		0		2		0		2	
Tinsmiths	0		0		0		2		2	
Engravers	0		0		1		0		1	
Coppersmiths	0		0		1		0		1	
Anchorsmiths	0		0		0		1		1	
Wireworkers	0		0		1		0		1	
Cutlers	0		1		0		0		1	
Total Metalworkers	1	2	12	14	19	15	26	13	53	13
Tailors	6		7		11		20		41	
Weavers	0		0		0		0		0	
Hatters	0		2		4		5		7	
Staymakers	0		0		4		6		9	
Milliners	0		0		0		5		5	
Stockingmakers	0		0		0		3		3	
Breechesmakers	0		0		1		2		2	
Quilters	0		0		3		0		3	
Collarmakers	0		0		1		0		1	
Total Cloth Trades	6	13	9	11	24	18	41	20	71	18
Bricklayers	3		4		2		14		20	
Plasterers	2		0		0		3		5	
Brickmakers	0		0		0		1		1	
Painters & Glaziers	1		3		2		5		9	
Total Building Trades	6	13	7	8	4	3	23	11	35	9

Ship Carpenters	1		3		9		5		15	
Caulkers	0		0		1		0		1	
Sail Makers	0		1		2		3		5	
Blockmakers	0		0		5		6		9	
Total Ship Building	1	2	4	5	18	14	16	8	32	8
Barbers	1		5		9		8		20	
Printers	1		0		2		3		5	
Bookbinders	0		0		0		3		3	
Total Service Workers	2	4	5	6	11	8	14	5	28	7
Butchers	1		6		7		9		20	
Bakers	0		1		2		5		7	
Brewers	1		0		1		1		3	
Total Food Trades	2	4	7	8	10	8	15	7	30	7
All Crafts	45	98	85	100	131	101	210	100	404	101

Note: For each row, the number of artisans in the four time periods does not equal the total number because some individuals' careers spanned more than one time period. Although many artisans appear in the records with more than one designation (e.g. tanner and currier or carpenter and joiner), no individual was counted in more than one craft.

Source: Adapted from Jean B. Russo, "The Structure of the Anne Arundel County Economy," section 5, Final Project Report, NEH Grant RS-20199-81-1955, "Annapolis and Anne Arundel County, Maryland: A Study of Urban Development in a Tobacco Economy, 1649–1776," table VIII, supplemented by material drawn from Research Files, Historic Annapolis Foundation, prepared by Nancy T. Baker, Research Director, 1972–82.

Table 7.3. Distribution of Occupations, 1665–1777, Decedent Population

	Anne Arundel		Annapolis	
Occupation	N	%	N	%
Planters	1340	83	12	5
Merchants	25	2	33	14
Woodworkers	53	3	32	14
Service trades	7	0	18	8
Professions	31	2	20	9
Government	8	0	17	7
Clothworkers	25	2	16	7
Tavernkeeps	11	1	14	6
Leatherworkers	21	1	13	6
Food trades	6	0	10	4
Building trades	3	0	8	3
Shipbuilders	13	1	5	2
Metalworkers	14	1	4	2
Miscellaneous	51	3	32	14
Total	1608	99	234	101

Source: Adapted from Jean B. Russo, "The Structure of the Anne Arundel County Economy," Section 5, Final Project Report, NEH Grant RS-20199-81-1955, "Annapolis and Anne Arundel Couty, Maryland: A Study of Urban Development in a Tobacco Economy, 1649–1776," table V.

Table 7.4. Urban-Rural Craft Divisions, 1655–1777
(in percent)

Craft Group	Anne Arundel	Annapolis
Woodworkers	74	26
Leatherworkers	52	48
Metalworkers	46	54
Clothing Trades	55	45
Building Trades	45	55
Ship Building	49	51
Service Workers	23	77
Food Trades	29	71

Source: Adapted from Jean B. Russo, "The Structure of the Anne Arundel County Economy," section 5, Final Project Report, NEH Grant RS-90199-81-1955, "Annapolis and Anne Arundel County, Maryland: A Study of Urban Development in a Tobacco Economy, 1649–1776," table VIII.

trades and crafts. In Annapolis, merchants formed the largest noncraft occupational group; planters who chose to reside in town represented just 5 percent of all inhabitants. A larger percentage of men in Annapolis (14%) worked in woodworking trades than worked in *all* crafts combined in the rural parishes (10%). The concentration of urban residents in the other craft sectors, even those strongly associated with rural areas (leather, cloth, and metal trades as well as wood), was similarly higher than in the countryside. Small though it was, Annapolis was nonetheless an urban community: Annapolitans engaged in mercantile, professional, or craft activities.

Early diversification and evolving specialization of the Annapolis occupational structure, culminating in the late colonial period when Annapolis artisans included practitioners of a wide variety of luxury trades and specialties found nowhere else in the Chesapeake except Williamsburg and Baltimore, resulted in two parallel craft structures in Anne Arundel County (see table 7.4). Marked differences existed between specialists catering to the urban environment and those working in the rural hundreds. The luxury trades, not surprisingly, were almost exclusively urban, as well as being late arrivals on the urban scene. The timing of their appearance in Annapolis underscores the reason for their failure to take hold in rural areas: they required a density of population and a level of wealth that even Annapolis did not achieve until late in the colonial period. Not until the 1790s did similar craftsmen begin to appear regularly in Talbot County, and then only with the growth of Easton as a town. Bakers, brewers, and butchers constituted another urban group. Planters and tenant farmers, who raised much of their own food, also processed it themselves; only the town dwellers needed to purchase enough of their food supplies to support purveyors of meat, bread, and alcohol.

Woodworkers, on the other hand, settled predominantly in the rural areas, close to their raw materials and close to the bulk of their customers.[33] Building and repair were continuous activities on rural plantations, with people, crops, and livestock needing to be housed in dwellings, kitchens, quarters, storage buildings, barns, and the like. Local carpenters performed much of the construction work and also made furniture and wooden portions of tools and agricultural implements. Plantations also generated steady customers for coopers' tobacco hogsheads, cider casks, and varied storage containers. Sawyers, the initial processors of wood, tended to live near ready supplies of timber. Together, those three groups in particular situated themselves primarily outside Annapolis.

The remaining craft sectors divided more evenly between rural and urban residence, but within the broad groups individual specialties frequently tended to be more skewed in their distribution. Ship carpenters were somewhat more numerous in the rural hundreds, while blockmakers, caulkers, and ropemakers worked in town. In rural Talbot, ship carpenters tended to do the work of blockmakers and caulkers, and it is likely that a similar lack of specialization occurred in rural Anne Arundel shipyards while a greater division of labor took place in Annapolis yards.[34] Shoemakers settled more heavily in the countryside, but saddlers tended to work in Annapolis. Specialty metal workers, such as brass founders, coppersmiths, and engravers, similarly appeared only in Annapolis, but blacksmiths resided more frequently outside the town. All the weavers lived in rural Anne Arundel, close to neighbors with yarn needing to be woven into cloth, but more specialized workers in clothing-related trades, such as hatters, milliners, quilters, staymakers, and stocking manufacturers, lived in Annapolis.

Tables 7.1 and 7.2 thus look very different, both in the specific trades listed and in the proportions of the total artisan population represented by different craft sectors. Woodworkers, who accounted for just over half the Talbot artisans, made up only one-quarter of the Annapolitans. Annapolis benefited from the services of twice as many metalworkers, but those men tended to be watchmakers or silversmiths, not blacksmiths. Town craftsmen also included twice as many men employed in the building and ship-building trades, drawn by the work of constructing the elegant brick mansions and by the ships calling at the port of entry to clear customs. Twenty barbers and twenty butchers, as well as more bakers and brewers, enabled the service and food trades each to claim a 7 percent share of the town's artisan population. With the exception of Talbot's weavers and its one fuller, all the craftsmen working in Talbot had their counterparts in Annapolis, but the converse was not true. Talbot had no engravers, coppersmiths, pewterers, wire workers, staymakers, stocking or breeches makers, milliners, quilters, rope makers, printers, or brewers. A rural craft population on one side of the bay that was heavily weighted toward building trades faced an urban work force on the other side that found employment in more evenly balanced sectors and more specialized crafts.

The presence in Annapolis of milliners and quilters points to another profound difference between opportunities in rural and urban areas. Only in Annapolis did women have a public presence as craft workers. Talbot women supported themselves and their families through their skill with a needle, but no record ever identified any Talbot woman as a milliner or mantua maker or quilter.[35] Annapolitans such as Elizabeth Crowder, Mary Anne March, Anne Griffith, and Catherine Futier occupied a different place in the local economy. While their work and that of women in Talbot may not have differed much in kind, a significant difference in degree did exist. The Annapolis women often advertised their trades in the newspaper, took in orphan children to be instructed in their skills, appeared in court in suits related to their work, and identified themselves by the craft work they performed.

Anne Griffith advertised quilting, "plain or figured, coarse or fine." In August 1745, Sarah Munro, widow of tailor Major Munro, offered "Quilting of all Kinds, . . . such as Bed Quilts, Gowns, Petticoats, &c. performed at her House in Annapolis, as well as in England, and much cheaper." Munro herself may not have been the quilter, for the following year she advertised for recovery of a runaway "English Convict Servant Woman, named Elizabeth Crowder, by Trade a Quilter." More than a year later, Crowder herself placed a notice in the *Gazette* to advertise her removal "to Mr. Carroll's Quarter . . . where she performs all sorts of Quilting." Mary Anne March sought students to learn "all Sorts of Embroidery," but also advised her Annapolis neighbors that she and her daughter took in "Quilting and any Needle Work, at very cheap Rates."[36] Catherine Futier, a free black woman who worked as a laundress, never advertised in the *Gazette* but undoubtedly acquired her customers by word of mouth. Futier sued Richard Starbue for payment of an account that included charges for twelve months of washing and mending. Futier also listed a payment to Jane Baker for making shirts for Starbue; Baker may have been a free black, working as a seamstress.[37]

Catherine Futier most likely was not the only free laundress working in colonial Annapolis but simply the only one who used the court to collect a debt and so left a record of her presence. She does appear to be, however, the only free black, male or female, documented as working at any trade in Annapolis before the Revolution. The absence of skilled free black craft workers characterized both the rural and urban work worlds. All Talbot artisans during the colonial period were free white males. Not until the 1790s did the first free black artisans appear in county records: Dick Johns, a barber who patronized Jesse Richardson's store in 1792, and hatter Lera Hall, who owned property in Easton and to whom the county court bound a young black boy in July 1796 to be taught the trade of hatter.[38] Joseph Gail, a mulatto carpenter, appeared twice in court in Anne Arundel County in the 1760s. As a defendant in March 1764, Gail received credit in a disputed account for making two scythe cradles; in June he sued merchant Henry Ward to recover six months' wages. His store account with Ward included credits for sawing nearly 1,800 feet of plank and two months of "work in the yard."[39] But Gail had no visible counterparts in Annapolis or even in Anne Arundel until the 1790s and early 1800s. On both sides of the bay, whether in rural or urban areas, free artisans remained exclusively or almost exclusively white.

Elizabeth Crowder's presence in the Munro household points to one area in which urban workshops did not follow the adaptive pattern employed by rural craftsmen. Annapolis artisans much more commonly called upon the labor of journeymen, apprentices, hired workmen, and bound laborers than did men working in Talbot County. In some instances, the additional workers followed their master's trade; in others, they offered related skills that allowed the master to expand his shop's offerings. Only a few years after his arrival in Annapolis about 1763 from Scotland, for example, cabinetmaker John Shaw entered into an agreement with Thomas Johnson to "work with him the said John in the Carpenters Business and Employment for and during the space of one year" for £30 current money wages. That the arrangement proved unsatisfactory, bringing the two men into court, does not alter Shaw's attempt to expand his operation by hiring a workman to assist him. Nor did Shaw abandon such efforts. By the early 1770s, Shaw not only formed a partnership with Archibald Chisholm as "Cabinet and Chairmakers," but their premises also housed Joshua Collins, a

"Musical Instrument-maker and Turner from Manchester," who offered flutes, hautboys, and fifes in addition to turner's work.[40] Similarly, blacksmith John Dennis owned two servants, one also a blacksmith and the other a collier; tailor Robert Pinkney employed enough workmen to give Richard Burland the status of foreman; and blacksmith Cornelius Howard advertised in 1755 that he had "lately engaged one of the best shoers and farriers in the province."[41] William Faris, who arrived in Annapolis from Philadelphia in 1757, over the next twenty years supplemented his own work as a watch and clock maker with the labor of convict servants, journeymen, and at least one slave who crafted clocks, silverware, jewelry, and chairs; in addition he trained three of his four sons as watchmakers, clockmakers, and silversmiths.[42]

The more elaborate organization of urban workshops had the further advantage of permitting someone not trained in a craft to continue the business in the event of the master's death. After the death of Gamaliel Butler, for example, his widow Mary, "having several good blockmakers" on hand, advised Annapolitans that she carried "on the business at the shop of her late husband."[43] When innkeeper Robert Johnson married widow Ann Golder after the death of her cabinetmaker husband, Johnson continued "the cabinet business . . . having furnished himself with the best workmen from London and Philadelphia."[44] Johnson himself needed no woodworking skills, only the ability to supervise the shop and handle the accounts. Talbot widows occasionally operated family craft businesses, but almost always had to rely on the skills of other family members; only rarely did the workshop include an indentured servant or journeyman who continued to fabricate the goods that customers sought.[45]

Similarly, urban entrepreneurs could shift from one craft to another in ways that rural artisans could never approach. William Roberts offers an extreme, but by no means unique, example. Roberts apparently started his career in Annapolis as a carter. In 1740, the indenture leasing a tanyard read "William Roberts, saddler." By 1745, he advertised watch repairs, the work being done by John Powell, an indentured servant. Within two years, Roberts was operating a shipyard, although commission book entries for two ships still identified him as a saddler. No later than 1748, Roberts also opened a dry goods store. In January 1750, Roberts advised his customers of the availability not only of dry goods but also of the services of both a blacksmith and a whitesmith. Nearly three years later, another *Gazette* notice declared that Roberts, no longer engaged in the ship-building business, would now carry on the "smith's business," having lately purchased a whitesmith. Nevertheless, in 1753, Roberts still employed or rented space to sailmaker William Bicknell, suggesting continuation of some ship-related activity. In the same year, Roberts purchased a blacksmith and farrier, possibly to replace John Miles, whom blacksmith Cornelius Howard described as the "late foreman of Mr. Roberts shop" when advertising his services in 1752. In 1755, Roberts also employed Thomas Aldridge, a carpenter and sawyer, and in 1758 acquired a "neat cutler, lately from England." Advertisements placed in the late 1750s described Roberts as carrying on "smith's work and carting, as usual." The final elaboration of his business appeared in a 1760 notice stating that he made "anchors of various sizes and all sorts of smith's work."[46] It would be difficult to declare with precision just what trades or crafts Roberts himself practiced: carter and saddler perhaps, but probably not watchmaker, shipbuilder, smith, carpenter, sawyer, or cutler. It would be even more difficult, though, if not impossible, to describe a similar career pattern for any rural artisan. Among all the craftsmen known to have worked in Talbot County, only one pursued two unrelated skilled crafts during the course of his career, and very few owned or hired additional skilled labor to offer a diverse array of products or services.

But Roberts was not unusual in Annapolis. Among the ships that Roberts owned, in January 1747 he launched one that he named the *Rumney and Long* after the builders, ship carpenters Edward Rumney and Sewell Long. Yet Rumney, the previous July, placed a notice in the *Gazette* that "having furnish'd himself with persons exceedingly well skill'd in the business of making earthen ware, . . . he [had] set up a pottery. . . . with all sorts of pots, pans, juggs, muggs, &c."[47] Gamaliel Butler worked variously as a carpenter, joiner, and cabinetmaker; he acquired the blockmakers who served his wife, as well as "everything necessary for carrying on the Blockmaker's business," in order to furnish blocks, repair pumps, and make carriages for guns.[48] When watchmaker William Knapp left town, silversmith William Whetcroft purchased "the servants lately belonging to Mr. Knapp with all the material for carrying on the watch and clockmaking business."[49] Another silversmith, John Inch, expanded his business in a dizzying array of directions: he "procured a watchmaker" in 1745, acquired a "compleat hand who understands the jeweller's business" in 1758, offered for sale in 1759 the remaining time of a Dutch servant who "understands tanning and currying," advertised a "very good mantua maker" in 1761, "provided himself with a very good house painter and glazier lately from London" in 1762, and owned a "good staymaker" in the same year.[50]

The career of Patrick Creagh encapsulates several of the facets of urban craftsmanship: additional workers to augment the master's skill, diversified workers to expand the shop's products, and continuity after the master's death. Creagh started his career in Annapolis in the 1720s as a painter and glazier, before branching out into ship building, construction, smithing, and trade. His various projects entailed the services not only of painters and glaziers, but also of an array of craft workers, some hired, some apprentices, and some bound servants: glazier George Gold, a convict servant in 1748 and 1749; sailmaker Samuel Osband in 1750; a "good brazier" at his smith's shop in 1751; Welshman David Jones, another convict servant, in 1752; sailmaker William Bicknell in 1753; and coppersmith Robert Rowan in 1756, who worked in Creagh's shop but placed his own notice in the *Gazette.* After Creagh's death in 1760, his son-in-law, merchant Richard Maccubbin, advertised that he carried on "the painting & glasing business at the shop of the late Patrick Creagh, having furnished himself with the proper artificers for those purposes."[51]

Only in the building trades could a master artisan working in Annapolis assemble a labor force that focused solely on a single sector of the craft economy. William Buckland came to the colonies in 1755 as an indentured servant of George Mason. Once released from service in 1759, Buckland worked for a number of wealthy planters on the Northern Neck of Virginia, including John Tayloe II of Mount Airy, whose son-in-law, Edward Lloyd IV, brought Buckland to Annapolis in 1771 to oversee completion of an unfinished town house purchased from Samuel Chase. Buckland then designed and supervised construction of a five-part home directly across the street from Lloyd for Mathias Hammond. During the course of his brief working career in Annapolis, Buckland employed at least sixteen artisans: two carvers, two carpenters, one carpenter and joiner, three joiners, one painter and glazier, five bricklayers, and two plasterers, men whose skilled hands can still be seen in the smooth brickwork, carved cornices, and delicate moldings that grace the two houses. Of these workers, two joiners and two carvers (including one journeyman and two servants, one a convict) accompanied Buckland from Virginia; in Annapolis, Buckland acquired additional indentured and convict servants and employed hired journeymen as well.[52] Buckland's Annapolis career, coming at the peak of the city's period of intensive private and public building, spanned less than four years, ending shortly before the Revolutionary War, and the subsequent eclipse of Annapolis by Baltimore turned the thriving colonial center into a quiet satellite of the burgeoning city on the Patapsco. Had he lived, Buckland too might have been hard-pressed to continue the specialization that served him so well in the early 1770s.

The careers of men like William Roberts, Patrick Creagh, John Inch, and William Faris point to one of the significant adaptive differences between rural and urban artisans. Annapolis was a major metropolis by Chesapeake standards but barely more than a village compared to cities like Philadelphia, Boston, New York, and Charleston. In the limited market offered not only within rural counties but also by the still-small urban center of Annapolis, few artisans could support themselves and their families solely through craft work. In Talbot County, most craftsmen also raised crops and livestock on land they owned or rented. Annapolitans did not have the option of planting tobacco to supplement their earnings, but could more easily diversify the products or services they offered, by keeping a tavern, operating a ferry, or investing in servants with different skills. Faris chose to focus on a cluster of related trades, clock and watch making and silversmithing, while also opening a tavern and briefly adding a chairmaker. Others, like Roberts, Inch, and Creagh, reached out into a wider assortment of businesses.[53] Either strategy, however, existed as a viable option only for the Annapolitans. No rural artisan pursuing similar paths of diversification would have found enough customers for his multiple offerings to warrant the expense of the workers and their tools.

One other characteristic markedly differentiated rural and urban craftsmen: their nativity. Once a predominantly native-born population became established in the late seventeenth century, the great majority of Talbot County's artisans were men born in the county or, less commonly, in the colony. Annapolis, on the other hand, experienced a steady influx of foreign-born artisans, as well as occasional migrants from other colonies. Fifty-eight (14%) of the town's free artisans can be documented as having immigrated to Maryland. Of this group, more than half (37) came from England, with most claiming London as their place of origin or training. Manchester supplied instrument maker Thomas Collins, watchmaker William Allen came from Birmingham, cabinetmaker John Anderson arrived from Liverpool, and sailmaker William Bicknell proudly informed Annapolitans that he had "served his time in his Majesty's Yard at Chatham."[54] Philadelphia made the next largest contribution, supplying nine artisans. Three men came from Ireland, and engraver Joseph Garton arrived from the West Indies. The rest relocated from other colonies, including saddler Henry Meroney from Charleston, cooper Nathaniel Bunker from New England, blockmaker John

Downes from New York, and two ship carpenters, Robert and Samuel Steele, from Salem, Massachusetts.

Immigrant artisans are distinguished by their concentration in the town's luxury and specialized crafts. Of the thirty men working in the food trades, only butcher Samuel Clayton from London immigrated to Annapolis. Just 8 percent of the wood and leather workers came from outside Maryland; with the exception of two coopers, all specialized in luxury branches of their sectors, as a carver or as makers of fine furniture, coaches and harnesses, instruments, and saddles. Immigrants accounted for between 10 and 20 percent of the building and ship building sectors, working as plasterers, painters and glaziers, ship carpenters, sailmakers, and blockmakers. The largest concentrations occurred in metalworking and clothing crafts, where immigrants made up about 25 percent of Annapolis artisans. No blacksmith appears among the non-native group; here again immigrants worked predominantly as silversmiths and watchmakers, as well as supplying both brass founders, and the sole anchorsmith, wire worker, and engraver. Annapolis became a magnet for skilled immigrant workers particularly in the years after 1740. Only three such men appeared between 1720 and 1740, when they represented just 4 percent of working craftsmen. In the following two decades, the number rose to seventeen and accounted for 13 percent of the town's artisans. During the nearly twenty years between 1760 and the Revolutionary War, thirty-seven immigrants swelled the city's population of artisans, contributing 18 percent of the total.

Only Annapolis offered a concentration of population and wealth sufficient to attract artisans seeking to exploit their status as transmitters of metropolitan standards and arbiters of the latest fashions. As newcomers, however, immigrants generally lacked ties to the local community and thus needed to make their presence known as rapidly and as widely as possible. They turned to the pages of the *Maryland Gazette* to announce their arrival, proclaim their knowledge of metropolitan skills and fashions, and solicit patronage from their new countrymen. George White, "painter and glazier from London" informed his neighbors that he "likewise papers rooms in the genteelest and neatest manner." Francis Hepbourne, "cabinet and chair-maker from London" advised that he "makes and sells in the most fashionable mode all kinds of cabinet and chair work." Samuel Rusbatch, a "coach and herald painter . . . and varnisher to their majesties and the royal family," also offered "painting in fresco, . . . decorated ceilings, . . . carved ornaments [and] house-painting."[55] Planters living in rural areas who could afford to patronize such men did so in

Annapolis, when they came to town to deliberate in the Assembly, hear cases in the courts, or conduct business. The ordinary planter relied on the skills of local artisans—native-born men who were their neighbors, friends, and, often, their kin—who did not put notices in the *Gazette* to advertise their services but depended on word-of-mouth and their place within a community network to supply their customers.

Artisans working in Annapolis enjoyed advantages not available to their counterparts in the rural tidewater region. They served a larger and much wealthier clientele, drawn from both town residents and members of the provincial elite who visited for governmental, business, or social purposes. This broader and more affluent patronage base supported a far wider range of craftsmen than did rural customers, enabling practitioners of an array of luxury trades to find sufficient customers for their wares. At the same time, the greater concentration of demand both encouraged operation on a larger scale than practiced in the countryside, with employment of additional trained workmen, and expanded opportunities for diversification into unrelated craft or business areas. Annapolis masters also benefited from the steady supply of bound laborers and journeymen who arrived in the port, just as new arrivals kept Annapolis consumers abreast of the latest metropolitan fashions and tastes. The steady infusion into the Annapolis workplace of men trained in the metropolis thus played a critical role in the town's development as the "genteelest . . . in North America." In Annapolis and the other small urban centers that developed toward the end of the colonial period, Chesapeake settlement finally achieved the conjunction of towns and handicraftsmen whose earlier absence had so dismayed the Reverend Hugh Jones.

The settlement of a land new to Europeans, devoid of familiar resources and institutions, necessitated an ongoing process of adjustment, accommodation, and adaptation. Within the contours of a colonial world shaped by the tidewater area's many waterways, the dispersed settlement fostered by tobacco cultivation, and the extensive trade networks of the Atlantic economy, colonists devised new ways of creating old forms. Both rural and urban areas faced this challenge, but solved it with different responses. Rural craftsmen practiced the same trades as did village artisans in rural England and accounted for similar proportions of the working population.[56] After the earliest years they were, for the most part, men native to the region, linked to their customers by ties of kinship and neighborhood. To accommodate the small size of their market and the limited pool of labor, Talbot artisans organized their workshops on a comparable scale, relying primarily on family members and apprentices for assistance, and worked as generalists within the disciplines of their raw materials. Urban artisans, on the other hand, exhibited characteristics more typical of their counterparts in English towns and cities: they pursued a wider range of trades, including luxury crafts virtually unknown in the countryside, and utilized larger workforces with more gradations of skill and training. In contrast to the rural craftsmen, who supplemented craft work with agricultural pursuits, they capitalized on greater opportunities for diversification into other fields. Their numbers included a markedly higher percentage of immigrant men and women than settled in the rural Tidewater. These newcomers arrived with few, if any, ties to the community, but with a local newspaper through which to announce their presence and to use the currency of their knowledge of metropolitan styles to bring customers to their doors.

Urban artisans provided one affirmation of metropolitan culture when they built the Georgian mansions, stitched the velvet suits, hammered the fluted silver soup ladles, carved the decorative moldings, and crafted the double harpsichords that catered to the needs of the region's gentry families. The rural craftsmen who mended tools, wove cloth, stitched shoes, fabricated barrels, and built tobacco houses offered a very different but no less important validation of the colonists' success in replicating the material culture of the metropolis. In their pursuit of the "art and mystery" of their trades, rural and urban craftsmen together produced the artificially made goods whose presence signified not an inchoate wilderness but a civilized society, despite the "fewnesse" of its towns.[57]

CHAPTER EIGHT

The Other "Susquahannah Traders"

Women and Exchange on the Pennsylvania Frontier

James H. Merrell

Have "thy Good wife . . . interpret": Re-viewing the Fur Trade

In the winter of 1748 two Moravian colonists, Bishop J. C. F. Cammerhoff and Joseph Powell, set out from Bethlehem on the Delaware River. They were bound for Shamokin, an Indian village at the Forks of the Susquehanna River where Moravians had a mission. Battling bitter cold and deep snow, ignoring locals en route who advised them to await better weather, the two pushed on, protected by "a special Providence." Among the providential signs of good fortune was that the travelers, no woodsmen, were able to "follow a trail [up the Susquehanna's east bank] left in the snow by . . . two Indian squaws, who lived fifty miles above Shamokin." Having visited a colonial mill just upriver from John Harris's trading outpost (modern Harrisburg), the native women were homeward bound. Passing these two, the famished, frozen colonists staggered into Shamokin at dawn on January 14, to be welcomed by Martin and Anna Mack, the missionaries stationed there. Two days later, still settling in, Powell had a visit from Esther Harris, widow of the first John Harris (their son now operated the family trading post and ferry). "Mrs. Harris" ran a store that winter not far from Shamokin.[1]

Esther Harris and those two Indian women were by no means unique. Perhaps, as Cammerhoff and Powell defrosted, the Macks mentioned how, visiting Shamokin three years earlier, they had met "French Margaret," of the well-known métis family of Montours, who with her Mohawk husband was passing through town en route to Philadelphia, driving ten packhorses laden with deerskins.[2] Nor was Esther Harris the first Pennsylvania woman to venture into the Indian countries bordering the province. More than half a century before her, Anne Le Tort—wife of one fur peddler, mother of another, herself a prominent trader—was living "remote in the woods" on her own.[3]

Even colonial women who did not venture out among Indians found that Indians often came to them, as a visit to a frontier settlement near the Susquehanna between Anne Le Tort's day and Esther Harris's reveals. One March morning in 1722, for example, Elizabeth Cartlidge "grieved almost to Distraction": an Indian had been killed, and now provincial officials were hauling her husband John, a trader, off to Philadelphia for questioning. As John was led away, "the Woman's sorrows being loud," several local Conestoga Indians, led by their headman, Tagotolessa (Civility), "went in [to the Cartlidge home] to comfort her."[4] Six years later, when Pennsylvania leaders wanted to talk to Tagotolessa about diplomatic business, they sent word to Adam Cornish, another fur trader out there, asking "that Eliz Cornish, who speaks the [Indians'] language, should privately between themselves enter into as close a discourse as possible with Civility about what news he hears or what he knows."[5]

Such moments speak volumes about everyday encounters between Pennsylvania women and native peoples. Since Tagotolessa spoke no English, his comfort either came by signs or else Elizabeth Cartlidge, like Elizabeth Cornish, spoke Conestoga. We do know that Mrs. Cornish not only knew that language but was more fluent than her own husband, for provincial authorities seeking a translator would tell him to have "thy Good Wife . . . interpret ye inclosed [letter] to" the Conestoga sachem.[6] We can only imagine the web of hidden contact that coaxed those Indians across the Cartlidge threshold to console a distraught woman and that dispatched Elizabeth Cornish to pump Tagotolessa for information.

Elizabeth Cartlidge and Elizabeth Cornish sitting down with that headman, Esther Harris running that store, Margaret Montour driving that packhorse train down the Susquehanna, two "squaws" headed the opposite way after visiting that colonial mill—these women fail to fit prevailing notions about exchange between colonists and Indians. The "fur trade," a catchphrase for the grand enterprise that (even before Frederick Jackson Turner launched his career by studying it) has been a central feature of American life and lore, has long had a simple plot: colonial men of dubious reputation ventured deep into Indian country to swap European goods for furs and skins native hunters brought. If recent scholars have made Indian and métis women more prominent players on the fur-trade stage, the older script, nonetheless, has kept its hold on the imagination.[7]

Bringing to light the likes of Margaret Montour and Elizabeth Cornish is hardly going to break that grip. But pondering their implications—the wider, deeper patterns of interaction they hint at—can do more than add a few names to the growing list of female traders, thereby further challenging conventional wisdom of the fur trade as a man's world. It also contributes to recent rethinking of the very term *trade,* recasting that seemingly simple word into something more complicated, more elastic, more inclusive—and more accurate a reflection of frontier realities.

In addition, awarding women other than cameo roles permits further consideration of two powerful metaphors that have captivated students of the colonial borderlands. Richard White introduced the first in 1991: exploring the Great Lakes region, White argued that natives and colonists fashioned a "middle ground," a physical and cultural space where creative understandings—and misunderstandings—enabled disparate peoples to get along, to swap ideas and goods, to forge diplomatic alliances and sexual liaisons. The second, coined by Kathleen Brown two years later, invited scholars to "think of cultures in contact as interacting along a *gender frontier,*" a site "of fierce contests for power" where one "gender system" collided with another.[8]

Both metaphors offer native women a leading role. They were, writes White, "in many ways the most influential creators of the middle ground," and Brown chronicles how Powhatan women were key figures on the gender frontier.[9] Neither middle ground nor gender frontier, however, has much to say about colonial women, any more than most studies of colonial women weave natives into their interpretive fabric. Yet because exchange brought women from colonial and Indian settlements onto the same stage, setting Anne Le Tort and Esther Harris alongside those two Indians in the Susquehanna snows is not only more faithful to the past, it not only prompts further explication of two evocative metaphors, it has the added advantage of pulling together in fruitful ways two heretofore distinct strands of scholarly inquiry.

Considering these women side by side suggests that trade, which engaged people in a common pursuit, nonetheless did not eliminate the divide between native and newcomer. Trade was indeed a precinct of the middle ground, a place where people from different worlds gathered to fashion mechanisms of exchange. But study of Susquehanna women traders reveals that few, if any, venturing onto that ground forgot where they came from or planned to stay long. Nor did the involvement of Indian and colonial women in exchange erase the gender frontier. Training bifocal lenses on the Susquehanna trade suggests that these women went about their business differently and kept a certain distance from one another.

"The *Common Course* of the *Indians* with their *Skins* and *Furr's*": The Susquehanna Valley

The Susquehanna Country is as good a place as any in colonial British North America (and better than most) to pick up women's tracks on the trading path. One appealing feature is size: the vast territory drained by the Susquehanna's two great streams, called by colonists the North and West branches, offers a large canvas on which to work. Another attraction drawing attention to the Susquehanna is its enduring centrality to intercultural exchange. Soon after William Penn started his colony in 1682, he learned that this thoroughfare was already "the *Common Course* of the *Indians* with their *Skins* and *Furr's* into our Parts . . . from the *West* and *Northwest* parts of the *continent.*"[10] To tap this flow of goods, several years later a French Huguenot named Jacques Le Tort arrived with his wife Anne and started trading with Indians, including Conestogas inhabiting the Susquehanna's lower reaches.[11]

Trade boomed as various groups—Conoys, Tuteloes, and Nanticokes from the south, Shawnees from the west, Delawares from the east, Iroquois from the river's headwaters—joined Conestogas there.[12] The Le Torts and other Pennsylvania traders moved to the banks of the Susquehanna itself around 1700 in order to be closer to these customers. Thereafter, even as Pennsylvanians followed the Indians (who in turn followed the game) up the Susquehanna into Iroquoia and westward across the Allegheny Mountains into the Ohio Country, they kept their Susquehanna River base and referred to themselves as "Susquahannah traders."[13] Not even the terrible frontier war that erupted in the 1750s could extinguish trade. At the behest of its Indian allies, Pennsylvania in 1756 opened a store under the walls of Fort Augusta, the colony's new bastion at the Susquehanna Forks, where Shamokin had stood. As late as 1763, Margaret Montour's daughter Catherine was following in her mother's footsteps, passing Forks and fort to swap goods with colonists farther downstream. Before the American Revolution, however, such rounds became a thing of the past. Nonetheless, trade's long life there offers an opportunity for studying the role women played in it over a span of time stretching from Anne Le Tort in the 1680s to Catherine Montour three generations later.

"Came Mrs Harris with three Traders": Retrieving Women from the Records

Even with the vast Susquehanna domain to explore and a century's span to traverse, it is hard to bring women traders out of the shadows. Colonial record keepers, almost always male, were so accustomed to thinking of traders as men that women earned scarcely a mention. Consider those two Indian women along the Susquehanna in January 1748. Cammerhoff said nothing more about them, even though the two were breaking trail for him, yet he went on at length about meeting a "large company of [male] traders at [John] Harris's."[14] The bishop's traveling companion, Joseph Powell, suffered from similar myopia. "Came Mrs Harris with three Traders," he wrote in his journal one day, omitting her from the ranks of "Traders" even though he knew she ran that store nearby.[15]

Provincial officials were no better than Christian missionaries at noticing native women, often labeling them only *Kyentarrah's wife* or *Job Chilloway and his wife* (or *his sister*).[16] Account books kept by colonial traders might perform the same sort of disappearing act. *Loossemans Wife, Mohican John's Sister, John Hill's Mother, The Hatt's Grandaughter, Woman with Hans Michael, Opihelay's Old Wife and young Wife*—these and other Indian women shall forever remain nameless.[17]

But if many pages of a ledger betray that blinkered male gaze, they also reveal that Indian women—*wife, daughter, sister; a Woman, a Squaw, an Old Woman*—were indeed walking into a trading post and striding up to the counter.[18] Nor were they all anonymous adjuncts to some man; many bore sobriquets akin to those of Indian men, ranging from tribal to Christian to descriptive names to monikers whose origins can only be imagined. With *Nanteycook Will* and *Connay Man* can be found *Mohickon Moll* and *The Mohickan Woman*, just as *Cate* and *Peggy* reside there with *Isaac* and *Jacob; Poet* came into the Fort Augusta trading post, and six weeks later *A Woman Poet* stopped by; *The Pockmarked Man, The Big Eard Fellow,* and *The One-Eyed Man* shared ledgers with *The Big Woman, the Flat-nosed woman,* and *The Strong Woman.*[19] Moreover, while many women were indeed identified (and obscured) by their relation to a man, the identity (and the obscurity) sometimes went the other way. *Mingo Man with Peggey, Malley's Husband, Bettys Bill, Burnt Woman's Son, Nance Sister's Husband, The farting Womans family*—clearly women of every sort of name, and many more given no name at all, were no strangers to intercultural exchange.[20]

Thus while women, native and colonial, are hard to see, they are not invisible. If their trail is hard to follow, nonetheless traces remain. Gathering what tantalizing glimpses and evocative moments survive, it is possible to suggest something of women's work, their lives, as "Susquahannah traders."

"I . . . gave the old grey headed mother 24 needles and six shoe strings. . . . She immediately gave me five small loaves": Redefining Trade

Recent scholars have argued that "the fur trade" as conventionally considered was actually, to natives, only part of a denser matrix of exchange that went well beyond account books, well beyond deerskins for matchcoats—and well beyond the standard scenario that has a colonial trader (male) sitting down amid piles of merchandise to haggle with an Indian hunter (also male). Such stock scenes, Richard White insists, cannot be "segregated from the wider spectrum of social relations and exchanges between Indians and whites."[21] That spectrum stretched in two different directions from the fur trade as it is usually understood. In both, women played a prominent part.

One direction led into foreign policy. Indians, drawing no sharp distinction between trade and diplomacy, often spoke of treaties and traders in the same sentence. The overlap was tangible: to Indians, negotiation without objects to make a point and cement a friendship was unthinkable, for these objects were powerful symbols of amity. If to provincial leaders it looked more like bribery than diplomacy, natives considered merchandise essential grease in the diplomatic machinery.

The people handing over the goods and making the speeches were almost always men, but women were never far from a treaty ground. Most Indian diplomatic delegations included (usually unnamed) women, and these women were deeply involved in the exchange. Some did a little trading on the side: in Philadelphia one day in 1712 the spouse of a Delaware headman left the council proceedings long enough to sell ten fisher pelts and an otter coat to a merchant, and in 1755 an Iroquois diplomat's wife in the same city got sixty pieces of eight for some deerskins she "gave" to a provincial official.[22] Other women at treaties picked up personal gifts or money, and still others left with rewards for "Services . . . to this Government." In 1728 Margaret Montour's aunt, the "celebrated" Madame (Isabelle) Montour, earned five pounds for advising colonists, and at councils a generation later Margaret herself received compensation—four kegs of rum, a horse, some cash—from grateful governors.[23]

Even when they stayed in the background, unnoticed (and unrewarded) by colonists, native women were leading actors on the diplomatic stage. By their very presence, as well as by their production of the pelts or wampum belts an Indian ambassador handed over to give his words weight, Indian women signified their consent to the proceedings. At councils in Indian country, too, women had an important if overlooked part. Preparing and serving the meals that punctuated negotiations, stringing the requisite wampum—without saying a word that found its way onto the page, Indian women were participating in the exchange of goods and ideas that lay at the heart of international relations.[24]

While their colonial counterparts had no comparable role in the diplomatic script, they were not altogether absent. Whenever a treaty convened in Pennsylvania, local women played hostess to native delegations. At the provincial capital in 1734, for example, Esther Hansen looked after twenty-three people—old and young, men and women—for more than a week, supplying everything from salt and turnips to bread and beer, from cordwood and candles to cabbage and pasturage. Even when a man submitted to provincial officials the accounts for bed and breakfast, it is unlikely that he was the one doing all the work.[25] Such receipts hint at a lost world of everyday contact between colonial women and natives. Isabelle Montour once mentioned that she often visited Philadelphia during councils and "was there very much caressed by the gentle women of that city, with whom she used to stay for some time."[26] Yet no record of those stays has survived.

Such habits of hospitality were not confined to diplomatic delegations, and this is the other direction in which "the fur trade" tended: toward encounters so mundane they were beneath the notice of colonial record keepers. As with trade and diplomacy, Indians drew no distinction between ordinary hospitality to anyone who happened by and the more formal trade sessions that so preoccupied colonists (and still preoccupy historians); both usually involved exchange of goods and services.[27] In the Susquehanna Country, native women took the lead in helping travelers. "Our Hostess set Victuals immediately before us" was a common refrain, as local women prepared cakes or bread, watermelon or venison for a hungry guest.[28] A colonist might call these gifts, but an experienced hand made sure he had something in his pack to repay the hostess.[29] When one colonial traveler gave a native woman "knives and thimbles" for "some spits full of venison," when another "gave the old grey headed mother 24 needles and six shoe strings" and she "immediately gave me five small loaves," the line between hospitality and trade blurs.[30]

Something that looked similar occurred when tables were turned and Indians ventured into colonial settlements. Traders with their wares, warriors heading home from a campaign, ambassadors en route to Philadelphia—these and other native travelers routinely stopped at Pennsylvania houses. Some lingered for a meal or a night; others stayed a few days; still others, falling ill—Owisgera, an Onondaga at the diplomat Conrad Weiser's frontier home in Tulpehocken; Kissakochquilla, a Shawnee headman at the trader Thomas McKee's Susquehanna place—stayed a season or more.[31] That the woman of the house was responsible for entertaining such guests can be assumed, even if her daily duties cannot be recovered. Doubtless most guests stayed outside—droves of Indian men, women, and children came so often to John Harris's entrepôt that he built board huts for them—but some had the run of the house, sleeping before the fire or sitting in some corner. As a result, many colonial women were, as Weiser said of his daughter Margaret, "somewhat used to the Indians."[32]

As the nursing of Kissakochquilla and Owisgera suggests, "hospitality"—the gift of food and lodging—shaded off into other activities, themselves forms of exchange. Like Weiser's wife Anna and McKee's wife Mary, Indian women nursed wayfarers, a "kindness" those men, once recovered, "remembered" with something tangible.[33] Other native women found a Pennsylvania trader's canoe or stored his wares, ferried him across the Susquehanna or fetched his horse—and might get something in return for the favor.[34]

Sometimes those favors were sexual, and here again the boundary with trade is more porous than usually thought.[35] The best evidence comes from Nicholas Cresswell, an Englishman starting out as a fur trader in the Ohio

Country in 1775. Cresswell's unusually candid account suggests how easily hospitality could take on new meaning in Indian country. Lost in the woods one day, he stumbled upon an Indian camp of three women and a boy. While "The youngest Girl immediately" looked after his horse and spread his blankets by the fire so he could sit down, the eldest made him a meal. That night, with the two women and boy discreetly "some distance away," "the youngest (she [who] had taken so much pains with my horse) came and placed herself very near me," then "began to creep nearer me and pulled my Blanket." Next morning, his "Bedfellow" found and saddled his horse, then guided him through the woods to his destination, receiving "a match coat" at parting. A few days later, Cresswell and his partner paired up with two Indian women, a connection that lasted more than a month. "Our Squaws are very necessary," he announced contentedly, "fetching our horses to the Camp and saddling them, making our fire at night and cooking our victuals, and every other thing they think will please us."[36]

Such arrangements would have been familiar in the Susquehanna Country. When, one summer's night at Shamokin in 1743, a rowdy band of Indians banged on a Pennsylvania trader's door and demanded rum, it was that trader's "squaw" who got out of bed to make the sale and send the revelers back into the darkness.[37] Fifteen years later another trader, Lawrence Burke, left his Delaware wife on the river's North Branch, where he had lived for several years, to visit the provincial capital.[38] How many other colonists made similar arrangements with an "occasional wife" is unknown. But when at one town "a drunken *Squaw*" came into the visitors' dwelling "frequently complimenting us and singing" while at another women were "infesting us with their company and bawling, in great good humour," it is likely that natives looking to swap sex for goods often made advances on colonial men, and that some of those advances were welcomed. The silence in the records might bespeak a colonist's reluctance to admit that he let the blanket be pulled off. Even Cresswell repeatedly felt compelled to defend his dalliances, admitting that "however base it may appear to conscientious people, it is absolutely necessary to take a temporary wife if [you] have to travel amongst the Indians."[39]

It seems like a long way from a Philadelphia council chamber to Nicholas Cresswell's bedroll. But a more elastic—and more realistic—definition of "trade" embraces all of this and then some. It was all exchange, all intercourse, whether diplomatic or sexual, whether lodging or nursing—and in all of it, women were near the center of things.

Nonetheless, the differences between native women and their colonial counterparts are striking. In the diplomatic realm, native women were essential. If their contribution was subtle, it was no less real for that, and it was in stark contrast to a colonial housewife, who had virtually no role beyond bed and board.[40] In the culture of hospitality, too, Indian and colonial women were worlds apart. Both fed, housed, and otherwise looked after foreigners. But a native woman setting food before a colonist did so out of a deeply rooted ethic of hospitality. If customary gift-giving brought this act closer to exchange, it remained a long ways from what a colonial hostess did: submit receipts to provincial officials in order to get reimbursed for every loaf of bread and jug of beer. Nor, as far as the records reveal, were colonial women as sexually adventurous as their native counterparts; no Pennsylvania woman crept toward an Iroquois or Delaware guest in the night.

Further testimony to the distance between Indian and colonial women can be found in the fate of those who did forge a liaison with a provincial trader. No colonist who took up with a native woman brought her to live in Pennsylvania. The "squaw" at that trader's Shamokin hut in 1743 never went with him to dwell on some colonial farm, nor did Lawrence Burke's Delaware spouse accompany him down the Susquehanna to Philadelphia. Thomas McKee's wife Mary, who did at least live on Pennsylvania's border, was the exception that proved the rule. Colonists, though occasionally calling her "an Indian wench," often enough considered her a white captive raised by Shawnees. Perhaps rumors of her natal identity gave her limited immunity to Indian-hating, enough at least to enable her to live where no native woman dared.[41]

"Several Indian Squaws Come into the House": Indian Women as Fur Traders

Even by conventional notions of the fur trade, that well-known portion of the spectrum of exchange, native women were more deeply involved than scholars usually assume. Men did the hunting, but trade was a family affair: kinfolk of both sexes and all ages made for hunting camps in winter; come spring they packed up and headed out to peddle the hunt's harvest.[42] Families were such a customary trading entity that Delaware diplomats keen to improve exchange with Pennsylvania talked of "Desiring . . . an open & free passage . . . for them, *their Wives & Children*, . . . yt they may Come to Buy & sell with" colonists.[43] And come they did. A Delaware man, along with his wife and two children, bearing furs to a frontier settlement; Mohawk and Delaware families back from another with horses hauling sacks of grain; clusters of Indian women, children, and men on shopping expeditions were a feature of the Pennsylvania landscape.[44]

Some Indian diplomats went beyond just mentioning native women to suggest that these women actually were shrewder than men, better able to fend off unscrupulous Pennsylvanians. Colonial traders "go up into the Countrey beyond their [Indian] Towns," intercept hunters en route home, then get them drunk and cheat them out of all their peltry "before they get home to their wives," complained some headmen in 1706, as if those waiting wives would put a stop to such shenanigans. Delawares are "in the Dark" when it comes to swapping goods with Pennsylvania, lamented one leader a decade later, and they feel "wholly ignorant how they had been Dealth [*sic*] with, or how they should Trade." Please explain colonial trading terms, he went on, so "that . . . they might at any time send their wives [in their stead] & be out of Danger of being cheated."[45]

Given these sentiments, no wonder native women also can be found trading on their own, not merely as a stand-in for a befuddled or addled husband, as part of a family, or as a Shamokin shop girl for some colonial trader. Take, for example, one December Saturday in 1760 at the Fort Augusta trading post. Capt. Peter, Nesheconickon, Keekechemo, Sunfish, and Aquatchenauy—all probably men—showed up that day to trade. But so did Salley, Nanse, and, near the close of business, two more Indians, both labeled "A Woman." Carrying venison and bearskins, tallow and fishers, these two left with goods ranging from saddles and bridles to blankets and matchcoats, from powder and lead to salt and flour, from bed lace and shirts to combs and awls. Of the ten customers that winter day, at least four were women, and those four bought more goods than the six other Indian traders combined.[46]

Or consider a summer's day at the same store in 1762, which began with one Indian woman plunking a dollar down on the counter for some rum. Then, around noon, the clerk struck a bargain with another in which she would "line a pair of plush britches" with "a thin Indian dress'd winter Skin," receiving in exchange some liquor to fill the bottle she carried. That evening saw a second visit from the would-be seamstress and, one observer reported, "several Indian Squaws" who had "Come into the [storekeeper's] House."[47]

Like those two unnamed women visiting a mill in the dead of winter in 1748, women from Indian country often pressed past the Susquehanna Forks and ventured into colonial neighborhoods to trade. Some had more than a miller's grain in mind; what to some colonists seemed an alarming number of them were after liquor. Provincial officials fretted that women from Susquehanna towns were "Coming to Philadelphia to Purchase & Carry up Rum," then "sell it amongst Their own People at excessive rates." Female liquormongers were so common that in 1731 Delaware leaders asked Pennsylvania "that some Rum may be lodged at Tulpyhockin & Pextan [Harris's], to be sold to them, that *their Women* may not have too long a way [to go from home] to fetch it." Whether this became provincial policy, it certainly was native custom to have women drive horses laden with kegs back into Indian country.[48]

"His Wife's trade": Colonial Women in the Trade

Pennsylvania women were equally busy. With husbands away for weeks, sometimes months at a stretch, wives ran the farm, home, and business.[49] Besides dealing with Indians who might stop by, these women left home, too, to deliver skins and pick up merchandise. If Anne Le Tort drew stares when she showed up in some Philadelphia store to swap hides from deer, bear, raccoon, elk, and otter for powder and lead, hatchets and jew's harps, beads and kettles, no gawking or whispering found its way into the record, probably because such a sight was so common. After all, her daughter-in-law Elizabeth went, too, as did James Patterson's wife Susanna and Henry Bailey's wife Martha.[50]

Back home, trading women were vital channels in the flow of goods and information across the frontier. In September 1730, anxious to get a better return on his investment, the Philadelphia merchant James Logan dispatched his protégé Edward Shippen to the Susquehanna to track down delinquent traders and funnel their wares Logan's way. "Call on Edm. Cartlidge . . . & know ye reason his Skins are not sent down. . . . See also H[enry] Baily's Wife & engage her to hasten down what she can."[51] Similarly, when Martha Bailey got instructions from Henry, still in Indian country, she would write to merchants in the capital to order the additional wares.[52] So extensive was such participation that women sometimes seemed to be trading on their own. Ask Jonah Davenport, Logan wrote Shippen one fall, what happened to the "effects he had for his Wife's trade."[53]

The first Susquehanna traders, the Le Torts, set the precedent. At times Anne operated so independently that Jacques, often away for years, faded into the background. In December 1693 one colonist mentioned "ryding by the house *of madam* Le Tort," and two months later she, too, talked of "*her* hous," going on to say that "the Indians are much indebted *to her.*" Meanwhile a native reported "that hee hath seen some strange Indians come to trade *with her.*" Summoned to vouch for these strangers, Anne Le Tort stood before the Pennsylvania Council—once on her own, once with her husband—to testify. Jacques stood silently by, apparently uttering no protest at talk of *her* house, *her* debt, *her* trade.[54]

Such women developed a confidence bred of capability. Martha Bailey, for example, addressed Edward Shippen about goods her husband wanted in a manner belying the fact that this merchant, prominent in his own right, worked for Logan, the most powerful man in the province. "I have heard from my Husband this week . . . ," she wrote, "and he desires me to write to you for 60 or 70 gallons of Rum which he will have Ocasion for[;] here is Now a Good Opportunity of Sending itt up and if you think proper to Send itt[,] well[,]" she went on; but "if not[,] I Desire ye favour of you Send me word that I may not be disapointed[,] for itt must be provided Some other place." Though she closed on a gentler note—"wth Respects to you & your family"—her request bordered on a demand.[55]

Shippen might not have liked the tone, but he and Logan literally and figuratively gave credit where credit was due: some women, they knew, had a head for business. When the Susquehanna trader James Hendricks lived with his wife, Mary, on leased land in an arrangement they worked out with Logan, the merchant was as confident of her abilities as he was worried about her husband's. "It is on *her* diligence and Care we Chiefly depend for the Rent," Logan fretted, "and E Shippen assures me I may Safely." When Mary dies, though, terminate the lease with the widower, for "I am Morally Sure that he cannot or at least will not so comply" with the agreement as well as she had done.[56]

Apparently these women were nothing compared to Esther Harris, whose reputation lived on for a century and more. "She was . . . the best trader of the two," her grandson recalled in the 1830s, reminiscing about Esther and her husband John. "Resolute, masculine, capable of writing," she was also a crack shot and a fine swimmer who could cover astonishing distances on horseback or by canoe. When not tearing pell-mell down some road or river, she "would box Indian chiefs' ears if they got drunk and unruly."[57]

Sharp, shrewd traders, with their husbands or on their own—here colonial and Indian women seem to have much in common. Yet in many ways their trading was profoundly dissimilar. Travel itineraries bear witness to the world of difference between a Margaret Montour and a Martha Bailey. Bailey might go to Philadelphia, but neither she nor any other Pennsylvania women besides Anne Le Tort and Esther Harris went in the opposite direction to trade in Indian country.[58] Colonial women involved in exchange—not alone or in pairs, not with husbands or children—virtually never ventured into a distant Indian village in the way that native women—alone, with other women, with kinsmen and children—so often headed for Pennsylvania.

"She . . . proceeded to insult them very rudely": Unruly Women

Esther Harris boxing Indian ears? Unlikely, but not impossible. Some women traders, native and colonial alike, were known for strong words and, occasionally, stronger deeds. If Esther Harris never cuffed an Indian, in 1737 county authorities did charge her with assault and battery on one David Priest. Mary Hendricks faced the same charges for attacking another man, and she seems to have annoyed a lot of people. "I am Sensible James [Hendricks]'s Wife . . . has been so unhappy in her Conduct as to stand but meanly in the Opinion of many," wrote James Logan elliptically in 1739.[59]

Anne Le Tort made folks unhappier still. In 1712 some Conestogas paid "a friendly visit to the old french women [*sic*], M. L. Torts' house; that without any provocacon she turned them out of doors, . . . & proceeded to insult them very rudely." Two decades earlier it was colonists who felt her wrath. In 1693 the fur traders Polycarpus Rose, Mounce Yokum, and Thomas Jenner were "ryding by the house of madam Le Tort" and "asked her hou shee did." "Where have you been," she demanded. Told they came from Peter Yokum's, another trader, Le Tort was furious. That fellow had been stealing her customers: though "the Indians are much indebted to her & Little to peter yokum," she later explained, yet "he came before her hous with Rum, & therwith enticed the Indians from her." Losing her business, she now lost her temper: "ther was no path for sweads or English rogues there," she cried, "for no English Rogue nor swead should come on her ground," then "run in a furie with a horse whipp &" drove off the terrified trio.[60]

Apparently Elizabeth Le Tort, James's wife, could be as formidable as her mother-in-law. In 1722 a grand jury charged that Elizabeth had stripped from Anne Le Tort's corpse a woolen petticoat, a linen girdle, and a silver buckle.[61] The hearing's outcome is unclear, as is exactly what dynamics—between Elizabeth and Anne, between Elizabeth and James, between Elizabeth and her neighbors—brought this to the authorities. That all was not well in the Le Tort marriage, however, is suggested by another cryptic document. "I think J Le [Tort] may venture into the woods with the Goods Sent up for him," wrote James Logan to Edward Shippen one fall day, "which thou may order into his hands." Getting Le Tort the merchandise and dispatching him westward were not going to be easy, however. For one thing, "Having borrow'd a horse that Stray'd from him . . . , he is on foot & wants . . . Shoes." For another, "He must keep out of Sight for fear of his Wif[e]"; she has sent someone "to look sharp after him," Logan concluded, so "assist him, for he must keep private."[62] The image of a cowed James Le Tort—unhorsed, unshod, hiding from his spouse—is one to conjure with, but nothing more can be said. At the very least, it further suggests that it was unwise to trifle with Elizabeth Le Tort.

Whether Logan was amused or alarmed by James Le Tort's plight is unclear. Certainly he was accustomed to trading with formidable women, who sometimes had as many transactions with him as their husbands did. But a woman with a head for business whom Logan might rely upon one year could also give him no end of trouble the next. When the Philadelphia merchant set about taking a trader's farm for overdue debts, he found the wife sometimes more trouble than the husband.[63] Certainly Jonah Davenport's spouse worked hard to keep the family home out of Logan's grasp. "I shall alwayes have a very due regard to the woman," an exasperated Logan wrote in 1731 as he sought to keep the Davenports from trying "to secure what they can from me" to avoid foreclosure; "but to be plain I am doubtful in ye mean time she will have too much [regard] for herself, & endeavour to convert what is by no means their own."[64] Three years later, the slippery Jonah Davenport finally gave up and signed over his farm to the merchant for debts past due. But the law required the wife's consent, too, and that, Jonah predicted, was not going to be easy. "Jonah tells me," Logan warned his agent on the Susquehanna, "he doubts [not] his Wife will make some Scruple" about signing, "& [he] will want thy Assistance to prevail with her. But," Logan went on sternly, "if she hesitates[,] be pleased to assure her from me that I Shall immediately cause the Sheriff to take both that [farm] & everything else by Execution, for I can doe it any day and she may take her choice of having it done in that public and very expensive manner, without having any title or pretence to farther favour, or in this Amicable quiet way, wch will still leave room for me to shew my regard to ye family."[65] Logan leaves to the imagination the scene at the Davenport house the day that Jonah, Logan's man, and the deed showed up.

When it was the Baileys' turn to pay up, Logan fretted that he would not be able to force Henry to sell horses and send the proceeds to Philadelphia. True, Martha had assured Logan's agent "that her husband would come and sign his Consent for the Sale of the Creatures," but Logan had his doubts. "They are a vile Couple," he stormed, "and if there be any difference, I think the advantage by no means lies on her Side."[66] And so it went, Logan lamented: Samuel Smith's wife at his door to complain about land, Susanna Patterson coming with her husband to sign a deal and then, widowed, trying to renege on it in order "to get the money into her own hands." The same skills that made these women effective traders also made them forbidding adversaries.[67]

Though they never faced the likes of Logan, Indian women, too, could be assertive in the course of trade. One "demanded" wares from a colonial trader. Another "takes up Goods at any rate and to any value," while in the provincial capital still another was so insistent on getting things that a weary colonist called her "a bold Beggar." Up at Fort Augusta, meanwhile, a woman known in the records only as Seeshocapee's mother was equally bold. When Seeshocapee got drunk one day and began to threaten the storekeeper, troops tied up the Indian and hauled him away. Close behind came his mother, "enraged," asking "what Right the White People had to tie her Son, Since they were the very people who Sold them the Rum."[68]

"The unhappy Woman": Reading Unruliness

Mrs. Davenport refusing to sign, Martha Bailey supposedly the worse of a "vile" pair, Anne Le Tort sending three men scampering, not to mention the legendary Esther Harris—such vivid images suggest not just shrewdness and stubbornness but command and control; they portray strong, independent women who knew, and spoke, their minds. Looked at another way, however, such behavior can be read as vulnerability, not power. The desperation of Seeshocapee's mother, as armed foreigners dragged her son away, is as clear as her fury. So, too, with that "bold Beggar," an Iroquois named Maryred: bold, perhaps, but also desperate. Marooned in Philadelphia during wartime when her husband died of smallpox, she lingered there for weeks, her fate in the hands of people she neither knew nor trusted. Ultimately Maryred "came so low down" that she was reduced to begging for a pair of stockings.

So, too, Anne Le Tort's outbursts can look like weakness rather than strength. French and female, she was doubly suspicious, doubly deviant, especially when she was effectively single for long stretches of time. That she was a successful fur trader only compounded her crimes in the eyes of her competitors, who in 1693 thought they could steal Indian customers from her very doorstep. When she resisted, they went straight to provincial authorities with stories that played to English fears of all things French: she was stirring up Indians against the province. Though other French Pennsylvanians, all men, were accused of dark talk and of entertaining unknown natives, only she was summoned to the capital to answer the charges "ag[ains]t Ann Le Tort &c." The case dismissed, Anne—perhaps to escape her accusers—moved to Delaware, only to find herself hauled into court there, too.[69] Back in Pennsylvania by 1700, she still felt beleaguered, as her outburst during the Conestogas' "friendly visit" in 1712 reveals. When the Indians objected to being thrown out, "she told them the house was her own, that that Land was hers."[70] Once again Anne Le Tort's insecurity about "her ground," "her house," and "her land" was almost palpable; she lived with the shadow of deceit, and defeat, always hovering about her.

Wives of other colonial fur peddlers fared even worse. In the spring of 1730 Ruth Cloud, widow of a trader, wrote from jail, begging to be released. When her husband died in debt, she had paid as many of his creditors as she could, but those still awaiting their due imprisoned her in late 1729.[71] Jonah Davenport's wife, too, suffered from her spouse's debts. Though she helped her husband keep Logan at bay, the merchant won in the end, and the end was unpleasant: evicted from the farm by early 1736, Jonah died soon after, leaving "the unhappy Woman and her Children" to fend for themselves.[72]

Perhaps not even Esther Harris was as independent or as powerful as her grandson recalled. One entry in Joseph Powell's 1748 Shamokin journal hints at trouble in that trading post nearby. On February 25 "Mrs. Harris Sent" word across the river to the missionaries, "Desiring wee.d immediatly both com over," Powell reported, for "hir Man Wm had beat hir & wanted to rob hir of hir Skins." Sending word back that "with Such a Matter We cannot meddle," Powell left it to the local headman to look into things—and left us to imagine the rest of the story. Whatever that headman found, the incident suggests that Esther Harris, legends notwithstanding, shared much with Anne Le Tort and other women.[73]

"She had bot. them with her own Money": A New Sort of Merchandise

The terrible war that swept through the Susquehanna Country in the mid-1750s brought a new trade item—people—to the valley. Did it also bring a new opportunity for women to cross, even erase, the gender frontier? Beginning in the fall of 1755, Indian warriors—backing France in its imperial contest against Britain and having scores of their own to settle with Pennsylvania—tore through the region, burning farms, killing farmers, returning home with plunder, scalps, and captives. Many of those captives, especially girls and women, were adopted by a family and lived out their lives among Senecas or Shawnees, Delawares or Wyandots.

The most famous of these prisoners was Mary Jemison, whose odyssey began near the Susquehanna in 1758 when a war party struck the Jemison farm. After killing and scalping her family, the raiders took sixteen-year-old Mary west and soon handed her over to two Seneca sisters. These two led the girl down the Ohio River to their village, where "all the Squaws in the town" went through the ritual of adopting her, complete with the Seneca name *Dickewamis* (Two falling voices). *Dickewamis* Jemison would remain—with her Indian family, including those sisters, along with brothers and a mother, and eventually with husband and children—until her death in the Seneca homeland (now western New York) more than seventy years later.[74]

At first glance, the tale Jemison told in 1823 suggests how her adoption eliminated the gender frontier between native and colonial women that trade in all its other forms had left intact. "Oh! she is our sister," Jemison recalled the two Seneca women crying during the ceremony. Indeed, she went on, "I was ever considered and treated by them as a real sister, the same as though I had been born of their mother." Dickewamis returned the feeling: "I . . . believe that I loved them as I should have loved my own sister had she lived," she concluded.[75]

The decades had softened Jemison's recollections—sixty-five years lay between her capture and her book—but it had not buried all of the evidence that even a "successful" adoptee always sensed a frontier between Indian and colonist in general and between native and colonial women in particular. Certainly at the outset, Jemison was no sister. The first she saw of the two women, after all, was when they "came and examined me attentively for a short time" as if she were a matchcoat or brass kettle. Even after adopting her,

Jemison's "tender and gentle" Seneca sisters constrained her. They "would not allow me to speak English in their hearing," she noted. And fully two years later, these same women "told me that I must go and live with" a Delaware man. "Not daring to cross them, or disobey their commands," Dickewamis did as she was told.[76]

Forbidden to do this, ordered to do that—no wonder Jemison remained, especially in her early years, ambivalent about her fate. Adopted, "settled[,] and provided with a home," with "no particular hardships to endure," she nonetheless was "constantly solitary, lonesome and gloomy," haunted by memories of her family's fate. A year later, traveling to Fort Pitt with her new relatives, her "heart bounded to be liberated." When colonists began talking with her, "my sisters became alarmed, believing that I should be taken from them, hurried me into their canoe," and took off downriver. The mere "sight of white people" had so "inspired me with an unspeakable anxiety to go home with them," Jemison said, that her sisters' spiriting her away "seemed like a second captivity, and for a long time I brooded the thoughts of my miserable situation with almost as much sorrow and dejection as I had done those of my first sufferings."[77]

"Time . . . ," Jemison claimed, "wore away my unpleasant feelings, and I became as contented as before." When she and her kinfolk visited Fort Pitt again, several years later, she found that her "anxiety . . . to be set at liberty . . . had almost subsided." Almost. In fact, throughout her long life Jemison remained somehow apart, marking herself—and being marked—as "the White Woman." She went off alone to whisper her catechism and other phrases in order to keep up her English. She named her children after her dead parents and siblings, and those children carried the Jemison name as well. She kept alive vivid memories of her colonial family's idyllic life and cruel death. Perhaps it was this abiding difference that led some Iroquois to accuse Jemison of everything from adultery to witchcraft to kidnapping her children from a white family.[78]

However Jemison felt, other women captured in the Susquehanna Country probably felt more like a commodity than kin as they were swapped for a horse or dragged hither and yon by an Indian mistress.[79] Marie Le Roy and Barbara Leininger, girls taken near the Susquehanna Forks in 1755 who lived among Indians for more than three years, talked after their escape of little but horror, hunger, and hardship. It was, they recalled, "the yoke of the heaviest slavery" that included "hard work of every kind." Apparently no bonds of womanhood connected these young women to their Indian counterparts. Asked "why she had run away," Le Roy replied simply: "her Indian mother had been so cross and had scolded her so constantly, that she could not stay with her any longer."[80]

Few in the Susquehanna Valley were more involved in the captive business than Margaret Montour and her daughter Catherine, longtime traders in the region. Though they purchased both men and women from passing war parties, the Montours tended to let the men escape but hold onto the women—sometimes for years—profiting from their labor while awaiting a propitious time to ransom them. Some Indians returned prisoners to provincial and Crown officials free of charge, as a sign of good faith and a token of friendship; Catherine and her mother would have none of that. When a colonial visitor suggested that she simply hand over Ann Carr, Carr's daughter Lizzy, and a teenager named Amy Brannon, Margaret Montour was outraged. "She had bot. them with her own Money," she protested, "& her Daughter had given £7- with 5 Strouds, 7 Shirts, & 3 pr. Stockings for one." Unlike Jemison, Le Roy, and Leininger, neither the Carrs nor Brannon ever told their story to a colonial scribe. But given Margaret Montour's recollection of precisely how much the prisoners cost, one wonders whether they identified more with Mary Jemison's sisterhood or Marie Le Roy's slavery.[81]

"My best Acquentances . . . speake . . . Disrespectfully of me, only . . . becase I spoke frendly with the Indians": The Susquehanna Trade's End

In the early summer of 1763, two years after Catherine and Margaret Montour finally relinquished their prisoners, a party of Indian women headed down the Susquehanna Valley with a cargo of skins. Led by Catherine Montour herself, the traders passed the Susquehanna Forks and Fort Augusta's trading post, bound for "the inhabitants" farther downstream. Reaching Paxton (Harris's), the party "appear'd in a friendly Way," stopping here and there in the neighborhood to peddle their wares for blankets and rum, lead bars and powder kegs. On the morning of June 26, their business done, Catherine and "her Company" retraced their steps up the West Branch toward home.[82]

Ordinarily such a mundane trading expedition never would have found its way into the records, but June 1763 was no ordinary time. That spring, Indian attacks against British outposts over the Alleghenies had sent shock waves through the Susquehanna Valley. At the Forks, jittery soldiers saw ominous signs. Indian traders at the store wanted to buy just one item: gunpowder. This "looked . . . a little suspicious," the fort's commander Samuel Hunter observed dryly. Another "bad omen" was that "The Indians is all gon off from about the Fort and all that was below us on the River [have] gon upwards." Frantically trying to get the dilapidated outpost ready for battle, Hunter had "No doubt but this place may be Attackt very soon."[83]

No wonder word of Catherine Montour trading for lead and powder triggered alarms. A posse went after the Indian women with orders to seize any arms or ammunition and haul the traders back for questioning. Catherine and her companions passed Fort Augusta—beyond which no Pennsylvanian that summer, however keen to see justice done, was likely to venture without an army at his back—just hours before their pursuers got there.[84]

Montour's shopping trip was among the last in a long line. Even as Samuel Hunter read bad omens in Indian behavior, so Susquehanna natives watched developments at the Forks that summer with growing "Uneasiness." The storekeeper not only stopped selling powder to any Indian, including locals who had traded there for years; he also moved his merchandise into the fort and dismantled the store. By early August, the clerk and his inventory were sailing downriver, never to return. If exchange had always been the lifeblood of friendship, its end meant only one thing.[85]

While trade ebbed, Pennsylvania attitudes hardened into hatred. One Paxton resident, William Patterson, a leading suspect in the investigation into selling powder to Montour, could not believe that "a groundless Rumer amongst the People" got him into trouble. "It gives me the gratest pain to think," he wrote, "that some of my best Acquentances shou'd speake so Disrespectfully of me, only upon bare supposition, becase I spoke frendly with the Indians." But now even an Indian woman so well known to Pennsylvanians that they called her *Cate* or *Catie* was suspicious; now any Indian was assumed to be "ye Enemy."[86]

Even with Catherine chased out of Pennsylvania and Fort Augusta's store abandoned, the Susquehanna trade died no sudden death. In 1768 a party of Indian men, women, and children were apparently hunting and trading below the Forks on the river's west side. That same year the Delaware Job Chilloway, a regular customer at the Forks, headed up a Susquehanna tributary, the Juniata River, and as late as 1800 was still venturing down from that stream's upper reaches to swap venison for bread and flour. But those Indian hunters met a grisly death at the hands of colonists, an episode that helped discourage further ventures in the vicinity. And Chilloway's lonely existence, numbed by liquor, was the exception that proved the rule. When a flood in the winter of 1768 swept boards from the huts "that were at the In[dia]n Camp" by John Harris's and some thief the next summer took most of the rest, it was the end of an era, of a time when that place was a center for the exchange of goods and information, when Indian traders, men and women, would stay amid colonial settlements for days or weeks on end.[87]

A newcomer wandering through the Susquehanna Valley in 1775 saw no Indians at all—the "Wood-surrounded Women" he met were all colonial—until he passed the Forks and headed up the West Branch toward the Montours' old village. Even in those parts, only shadows of the trade remained: one colonial trader with a packhorse and servant, two young Indian men "going downwards with Skins." So unusual were these, so much a vestige of another time, that the colonists "startled" the traveler while the Indians robbed him of "a Pleasant Feeling."[88] There were no signs of women, Indian or Pennsylvanian, in the trade at all.

"Traces can yet be plainly seen": Parallel Paths

In 1855, a Susquehanna Valley antiquarian named U. J. Jones reported that "the great western highway" running up the Juniata River from its junction with the Susquehanna had not altogether vanished. "Traces" of this trail that was "famous . . . in its day" "can yet be plainly seen," he wrote. "Though filled up with weeds in the summer-time," nonetheless "the indentations made by the feet of thousands upon thousands of warriors and pack-horses which traveled it . . . are still plainly visible. . . . In some places," Jones went on, "where the ground is marshy, . . . the path is at least twelve inches deep, and the very stones along the road bear the marks of the iron-shod horses of the Indian traders." Still, even the enthusiastic Jones had to admit that what "traces" remained were most likely to be found "in the wilds of the mountains." And even he was left with little more than mute marks—ruts beside a stream, weed-choked paths, stones scored by iron—that left him imagining, rather than studying, the "dusky warrior," the packhorse train, the "foot-men" who had made that trail.[89]

Searching for women who were Susquehanna traders can evoke the same nagging sense of mystery, of an elusive quarry more easily imagined than examined. Of their lives and labors, only traces remain in the remoter "wilds" of the documents. It is hard, picking up those traces, to discern the underlying structures of frontier life, to set these gleanings into their proper context, to divine what rendered them, to contemporaries, routine rather than remarkable.

But if the tale resists the telling, turning the spotlight away from men and toward women does offer instructive lessons. One is that the longstanding idea that trade was a man's job must be abandoned, as Esther Harris, Margaret Montour, and other women can attest. Another is that "the fur trade" is at best misleading, at worst simply wrong, since it fails to encompass the range of activities and encounters that comprised cross-cultural exchange, a range that included diplomacy and hospitality, nursing and sex. A third lesson is the abiding distance between the two worlds trading up and down the Susquehanna Valley. Bringing Indian and colonial women together via exchange only helps measure how far apart they remained.

It is telling that trading women left no residue of an attachment akin to the "sisterly relations" that, Jane Merritt has found, German, Delaware, and Mahican women forged in Moravian towns along the Delaware River. There—at the very time Esther Harris, Margaret Montour, and the rest were plying their wares beside the Susquehanna—colonial women were attending Indians in childbirth, serving as godmothers to those children, and in other ways developing "emotional bonds" with native women from shared "personal circumstances." No hint of such bonds survives from the Susquehanna Country. Perhaps the records there are simply too fragmentary. Perhaps trade, more adversarial than cooperative, could not be the glue that a shared spiritual yearning was for Moravians. Perhaps the character of Moravian communities—with residence and ritual often segregated along gender lines, with a spirituality "that celebrated femaleness"—helped foster bonds of womanhood across the cultural divide. Certainly those Christian women spent more time together, season after season, than their peripatetic sisters pursuing whiskey or peltry.[90] Whatever the explanation for this striking difference between neighboring valleys, one thing is clear: a "gender frontier" endured in the Susquehanna Country, not just between men and women, not just between native and European gender concepts and constructs, but between Indian women and their colonial counterparts.

Part III / Politics and Identity

CHAPTER NINE

A Death in the Morning

The Murder of Daniel Parke

Natalie Zacek

The summer of 1710 was a time of great tension for the residents of the English colonies of the Leeward Islands. The governor and commander-in-chief of the Leewards, Colonel Daniel Parke, was at loggerheads with the majority of his subjects, especially those in Antigua, in whose capital, St. John's, he had his seat of government. From the moment of Parke's first appearance in the islands in 1706, when he arrived from England to take up his post, governor and governed had come into conflict. The governor was a proud, hot-tempered man who had hoped that his close friendships with influential members of the English court and with Queen Anne would earn him a powerful and highly paid position in the colonial administration such as the governorship of his native Virginia, in which position he might wield authority in the manner of his mentor, the highly controversial Governor Edmund Andros. Instead, Parke found himself dispatched to the remote eastern edge of the West Indies, serving as the lowest paid of colonial British America's royal governors. To add to his sense of grievance, his new subjects were "People of such turbulent Spirits and Loose Principles," who were intensely hostile to his repeated attempts to impose order upon them and to remedy what he saw as their "defective and corrupt laws."[1]

For their part, the Antiguans considered that it was they, rather than Parke, who had been ill-used. In their eyes, from the moment of his arrival Parke did nothing but abuse, frustrate, and menace his subjects. He neglected the security of the islands in the face of the threat of an attack by the French, and used the royal troops stationed in the islands less as a bulwark against invasion than as a personal standing army. He undertook a sustained endeavor to curb the powers of the island assemblies by launching concerted efforts to prevent them from holding their sessions and by challenging their claims to long-held privileges. These chilling threats to individual and corporate security were matched by others of a more private nature. Parke allegedly entered into sexual relationships with the wives of a number of Antigua's wealthiest planters, including members of the local legislature, and when one angry husband confronted him, the governor publicly humiliated the man, then attempted to frame him for murder. Later, as Parke became aware of the depth of his unpopularity among the Antiguans, he took to walking the streets of St. John's at night in various disguises, leading people to believe that he was spying upon them. By the spring of 1709, planter patience was exhausted. Determined to defend themselves, leading activists sent William Nevin, a member of the Antiguan assembly, off to London bearing a petition to Queen Anne, which described the "highest acts of Injustice" that Parke had committed and pleaded that she remove this "Yoke of Oppression" and grant the islanders "such Reliefe as yo[ur] Ma[jes]tie shall thinke fitt . . . to afford us in these our Dismall Melancholy Circumstances."[2]

During the spring of 1710, news arrived in Antigua that the islanders' appeal had met with a receptive ear. On February 11, the Queen had decided that their "Complaint . . . of great Oppressions and Mal-Administration" was sufficiently serious in its nature that she ordered Parke to give up his office, leave the island, and make his way to London to answer the charges against him.[3] But the Antiguans' relief was short-lived. When Parke heard the news of his recall, he simply refused to resign or depart, pledging that he would remain in the islands at his pleasure and force the inhabitants to recant their testimony against him. By early summer of 1710, as hurricane season approached the West Indies, this equally menacing political storm was brewing in Antigua, as the governor and his subjects confronted one another. As great as anticipatory tensions were, however, neither Parke nor his enemies could have imagined that the following months would see the governor lose the use of his right arm in an assassination attempt carried out by one of his opponents' slaves, and that the governor would employ royal troops to break up a legislative session at bayonet point. Least of all could anyone have imagined that two weeks before Christmas the governor would be dead at the hands of his subjects.

Much of the scholarship on the English Caribbean settlements, including both recent works and older monographs, has chosen to pass a harsh verdict on these colonies, evaluating them not on the basis of their own successes and failures, but through comparison with idealized images of the supposedly far better ordered societies of the mainland colonies.[4] In the eyes of these scholars, the West Indian colonies failed to develop even the most rudimentary forms of local political ideology, identity, or practice by which they might have promulgated English norms and values of citizenship and governance.

The residents of these islands, however, disagreed strongly with this judgment. In their eyes, their plantation-based settlements were model *colonial* worlds in terms of their economic development and social structure, and at the same time societies that had succeeded in developing a set of identifiably *English* political institutions and a corporate identity that centered upon allegiance to the metropole and replication of that metropole's most cherished norms of behavior and identity.[5] Eighteenth-century West Indian colonists such as Edward Littleton maintained that the "Plantations" in which they lived were "meer Additions and Accessions to *England,* and Enlargements of it . . . only herein lies the difference, that there is a distance and space between *England* and the Plantations"—in other words, that the islands were thoroughly English polities, and that the only difference between Antiguans or Barbadians and Yorkshiremen or Londoners was that the islanders were physically farther distant than the latter from the seat of government and of civility alike. As Jack Greene has observed, these colonists "took great pride that their 'Form of Government' was 'as nigh as conveniently can be to that of *England.*'"[6]

In this essay, I explore the formation of a political ideology and attendant variety of behavior among the white residents of the Leeward Islands through which they articulated a strong sense of British identity and an "overwhelming desire to be judged according to British values."[7] Through close examination of an instance in which Antiguan settlers resorted to verbal, legal, and, eventually, physical attacks upon an individual whom they believed was attempting to undermine what they saw as their most cherished natural rights, I will show the extent to which the articulate white residents of the Leeward Islands identified themselves as Englishmen, with all of the responsibilities and privileges that such an identity vested in them. Previous commentators have seen the story of Governor Daniel Parke's murder by his subjects as an example of the brutality and depravity of English West Indians when he attempted to impose order upon them. I view the incident as one in which a group of English subjects, having exhausted all legal means by which to rid themselves of a commander who had repeatedly "Exercis'd the highest Acts of Injustice . . . and Violence and Dispensed with and Trampled on [their] Laws," resorted to violence in order to save themselves and their community from a tyrant whose every action over several years had displayed his conviction that the residents of the Leeward colonies possessed no English rights that he was bound to uphold.[8] Convinced as they were of the legitimacy of their claims to English rights and the importance of defending these rights against anyone or anything that appeared to threaten them, the Leeward colonists were willing to take highly assertive and even violent action in order to proclaim and defend their political and legal identity as Englishmen. By setting the history of Governor Daniel Parke within a framework of the politics of colonial and metropolitan identity, I remove Parke's story from the realm of scandal and mindless violence, where previous accounts of English settlement in the West Indies have lodged it, and redeploy it as a lens through which to examine issues of national identity, governance, and social order.

The Structure of Government

The structure of government in the Leeward Islands was on the whole quite similar to that which prevailed throughout colonial British America in the late seventeenth and eighteenth centuries, particularly in the southern and island colonies. The several local administrations replicated in miniature the structure of government present within the mother country; each of the individual Leeward Islands possessed a council whose functions were parallel to those of the House of Lords, and an assembly that played the role of the House of Commons, while the royal governor served as the local representative of the monarch, holding a commission directly from him or her.[9] The membership of the council and of the assembly was drawn from among the more prominent inhabitants of each of the islands, while the governor was appointed by the sovereign from among his or her protégés or their clients. The men who formed the membership of the council were also technically royal appointees, because they obtained their seats via the royal mandamus, but the selection process for these offices, unlike that for the governorship, did not lie exclusively within metropolitan control. In many instances, members of the islands' elites either enlisted the assistance of their governors or wrote to the Board of Trade or to influential friends and relatives in Parliament or at court, requesting that they, or those they supported, be considered for vacant seats on the council. Because monarchs were almost always unfamiliar with the individuals who constituted the island elites, they generally made appointments to the council based upon the recommendations of their advisers, or upon those of the local governor. In practice, all that was required of a councillor was that he should possess a substantial estate and be free of debt.[10] Once appointed, councillors had staying power. No governor could remove a councillor without sufficient cause, and any such removal had to be reported at once to the monarch. This rule allowed councillors to claim legitimacy simultaneously as representatives of their communities and as participants in imperial politics.[11] Moreover, although the governor, as the monarch's representative, was on paper invested with considerable authority, he was obligated to gain the agreement of the members of the council in order to carry out many of the responsibilities of his office.

In the Leewards, as throughout colonial British America, the interests of the royal governor frequently came into conflict with those of the council and the locally elected assembly. At first glance, it seems as if the settlers' repeated declarations of their innate Englishness at both the individual and the societal level should have prevented such problems from arising. If, as Edward Littleton claimed, the only difference between metropole and colony was that of "distance and space," and if there was no essential difference between a man born in Antigua and one born in London, why should it matter whether the governor were a local leader or a royal appointee sent out from England? In reality, the source of tension was less a result of a perception on the part of the council and assembly of the governor's foreignness than it was of their resentment at being consistently denied the opportunity to hold this, the highest office within their polity.

Although the planters of the Leewards, even those who had never visited the metropole, eagerly professed their Englishness, they simultaneously stood convinced that no man could properly understand the economic, political, and social realities of their islands who had not lived in them for at least a few years. What, they demanded, could an outsider know of the tremendous risks and great expense involved in the production of sugar, or of the constant fear that their small and isolated settlements might fall victim to a slave revolt or an attack by a foreign power? Though islanders were proud to conceive of themselves as Englishmen overseas, they were aware that the realities of daily life in the West Indies were very different from those that characterized Britain. The vagaries of a tropical climate, the frequent appearance on the horizon of threatening French vessels, and the sense of unease generated by living amid a host of black slaves were normal to islanders, but to outsiders often seemed sufficiently disconcerting and unwholesome to prompt both censure and anxiety. Such newcomers might possess the advantage of access to persons of influence at Whitehall, but this did not, in the eyes of the planters, compensate for their lack of island experience, and certainly did not justify the decision to allow them to supplant knowledgeable and capable local residents in taking the position of governor.[12]

The majority of West Indian planters were aware, often passionately and angrily so, of the low esteem in which many metropolitan Englishmen held them: that their norms of sociability and consumption appeared to English eyes as profligacy and decadence, their carefully achieved control over their slaves as wanton cruelty, and their wealth as the ill-gotten gains reaped by the corrupt descendants of the dregs of English society.[13] Unsurprisingly, they were frustrated and infuriated by the fact that their wealth and their frequently professed devotion to England and all things English did not win them the degree of metropolitan respect that they believed to be their due. They recognized, of course, that they were hardly unique among Britain's American colonies in having imposed upon them an unwanted and unfamiliar governor over whose appointment they had little or no control, but many among them felt that the antiquity of their settlements and their profitability among Britain's American colonies ought to have exempted them from bearing some of the more onerous burdens heaped upon them by metropolitan elites. To the planters, the presence of an outsider as governor epitomized metropolitan distaste and skepticism toward the West Indian colonies, implying that, despite their wealth, their ability to prosper under challenging circumstances, and their strong sense of Englishness, they remained unworthy and incompetent to select their own leaders.

In addition to these grievances, the political elites of the Leewards resented gubernatorial incongruities between personal wealth and the status of political office. Of all the royal governorships of British America in the early eighteenth century, that of the Leewards was by far the lowest paid. Despite the smallness of his salary, however, it was crucial that the governor maintain an appearance of affluence, renting or purchasing a commodious residence, dressing with elegance and style, and offering lavish and open hospitality. Eighteenth-century English commentators and modern historians alike have ridiculed the flashy style in which West Indian planters and their wives and daughters dressed, finding them gaudy in their tastes and naïve in their belief that the possession of fine clothes was an indication that their wearer was wealthy and reputable, but in societies such as those of the Leewards, in which even the greatest holders of land and slaves were constantly dependent upon the extension of credit, maintaining a luxurious lifestyle served as evidence that one was solvent, and thus a good risk for the extension of loans or credit.[14] A governor who possessed a substantial private income could be relied upon to cut the right sort of figure among the local planters. Importantly, too, he would not need to resort to cheating or embezzling from public funds, "grinding and fleecing" his subjects.[15] His wealth would render him independent, in the sense that he would be his own man and need rely on none but himself for financial support—a central tenet of British metropolitan and imperial political culture, which limited electoral participation to those who possessed sufficient land or income to rank among the independent men of a community. Finally, a rich governor might be a source of patronage, spreading his wealth amongst those he favored, which would both increase his influence, thus raising the power and prestige of the government, and yield tangible benefits to at least some of his subjects. The governor was, after all, the representative of the monarch, and it behooved him as ill as it did a king or queen to appear either penurious or parsimonious. In such a milieu, a man such as Daniel Parke, who combined a small purse with an inflated sense of self, was likely to become a target of his subjects' envy and mistrust.

Interpersonal tensions often flared high in these inescapably intimate societies, in which a man's honor was as prized an attribute as his slaves, his land, or his money, and in which the loss of that honor would be known to the entire community and reflected in a concomitant diminution in personal and familial prestige. In the Leewards, social mores centered upon individual honor and the necessity of constantly defending that honor from overt or implied challenge. Even the most trifling insult was difficult to overlook, because to be insulted was to lose control over one's sense of selfhood and place in the social order, and if an individual possessed less than complete control over himself and his societal role, even for a moment, how might he maintain control over his family, his finances, or his slaves? This pressing need to control not only one's own speech and behavior but that of others, combined with concerns relating to the fragility of territorial and internal security, encouraged those who wielded formal authority to demand obedience, respect, and even deference from those they governed.[16] As Joanne Freeman has noted in the context of the early American republic, "the small-scale, localized political realm magnified this obsession with reputation."[17] In polities whose participants at any moment might number only a few hundred adult white males, it was personalities rather than parties that mattered. What might appear to be a trivial instance of individual self-aggrandizement could reverberate throughout the entire local political community.[18]

Overbearing behavior on the part of governors, added to the inevitable tensions that arose between metropolitan and colonial authority, aggravated political disputes in the islands to the point at which they prevented the local elites from either overlooking such quarrels or resolving them peacefully.[19] The governor's formal authority was considerable, but "it was not so much the legal powers possessed by a Governor that mattered as the capacity of the man who filled the post." Because his inadequate salary and lack of powers of patronage prevented him from developing significant informal authority within his polity, an incumbent governor could gain real community influence only by "provid[ing] effective and persuasive public leadership and . . . perform[ing] his duties in a way the society approved."[20] Some Leeward governors were successful in carrying out this delicate balancing act, but others enraged island residents by committing actions that the islanders saw as encroaching upon the security of their liberty and their property alike. In 1690, Dalby Thomas wrote that "the great discouragement those [West Indian] Collonies lye under, is the Arbitrary Power and practices of their Governours there . . . which some have felt to their undoing and all are liable to," a complaint that Leeward residents echoed frequently over the course of the seventeenth and eighteenth centuries.[21] The colonists staunchly believed that "the Greatest and Best of Kings never gave any one of his Subjects Authority to oppress the rest," as when "a Person whom he imploys to take Care of them . . . shall by Virtue of that Authority . . . assume a Power of doing such Things as will only answer Purposes diametrically opposite to those his Duty obliges him to Promote."[22] When such a person seemed to threaten the security of their persons and their property, colonists drew upon the Lockean idea of the right of resistance that became explicit in the Glorious Revolution and remained implicit in the settlement that that revolution generated. In a struggle between official prerogative and local practice, the stakes were high, and in a political culture that valorized individual honor and self-assertion over cooperation and compromise, they became still higher.

The "Great Oppressions and Mal-Administration" of Colonel Daniel Parke

Daniel Parke would have been a problematic choice for the governorship of any colony. Born in 1664 into one of tidewater Virginia's leading families, he used his wealth and family connections to climb the ladder of public office, and by his thirtieth birthday sat on Virginia's council, simultaneously holding such prestigious offices as collector of revenue and colonel of the militia of York County, of which he was the principal landowner.[23] He had spent his youth in the pursuit of dissipation, and had developed a reputation both in Virginia and in England as "a complete sparkish Gentleman" whose "quick resentment of every the least thing that looks like an affront or Injury" made him "the greatest Hector [aggressive individual] in the Town," whether that town was Williamsburg, London, or St. John's.[24] Put plainly, Parke was a womanizer and a spendthrift who displayed little concern for the personal embarrassment or financial difficulties to which he subjected his wife and family. He was also a close friend and ardent admirer of Governor Edmund Andros of Virginia, an intensely autocratic military man whose aggressive style of leadership so alienated his subjects that he was recalled successively from the governorships of both Massachusetts and Virginia. Parke himself was sufficiently hot-tempered to have taken a horsewhip to Francis Nicholson, the governor of Maryland, when that gentleman accused him of lying.[25] When he became embroiled in a quarrel with the Reverend James Blair, Virginia commissary of the Bishop of London, Parke was frustrated by the fact that a clergyman could not be challenged to a duel, but managed to cast a slur upon Blair's honor by storming into Williamsburg's Bruton Parish Church in the midst of the reverend's sermon, seizing Blair's wife by the arm and dragging her from her pew and out of the church.[26]

Outbursts such as these rendered Parke persona non grata in Chesapeake society and encouraged him to quit Virginia and to seek his fortune and pleasure in England, where, after an unsuccessful attempt to enter the House of

Commons, he joined the English army, which was then fighting the War of the Spanish Succession.[27] Parke became aide-de-camp to John Churchill, the Duke of Marlborough, and found his great opportunity in 1704, when Marlborough dispatched him to Queen Anne to bring her the great tidings of the victory at Blenheim. So delighted was Anne by the news that she rewarded Parke with a purse containing the vast sum of a thousand guineas, as well as with a miniature portrait of herself, encrusted with diamonds. Apparently the Queen was also taken by Parke's physical attractiveness and the undoubted charm he could display when it was in his interest to do so. When the post of Governor of the Leeward Islands fell vacant some months after the battle of Blenheim, at the death of the incumbent, Sir William Mathew, Anne appointed Parke to the post.[28]

Neither Parke nor the planters of the Leewards viewed this turn of events with particular enthusiasm. For most of the preceding two decades two governors named Christopher Codrington, father and son, had presided over the islands' government. In the process, they had angered many West Indians with what island residents perceived as the Codringtons' arrogance and selfishness.[29] The planters' tempers had cooled little after many years in which the Codringtons had continually frustrated them by transacting most political business through a general assembly representing all four islands, while ignoring the four local assemblies and denying them a voice in the proceedings.[30] Few in the Leewards welcomed the arrival of a new governor, and Daniel Parke's reputation encouraged many to mistrust him long before they met him and confirmed their preconceptions. Parke's known support of Edmund Andros's governing style smacked uncomfortably of the Codringtons. But the Codringtons at least were Leeward residents, having moved from Barbados to Antigua in 1674, and were possessors of vast island estates and a substantial private income. Parke, by contrast, was a Virginian by birth and a Londoner by temperament, a man whose taste for high living had depleted his income and rendered him dependent upon his salary and any other perquisites he could draw from his office.[31] The circumstances of Parke's appointment were also suspect in the eyes of many of his new subjects, who failed to discern in him any of the personal qualities of intellect, valor, or leadership that might have rendered him worthy of his office. Parke's reputation as a ladies' man and a social climber suggested to many that he owed his success to Queen Anne's having developed something of a passion for him. Although even the most scurrilous gossips stopped short of accusing the matronly and middle-aged monarch of having entered into any kind of a sexual relationship with Parke, some feared that Parke's attractiveness had clouded Anne's judgment, which many already considered faulty due to the Queen's blatant display of favoritism toward the much-detested Sarah Churchill, Duchess of Marlborough, whom public opinion in England and the colonies execrated as a vulgar, scheming harlot.[32] The colonial public, like that of the metropole, tended to be suspicious of those who occupied the position of royal favorite, and resented such individuals' reaping what it saw as entirely undeserved rewards in the political, financial, and social spheres. Parke's connection with the Marlboroughs and the nebulous nature of his relationship to Queen Anne, in combination with his reputation as a spendthrift, a rake, and (through his involvement with a bribery scandal) a suborner of parliamentary integrity, made him suspect to those Leeward residents whose London connections allowed them to gain information about him before he arrived in the islands.

For his own part, Parke arrived in the islands a disappointed and bitter man. He was far from enthused about becoming governor of the Leewards, an office with a low profile and an inadequate salary that would banish him to a remote locale far from the sophisticated pleasures and possibilities for personal advancement he sought in London. He had hoped that Anne would appoint him governor of Virginia, perhaps imagining himself returning in triumph to rule over his old adversaries. Indeed, the Duke of Marlborough had at one point promised to obtain the Virginia post for Parke, but later encouraged Anne to grant it to George Hamilton, the Earl of Orkney, who, unlike Parke, had played a crucial role in the battle of Blenheim.[33] Denied the plum he desired, Parke was furious to find himself bound for the West Indies to take up a position that he saw as far beneath the dignity of a member of one of Virginia's most prominent families, an intimate friend of the great military hero Marlborough, and a protégé of the Queen herself. As he sailed from London toward the Leewards, Parke described himself disgustedly as an "unfortunate Divel here to be roasted in the sun, without the prospect of getting anything."[34]

Parke was clearly unhappy as he took up his post, and his new subjects were similarly unenthusiastic about his becoming their governor. After Parke's arrival in 1706, tensions between governor and governed quickly escalated. The islands were already suffering the effects of the continental war: there was a constant threat of French attack, privateering vessels lurked in nearby waters and preyed on island shipping, and many colonists were convinced that

Britain was doing far too little to assist its colonies in a war that had resulted from European dynastic politics and imperial rivalries rather than from local concerns.[35] In such a situation, decisive actions on the part of the governor would not necessarily have been unwelcome. But Parke's initial actions, though decisive, served almost immediately to alienate his constituents, including Christopher Codrington the younger, who had succeeded his late father as governor, and had unsuccessfully lobbied the Board of Trade to gain reappointment to the position after the death of his successor, Mathew. With his ambitions frustrated by Anne's selection of Parke, Codrington had good reason to resent the new governor, seeing him as a scheming upstart who had obtained his office through his cunning manipulation of royal favor. Parke, in turn, realizing that "that Machiavell" Codrington was a powerful and implacable opponent, decided to preempt any malfeasance on the latter's part by striking at him first.[36] Parke confiscated Codrington's enormous estate on St. Kitts, challenged "by what authority, he the said Codrington did hold the island of Barbuda," and brought suit to force Codrington to give up the vast amount of prize money he had acquired in the early years of the war against France.[37] Parke also missed no opportunity to defame Codrington, writing in an official letter to the Board of Trade that a local woman, Kate Sullivein, "as formerly Coddrington's Wench, and she layd two Bastards to him, but she giving him the Pox he turned her off."[38]

Parke made a serious miscalculation when he attacked Codrington. He may well have believed that by harassing Codrington he would both subdue his greatest enemy and win himself favor among the islanders, many of whom had resented Codrington's imperious ways during his governorship and had not been displeased when the Board of Trade recalled him in 1704. Ardent royalist that he was, Parke may have thought that by attacking Codrington he would demonstrate the power of the monarch, as channeled through her representative, to prevent certain over-mighty subjects from aggrandizing themselves at the expense of their humbler neighbors. In fact, Parke's repeated assaults upon Codrington's property and reputation encouraged Leeward residents to alter their opinions of the latter and view him henceforth less as a self-promoting quasi-tyrant and more as a fellow sufferer at the hands of the new governor. If Parke could use his royal prerogative to attack a man such as Codrington, with his wealth, his title, and his influential friends in London, who could consider himself safe from the governor's aggression? Parke's attempts to divest Codrington of the lands he held in St. Kitts and Barbuda were particularly appalling to island residents because such actions implied that the governor could call into question long-established and previously unquestioned titles to real property, thus potentially threatening to dispossess all local landholders. This action posed a tremendous threat in these small islands in which all lands suitable for the cultivation of sugar had long since been engrossed; if a planter's land were confiscated, he had no hope of acquiring any to replace it. Through his dealings with Codrington, Parke created a situation in which his subjects became inclined to view *him* as the over-mighty metropolitan oppressor and the previously feared and detested Codrington as the harassed colonial victim.

Parke might have defused the threat Codrington posed without inflaming public opinion against himself, had he not simultaneously embarked upon a program of what he claimed was much-needed administrative reform, but which appeared to many local planters to be a blatant attack on what they saw as their inalienable right to govern themselves. Within a few months of his arrival in the Leewards, Parke began to reshuffle the lieutenant governors of the four islands and to increase the membership of the island councils beyond their prescribed limits. His general motive was to place those who supported him in positions of authority, particularly so that they might aid him in his efforts to stamp out the illegal but lucrative trade that many islanders carried out with the nearby Dutch and French islands.[39] The Lords of Trade reprimanded him for these actions, which ran contrary to the instructions they had sent him, but reluctantly gave their assent to the various conciliar appointments, hoping that Parke might restrain himself in future from interference in matters that lay beyond his sphere of influence.[40]

No such restraint was forthcoming. Instead, Parke intensified and broadened the scope of his contemptuous behavior toward the people he governed and the laws and institutions upon which they relied for protection against the abuse of gubernatorial prerogative. The activities that rendered Parke most notorious on both sides of the Atlantic were the sexual depredations he committed in the Leewards. In the few years in which he resided in the islands, Parke embarked upon sexual relationships with a large number of married women, and made little attempt to hide these relationships from their husbands, let alone the general public. Parke's sexual behavior inflamed Leeward public opinion because it challenged strongly established ideals of masculine honor, feminine virtue, and patriarchal order. These flagrant personal misdeeds have played the largest part in the conception of Parke as an historical personage, but these transgressions were merely one aspect of his apparent hostility and disdain toward the people he governed. At the same time that Parke repeatedly ignored established values relating to familial and sexual conduct, he continued to infringe upon what his subjects viewed as their political rights as Englishmen.

The ways in which the personal led to the political are best illustrated by Parke's treatment of Edward Chester, a prominent merchant and member of the Assembly of Antigua. Among Parke's various "amours with . . . planters' wives" was a particularly indiscreet liaison with Chester's wife Catherine. Subsequently, Parke accused Chester of the murder of Thomas Sawyer and "direct[ed] his instrument the provost-marshal to impanel a jury of certain persons, from whom he doubted not to obtain Chester's conviction," thus contravening the right of all Englishmen to be tried by an impartial jury; "the execution of this innocent and injured man would undoubtedly have followed, if the evidence in his favor had not proved too powerful to be overborne; so that the jury was compelled to pronounce his acquittal."[41] In an interesting piece of hypocrisy, Parke claimed that the Leeward planters, particularly those of Antigua, were guilty of countless acts of sexual depravity; in his opinion, the only way by which he could force the locals to adopt better morals was by patrolling the streets of St. John's by night, "in order to set a decorous example."[42] Not surprisingly, local residents interpreted the Governor's nocturnal wanderings "in different disguises" as evidence that he was spying upon them, subverting the political order by illicitly gaining information about his opponents.[43]

Still more ominously, Parke began to strike at the authority of the island assemblies, particularly that of Antigua, which was widely known for its assertiveness against gubernatorial aggression.[44] He tried to force the Antiguan assembly to pay for the hire and maintenance of two sloops for use in the service of the island, but the House refused to do so on the grounds that Parke had engaged these vessels without the assembly's prior consent. Parke obstructed the passage of an electoral law that would have obligated him to summon the assembly at least once a year, and refused to allow either the General Assembly or the island legislatures to appoint their own clerks, as had "been the constant practice, sue, and custom of the General and several Assemblies from the first settlement of these islands," an action that encouraged the islanders to fear that Parke might construct false records of their sessions that would defame them when he sent them to the Board of Trade.[45]

Taken individually, none of the charges against Parke was tremendously damaging. In combination, however, they served to create great alarm among the Leeward planters and to convince many of them that Parke was conspiring against his subjects' natural rights as Englishmen to liberty and property. If Parke were innocent of any malfeasance, they reasoned, why would he try to prevent the assemblies from appointing their own clerks? What well-intentioned governor would refuse to call an annual meeting of the assembly? What blameless motives could lead Parke to don a disguise and ramble about at night armed with "a small ponyard, and a case of pocket-pistoles"?[46] As the islanders brooded over these questions, every action Parke took, or was reported to have taken, acquired sinister implications. When he withdrew the royal regiment, ammunition, and provisions from the recently erected fort at Monk's Hill, Nevis, and reinstated them in the fortifications around St. John's, public opinion insisted that he had done so because he cared only for his own security and that of the lavish Government House he had just had built, although the regiment's colonel had issued a report that the design of Monk's Hill was so flawed as to render the fort useless, and that it made more sense to fortify the Leewards' capital city.[47] Even the most passing rumor inflamed public opinion against Parke. In a whispering campaign, Parke's critics claimed that he had had the seal of the Leewards melted down and made into a tankard for his own use, an action that, if true, symbolized the depths of Parke's contempt for the colony and its inhabitants.[48]

By the beginning of 1709, the planters' patience was exhausted; seventeen of the twenty-two members of the Antiguan assembly affixed their signatures to a petition to Queen Anne in which they beseeched her to recall Parke for his misgovernment. They accompanied it with a document listing twenty-five articles of impeachment against the governor. The articles were a catalog of grievances that represented Parke's most galling actions against the planters. In addition to the complaints mentioned before, the petitioners charged that Parke "did menace and otherwise endeavor to scare, frighten, and discourage Witnesses from testifying the Truth in the Case of Edward Chester"; he "employ'd Parties of arm'd Soldiers . . . in ejecting Persons out of their Freeholds and Possession," and "order'd several groundless and unwarrantable Seizures to be made Where no offence has been committed."[49] As alarming as these incidents were, they paled in comparison with Parke's apparent disregard for the island's laws. The articles accused him of "frequently and publicly declar[ing], That he had assurance from my Lord High-Treasurer of

England and the Duchess of Marlborough, that he should be supported and protected, let him do what he would . . . to awe every Person under his government into the utmost tame and servile Submission to whatever he should do."[50] Furthermore, Parke had allegedly declared that in his role as head of the Court of Chancery he "would be guided by no Laws or Precedents whatsoever, in making his Decrees . . . so that he is rather a Law-Giver, than a Judge," and that, in response to the Assembly's assertion of "that undoubted Privilege of their House, to enquire into, examine, and represent Grievances to him and his Council, for Redress, He in Answer . . . flatly declar'd, he knew no Privileges they had."[51] These charges reflect the Antiguans' profound anxiety that they were completely at the mercy of a man with highly placed supporters at court, who had no respect for them and who believed that he lay under no obligation to play by the rules that they had carefully developed to forestall the rise of tyrants among them. To the petitioners, their governor showed no solicitude for them, but had instead "frequently and publickly declar'd his implacable Malice against the Island of Antegoa and . . . that if it were not for a few Friends, he would send the Island . . . to the Devil."[52] The planters feared that they might reap terrible consequences simply by drawing upon their right as Englishmen to request a redress of grievances from the Queen, for had not Parke announced "that if he knew any Person that was going home to complain of him to the Queen, he would clap them up in a Dungeon and there they should perish"?[53] It was with considerable apprehension that they dispatched one of their number, William Nevin, to London to present their grievances to the monarch and the Board of Trade.[54]

In the months between Nevin's departure and Whitehall's response, tensions rose still higher between Parke and the Antiguan planters, and a number of the latter responded to this charged atmosphere with intimations of violence. In February the brothers Barry and John Tankard armed their slaves and posted them as guards on all paths running through their estates in order to prevent Parke from executing any warrant against them. A few weeks later, Barry Tankard organized a gathering of prominent locals, "who were all armed . . . [and] all inimical to Parke."[55] The summer hurricane season passed tensely but without violence, but this uneasy truce was ruptured at the beginning of September, when Sandy, a slave belonging to John Otto-Baijer, who with his brother Bastian was one of Parke's bitterest opponents, attempted to assassinate the governor, leaving Parke alive but with a shattered left arm and a reinvigorated desire to block his subjects' increasingly desperate attempts to rid themselves of him by fair means or foul.[56] The fact that some planters had resorted to arming their slaves illustrates just how far the situation had deteriorated; under ordinary circumstances, slaves were absolutely barred by law and custom alike from having or using firearms, but in 1709 the threat Parke posed seemed far more frightening than the idea of black men with weapons.[57]

In March 1710, news arrived from London that most Leeward residents greeted with joy. On February 5, the Privy Council had issued a proclamation demanding that Parke return to England to answer the charges his subjects had presented against him. On February 25, the Crown had revoked Parke's commission as governor. Further instructions ordered him to resign his office immediately in favor of Colonel Walter Hamilton, Lieutenant Governor of St. Kitts, and to "leave those Islands and return into Our Presence prepared to make your Defence before Us in Council."[58] The islanders' rejoicing, however, was short-lived, as Parke refused flatly either to relinquish his commission or to return to England, declaring that these orders "did in no ways damp my mirth, but added to it, for now I shall have an opportunity to expose their [the petitioners'] perjury's and villainy's and prove they assasinated first my reputation."[59] In frustration, the Assembly invoked its power to refuse to grant the governor military supplies, despite the rumored approach of a French fleet, a decision that, like the arming of slaves, indicates the level to which tensions had risen. As tempers frayed further, Parke made his most audacious strike yet against his subjects' liberties by admitting a party of royal grenadiers into the Assembly's chambers in St. John's Court House and ordering the soldiers to disperse the legislators at bayonet point.

At this juncture, the situation passed from tense to lethal. The dismissed assemblymen and their supporters passed the next few days roaming the streets of St. John's, making speeches, gathering weapons, and organizing a demonstration by which they hoped to serve Parke with "such a pill . . . as he should not digest," and to attack him "by such a force . . . as would drive him and his grenadiers to the devil!"[60] Parke withdrew from public view and sequestered himself with a small band of his supporters in his house, which he garrisoned with his seventy grenadiers and fortified with five cannon. On the morning of December 7, 1710, a mob estimated to have contained four to five hundred people, many of whom had recently made their way to St. John's to confront the governor, surrounded Parke's residence and demanded that he dismiss the soldiers, resign his position, and depart the island immediately. When Parke refused to "quit the Government with which he had been entrusted by his Royal Mistress," his opponents formed themselves into two assault squads. Captain John Piggott and his men attacked the governor's mansion from the front, while those under Captain John Paynter advanced upon it from the rear.[61] Parke commanded the troops to fire upon the attackers, but the mob, which outnumbered the defenders by at least six or seven to one, soon managed to overwhelm the grenadiers and gain entrance to the house. When they found that Parke had locked himself in his bedchamber, Piggott and his followers broke down the door. Parke responded instantly by shooting and killing Piggott, but was immediately felled by a bullet to the thigh.

At this point, the story grows murky. The most restrained accounts assert that Parke's wound was fatal and that Piggott's men allowed some of the former's defenders to transport him to the nearby house of a Mr. Wright, where Doctor Gousse Bonnin bandaged the wound, but his ministrations came too late to prevent Parke's death shortly thereafter.[62] A number of alternative versions, however, claim that Parke met a far bloodier end. One variant concurs that Parke died in Wright's house under Bonnin's care, but states that after Parke was wounded the mob refused to let his friends evacuate him. Instead, they stripped him of his clothes "with such violence that only the wrist and neckbands of his shirt were left on him." They then dragged him down the steps of his house and into the street, where his assailants, after indulging their hatred by insulting and reviling him, left Parke to die of his wounds and of thirst in the noonday heat. At this point, Wright and Bonnin were allegedly permitted to ease his end.[63] Other accounts depict the attackers as rending apart not only Parke's garments, but his body. They "dragged him by the members about his house, bruised his head, and broke his back with the butt end of their pieces," or, still more violently, "drag'd [him] naked on the coarse, gravelly, and stuff clayey Street, which rak'd the Skin from his Bones."[64] Another version is gorier still, maintaining that after Parke received his leg wound, he was "then torn into pieces and scattered in the street."[65]

It is impossible to discern which, if any, of these accounts gives an accurate description of Parke's death. The fighting was close, and the witnesses, among both Parke's friends and his enemies, had ample reason to exaggerate or minimize the wounds and tortures supposedly inflicted upon him. The final version of the story, however—the one that claims that the mob mutilated Parke's body before rather than after his death—is the one that has captured the imagination of later chroniclers and historians. The narrative of dismemberment resonated because it fit so well with what contemporaries and scholars alike know of Parke and the threat he appeared to pose to the integrity of the body politic. The idea that Parke's body natural was destroyed, cut or ripped into pieces, at the hands of a crowd that represented the body politic contains a kind of poetic justice. As Lorna Clymer has observed,

> fragmenting the living body of one who dared to challenge the integrity of the body politic was a common means of British punishment for treason and sedition. Heads and the body parts generated by the execution method of drawing and quartering were commonly displayed during the sixteenth and seventeenth centuries on London's gates and public buildings. Several of the forty-one identified as regicides were executed in the fall of 1660 according to what were already standard forms of punishment for treason: they were first hung [*sic*], their members were cut off, their bowels removed through abdominal incisions, and the various quadrants of their bodies were drawn and then displayed throughout the city.[66]

It is not possible to verify the accuracy of the story of Parke's dismemberment. The importance of the story lies not in its verisimilitude, but in its appearance and reappearance in various accounts of the governor's death. To the Antiguan pamphleteer George French, Parke's staunchest defender, the mutilation testified to the "turbulent Spirits and Loose Principles" of the "fomenters of the Rebellion," and French invoked the rending of Parke's body as an appeal to Parliament to mete out severe punishment to the guilty.[67] To Bryan Edwards, writing nearly a century later, the mutilation of the body was a harsh but necessary response on the part of the long-suffering Antiguans. The fact that the anecdote appears in the writings of French, Parke's principal apologist, and of Edwards, who execrated him, does not prove that it accurately represents Parke's fate. What it does demonstrate is that many people considered such a punishment to have been imaginable in light of Parke's particular offenses.

Parke and Polity

According to Richard Dunn, "the murder of Governor Parke . . . was not an isolated or accidental event. It summed up many long years of life on the tropical firing line."[68] To Dunn, Parke's murder is just another example, albeit an exceptionally bloody one, of the "disastrous social failures" of the West Indies, as precipitated by the supposedly violent and uncivil people who populated them.[69] In perspective, however, the murder was a singular event. Leeward white society, though certainly replete with prejudices and insecurities, was in many instances willing and able to incorporate various types of initially suspect groups and individuals—including Irish Catholics, Scots, Sephardic Jews, Quakers, and unmarried couples—into their island worlds. As long as such people did not challenge the norms and ideals that Leeward residents most valued, particularly their sense of their innate Englishness and the natural rights that they considered to be an integral component thereof, idiosyncratic behavior received relatively little censure.

In these circumstances, the Leeward planters had to deal with other officials, including the two Codringtons, whose mode of governance was high-handed and self-aggrandizing. What was unusual about Daniel Parke, and which led directly to his death, was that he appeared to be bent upon denying the colonists many of the rights of Englishmen, especially those connected to the security of person and property. From the islanders' point of view, every aspect of Parke's background, character, and actions proved that he was intent upon subjugating the Leewards to his arbitrary rule and denying them the exercise of their vaunted English rights. His veneration of the authoritarian Andros, his ardent royalism, and his involvement, through bribery, in an attempt to undermine the integrity of Parliament, all showed him to be a man who would support royal or personal prerogative over the rights of his subjects. In four years as governor of the Leewards, Parke had threatened his subjects' rights to their property by questioning land titles, and, as in the Chester case, had interfered with their right to trial by jury. He had attempted to intimidate them by wandering in disguise through the streets of St. John's. He had used royal troops, who had been stationed in the islands to protect them from slave uprising and foreign attack, as a sort of private standing army to do his bidding and, in the last extremity, to serve as his guard against his subjects. He had manipulated symbols of power in order to elevate himself, ordering the erection of the grandiose and expensive Government House to serve as his residence, and apparently taking the island's seal, a symbol of imperial authority, and transforming it into a drinking vessel for his own use. Most menacingly, he had used all means possible to minimize the power of the assemblies, which the islanders viewed as their bulwarks against gubernatorial tyranny. By ridding themselves of Parke, Leeward whites believed that they were saving themselves from an unprincipled attacker who clearly had no respect for them either as individuals or as a group. It would have been bad enough if Parke had merely insulted them, as he had done through his sexual transgressions, but the crux of the matter was that, by impugning their rights as colonists, he implied that they had none of the rights of Englishmen. Parke's murder implies not that Leeward settlers were perpetually in rebellion against lawful authority but that, on the contrary, they attempted to uphold their rights by using less confrontational tactics, and moved toward violence only when they believed that all other options had been exhausted. In their view, they had used all means legally available to rid themselves of Parke without resorting to violence. But his refusal to leave the islands, even at the Queen's command, and his deployment of royal troops as a personal army had undermined public affairs to the point that islanders felt that they must destroy him before he destroyed their polity.

CHAPTER TEN

Enjoying and Defending Charter Privileges

Corporate Status and Political Culture in Eighteenth-Century Rhode Island

Edward M. Cook, Jr.

> The bitterness of party strife is often developed in an inverse ratio to the intrinsic merits of the controversy. No hostility is so keen as that which has for its basis persons, rather than principles, or more unrelenting than one that, without just foundation, arrays men against each other, in something like a war of classes, upon local divisions or differences of position, whether geographical or social. When position becomes the criterion of party, principles soon perish in the conflict.
>
> SAMUEL GREENE ARNOLD, HISTORY OF THE STATE OF RHODE ISLAND

During the first half of the eighteenth century, Rhode Island developed a distinctive pattern of politics and a political culture unique among the American colonies. As colonial politics supplanted town politics as a central concern, colony-wide elections became first important, then competitive. By the 1730s at the latest, and perhaps as much as two decades earlier, electoral factions reached out from Newport to align and mobilize voters in hinterland towns. Electoral procedure became increasingly sophisticated, including central regulation of the admissions of freemen, the circulation and collection of written ballots for election, and by the 1740s the use of printed ballots. In peak periods of competition, as many as 80 percent of the likely eligible voters actually turned out. High levels of mobilization were stimulated by election manifestos, issue appeals, expenditures of campaign funds that sometimes amounted to bribery, and intensive precinct work. This system of politics reached its height in the famous "Hopkins-Ward Controversy" of the 1760s, during which for a decade more than four thousand freemen regularly turned out for elections decided by fewer than two hundred votes. Through all of this, the participants vehemently denied that they were violating eighteenth-century norms of nonfactional, disinterested, and deferential politics.[1]

The distinctly modern cast of this system, as well as its limits, became clear after the Revolution. Following a period of coalition and nonpartisan politics during the crisis, parties reformed in the mid-1780s. The precipitating issue was state taxation and the disenchantment of the agrarian majority with the property tax policy favored by the governing elite. Remembering the political tactics they had learned during the Hopkins-Ward years, the farmers formed a "Country Party" and swept to power in 1786. They infuriated traditional elites by substituting machine-style organization for the appeals to common good that were the foundation of respectable politics, and they imposed commercial taxation and paper money on the mercantile and gentry minority. The Country Party leadership also dragged its feet on the 1787 Constitution, which they recognized was not intended to serve the ends of insular, agrarian groups. Once the new government was in place, Country and Minority reached a modus vivendi by which the Minority, now styled Federalists, took charge of national politics while conceding a predominate voice in local affairs to their erstwhile opponents.

The local-national compromise worked well until a rival popular voice emerged in national politics. After supporting Adams for president because he was a New Englander, late in 1800 the Country Party warily proclaimed themselves Republicans. Their constituency remained firmly agrarian and landowning, and they quickly became disenchanted with the broader democratic focus of the national Republicans. When nonagrarian Republicans began to claim a voice in state politics, the Country joined a formal coalition with the ostensibly hated Federalists, dividing places on the annual electoral ticket with them. Increasingly their program linked defense of an archaic, agrarian apportionment of the General Assembly and a rigid land-holding franchise to their traditional opposition to legal facilitation of commercial and industrial change. By the 1830s the old Country Party formed the core of a "law and order" movement drawn together to resist democratic and constitutional reform.[2]

This brief excursion into the nineteenth century may help to explain why historians have found it difficult to grasp the nub of eighteenth-century political culture. A first line of interpretation, labeled "Rhode Islandism" by David Lovejoy, stresses the individualism, unapologetic contentiousness, and aggressive pursuit of advantage that were the colony's heritage from the seventeenth century. A second line stresses sectional and economic interests, notably the mid-eighteenth-century rise of Providence to commercial rivalry with Newport, and the formation of a Providence political hinterland within its economic orbit.[3] A third line, advanced recently by Sydney James in a long-awaited and posthumous work, stresses the slow elaboration of a rationalized colonial institutional structure as a framework within which competitive central politics expressed the colony's legacy of contentiousness.[4]

None of these interpretations is wrong, and all overlap in important ways. All are tantalizing because of the affinities of Rhode Island political culture to modern American interest politics. Nevertheless, there is an additional perspective that perhaps best explains why Rhode Island political values advanced so rapidly toward a competitive paradigm that was popular but not democratic, and at the same time resisted other common features of the emerging American political system. That perspective centers on the corporatism that was both inherent in the colony's chartered institutions and congenial to its social situation. Rhode Islanders, like most colonists, were provincial Englishmen. Indeed, their rejection of many of the peculiar religious and social institutions of puritan New England accentuated their ties to the mother country. The direct context for Rhode Island political development was an appeal to English authority and an affirmation of English practices—political, economic, social, and individual—against the puritan communalism of their neighbors. Of course, the unique provincial circumstances of the colony insured that the selection of metropolitan institutions and ideas would be highly nuanced. Political practices had to be inclusive of the independent property holders and frankly individualistic, while shaped by the special claims of local elites. The tension between inclusiveness and elite recognition was effectively meditated by the notions of privilege and privatism central to English corporate institutions. These notions came to hold a central place in the colony's political values.

Colonial Corporatism

Eighteenth-century Rhode Island political culture began with the colony's seventeenth-century charter. Granted in 1663 as part of an imperial effort to strengthen the smaller colonies against the New England colossus, Massachusetts Bay, the charter established the framework and set the tone for later politics. In form it created a corporation that was a cross between the small municipalities that dotted the English countryside and a business company. Like a borough, the charter created a named group of freemen who were invested with a specific set of political privileges and governmental powers. These freemen were entitled to admit others to share in the conduct of their government and in the enjoyment of their privileges.[5]

The exact structure of the Rhode Island government, however, owed much more to the old-model joint-stock corporation than to the more numerous municipal corporations and represented one of the small number of hybrid colonial incorporations. As a colonial corporation, the charter established a fuller framework of government than most municipal corporations and a range of grants and exemptions that came later to look more like political rights than the particularistic privileges characteristic of boroughs.[6] Nevertheless, the confluence of the late-seventeenth-century experience of English corporate regulation and the peculiarities of Rhode Island's colonial situation made the more particularistic model of corporatism a compelling frame of reference to Rhode Islanders, perhaps more so than in nearby chartered colonies like Connecticut and Massachusetts Bay.

In seventeenth-century England, the dominant form of chartered corporation was the municipal borough. Although institutional forms differed so much as to make generalization hazardous, a borough was typically a town, and its institutional elements a mayor, a council of aldermen, and a body of freemen drawn from householders, local guilds or business groups, or a range of constituencies that made local sense. A borough might or might not have an assembly or common council through which freemen participated actively in governance. The core purpose and power of a corporation was to facilitate some local objective, such as a market day or the management of local charitable endowments. Broader governing powers such as the right to dispense justice and enforce order were negotiable features of the chartering process. The fullest form, creation within the borough of a commission of the peace through appointment of some or all of the municipal council as justices of the peace, was a much-prized privilege of larger and stronger boroughs. Similarly, general taxing power, beyond the ability to assess business groups for the core market or local facility, was not a given but also a much-desired objective.[7]

Variations in the degree of governing authority accorded to corporations stemmed from their nature as "bodies politic" or "private bodies with public functions." Boroughs were not comprehensive units of government, but literally fictive persons with a balance of private interest and public concerns like any enfranchised person of the time. Within these fictive bodies members pursued their individual private interests as well as their public concerns. As we shall see, it was in a sense only the public side that was "political."[8]

There were some two hundred of these incorporated bodies in the seventeenth century, created over the centuries by letters patent from the Crown. Formal, legal procedures existed for the regulation of corporations and for forfeiture of mismanaged boroughs, but at most times these were little used. Instead, regulation took place through informal, socially informed means. A corporation that incurred the displeasure of the king, or even of locally powerful gentry or nobles, would soon learn of its vulnerability and would look to its best interests. These interests might well include finding a patron who would negotiate the surrender of the charter, usually in return for the promise of a new one with enhanced privileges. Thus the offending corporate powers, or more likely the offending officer of the corporation, could be given up in an effusive display of loyalty and in return for the receipt of new and valuable local benefits. A borough might well defend its privileges, in court perhaps, but usually in the context of business rivalry or local dispute, and rarely in a contest with higher authorities that later observers would label "political" or "constitutional."[9]

Threats to the continuity of charters were usually individual and associated with local and idiosyncratic causes, but there were periods of broad challenge to the underlying privileges of the boroughs. Two of these, during the Interregnum and in the mid-1660s, involved the widespread perception by local governors and the central authorities of a need to exclude the religiously dangerous, as currently defined, from a share in power. Regulation of charters in these periods, despite the threat of wholesale forfeiture, was usually accomplished by informal means, and often with new gains in local power and privilege. A third and climactic threat to chartered liberty came in the early 1680s and in the wake of the social turmoil of the Popish plot and of the broad political movement to exclude James, Duke of York, from the succession to the throne.

Historians have always understood the connection between the broad attack on charters and the electoral franchises of boroughs as exercised for the Exclusion parliaments, and have usually emphasized the threat to political liberty in the manipulation of Parliamentary boroughs. Only recently have English historians come to appreciate the equal concern of the Crown with non-Parliamentary boroughs and how and by whom local authority was exercised to maintain (or threaten) order. As in the past, challenges to chartered powers were often initiated by local factions, with central encouragement, with an eye to ridding themselves of opponents. Now some boroughs saw multiple surrenders and re-grants—perhaps one under Charles II by Anglican royalists to depose Exclusionists, and a second under James in favor of Dissenters and Catholics. Thus the campaign of the 1680s had even broader implications than the threat to Parliamentary liberty, raising fundamental issues about local stability and the continuing distribution of privilege and privileges.[10]

The charter revisions of the 1680s also saw a revived application of the process of legal forfeiture, which had remained largely a threat through much of the seventeenth century. The main legal device, quo warranto, was an ancient royal writ by which the Crown challenged the right or "warrant" of a corporation to exercise some or all of its powers. Although legal ingenuity had devised forms of quo warranto that only amended a challenged charter, quo warranto proceedings—and a related and more radical writ, scire facias—carried the threat that the charter would not be amended or surrendered in return for a negotiated regrant, but terminated, voiding all the privileges of the chartered community back to the earliest days. With the forfeiture of the charter of the great city of London in a 1683 test case, the possibilities seemed quite stark, both for political liberty and local privilege. The holders of local privilege had strong reasons to look to the security of their charters and to consider the desirability of surrender and negotiation under pressure in the face of the much wider dangers of forfeiture.[11]

Although colonial corporations like Rhode Island were not boroughs, the facility with which they were swept into the process of charter revocation in the 1680s is indicative of the habits of thought that considered colonization charters as variations on a theme. As suggested above, colonial corporations were clearly different from municipal boroughs. Those that survived the initial period of colonization were more public, more distinctly established governments, and more often framed powers as rights. Those distinctions became clearer in the eighteenth century when colonial governments patterned themselves more regularly on the central institutions of the mother country, and appeared less and less like the more limited borough form, at least in the eyes of colonists. Even down to the Revolution, of course, policy makers in England continued to tie colonial governments to the limited municipal model.[12]

It is far from clear how colonists understood their anomalous corporations.[13] Presumably there was a spectrum. As in all things, the extreme case seems to have been Massachusetts Bay. As early as the 1630s, Massachusetts men claimed that their charter had an ill-defined quality that denied officials in London power to intervene in their affairs. The king could grant the charter, but once granted he could not change it or interpret its scope. Instead, they claimed it gave them almost absolute autonomy. To some extent this pose, and attendant episodes of defiance of central authority throughout the seventeenth century, reflected a hard-nosed evaluation of the difficulty and cost to the Crown in supervising a large corporation located three thousand miles away.[14] But there was also a strand of opinion in Massachusetts that believed that it had broad autonomy in principle, not just in practice. This opinion seems to have informed the decision to defy the quo warranto proceedings in the 1680s, even if only through the belief that legal proceedings could be stymied by refusing to produce the parchment charter. It also seems to have informed the actions of the Massachusetts General Court in the 1720s, when the General Court made a point of formally accepting the unpalatable Explanatory Charter, issued after another episode in which the colony claimed exorbitant power under its now second charter.[15] Formal acceptance was better than admitting that the Crown could make changes. Characteristically, it was Massachusetts in the 1760s and 1770s that made the strongest claims about its charter, of the sort that a few years later would be classed as constitutional.

If Massachusetts Bay was at one end of the spectrum, Rhode Island was at the other. Too small and weak in the 1680s even to consider defending its charter, Rhode Island submitted to the Dominion of New England and allowed the charter to go into abeyance. Over the next few years, the colonists were schooled in the intricacies of charter politics. Submission was the first step; resuming the charter after the Glorious Revolution was the next; doing nothing controversial while seeking confirmation from the Crown was the third. When the governors of surrounding colonies sought to mobilize Rhode Island troops, the colony pleaded hardship while appealing to the king to uphold the privileges his predecessor had granted. Protecting the charter became an art form, all the more so because the disgruntled Newport supporters of the Dominion kept up a constant campaign to have it voided.[16] Rhode Islanders increasingly valued it for the autonomy it accorded them from aggressive neighbors and the privileges it defined, including the famous one to "hold forth a lively experiment in religion," a clause that could only be framed in 1660s London as an idiosyncratic privilege.[17]

Defending the Charter

When Rhode Islanders received King Charles's new charter in 1662, they little realized how important the document would become in the life of the colony. Rhode Island had originated as four entirely autonomous towns composed of fractious individuals unable to bear the government of the surrounding colonies. Inclined to maintain the widest possible sphere for individual action and to cooperate only to the limited degree necessary to preserve their liberties from natural hardships and from the political pressure of their more powerful neighbors, the settlers of the four towns had reduced a series of compacts, patents, and charters to near nullity. Power in Rhode Island, insofar as there was any, had flowed up from the settlers, who had given their delegated governors the bare minimum necessary to keep order.[18]

Although the royal charter set out to reverse the flow of power by vesting authority in the governor and company and allowing them to establish town governments and enfranchise whom they saw fit, in practice the colony fathers found it expedient to recreate something close to the old system. They threw freemanship open to the settled male inhabitants of the towns, and acquiesced when town autonomy resumed its course. Warwick started out by flatly refusing to pay the taxes levied to pay the expenses of securing the charter, and Providence continued and even intensified its internal bickering over the town's proprietary lands. Many of the inhabitants of the Narragansett Country, the area on the mainland south of Warwick that had been secured within the charter bounds, conspired to annex themselves to Connecticut. That the charter promised the freemen an inheritance of political liberties and material privileges was little grasped by the generation that received it. But the perception would grow apace in the decades that followed.[19]

The charter's value began to become clearer when royal officials started to tighten their supervisory bonds in the last decades of the century. In 1686, following the annulment of the Massachusetts Bay charter and the institution of an autocratic government in Boston, Rhode Island received notice of a legal challenge in England to its own charter. Realizing the futility of resisting Crown authorities intent on change, the governor and assembly decided to submit without further formalities. Accordingly they drafted an abject address to King James II, pleading for the substance of their privileges, dispatched an emissary to England, and adjourned sine die.[20]

For the next three years they were subject to the appointed local agents of the Andros regime, several of them longstanding opponents of local autonomy. This clique supported outside claimants to Rhode Island lands, attempted to limit the scope of town meetings, and levied taxes by fiat. One thing the Andros cabal did not do was to collect up the charter and the records of its government, which remained safely in the hands of the last elected governor, Walter Clarke. When Andros was overthrown and imprisoned in Boston, Clarke advanced the theory that since the charter had never been condemned in court it was still in force, and recommended resumption of "our ancient privileges and former methods." Accordingly, provincial leaders convened an election meeting in May 1689 and resumed their government. Later that year governor and assembly dispatched a petition to the new monarchs, William and Mary, rehearsing their zeal in apprehending an escaped Sir Edmund Andros "to prevent New England from partaking in Ireland's miseries" and pleading for a confirmation of the charter.[21]

There followed six years of uncertainty, as the colony awaited firm word about the shape of government to come. The decision to resume government was not without its risks, both for the men involved and for whatever credit the charter retained in England. At worst, unauthorized rulers might be treated like Captain Leisler in New York, but that threat receded quickly. More realistically, a too-confident use of the charter might undermine the posture of loyal waiting on the king's pleasure. The result was a show of irresolution that underscored the provisional nature of government. Within months of his restoration, Governor Clarke had ceased to act, leaving government in the hands of his deputy. The next spring that gentleman refused promotion to the governorship, forcing an entirely new choice. When the new administration asked Clarke to turn over the charter and records, he questioned their authority and refused. Seemingly, the colony's privileges were safer with the charter in the custody of the last unchallenged governor and practical government in other hands. The 1690 governor in turn declined re-election after a year, forcing another new choice.[22] Exactly what happened then is uncertain, because the governor and assembly held only two recorded sessions and seemingly no election from the spring meetings of 1691 to the summer of 1695.

If the surviving records are at all accurate, the sole business of the two sessions was to meet a new challenge to the colony's autonomy. Shortly after his appointment as governor of Massachusetts, Sir William Phips informed the neighboring colonies of his commission to command the united militias of New England. Militia policy was a particularly touchy point for Rhode Island, not only because of the extraordinary risks and costs imposed by the wars of the 1690s but also because of the need to accommodate the pacifist sensibilities of the colony's Quaker population. Moreover, Phips' demands raised questions about the colony's privilege of managing a militia under the Charter. And the assembly clearly saw the relationship between these powers and privileges and private advantage. "We humbly conceive the principall ground of these matters are occasioned by private interest," the assembly reported to the king and queen, because "some of the principall persons of his Excellency Sir William Phips, his Councillors" had interests in Narragansett lands, so "that by reasons of these overtures in the militia, as aforesaid, several persons in Kingstown" had been induced to riot against the Rhode Island government. The assembly hastened to reconstitute the militia under leaders of its own choosing and dispatched an agent to England to defend their chartered right to do so. In due course the mission evoked a ruling by the attorney general that the Rhode Island charter had indeed survived the quo warranto challenge of 1685, and that among the "liberties, franchises, and privileges" contained in it was a power "to Trayn and exercise the inhabitants of that Collony in martial affairs."[23]

On the strength of this reassurance Rhode Island elected new officers and resumed full self-government in 1696, returning the redoubtable custodian of the charter, Walter Clarke, to his old post as governor. Clarke continued to spar with his opponents of Andros's days, who now were rewarded for their long-standing advocacy of royal government with appointments to enforce the customs laws. When Peleg Sanford appeared before the council with a commission as vice-admiralty judge, Clarke informed the lower house that the commission "was a violation and infringement of the Charter right and privileges, and if they allowed thereof, he would take his leave of them, and there would be no more choice or Election according to their Charter." A few days later, Clarke, on the strength of his Quaker principles and charter loyalties, refused the oath to uphold the customs laws required by a recent act of Parliament.[24]

Clarke's unbending defense of privilege was in itself a threat to its continuance. Sanford, Customs Collector Jahleel Brenton, and that nemesis of New England governments, Edward Randolph, peppered London with memorials alleging that Rhode Island defied the customs laws, harbored pirates, and played fast and loose with the terms of its charter. Faced with a threat of investigation, the colony adopted a tactic that would serve it in good stead in many a crisis: it changed governors. Sometime in 1697 Walter Clarke resigned and was replaced with his much smoother nephew, Samuel Cranston. When Massachusetts Governor Lord Bellomont rode into Newport in September 1699 with instructions to investigate the misgovernment of Rhode Island, he was escorted to Cranston's stylish house by the governor and a troop of horses, and was genteelly assured that his demands for copies of the colony's charter, laws, and proceedings would be met as quickly as possible. Cranston also took the oaths prescribed for governors by the navigation acts, and politely insisted that he had dealt with the problem of piracy.[25]

He was as firm as Clarke ever had been, however, though more diplomatic, in resisting demands that conflicted with the Rhode Island view of its charter. Bellomont, acting on the assumption that colony charters were subordinate documents subject to modification by every subsequent act of Parliament, challenged Cranston to take the Test Oath and the oaths prescribed by Parliament after the Glorious Revolution, and further pressed him for evidence that the king had approved his election as governor. Rhode Islanders had a much higher opinion of their charter, holding that it exempted them from outside interference in matters defined by it. When pressed by Lord Bellomont, Cranston brought out a statute book to show his awareness of the provisions in question, but insisted that "their Charter empower[ed] them to establish forms of oaths and attestations," and that he needed no approval to govern "otherwise than by virtue of their Charter." Within a few weeks of Bellomont's return to Boston, Judge Peleg Sanford was reminding him that Rhode Islanders held that "what commissions are immediate from his Majesty is an infringement of Charter privileges; and the persons accepting the same are reputed enemies unto their free state or unlimited power."[26]

Cranston saw to it that the "free state" was defended by more than appeals to charter privilege. Tangible irritants like bad roads and a chaotic law code got attention, and the colony contributed with ostentatious enthusiasm to the imperial forces in Queen Anne's War (1702–13). The colony also conceded the Crown's power to exercise admiralty jurisdiction, and justified the last few incidents of conflict over privateering on grounds of emergency rather than of right. Such substantive accommodations to imperial interests helped to draw the attention of London officials away from the charter and blunted the attacks of the local prerogative clique.[27]

Governor Joseph Dudley of Massachusetts made a last effort in 1704 and 1705 to rally the Board of Trade behind his claim to command the militias of the colony, pulling out the old charges of harboring pirates, violating the trade laws, and exercising jurisdiction beyond the scope of a municipal charter to buttress his memorial. The law authorities responded with an opinion asserting the queen's right, "upon extraordinary exigency," to override the usual governance of any colony, but implicitly rejecting the claim that the charters could be swept away on simple grounds of good policy. Rhode Island, in common with the similarly chartered colony of Connecticut, employed skilled counsel in London to rebut interpretations of colonial charters as nothing more than municipal grants with powers to make narrow bylaws. The effective measures taken by the colony's government, together with the declining political fortunes of the proponents of charter reform in England, led to a rapid decrease in fears for the charter and its privileges, and to a period of political peace and prosperity that lasted through the long administration of Governor Cranston.[28]

The harmony of Cranston's later years drew strongly on developments in the internal condition of the colony. The rapid growth of Newport provided economic grounds for political change. From an agricultural community with some mercantile interests in the late seventeenth century, Newport blossomed into a full-fledged commercial city by the 1720s. Privateering during the wars at the turn of the century, and the conniving at piracy that royalist agents complained about, were part of the means by which Newport merchants gathered capital, but the lasting basis of the town's prosperity was the West Indies trade. Increasingly after 1700, Rhode Islanders pulled away from Boston and established an independent presence in the Caribbean. The commodities for this trade—provisions, livestock, and lumber—flowed from the growing towns along the margins of the bay, and from neighboring parts of Connecticut and Massachusetts. Before long secondary forms of economic activity—shipbuilding and rum distilling—sprouted in the little city. The complementary economic strengths of Newport and the rest of the colony fostered the growth of a symbiotic relationship. From a position of simply the largest of a set of equal and competing towns, Newport overshadowed the other communities, becoming an entrepôt city with the others as its hinterland. During the first quarter of the eighteenth-century Rhode Island became virtually a city-state.[29]

Newport's commercial primacy allowed her leaders to exercise unprecedented power in the colony. Since the arrival of the charter in 1663, Newport had been the official capital of the colony, and every governor from that time to 1727 was an inhabitant of the town. During the first half of Samuel Cranston's incumbency a Newporter was deputy governor as well, and local men held the majority of the central offices of secretary, general treasurer, attorney general, and sheriff. The town's deputies and assistants also exerted disproportionate influence in the general assembly. As Sydney James has demonstrated, Newport's combined political and economic power lay behind Cranston's leadership in settling the colony's longstanding divisions over the proprietorship of land. A political *Pax Newportanica* sank the older factional divisions and created what scanty surviving sources suggest was a period of political harmony unique in Rhode Island history.[30]

Toward the end of Cranston's administration, a new division among the Newport elite raised anew questions about the charter and its privileges, and laid the basis for the political controversy that would dominate Rhode Island politics down to the Revolution. The issue was paper money. In 1710 and 1711 Rhode Island had followed the lead of Massachusetts Bay in issuing small amounts of bills of credit as a way of funding the local offshoot of the War of the Spanish Succession. In 1715 this monetary program expanded dramatically with the issuance of a land bank of £30,000, by which bills were loaned to landholders on the security of mortgage deeds. The loans were due in ten years and bore interest of 5 percent. Similar "banks" followed in 1721 and 1728. Meanwhile the borrowers had discovered the inconvenience of repaying the principal and had forced a series of postponements in the redemption of the banks.[31]

Actually, floating more and more currency served the colony well. Farmers in the country towns had never willingly paid central taxes, and one of the strong points in Newport's assumption of political dominance was its willingness to bear the costs of government. The interest on the loans, which seems to have been collected fairly efficiently, paid the ordinary charges of government, enabling the colony to dispense with direct taxation after 1715. The bills themselves passed from hand to hand, facilitating trade, and circulated into the neighboring colonies. Within a few years there was a New

England–wide currency pool, with issues of the four colonies circulating freely across borders and bearing equal value. The pool multiplied Rhode Island's economic benefit, because by the 1720s Massachusetts came under pressure from the London authorities to curb its emissions. Unrestrained by direct English supervision, Rhode Island was left to fill the currency needs of the whole region.[32]

The land banks were precisely the kind of private enterprises conducted for public benefit that were the hallmark of English corporate bodies. The colony's unrestrained ability to issue bills of credit derived from its chartered exemption from submitting its legislation to the Privy Council for review. Little evidence survives from the 1710s and 1720s to indicate how the proponents of paper money argued the case, but the fulsome address on the accession of George II, praising that king for "continuing unto us the quiet enjoyment of our ancient charter privileges," and the shrill dispute that erupted after 1731 over which faction was endangering "charter privileges" make it clear that Rhode Islanders well understood that political accident had bestowed on them a valuable economic asset.[33]

Charter privilege made possible the payment of public charges through the corporation's management of a kind of private business. Beginning with the 1715 issue, the assembly established a "Grand Committee"[34] of six trustees (one of whom eventually became the single "Keeper" who actually ran the office) to manage the currency, supervise the mortgage loans negotiated by agents in each town, and oversee the payment of the interest money into the colony treasury. Although investigative committees from the 1740s would inevitably stress the accumulated administrative laxness and confusion of record keeping, the system was efficient enough to eliminate the need for colony-wide taxation from 1715 until further emissions of currency were forbidden by the New England Currency Act.[35] This public benefit at the center was matched by private benefits to the recipients of the mortgage loans in the towns. These loans were dispersed widely among the substantial landowners, virtually all of whom were freemen of the corporation.

One would wish to be able to examine closely the politics of the early land banks, both centrally and locally, but the paucity of sources makes possible only the most fragmentary understanding of the period before 1730. Much of what can be discerned comes through sensitivity to changes in the structure and process of government. These patterns allow a view of when decisions were contentious and of who was centrally involved, but little sense of fine-grained detail.

Some discussion of the shape of the Rhode Island government and governing process is therefore in order. The Charter provided for a general assembly that was to meet at least twice a year, and which held general power for electing officers, enacting laws, and making decisions. Within the assembly was a council of twelve assistants who were to defend the colony and execute its laws during intervals of the general assembly. The head of the council, designated governor, or his alternate, designated deputy governor, was charged to convene meetings of the council and general assembly and to preside at them, but had few other formal powers to distinguish him from the other assistants. Each of the four existing towns in 1663 received fixed quotas of seats (Newport, six and Providence, Portsmouth, and Warwick, four each), and all subsequent towns were to have two deputies. From the beginning, the deputies were in a position to dominate the government by dint of numbers. The council received a procedural veto when the two houses sat separately for ordinary legislation after 1696, but their negative did not carry over to those important decisions, including the hearing of petitions and the election of all other officers of government, that were taken in a joint session called a grand committee. The membership of the council was allocated among the towns by convention, although the distribution necessarily changed rapidly in the eighteenth century as the number of towns grew. There were nine towns in 1700; eighteen in 1745, created mainly by additions to the settled area of the colony; twenty-four in 1750, created mainly by the annexation of territory from Massachusetts; and twenty-nine in 1770, all as a result of the division of existing, settled towns.[36]

The charter prescribed the election of governor, deputy governor, and assistants at a general election meeting of the freemen of the corporation, to be held at Newport on the first Wednesday in May. By convention, the colony added the secretary, general treasurer, and attorney general to the slate elected at large. From the inauguration of the Charter, freemen had the option of submitting written, signed proxy ballots at the town meeting immediately preceding the general election, and those ballots were carried to Newport by a local magistrate, opened and counted. Freemen from all towns retained the right to vote in person at Newport. By 1700 these ballots, called "proxes" were an established part of the political process.[37]

The first twenty-six freemen were named in the Charter, and they were empowered to admit others to the corporation, with no restriction as to criteria or procedure. In keeping with the popular character of early Rhode Island government, the assembly authorized the admission as freemen who were "of competent estates, civil conversation, and obedient to the civil magistrate," empowering town officials to nominate such men, with specific testimony as to qualifications. This was not a general enfranchisement. Each freeman was elected, by name, to the freedom of the company in open assembly, at the outgoing assembly convened in Newport each year on the day before the General Election. The assembly also admitted freemen at other sessions. The assembly set the required estate at £100 in 1723, increased it to £200 in 1729, and subsequently restated it periodically to allow for fluctuations in the value of currency. The rules for "making freemen" were not restrictive, allowing 70 to 80 percent of the free white adult males to qualify, but they were structured to remind freemen that they were members of a formal, privileged company.[38]

Sydney James is probably correct in concluding that the 1715 Land Bank was the occasion for an escalation in political conflict, and the first sign of political patterns that would dominate the colony for the rest of the colonial period. The sudden large turnover in the membership of both houses in 1714 and 1715 points to that conclusion. But the formlessness of the electoral turnover over the next fifteen years, occasional surges in the admission of freemen, and intermittent spikes in the turnover rates of assistants suggest that change was gradual. Central to the development of partisanship was the rise to political leadership of Newport merchants and ship captains John and William Wanton. During the teens and twenties, the Wantons clearly aspired to the position at the head of Newport political society long held by Governor Cranston. In forming an opposition first against Cranston and then against Newport merchant and provincial secretary Richard Ward and ex-Providence resident Joseph Jenckes, the Wantons played an insurgent, almost populist role. They were clearly involved in the currency emissions in 1721 and 1728 as well as that of 1715. One of John Wanton's critics noted his talent "for keeping up the rage and humor of the mob." Decades later, Moses Brown recalled that "the violent hostility between [Stephen Hopkins and Samuel Ward] grew out of a private feud, which had long existed between William Wanton and R. Ward, and that to this cause alone was the political war waged for so long a period."[39] If such a feud has recoverable roots, the politics of this period seem the most likely origin.

Beginning in 1730, the political temperature began to rise. Admissions of freemen, which had averaged seventy from 1725 to 1729, averaged 105 from

1730 to 1733. In June 1731 politics boiled over when the Wanton leadership pushed through a fourth paper money bank, the largest yet at £60,000. The established faction in Newport had grown increasingly restive as the issues of currency grew larger, and they now persuaded Governor Joseph Jenckes to withhold his participation in the legislative process and to enter a dissent, intended to function as a veto.[40] The written dissent was apparently added to the bill and filed in Secretary Richard Ward's office the day after the assembly rose from the session. Shortly afterward, members of the Newport establishment, along with the small group of royal officials who had for thirty years petitioned the Crown to revoke the Charter, began to gather official documents to support a memorial to London.

When Deputy Governor Wanton learned of the dissent and the intended memorial, he called the assembly, over the objections of Jenckes, into a session that passed legislation affirming the paper money act, rejected Jenckes' dissent as "null and void," confiscated official copies of documents the memorialists had obtained from Ward, and attempted to intimidate the memorialists from sending their address home. In response, Jenckes prepared a letter to the king rehearsing his responsiveness to royal instructions (including implicitly those against paper money), denouncing the Wanton brothers as "two members of our general council, gentlemen desirous of popularity and to be accounted the prime agents in preserving of our charter privileges," and who "caused the news thereof to spread throughout the colony, declaring that the governor had endangered the loss of our charter by ordering the colony seal to be sett to a complaint against the government," and appealing for a ruling upholding his innovative veto. The memorialists supported Jenckes with an appeal to the king for an order putting an end to all bills of credit.

There were now two sharply contrasting theories on the table as to how to safeguard charter privileges: the accommodationist approach of Jenckes, which offered concessions to preserve what was left, and the more blunt approach of the Wantons, which saw safety in the Crown's knowing as little as possible about the colony's business. The Newport establishment was stunned to learn that the law officers in London, in effect, backed the Wantons. "In this charter," Attorney General Yorke and Solicitor General Talbot reported, "no negative voice is given to the governor, nor any power reserved to the crown of approving or disapproving the laws made in this colony. . . . The crown hath no discretionary power to repeal laws made in this province; but the validity thereof, depends upon their not being contrary, but as near as may be, agreeable to the laws of England. . . . Where this condition is observed, the law is binding; and where it is not, the law is void as not warranted by the charter." Only on the subsidiary question of authority to send papers to England did the officers side with Jenckes.[41]

Reconfiguring Politics

The conjunction of charter and paper money concerns in 1731–32 marked a change in politics. The Newport establishment's claim that the best defense of the colony lay in their mastery of smooth-tongued diplomacy lost credence, and, more broadly, Newport leaders were put on notice to consider the special interests of the rest of the colony; the Wantons' support for paper money came from secondary port towns such as Westerly, Warwick, and East Greenwich, as well as from their minority faction in Newport.[42] The freemen were now free to exploit their privileges in promotion of common and individual ambitions and to compete as unrestrainedly as they wished to pursue their ends. And they did. In 1734 admissions of freemen jumped to a record 246, and from 1734 to 1739 averaged 189. These were years of disciplined political competition. The phenomenon of assistants chosen from among the deputies virtually disappeared. Whereas 58 percent had been so chosen in the decade 1710–19, and 32 percent in 1720s, the proportion dropped to 4 percent between 1730 and 1762. That represented five cases, of which two were mid-year replacements for deceased officials. In 1732 William Wanton replaced Jenckes as governor, so that for the next two years the brothers held both top offices. John Wanton succeeded as governor upon his brother's death in 1733, and served until his own death in 1740.[43]

Despite the continued success of the Wanton faction, elections were sharply contested in these years. For the first time the actual returns are recoverable for several of these years, scribbled by harried clerks on the flyleaves of the Journals of the House of Deputies. In 1734 Richard Ward contested the governorship with John Wanton and polled 840 votes to Wanton's 1065. Competition the next year was less intense, with Wanton besting Jahleel Brenton 958 to 320. In 1736 Wanton again defeated Ward by the narrower margin of 1159 to 1017. The 1737 scribblings record the margins only for some of the assistants down the ticket. For fifth assistant, the vote was 1015 to 860, and for seventh assistant, 936 to 734.[44] These voting totals reflected a very high level of participation. Using a somewhat optimistic set of criteria for estimating the lifespan of admitted freemen, Lowther concluded that the turnout of freemen in 1736 was 82 percent. A more conservative calculation that estimates the adult males in an eighteenth-century census population at one-fifth, and uses the 1730 census as a base, yields a figure of 71 percent for 1736 voting by the colony's white, adult males.[45] These are high rates, comparable to the percentages reached in the Hopkins-Ward era, and comparable also to much later periods. In these contested elections, campaign finance and election chicanery reached considerable sophistication. A surviving letter from William Wanton to "Gentlemen," apparently in Providence, asks "the Gov[ernment] men to contribute to [Jonathan Jenckes'] Support as he is upon Service that Immediately concerns them," to do otherwise would discourage "the main affair." Similarly, James Brown, probably of Providence, wrote cryptically to Richard Ward about his "Chief friend in Government affairs . . . You may see by enclosed that he is able to Govern his purse (if not his word)." And freemen at Westerly submitted a deposition reporting that James Babcock was distributing deeds "to make freemen," that is, to qualify them for admission.[46] The elaboration of methods of voter mobilization stretched the conception of the freemanship as a privileged group of chartered gentlemen.

Only for the year 1736 do the voting tallies break down the results of proxing by town. These refute the idea that any simple regional interest division informed the voting. All of the towns were contested, with the most lopsided results running two to one for one candidate over the other, and the closest running a margin of less than 10 percent. Wanton carried commercial towns like East Greenwich and Warwick, but lost in Westerly, where Ward owned land and his son Samuel would later establish an estate. Providence, which in the Hopkins-Ward era would vote almost unanimously for Hopkins, divided 124 to 87 for Wanton. The three rural towns that had separated from Providence in 1731 divided, with Glocester voting for Wanton, but Scituate and Smithfield for Ward. There were no discernable differences in material interest among these towns. The expansion of political alignments incorporated newly developed towns, but in doing so did not erode the mixture of interest politics and of factional rivalry among the colony's gentry.

Vivid expressions of political competition continued in the mid-1740s. Although Ward succeeded quietly as governor after John Wanton's death, his nephew, Gideon, who had served as treasurer of the colony from 1733 to 1742, conducted several political duels with Ward's relative and successor, William Greene. Admission of new freemen leapt from the low 100s in the early 1740s to the middle 200s for 1744–46. Wanton and his party swept into office in 1745, turning over eight of the twelve members of the upper house and a large number in the assembly. The following year Greene and his party replaced Wanton and all but one member of the upper house. The same cycle repeated itself in 1747 (Wanton) and 1748 (Greene).[47]

For reasons that are not entirely clear, Greene's solid victory in 1748 led to a period of reduced partisanship. One contributing circumstance was that issues that had divided the two parties, such as the protocols of address between the colony and its English agent, and raising the property qualification for voting in the face of currency inflation, proved transitory. Another factor was that Greene himself appears to have been a less enthusiastic partisan than either his Ward allies or the Wantons. His administrations gave prominent places to some old Wanton partisans, including notably Daniel Jenckes and Stephen Hopkins of Providence. It may be that this recognition of Providence leaders' aspirations temporarily quieted their competitive fervor.[48] A third factor was that, when Gideon Wanton faded back into the second rank of leaders as quickly and mysteriously as he had moved to the front, Hopkins in particular emerged as the leader on the Wanton side. For a time neither party spokesman was directly engaged in the Newport family rivalries that were a key part of the old alignment, and it took some time for new personal rivalries to emerge.

While Greene was in office, the Parliament in London passed the Currency Act of 1751 depriving Rhode Island, along with the other New England colonies, of the single material issue that had most influenced the old alignment. Rhode Island helped to provoke the act by issuing a final bank of paper money in March 1750, after it was clear that the ministers were seriously concerned about the issue.[49] Thereafter the assembly was forced to take effective measures to clear the accounts of the Grand Committee and close out the mortgage loans that backed the currency. Although partisans would try for another decade to score points by manipulating the currency issue, it became less and less clear what constituency was being served.[50] Increasingly, politicians were forced to make their presentations in other ways.

A new and extraordinary intensification of partisan divisions began with Samuel Ward's well-known indictments of Stephen Hopkins's role at the Albany Congress and in raising provincial troops for the French and Indian War. Out of this personal and paper war were born ten successive annual election confrontations beginning in 1758—the famous Hopkins-Ward controversy. During that series, Hopkins prevailed seven times and Ward three times in a sequence of elections that historians have rightly analyzed in the context of later partisan politics and examined for their indirect connections with the imperial conflict of the 1760s.[51] Party leaders mobilized voters for these elections on a scale that would be rare in American state politics after the Revolution, and even rarer in federal politics until the second quarter of the nineteenth century.[52] Actual voters totaled an average of slightly over four thousand a year during the eight years of Hopkins-Ward elections for which fairly complete tallies are known. This represented about half of the free adult males of the colony, and close to 70 percent of those estimated to meet the criteria for freemanship. These results were facilitated by the closeness of the elections, year after year. Winners' pluralities averaged 159 over the ten years, or about 4 percent. Ward won by sixteen votes in 1762 and Hopkins by twenty-eight in 1764.[53] Both parties developed extensive campaign organizations with contacts throughout the colony. Both parties mounted costly programs of campaign finance, with large sums disbursed in towns with pools of swing voters. Outright bribery was illegal, of course, and sanctioned by the threat to discard the corrupted ballots, which could be done because the ballots were signed by each voter and preserved in Newport until the election was certified by the General Assembly. But bribery of voters was largely unnecessary (although regularly charged by each party against the other) because a more promising approach was to persuade likely opposition voters to "lie still" by employing them for work that would keep them away from town meeting on proxing day. Large sums were also spent on rum for the customary practice of treating the voters. Of course newspaper articles and broadsides were employed to rouse supporters and attack opponents.[54]

Historians have identified a series of interest divisions behind the Hopkins-Ward contests. For the long run, there can be no doubt that the rise of Providence as a population center and commercial city was central to the reshaping of politics from the 1740s on. Providence provided the Wanton-Hopkins party with a voting stronghold that offset the Ward majority in Newport and made the elections competitive. Partisan writers never tired of energizing local voters by claiming that the opposing candidate was hostile to the interests of north or south, Providence or Newport.[55] Occasional issues, such as the siting of the College of Rhode Island (later Brown), came down to direct choices between the rival towns. Political patronage and the profits of office were a constant focus of rivalry, especially because officers of the central government were elected annually by the Grand Committee of the assembly in a winner-take-all orgy. Appeals to personal and regional interest, as well as the growth of an almost prescient process of political mobilization, tie the politics of the 1750s and 1760s unmistakably to the political future.

At the same time, however, these developments were deeply embedded in a politics of privilege, social connection, and family prestige. While Stephen Hopkins seems not to have been closely related to the traditional gentry and mercantile elites, all the other key partisans were. The rivalry of the Wanton and Ward families entered at least its third generation with the emergence of Samuel Ward and Joseph Wanton, Jr., as Newport leaders. Members of the Brown family of Providence were key partisans on both sides of the political divide. William Greene was closely related to the Wards by marriage. These family connections reached out into the country towns, both invigorating rivalry and reducing the salience of a more impersonal interest politics. Campaign correspondence is replete with conversations with familiar connections, reports of rivals' boasts, and concerns about betrayal—"you know the man and Can Judge of his Sincerity."[56]

The reach of family connections is clearly illustrated in the management of campaign funds. Campaign finance was very much the province of elites. The Hopkins campaign fund for 1765 was subscribed by twenty-five gentlemen to assist "the free Votes of the poorer Sort of Freemen in this County . . . particularly them Who's Sircumstances does not admit thar time to ye Injury of their Familys Tho for ye good of the Government." Ward funds and the Wanton money raised in Newport worked much the same way. It mattered very much who was entrusted with the funds in the country towns, since these decisions reflected gentry family ties, not only with the leaders, but with the "poorer Sort" who were in the personal patronage networks of local magnates. Leaders had to be careful not to offend and alienate local contacts through decisions that would upset local social networks and reflect on the honor of local gentlemen. The ubiquitous distribution of liquor for treats was freighted with the same symbolic burden of local respect.[57]

The force of local networks and local rivalry combined with the closeness of the party division to mitigate the force of large-scale interest politics. Although partisans talked as if one party represented Newport and the other Providence, each side was dependent on supporters from the others' region for victories in elections that were routinely decided by fewer than one hundred votes. The northern towns of Providence and Cumberland voted almost unanimously for Hopkins, but were nearly unique in that respect.[58] Elsewhere, the minority vote rarely fell below a third. These minorities were sustained by the prestige of party victories on a colony scale, and by the patronage that flowed to them when their allies triumphed. In these circumstances, the parties were never able to pursue regional interest on a large scale. Throughout the 1760s, partisan Assemblies made a show of skewing the assessment of property taxes toward opposing towns. Of course the victims howled about "Despotism," but more effectively they revived the old tradition of tax resistance and simply refused to pay. Neither party could afford the price of enforcing the tax schedules, and the offending charges were predictably reversed at the next change of party.[59]

Considerations of prestige and honor were also central to the proposals for "peace," or partisan compromise, that were a perennial feature of the competition. Virtually every year one party or the other proposed a formula under which the two parties would end contention and share the offices. Typically these proposals were disingenuous campaign ploys, designed to provoke rejection and to score points with whatever freemen found partisan competition distasteful. Hopkins's 1767 proposal, for example, was premised on the near approach of anarchy under Ward, and on encomiums to Hopkins's wise rule. More concretely, they were built around technical details designed to advantage the proponents and humiliate opponents. Hopkins's 1764 proposal invited Ward to take office under him as deputy governor, and Ward proposed in 1767 that his allies nominate the governor, while Hopkins's allies chose the deputy. Ward habitually proposed variants on an obsolete early eighteenth-century formula that required the choice of a governor from Newport, paired with a deputy governor from Providence.[60] Most of these proposals, in suggesting that the parties nominate assistants alternately, were carefully structured to force the adverse party to include the few neutral assistants in their allocation. When coalition was achieved in 1768, it was on a Hopkins proposal that his friends choose a governor from Ward's supporters, while Ward's side would choose a deputy governor from his. This led to nominees with the weakest possible partisan ties, but predictably a resident in the party's stronghold. The effect was to force each party to protect supporters in its core area and to sacrifice its minority component. Joseph Wanton rebelled directly, and ran a doomed campaign against the coalition, while Elisha Brown warned Ward that the coalition would destroy his interest in Providence County and proceeded to retire.

The 1768 coalition responded in part to the growing imperial crisis. Through most of the 1760s, colony politicians had exploited their privileges under the Charter without much concern. The charge that the opposition was endangering charter privilege was a stock claim, but not one to be taken too seriously. Actually, the main challenge came from the Newport Junto. This little knot of merchants, professionals, and imperial office holders, largely detached from local politics, continued the principled opposition to colonial charters that had subsisted since the Glorious Revolution. Beginning in earnest in 1764, the Junto peppered the newspapers with critiques of charter government, contrasting the turmoil of contention, the corruption and indecorum of campaigns, and the moral untidiness of competitive government with an idealized version of royal government that might follow the revocation of the Charter. Although the Crown paid little attention to the Junto, the increasing crisis in the Empire seemed one more reason to dampen the competition that charter privilege justified.[61] It remained for Governor Joseph Wanton, the son of Governor William Wanton who was elected first in 1770 with the support of the Hopkins party, to carry his defense of the charter to a length other Rhode Islanders rejected when he defended his refusal to implement the measures of the Revolution as "calculated to serve Purposes of Party" and to threaten "our invaluable Charter Privileges." Even in May 1775 Wanton lectured the assembly that "your charter privileges are of too much importance to be forfeited" by challenging the colony's "connexion with Great Britain."[62]

In the first six decades of the eighteenth century, Rhode Island developed a political culture that was vigorous, popular, and competitive. During these years they worked out a set of political practices and expectations that were pushed to their limits during the decade of competition between Hopkins and Ward. Even with the relatively plentiful records for the 1760s, historians struggle to understand the factors that moved both the partisans and the mass of voters they mobilized—the issues and social cleavages that could explain the intensity of partisan competition. Yet issues and hard social divisions largely fail to explain what went on; and a culture of competition, revolving around personal and group rivalries and a socially coded sport of political contestation, goes far as an explanatory device. This culture of competition derived from the unique adaptation of English institutions and practices to a small, religiously and socially fragmented colony. By the turn of the eighteenth century, Rhode Islanders seized on their charter of privileges as a key ground for justifying their liberties and for the frank contentiousness with which they exploited their liberties as a small and poor colony in a great world. As a "private body with public functions," the corporate colony was able to advance its collective interests through expedients like the issue of large sums of currency, and to place its privileges at the disposal of its freemen in their more strictly private interests. Under the banner of "charter privilege," the colony was able to advance a politics that was competitive and broad-based without challenging the core values of received political culture. As an exercise of privilege, politics could be inclusive without challenging the priority of property and social order. If local politics was at least partly private, contention only partly challenged the notion of a larger politics that was to be disinterested. It was characteristic of colonial society that Rhode Islanders made a distinctive adaptation of English institutions that was both shaped by the imperial connection and became the framework for its rejections.

CHAPTER ELEVEN

Native Americans, the Plan of 1764, and a British Empire That Never Was

Daniel K. Richter

For a brief moment after the Seven Years' War, a handful of British officials on both sides of the Atlantic struggled to imagine an empire where Native Americans and Europeans might coexist. Their ideas spawned an ill-starred document known as the "Plan for the future Management of Indian Affairs," which the British ministry circulated for transatlantic comment in 1764. To set this "Plan of 1764" in context, and to explain both the logic of its vision and the reasons for its failure, requires an eighteenth-century prologue reminiscent of *Tristram Shandy*, for the perceived problems that the Plan tried to address are as significant as the flawed prescription it offered. As both perception and prescription, the Plan reveals tensions at the heart of the Empire as it was, even as it struggled to envision an empire that never was to be. Paradoxically, the Plan's utter rejection—the apparent irrelevance of its scheme for British-Indian coexistence—may be its greatest historical relevance.[1]

An Uneasy Connection

The secrets to a successful imperial relationship with Native Americans, as Superintendent for Indian Affairs William Johnson once complained, lay in "a

Terra Incognita, inaccessible to the Generality of even enquirers."[2] Yet, as the Seven Years' War drew to a close, Britons who approached that mysterious landscape agreed on four basic principles. First was the need for an enforceable boundary to defend Native lands from unregulated Euro-American expansion. "The Indians ought to be redressed or satisfied, in all their reasonable & well founded complaints of enormous & unrighteously obtained Patents for their Lands and Treaties of Limitations with the respective Provinces agreed upon & religiously observed," Johnson breathlessly concluded as early as 1759.[3]

The second principle was particularly vital for an empire whose national identity was deeply rooted in commerce: the need to find some workable system to regulate trade. Among what South Carolina's agent to the Creeks called the "several irregular Practices and Abuses" that had "crept into the Indian Trade" were shoddy goods, rigged scales, usurious debts, and outright theft. Alcohol, as the key weapon in crooked traders' arsenals, the most lucrative of commodities, and the lubricant of murderous violence when things went wrong compounded Native grievances. The persistence of noncapitalist ideas about reciprocity and redistribution and the Indian expectation that much of what Europeans considered commerce should take the form of gift-giving only deepened Native perceptions that the entire system was corrupt. The real or imagined presence in Indian country of competing French and Spanish traders who were presumably eager to capitalize on British lapses to divert merchandise to New Orleans multiplied the potential for trouble.[4]

And trouble, in all its varied forms, undergirded the third great issue in British-Indian relations: boundary lines and trade regulations would remain meaningless unless some mutually acceptable system of resolving disputes between Native people and Europeans—some workable mechanism of cross-cultural justice—could be found. Finally, none of the other issues could be addressed effectively without centralized administration in the hands of agents who could speak reliably on behalf of the Empire as a whole. It was vital, said Johnson, for "the Superintendency & Direction of Indian Affairs & Trade, to be under an Authority from the Crown" rather than the fractious individual provinces.[5]

Most Native Americans of the continental interior probably would have agreed with this four-part analysis. Paradoxically, the utter breakdown of Indian-British relations in "the war named Pontiac's" demonstrates the importance Native people attached to boundaries, trade regulation, dispute resolution, and centralized imperial authority.[6] The religious teachings of the

Delaware prophet Neolin—the ideological glue binding the varied Indian attacks on British forts in the Great Lakes and Ohio countries in 1763—centered on what a more secular vocabulary would call the need for a clear territorial boundary. "This land where ye dwell I have made for you and not for others. Whence comes it that ye permit the Whites upon your lands?" the Master of Life supposedly demanded of Neolin.[7] Such rhetoric mobilized very real grievances. During the Seven Years' War, British and provincial officials in the north had repeatedly pledged that colonists would be barred from Indian territory west of the Appalachians and had denied any plan to build permanent military posts at strategic spots formerly held by the French. Yet after 1760 squatters crossed the mountains at the first opportunity, and the British army dug into a string of garrisons from Fort Pitt to Detroit to Michilimackinac. "They say We mean to make Slaves of them, by Taking so many Posts in their Country," the commandant at Detroit reported in April 1763. Indians were convinced "that they had better Attempt Something now, to Recover their Liberty, than Wait till We were better Established."[8]

For Delawares, Shawnees, and Iroquois who lived in the Ohio Country, the apparent immediate provocation for war was the murder of the Delaware leader Teedyuscung. He was a controversial figure, and certainly not recognized by all Delawares as the "king" he purported to be in his sober moments. Yet throughout the Seven Years' War he had defended the lands of a diverse community of several hundred Indians in the Wyoming Valley (the vicinity of present-day Wilkes-Barre, Pennsylvania), while relentlessly criticizing the behavior of the Pennsylvania government and the Six Nations Iroquois in the "Walking Purchase" of 1737, which had dispossessed Delawares of their homes farther east. Having established his credentials in raids against squatter settlements in 1755–56, Teedyuscung later helped to broker peace negotiations between Pennsylvania and the Ohio Country Indians. In reward for his services and in token of promises to defend Indian lands, the provincial government built a house for him at Wyoming. When persons unknown burned that house down around him and set fire to the rest of the village, whatever Delaware trust in British guarantees of Native land claims remained also went up in smoke. Within weeks of the arson-murder, across a vast stretch of trans-Appalachian territory bordering Virginia northward through Pennsylvania, colonists who had squatted in Indian country or settled under patents Indians did not recognize were slaughtered or sent fleeing to the east by Delawares and their allies among the Ohio Country Shawnees, Cherokees, and Iroquois.[9]

Trade grievances inevitably intertwined with threats to Indian lands. Neolin prophesied a future in which Indians would abandon their addiction to European goods, and many of his followers ritually purged themselves of foreign corruption. Yet for most of those who went to war in 1763 the crucial questions involved the quantity, quality, and price of British commodities and the behavior of those who supplied them. "It is important for us, my brothers, that we exterminate from our lands this nation which seeks only to destroy us," Pontiac reputedly told his followers. "The English sell us goods twice as dear as the French do, and their goods do not last . . . ; and when we wish to set out for our winter camps they do not want to give us any credit as our brothers, the French, do."[10]

Commander-in-Chief Jeffrey Amherst's policies for the Ohio Country and Great Lakes regions exacerbated the commercial squeeze. Trade was to take place only at British army posts—Fort Pitt, Niagara, Detroit, Michilimackinac, and about a dozen smaller garrisons—and only those provincials who held licenses from Superintendent Johnson and pledged to follow price lists drawn up for each station were to engage in commerce.[11] Rum was, in theory, completely banned from the marketplace. Powder and lead, Amherst reasoned, should purposely be kept "scarce, . . . since nothing can be so impolitick as to furnish them with the means of accomplishing the Evil which is so much Dreaded."[12] The "Evil" that broke out in 1763 only became more likely when both French voyageurs (whom Great Lakes Indians had long trusted) and British traders (whom Ohio Country Indians seldom had) ignored Amherst's and Johnson's regulations and flocked into Native villages. Floods of rotgut rum and shoddy goods at high prices combined with shortages of officially sanctioned alcohol and of the ammunition crucial for hunting to convey an impression of British mean-spiritedness, if not outright aggression.[13]

That impression took deeper root as Amherst also abandoned the century-old diplomatic tradition of using ritual largesse to demonstrate the benefits of alliance with imperial power. "You are sensible how averse I am, to purchasing the good behavior of Indians, by presents" the commander-in-chief wrote to Johnson. "I think, it much better to avoid all presents in future, since that will oblige them to Supply themselves by barter, & of course keep them more Constantly Employed by means of which they will have less time to concert, or Carry into Execution any Schemes prejudicial to His Majesty's Interests."[14] Having refused to "purchase" Indian allegiance, Amherst ensured that the "Schemes" would thrive. "All the Indian Nations were . . . become verry Jealous of the English, who had erected so many Posts in their Country, but were not so generous to them as the French, and particularly gave them no Amunition, which was the cheif cause of their Jealousy & Discontent," Johnson's subordinate George Croghan reported from Fort Pitt in early 1763.[15] During Pontiac's War, these issues echoed in symbolic messages left with the bodies of slain squatters. Corpses mutilated with awls, pitchforks, even door hinges, spoke volumes about the role such trade goods played in Native rage.[16]

British material parsimony transcended issues of supply and demand; it cut to the heart of Native expectations about political behavior. The diverse Indian villages of the Great Lakes had long participated in a cross-cultural political order that portrayed them as metaphorical "Children" of the French "Father." In the matrilineal kinship systems of many of the region's peoples, the child-father metaphor did not imply coercive dominance. When mothers' brothers rather than mothers' spouses were the figures who exercised male authority over youngsters, fathers could earn deference partly from their superior age and wisdom, but more through their roles as dispensers of advice, sources of material benefits, mediators of disputes, and keepers of the peace.[17] The diplomatic metaphor of fatherhood implied similar bases for respect, earned through peacemaking and the distribution of diplomatic gifts, especially the condolence presents necessary when people died by war or murder. Yet, as a Chippewa orator informed Scottish fur trader Alexander Henry at Michilimackinac in 1761, "your king has never sent us any presents, nor entered into any treaty with us, wherefore he and we are still at war; and, until he does these things, we must consider that we have no other father, nor friend, among the white men, than the king of France."[18]

The collapse of the system of fatherly peacemaking rippled through villages everywhere in Indian country. The failure of British beneficence in turn made it impossible for Native headmen who had formerly relied on French patronage to use their own powers of redistribution to restrain warriors inclined to seek justice through violence. In the months leading up to Pontiac's War, chiefs repeatedly showed up at British posts, desperately seeking some token of generosity they could take back to their people to convince them that a workable political order was possible with the British. At Fort Pitt, Croghan reported that Indian visitors were "very unesey att our Not Suplying them with Amunishion & Nesereys." Attempts to make up for the shortfall personally cost Croghan "above a years Salery within this twelf Months in trifles,

More then the officer Coimmanding heer wold aLow them In order to keep them In Temper."[19]

In the effort to cool tempers, the same alcohol that at other times caused grief assumed particular significance. In April 1762, the commandant at Niagara, having locked up in his storehouse a "very Large" cache of rum confiscated from traders, had an awkward conversation with an unnamed Native leader who was an "old friend" of William Johnson. "Beging" for an order to "allow the traders to sell their people a Little Rum for their Refreshment," the Indian man refused to take no for an answer. Finally, in consideration of the "great number of his Tribe with him," the officer "made him a preasent of three two-gallon Cags of rum to take whome with him."[20] A little over a year later, as war was breaking out, "Wapackcamigat, the Chief of all the Indians here abouts," enacted a similar scene at Niagara. The commandant reported that, when the headman was denied the gift he sought, he "said he would come here once more, and if he was Refused Rum (as he only asked a little) We must take Care of the consequence . . . & he was afraid that We should soon hear bad News." That news arrived soon enough; a few days later, as the entire region erupted in violence, a party of Chippewas attacked six traders' boats near the fort, killed three of the passengers, and took several others prisoner.[21]

That many such local scenes combined to spark region-wide bloodshed points to the final dilemma of British-Indian relations in the period of Pontiac's War. The diplomatic metaphor of fatherhood had meant many things to Native people, but among them surely was the importance, for better or worse, of an empire that spoke in a single voice. Thus Indians also shared with the handful of British officials who thought about such matters the desire for centralized administration, albeit an administration whose fatherly responsibilities Native people defined very differently than did their imperial counterparts. The desire was just as strong among Native people who had remained allied to the British as among those who had fought against them in the Seven Years' War and the battles of 1763. Indeed, disinterested royal mediation was the great hope of many who despaired of dealing with land-hungry provincials through any other means. Teedyuscung, for example, in making peace with the king's Pennsylvania subjects in 1757, had "desired that all Differences between the Indians and Your Majesty's Subjects might be referred to Your Majesty's Royal Determination, and that the same might be publish'd throughout all your Majesty's Provinces."[22] In the 1760s Mohawks, Narragansetts, Wappingers, and others all similarly tried to go over the heads of provincial officials in hopes that their land claims and other grievances might gain a more impartial hearing at Whitehall.[23] As Johnson explained later, such petitions to the Crown were "founded on a certainty that they could expect no redress elsewhere."[24]

An Illusion of Boundaries

In late 1763, as Pontiac's War sputtered to an end and British and Native leaders began to rebuild their uneasy connection, none of the basic problems had been solved. Only the most rudimentary skeleton of a centralized administration existed. Since the early days of the Seven Years' War, the right to speak in the name of the Crown had in theory rested in two regional superintendents of Indian Affairs. Johnson had held the northern post since 1756. John Stuart of South Carolina had succeeded to the southern office in 1762 after the death of Edmund Atkin, whose proposals had convinced Whitehall to create the superintendencies in the first place. Yet independent diplomacy by provincial governors and especially the military's control of the superintendents' budgets stymied many of Johnson's, Atkin's, and Stuart's efforts to keep Indians in the British camp. This was most powerfully demonstrated when Amherst overruled Johnson's objections to the policies that helped provoke the carnage of 1763. In September of that year, the Board of Trade concluded that Amherst's decisions were "the causes of this unhappy defection of the Indians" and that "nothing but the speedy establishment of some well digested and general plan for the regulation of our Commercial and political concerns with them can effectually reconcile their esteem and affections."[25]

On that, there may have been widespread consensus in government circles, but less agreement prevailed on what should, or could, be done about boundaries, trade, and keeping the peace. To the extent that British officials supported the general concept of a boundary between Natives and Europeans, they seemed motivated less by a quest for justice toward Native Americans than by a desire to impose some order on land titles among Euro-Americans. A coherent land tenure system would capture for provincial and imperial governments the filing fees and quitrents, and for large proprietors the purchase prices and land rents, that they so much desired and that squatters and freelance purchasers so frequently denied them. Talk of a British-Indian boundary line was almost always inseparable from schemes to remove the authority to make future purchases (or uncompensated expropriations) of Indian lands from individual colonists and place it safely in centralized government hands.[26]

The stress on Euro-American rather than Native American real estate rings clearly in the royal Proclamation of October 1763. Although it was issued a few days after Whitehall learned about Pontiac's War, the Proclamation had been in the works for months before the ministry knew anything about the troubles in the Great Lakes and Ohio Country.[27] The text of the Proclamation begins not with lands belonging to Indians but with "the extensive and valuable Acquisitions in *America*, secured to Our Crown by the late Definitive Treaty of Peace" that brought the Seven Years' War to an end. The bulk of the document deals with establishing the new colonies of Grenada, East Florida, West Florida, and Quebec and with annexing conquered territory to Newfoundland, Nova Scotia, and Georgia. Next comes a scheme for distributing lands to war veterans in both new and old colonies.[28]

Only then, not quite as an afterthought, does the final third of the Proclamation turn its attention to "the several Nations or Tribes of *Indians*, with whom we are connected, and who live under Our Protaction, [and] should not be molested or disturbed in the Possession of such Parts of Our Dominions and Territories as, not having been ceded to or purchased by Us, are reserved to them . . . as their Hunting Grounds." Royal and proprietary governors must not "pass any Patents for Lands beyond the Bounds of their respective Governments, as described in their Commissions" or "beyond the Heads or Sources of any of the Rivers which fall into the *Atlantick* Ocean from the West and North-West, or upon any Lands whatever, which, not having been ceded to or purchased by Us as aforesaid, are reserved to the said *Indians*." British subjects "who have either wilfully or inadvertently seated themselves upon" the reserved lands were "forthwith to remove themselves." In future, "no private Person" would be allowed to purchase lands from Indians on either side of the line. Instead, the Crown directed that, "if at any Time, any of the said *Indians* should be inclined to dispose of the said Lands, the same shall be Purchased only for Us, in Our Name, at some Publick Meeting or Assembly of the said *Indians* to be held for that Purpose by the Governor or Commander in Chief of our Colonies respectively, within which they shall lie." Clear British legal titles were a principal objective, and, with the continental interior off limits, Euro-American expansion could be more profitably channeled into such places on the Atlantic rim as Nova Scotia and the Floridas. Imperial aims and the exclusion of Europeans from Indian country ("reserved to" but not technically owned by its inhabitants) happily converged.[29]

The Proclamation's language revealed the multiple complications that would bedevil every British effort to envision, much less enforce, a boundary line. In 1763, Euro-American squatters already lived west of the Proclamation Line and would continue to do so despite royal edicts, threats of forced removal, and even the occasional cabin-burning by provincial or regular troops.[30] Moreover, powerful interests in every province had long been speculating in western lands and in schemes to plant entire new colonies in the continental interior. These men (who of course had no sympathy for the squatters who already occupied some of the lands in question) were those for whom the otherwise toothless edict of 1763 had a real impact. They could not obtain legal possession of the lands they coveted and, just as important, faced tough questions about their titles to tracts east of the line privately purchased from Indians under questionable circumstances.[31] Yet they were patient and determined. "The majority of those who get lands, being persons of consequence in the Capitals, . . . can let them lye dead as a sure Estate hereafter," observed Johnson. "Tho' Proclamations are issued, and orders sent to the several Governours[,] experience has shewn that both are hitherto ineffectual and will be so, whilst the Gentlemen of property and Merchants are interested in finding out evasions or points of Law against them."[32]

The lands in question were not only vast but almost impossible to map coherently. One of the most problematic phrases in the Proclamation was its seemingly simple prohibition on the various governors granting lands "beyond the Bounds of their respective Governments, as described in their Commissions." Those commissions almost universally conflicted with each other. On the northern half of the continent alone, nearly every inch of territory east of the Proclamation Line and west of what provincials called "the settled parts" was subject to bitter intercolonial dispute. In 1763, Charles Mason and Jeremiah Dixon were only beginning to survey the border that the Penn and Calvert families had recently agreed upon to end their decades-long controversy over proprietary ownership of a third of modern Pennsylvania and most of Maryland. And, whatever may have been recorded on paper and carved on surveyors' stones, all conceptual clarity broke down when the projected line reached the headwaters mentioned in the Proclamation of 1763. There Pennsylvania and Maryland both transgressed Virginia's extensive land claims—the same claims that in 1754 had led George Washington to Fort Necessity and ignited the Seven Years' War. The crossroads then known as "Redstone"—around modern-day Bedford, Pennsylvania—was a particularly contentious place, claimed by both Pennsylvania and Virginia and inhabited by a thriving community of squatters on lands never publicly purchased from Indian owners. Thus, at precisely the geographic point where Whitehall most needed a neat division between the British and the Indians, rival British provinces bitterly contested ownership in a way that mocked the Crown's vision of orderly real estate transactions.[33]

Northward along the east side of the Proclamation Line the situation was just as confused. Pennsylvania and New York had for decades contested a sixty-mile swathe of what would eventually become part of the Empire State. More pressing, however, was Connecticut's pretension, under the terms of its 1662 sea-to-sea charter, to territory that now comprises the northern third of Pennsylvania. This Connecticut claim was the basis for the aggressive efforts of the Susquehanna Company, chartered in 1753, to plant colonists in Teedyuscung's Wyoming Valley. To stave off the New Englanders, at the Albany Congress of 1754, Pennsylvania delegates secured a purported deed to the lands, signed by a handful of headmen who apparently had no authority to engage in the transaction, and worded in a way that appeared to include not only Wyoming but much of the territory southwestward to Virginia's claims at Redstone and on the Ohio River.[34]

Similar controversy reigned in the Hudson Valley. Tenant uprisings that had occurred in 1751–57 and would erupt again in 1766 capitalized on longstanding border disputes among New York, Massachusetts, and the Stockbridge Indians to call into question the manorial titles of New York grandees.[35] The upper Hudson and Lake Champlain watersheds were likewise a legal no-man's-land contested by New York and New Hampshire, the fate of which would not be decided until after white inhabitants proclaimed the independent state of Vermont in 1777.[36] To the west, in the Mohawk Valley, New York's legal authority was unchallenged by any other British province, but real estate chaos nonetheless remained the order of the day as a result of massive, overlapping, and often fraudulent land grants made earlier in the century. The mother of all such controversies centered on the 800,000-acre Kayaderosseras Patent, a half-century-old legal quagmire that threatened to dispossess the Mohawk Iroquois of almost their entire homeland and to provoke war between the Six Nations and New York.[37]

And so it went, wherever one looked. The only semblance of legal order emerged at the forty-fifth parallel, where governors Henry Moore of New York and Guy Carleton of Quebec would amicably meet to settle the boundary between their jurisdictions in late 1766. But the orderly scene was nevertheless troubled by "several French Gentlemen . . . from Quebec" who requested that Moore confirm their pretensions to seigneuries well south of the border, "which were granted to them before the conquest of Canada" and included at least two tracts of 100,000 acres or more.[38] Similar problems could be found almost anywhere along the Appalachians from that point south to the Carolinas, even in areas where the claims of provinces and grandees were not in dispute. For smallholders, land titles were difficult to acquire, clear patents rare, rules stacked in favor of well-connected easterners, quitrents paid only by the excessively scrupulous, property rights defined variously by ethnic traditions, leases available from a variety of Indians and Europeans with a variety of claims to ownership.[39] For British officials, then, the boundary problem rested on nothing so simple as mere land hunger. It sank into a quicksand that made the bounds of any individual Euro-American farm—much less anything so grandiose as a line tracing "the Heads or Sources of any of the Rivers which fall into the *Atlantick* Ocean"—profoundly unstable.

An Ungovernable Trade

The nightmares plaguing enforcement of a boundary line were matched by those afflicting rational regulation of British-Indian trade. On a local scale, the commercial problems were quite old, and various British provinces had long attempted to deal with them. New York and South Carolina—not coincidently the homes of superintendents Johnson and Stuart—had the most experience and, between them, provided a range of tested options. Since the 1670s, New York had relied with some success on a plan that required all merchants to set up shop in public markets at specific military posts, first Albany and then Oswego. In theory, Indians came to the traders, not vice versa, and the worst excesses of price-gouging, short measures, and transactions under the influence of alcohol could be policed, although hardly eliminated. Yet the viability of the New York system depended on three distinctively local factors that did not apply to the broader continental stage: leaders of the Six Nations, New York's primary trading partners, almost universally agreed that pedlars were best kept out of their villages; Albany and Oswego were close enough to those villages that shopping trips were not a major inconvenience; and any traders who might venture elsewhere had to enter hostile territory dominated by the French and their Native allies.[40]

The stay-at-home New York model contrasted strikingly with the policies that South Carolina had attempted to enforce on its much more far-flung commercial system in the early eighteenth century. Traders had to apply for licenses issued by a board of commissioners that granted each the right to set up shop only at a particular Indian town. Provincial oversight rested on requirements that traders appear annually in Charleston to renew their permits and post bond for compliance with regulations. In addition, a government agent, instructed to spend at least ten months a year traveling in Indian country, was armed with a justice of the peace's powers to mete out penalties in minor cases, take testimony under oath, and send major offenders to Charleston for trial.[41] On occasion, the Carolinians had superimposed on this basic model a government monopoly over particular trades. Most recently, in the wake of the Cherokee War of 1759–61, a board of "Directors of the Cherokee Trade" assumed control of commerce with that nation and appointed a factor to manage its operations in the town of Keowee. A regular but almost impossible to enforce feature of both South Carolina systems was an official "tariff," or price list for staple items.[42]

Amherst's approach to trade in the Great Lakes and Ohio countries on the eve of Pontiac's War attempted to combine New York's military posts with South Carolina's licenses and tariff schedules. But neither of the two British provincial models was familiar to most of the region's Native peoples. For over half a century, the French had managed the region's trade as a set of local monopolies controlled by those who held government office. These officers in turn contracted with companies of merchants and with the voyageurs who transported goods into the continental interior and fanned out from military posts to deal with Indian customers. For New France as a whole, a company of merchants leased the right to export beaver furs and the concomitant obligation to buy at a fixed price all the pelts offered. Those who transported goods westward from Montreal similarly purchased the right to do so, under licenses that minutely described their destinations and privileges. Forts Frontenac, Niagara, and Detroit had been "king's posts" that often operated at a loss in order to keep prices competitive with the British. At smaller forts, the commandant usually leased the right to trade, which he then exercised in partnership with a few merchants and by contract with those who traveled to surrounding villages; these establishments were supposed to support themselves from the profits. Only at Michilimackinac did anything resembling free trade exist, on the theory that competition might lower the price of goods otherwise inflated by the vast costs of transportation to that distant post and its far-flung hinterland. Everywhere in the French system, the pursuit of private profit was subordinated to the need to maintain strong alliances with Native people.[43]

As Pontiac's War demonstrates, no one recognized the virtues of such a system more than Indians themselves. Yet after the British conquest, several unprecedented factors made the French trading model only slightly more workable than those of New York or Carolina. First was the sheer geographical scale of the problem that confronted British policy makers. Johnson—rightly concluding that "Traders will be more cautious of committing Frauds under the Eye of a Commanding officer of some Rank"—never quite seemed to grasp the ludicrousness of attempting to export the New York system of military marketplaces to the wide expanses of the Great Lakes and Ohio countries. Native people, he kept trying to convince himself and Whitehall, would "think nothing of comeing to the Posts," no matter how long the trip.[44]

New France had confronted the problem of geography by combining trading posts with mobile voyageurs, all loosely supervised by the interlocking quasigovernmental monopolies that tied the *pays d'en haut* to Quebec City. After the conquest, however, competing lines of authority crisscrossed the continental interior. Traders from Quebec, New York, Pennsylvania, Virginia, the Carolinas, Georgia, and the Floridas all considered themselves free to enter the fray. The Proclamation of 1763 made the problem worse when it opened commerce "to all . . . Subjects whatever; provided that every Person, who may incline to Trade with the said *Indians*, [d]o take out a Licence for carrying on such Trade from the Governor or Commander in Chief of any of . . . [the] Colonies respectively, where such Person shall reside." Governmental monopolies such as that still in effect for the Carolina-Cherokee trade became illegal, and licenses granted under the Proclamation, unlike those previously issued by South Carolina or New France, placed no restrictions on where traders could peddle their wares. This, combined with the availability of permits in any province, rendered nearly meaningless the Proclamation's proviso that licensees "give Security to observe such Regulations as . . . Commissaries to be appointed for this Purpose" might contrive.[45] To make matters worse, Pennsylvania and Virginia, in contrast to Quebec, New York, or South Carolina, had almost no tradition of effective regulation of Euro-Americans who ventured into Indian country. Employed by politically influential eastern merchants, vagabond traders from those two provinces operated much as they pleased.[46]

A Fugitive Justice

So the hope of policing the trade took up residence in the same fantasy land as the dream of enforcing boundary lines. Joining them there was any vision of peacefully resolving disputes. A solution to this problem would have to depend either on the British Crown somehow exerting real sovereignty over Native Americans or on a successful attempt to blend two very different cultures of justice. Pontiac's War had demonstrated the folly of treating Indians like British subjects. "Many mistakes arise here from erroneous accounts formerly made of Indians," Johnson pointed out. "They have been represented as calling themselves subjects, although, the very word would have startled them, had it been ever pronounced by any Interpreters; they desire to be considered as Allies and Friends." The British had to play along with the rhetoric of alliance at least "until in a few years we shall become so formidable throughout the country, as to be able to protect ourselves." Or perhaps much longer. Indians "can not be brought under our Laws, for some Centuries, neither have they any word which can convey the most distant idea of subjection," Johnson observed on another occasion. "Should it be fully explained to them, and the nature of subordination punishment ettc, defined, it might produce infinite harm, but could answer no purpose whatever."[47]

Hope for permanent peace therefore depended on accommodating European and Native American ideas about justice: on the one hand, the requirement that courts try, punish, and perhaps execute the perpetrator and, on the other, the demand that victims receive compensation either through revenge or, preferably, condolence gifts. At various times and places—early eighteenth-century Pennsylvania, occasionally on the frontiers of South Carolina—the two systems had achieved at best a fragile balance, resting on a usually unstated agreement that each side would police its own and that, when Europeans killed or robbed Indians, both condolence gifts and judicial trials would have their day.[48] With sufficient diplomatic skill and financial resources, the condolence gifts necessary for such satisfaction could be managed. But the real British problem centered on the need to police their own in a way that would minimize the need for such gifts—and the potential for warfare that each such need represented.

The problem was fundamental. How could Euro-Americans who cheated, robbed, or killed Indians be forced to face charges in a British court and be convicted by a jury of their peers? The political support the Paxton Boys enjoyed in Pennsylvania after their massacre of the Conestoga Indians in 1763, along with numerous other examples of whites who literally got away with murder in the 1760s, demonstrate the enormous barrier that racial hatreds placed in the way of Indians seeking redress from British American juries. When no one in Lancaster professed to know who broke into the town workhouse and gruesomely slaughtered those who escaped the attack on Conestoga, and when a similarly mysterious mob sprang Frederick Stump and John Ironcutter from the Carlisle jail before they could stand trial for the murder of ten other Indians, the prospects for justice east of the Proclamation Line, much less west of it, were slim indeed.[49]

But even if racism were tamed, vigilantes restrained, and juries forced to do their job, daunting systemic problems stood in the way of bringing what Commander-in-Chief Thomas Gage referred to as "Lawless Banditti" to justice.[50] If perpetrators effortlessly escaped justice in Pennsylvania's Lancaster and Cumberland counties, how much more easily could they vanish into the *pays d'en haut* or the Creek country, where legal pursuit would require direct exertion of the British sovereignty that Indians almost universally resisted? And even if somehow the perpetrator were arrested at a military post, he would still have to be shipped east to be tried in a proper court—preferably far to the east in a provincial capital where there was more hope for an impartial jury than in places nearer the line. "In the course of a long and tedious journey," it was more than likely that the accused would be "suffered to escape either by the neglect or connivance of their conductors," New York Governor Henry Moore complained.[51] But even if the trip could be safely made, which provincial capital should be the destination? A good lawyer could easily make the case that a New York court, for instance, had no jurisdiction in Indian country, which the Proclamation of 1763 had purposely "taken out of the Jurisdiction of the civil Government."[52]

Whatever the destination, not only the perpetrator but witnesses would have to undertake the voyage. Often, the most important evidence would have to come from Indians who—even if they swallowed their scruples about sovereign British courts and endured the journey—were almost universally barred from testifying, largely due to racial prejudice but also because, as non-Christians, they were presumed to have no fear of the divine power behind the oaths that guaranteed nothing but the truth. Oaths were only one of myriad aspects of the common law that stacked the deck in favor of Anglo-Americans who knew them and who could support their arguments with written documents, however tainted those might be.[53] "Is it possible to suppose that the Indians, to whom (according to the account of the Traders) it is not at all convenient to come even to the outposts to Trade, should be able to go at least 5 or 600 miles, still farther to the capitals for Justice; and admitting that some of them should know of this method, and do so, how are they to obtain Justice?" Johnson rightly asked. "The Courts of Law, cannot admit of their evidence, nor is there any reason to expect it from many Jurys, the prejudices against Indians being too strong, and their regard for their friends to[o] powerful, if these insurmountable bars did not exist."[54]

There were only three possible, and unpalatable, solutions. Traders in Indian country could be subjected to courts-martial at the western posts, but this was a dangerous proposition to make in a British-American climate of protests in the streets against admiralty courts and in a culture where everyone cherished the rights of Britons. More realistic would have been to grant British officials in Indian country the powers of justices of the peace, as had long been the case with South Carolina's agent. But justices had summary powers only in minor cases. The capital crimes most likely to provoke an Indian war would still need to be bound over to courts in the provinces. And the rights of Britons required that any case have the right of appeal. "As the Indians come from a great distance, to Trade, and at all times lead an ambulatory Life in Hunting, any delay of Justice, is in effect a denial of justice as to them" concluded New York Lieutenant Governor Cadwalader Colden. "Allowing of appeals, cannot be proper in controversies, between the Traders and Indians themselves," because "there is reason to suspect, that . . . when the judgment goes against the Trader he will on any pretence appeal"[55] The third option—seriously, if desperately, advocated by Johnson—would be to erect full-fledged British provinces with their structure of courts and juries in the Illinois Country, at Detroit, and perhaps elsewhere. How this might be reconciled with protecting Indian lands was never made clear.[56]

A Plan Made in Whitehall

These were the convoluted problems the Board of Trade hoped to solve with the Plan of 1764. Drafted in the summer of that year under the leadership of the Earl of Hillsborough, building upon Atkin's scheme for regional superintendencies, and drawing on advice in countless wartime letters from Johnson,

Stuart, provincial governors, and others, it had "for its object the regulation of Indian Affairs both commercial and political throughout all North America, upon one general system, under the direction of Officers appointed by the Crown, so as to sett aside all local interfering of particular Provinces, which has been one great cause of the distracted state of Indian Affairs."[57]

The Plan assumed "that all laws now in force in the several Colonies for regulating Indian Affairs or Commerce [would] be repealed." In their stead, the eastern half of the continent would be divided into two administrative districts, defined less by geography than by lists of Indian nations that the Board of Trade, with minimal ethnographic knowledge, presumed to live north and south of the Ohio River. Each district would be the responsibility of one of the existing superintendents, appointed directly by the Crown to "have the conduct of all public Affairs relative to the Indians." Except in emergencies, the commander-in-chief of the British army and the provincial governors were to be forbidden to conduct treaty councils or send official messages to Indians without the consent of the superintendents, who would nonetheless "advise and act in Council" with the governors and sit as provincial "Councillors extraordinary within each Colony in their respective Districts."[58]

A similarly awkward rationalization of lines of authority would extend outward into Indian country. In the south, each town was to choose, subject to the approval of the superintendent, "a beloved man . . . to take care of the mutual interests both of Indians & Traders." These town representatives would in turn "elect a Chief of the whole Tribe" to act "as Guardian for the Indians and protector of Their Rights." In the north, parallel arrangements were to be made to the extent "the nature of the civil constitution of the Indians in this District and the manner of administering their civil Affairs will admit."[59] This system envisioned something vaguely similar to the form of indirect imperial government being worked out at the same time around the globe in South Asia, and the result might well have evolved into something more resembling the raj than the rez.[60]

Within the system of centralized communication and indirect authority thus established, the crucial business of negotiating workable boundaries between Native and Euro-American territory was to fall into place. With "the consent and concurrence of the Indians," the superintendents were "to ascertain and define the precise and exact boundary and limits of the lands which it may be proper to reserve to them and where no settlement whatever shall be allowed." On either side of the line, private and corporate purchases of Indian lands were to be forbidden and, east of it, restricted to proprietors or corporations who held grants from the Crown. New purchases on behalf of the Crown or any of the colonies were to be negotiated only by the superintendents in open councils with "the principal Chiefs of each Tribe claiming a property in such lands." To prevent fraud, any ceded territories were to be "regularly surveyed by a sworn surveyor in the presence and with the assistance of a person deputed by the Indians to attend" and platted on "an accurate map . . . entered upon record with the Deed of conveyance."[61]

Within the newly defined limits of Indian country, commerce would "be free and open to all his Majestys Subjects," but allowed only at specified Indian towns in the south and forts in the north—thus extending the oversight systems traditionally used by South Carolina and New York to their respective districts. Traders would have to apply for annual licenses from the governors of the provinces from which they imported and exported. Licenses would be valid only for specifically named traders at a single location and subject to bonds for good behavior. Each trading town or post would be staffed by a commissary, interpreter, and smith who reported to the regional superintendent. These were to be civil officers, independent of military command, and forbidden to engage in trade on their own behalf. The commissaries would enforce prices according to tariffs established in consultation with both the traders and their Indian customers, prohibit the sale of "rum, or other spirituous liquors, swan shot or rifled barralled Guns," and nullify the debts of any Indian to whom traders extended credit beyond the sum of fifty shillings.[62]

In enforcing these regulations, commissaries would act as justices of the peace. They would bear the "full power of combating offenders in capital Cases in order that such offenders may be prosecuted for the same" and the capacity to declare summary judgments in civil cases between Indians and traders and among traders to the value of £10 sterling. Appeals would be allowed only to the superintendents, whose decisions were to be final. Indians were, "under proper regulations and restrictions," to be allowed to testify in cases tried by the superintendents and commissaries, as well as in trials before provincial courts. The elected national chiefs would have the right "to be present at all meetings and upon all hearings or tryals relative to the Indians." The annual costs of the entire administrative and judicial apparatus—wildly underestimated at £20,000—would be funded by "a duty upon the Indian Trade, either collected upon the exportation of skins and furs (Beaver excepted) from the Colonies or payable by the Traders at the Posts and Places of Trade."[63]

As requested, Johnson and Stuart filed detailed comments on the Plan. The northern superintendent's main reservation concerned the unworkable scheme for Indians to elect national representatives. Attempting to explain to the Board of Trade that in Native polities multiple clan headmen had equal voices in consensual councils, he suggested that a scheme for inviting "A Chief of every Tribe [clan] in a Nation to attend occasionally for the purposes in this article, would . . . appear more satisfactory."[64] Stuart was somewhat more critical than Johnson, setting the Board of Trade straight on the ethnography and geography of the Indian nations assigned to his district, objecting to the provision allowing individual governors to issue licenses—which, he feared, would encourage "Competition and Jealousy between the provinces or the Trading people . . . incompatible with good Order and Government among Indians"—and proposing that the number of permits be strictly limited to avoid the "Confusion arising from Crowds of Traders and Packhorsemen being Sent indiscriminately from the different Provinces."[65]

Yet despite these imperfections (and others that Native people, had they been asked, might easily have pointed out), the superintendents enthusiastically supported the basic outlines of the Plan, which seemed to address comprehensively all four of the great issues in British-Indian relations. With excessive optimism about the proposal's Parliamentary prospects and with Gage's encouragement (and cautious expenditure of military funds), the superintendents set about their work as if the Plan was certain to become law, and waited for Whitehall to confirm their authority to do so.[66]

In the interim, the superintendents devoted much of their attention to undoing the damage Amherst had inflicted on relations with Native people late in the Seven Years' War. Already at the Treaty of Augusta in November 1763, Stuart had resurrected something like the prewar system of diplomacy. Governors from Virginia, Georgia, and both Carolinas and spokesmen for substantial segments of the Catawbas, Cherokees, Creeks, Chickasaws, and Choctaws confirmed peace, exchanged gifts, discussed trading arrangements, and made considerable progress toward fixing a boundary line between the Creeks and Georgia and the Carolinas.[67] In the north, meanwhile, peaceful diplomacy also reemerged as the troops Gage dispatched to pacify Indian country in 1764 negotiated more often than fought and presided over a series of treaty councils with Great Lakes and Ohio country Natives. In the spring of 1765 at Johnson's Mohawk Valley home, headmen from throughout the region brought Pontiac's War to a formal end. A year later, Pontiac himself participated in a treaty with Johnson at Oswego and subsequently pronounced himself a great friend of the British.[68]

Beyond the treaty grounds over which the two superintendents presided, however, there was little evidence of friendship. In July 1765, the same month Johnson hosted his grand peace conference, he complained that "the Frontier Inhabitants of *Pensilvania, Mary Land* & *Virginia*" had attacked convoys carrying Indian trade goods to Fort Pitt, "form[ed] themselves into partys threatning to destroy all Indians they met, or all White People who dealt with them," and attacked "a small party of His Majesty's Troops on the Road." With similar mayhem occurring on the Carolina frontiers, Indians everywhere saw "themselves attacked, threatened and their property invaded by a sett of ignorant misled Rioters who defy Government itself."[69]

Thus, when the superintendents were not trying to patch things up with increasingly frustrated Native leaders, they were writing letters "home," bewailing their inability to implement the rest of the plan and their nearly complete loss of control over the Proclamation boundary, trade regulations, and disputes between Indians and Europeans. What Johnson and Stuart most desired was a clear grant of the royal powers they needed to exert their authority over Indians, colonists, and provincial governors alike. Until "the plan formerly proposed by your Lordships Board be carried in to Execution . . . ," Johnson concluded in the summer of 1766, "I cannot see how it is possible to remedy the foregoing evils."[70]

The lack of royal power in North America was, of course, the great issue of a period marked by the chaos of the Stamp Act and Townshend Duties crises in the provinces, the Wilkes affair in Britain, and revolving-door Whitehall ministries too consumed by domestic politics to concentrate on the vexing, but to them relatively minor, question of relations with Native Americans. Even before the Plan of 1764 had been drafted, George Croghan, who was in London to press the importance of Indian affairs (and the interests of speculators in Indian lands), lamented that "No one thing has been Don Except the affairs of Mr. Wilks & Liberty which Draw the attension of the Nation and has Imbarrest the pres[e]nt Ministry Much." With "the Grate ones but Sqübeling & fighting [to] See who will keep in power[,] the publick Intrest is Neglected to Serve privet Intrest," and the ministers appeared to be "all R——g——e——s aLicke."[71]

Rogues or not, the members of the Board of Trade confessed in July 1766 that "a great variety of considerations of the most difficult and extensive nature" had made it "impossible for us, amidst the other pressing business that has occur'd, so to prepare our thoughts & opinion upon this important Subject." A year later, Secretary of State Shelburne still professed that "the System of Regulations" in Indian relations was "a measure of so great Importance as to require the utmost Deliberation." Whenever a moment could be spared for the project, ministers were bombarded with protests from merchants against any restrictions on Indian trade and from governors—particularly James Murray and his lieutenant and successor Carleton of Quebec—against infringements on the powers of their provinces.[72] As a result, four years of vital time was lost in North America, and squatters and free traders imposed an irreversibly chaotic regime on the landscape that made the Plan of 1764 a dead letter. "Had it been put in execution immediately, I am of opinion, it would have had all the effects expected from it," Johnson bemoaned; "the longer it continues unsettled, the greater will be the opposition."[73]

The Stamp Act crisis, in particular, was an important factor in both the delays in implementing the Plan and the inability of Johnson and Stuart to control the situation, if only for the ways in which it paralyzed the machinery of government. In New York in 1766, for example, Governor Moore refused to issue any trading licenses because they could not be engrossed on stamped paper. As a result, the province's traders either went to Quebec to get the permits allegedly handed out by the sheaf there, or, more likely, headed west with no papers at all. "I am under no small difficulty in preparing such regulations for the ensuing season as I think can be enforced," Johnson confessed in the spring of the next year. "The Traders have got such a habit of late of passing the Posts, and trading where they please, that it is impossible for me to prevent them."[74] For varying periods in many colonies, meanwhile, courts were closed, preventing prosecutions of unlicensed traders, and the proroguing of rebellious assemblies prevented legislation that might have established effective licensing systems, punished squatters, or otherwise strengthened the hands of Johnson and Stuart—not that there would have been much hope for such action anyway.[75]

Perhaps most important, the Stamp Act crisis instilled habits of contempt for royal authority that doomed any efforts to police British frontiers. "I do not apprehend the Colonists are extremely fond of supporting officers immediately under the direction of the Crown," Johnson understated.[76] The superintendent learned his lesson firsthand in late 1766, when he tried to evict a man who had squatted on Mohawk land. Johnson had, he said, "repeatedly (at the earnest request of the Indians) wrote to him, and personally shewn him His Majesty's Proclamation of 1763, and laid the matter before the Governour in Council and the Attorney General, all which he laughs at, well knowing the party that is ready to suport him, in so much, that it would only weaken the prerogative to prosecute him, as may be evinced in many similar cases."[77]

No wonder that, as Thomas Penn reported from London, when the topic of Indian affairs came up, "Every one" was "out of Humour with the Americans."[78] In early 1768, in the midst of the Townshend Duties crisis, another shuffling of the British ministry brought Hillsborough into the government as secretary of state for the colonies, a new post assuming functions formerly exercised by the secretary for the Southern Department. One of his first acts was to help kill the Plan he had originally sponsored. Several months earlier, the ministry, "observing the expences of North America to be enormous, and to arise in a great measure from the present manner of manageing Indian Affairs, by the intervention of Superintendants who necessarily have a power of drawing for such sums as they shall judge expedient," had urged the Board of Trade to pull the plug.[79]

In March 1768 it obliged, and a month later Hillsborough announced the cabinet's final decision. Of the comprehensive program envisioned in 1764, only the negotiation of a boundary line with the Indians (which would be completed by Johnson at the Treaty of Fort Stanwix and by Stuart at the Treaty of Hard Labor later that year, only to be torpedoed by lack of provincial cooperation) remained a goal "essentially necessary to . . . preserving the tranquility of the Colonies." Otherwise, the powers of the superintendents would henceforth be limited to matters that, "as they have reference to the general interests of the Indians, independent of their connection with any particular Colony, cannot be provided for by the Provincial Laws." Among these were "the renewal of antient Compacts or Covenant-Chains . . . ; the reconciling Differences and disputes between one body of Indians and another; the agreeing with them for the sale or surrender of Lands for public purposes not lying within the limits of any particular Colony; and the holding interviews with them for these and a variety of other general purposes which are merely objects of Negotation between your Majesty and the Indians."[80]

The key word was "merely." Individual provinces now regained the upper hand in nearly everything that mattered. Determining "that no one general Plan of Commerce & Policy . . . can be applicable to all the different Nations of Indians of different interests and in different situations" and "that the confining Trade to certain Posts and Places" was "evidently disadvantageous inconvenient and even dangerous," the government concluded that "intrusting the entire Management of that Trade to the Colonies themselves" would "be of great advantage . . . as a means of avoiding much difficulty, and saving much expense." Admitting that in the past provincial mismanagement of the trade had "contributed not a little to involve us in the enormous expences of an Indian War," the Board of Trade somehow found confidence that "the ill effects of such inattention and neglect, will induce all of them to use more caution and better management for the future." Moreover, with trade free and decentralized, there would be no need for the vast expense of western forts, the majority of which could be dismantled. The few that remained, "being formed under Military Establishments and ever subjected to Military Authority" did not "require any other Superintendance than that of the Military commanding at these Posts." This was as close as the new non-plan came to dealing with the vital issue of judicial powers. Concerning mechanisms for resolving everyday disputes between Natives and Euro-Americans, the ministry was silent.[81]

An Empire That Never Was

On the surface, the demise of the Plan of 1764 is easily explained by its cumbersome features, by prerevolutionary chaos in British North America, by political pique in Whitehall, and by empty purses everywhere. Yet deeper still (although no one at the time apparently made the connections), the scheme engaged nearly every great constitutional and ideological issue that defined the imperial crisis. Funding for the Plan—the ballooning annual figure that provided the excuse for killing it—was to come from a levy on fur and hide exports, a form of taxation without representation not unlike the Townshend Duties that nearly brought the Empire to its knees. The Plan's tariff schedules, licenses, and trade regulations flowed from the same basic mercantilist assumptions as the Navigation Acts, assumptions to which Euro-Americans were only just beginning to articulate their gut-level revulsion. The Plan's grant of justice-of-the-peace powers to officials outside the purview of assemblies, its limitations on judicial appeals, and its requirements that provincial laws regarding Indian testimony be overridden would—if anybody seriously examined them—have horrified those who cherished the common law, the independence of courts, and the power of juries. And the shortest of the forty-three articles in the Plan was in some ways the most explosive in its implications. What could more fully assault the privileges of provincial assemblies, more deeply threaten the powers of Euro-American elites, more thoroughly undermine the ambitions of merchants and traders, landlords and landless, speculators and squatters—more concisely sum up the issue of imperial centralization—than the bald assertion "that all laws now in force in the several Colonies for regulating Indian Affairs or Commerce be repealed"?[82]

Beyond these political and ideological issues, the Plan of 1764, in its ham-handed even-handedness toward Indians, also cut to the heart of an emerging British-American racial identity. Like the Proclamation that preceded it, the Quebec Act that followed it, and the vetoes of schemes for western colonies that surrounded it, the Plan suggested that at least some British imperial officials in both Whitehall and North America actually considered Native people to be something resembling subjects of the Crown who had rights and interests that had to be protected, even if those rights and interests came into conflict with subjects of European extraction. Taking root in the 1760s, this alarming potential for imperial racial fairness would convince many provincials that the Crown was not only guilty of an unpopular program to keep Native American lands out of their hands but enmeshed in an unholy alliance with racial others to deny them their lives, liberty, and property. Accordingly, Thomas Paine would assert in 1776 that there were "thousands, and tens of thousands, who would think it glorious to expel from the continent that barbarous and hellish power, which hath stirred up the Indians and Negroes to destroy us."[83]

The Plan of 1764, then, was not just any vision of a British Empire that never was, not just a bureaucratic fantasy in which centralized administration would allow trade to flourish, property to be protected (at least until it accumulated in proper elite hands), and peace to be preserved between Euro-Americans and Indian subjects (although the latter were not to be openly called by that name). The flood of petitions lodged against the Plan, and the constitutional, economic, and racial issues it so thoroughly engaged, suggest instead that it reflected a vision of empire deeply threatening to Euro-Americans who would ultimately reject any imperial future that they themselves could not control. This was indeed an empire that never was. *That* it never was speaks volumes about the imperial structures that actually did emerge, in North America as well as in Britain, during the generation after 1763.

CHAPTER TWELVE

Between Private and Public Spheres

Liberty as Cultural Property in Eighteenth-Century British America

Michal Jan Rozbicki

Liberty, as we all know, was both the central metaphor of the age of the American Revolution and the conceptual axis of its ideology. At times this has diverted our attention from the fact that this ideology, produced and supplied by the elites to the wider public, was a political and cultural instrument rather than a measured description of the essence of the Revolution. Patriot speeches and sermons on liberty were depictions of ideal models rather than representations of the revolutionary process, but commentators often have not made a clear distinction between the two. The two currently dominant historiographical models explaining revolutionary change are both premised on the meaning of liberty as an inclusive notion of the universal rights of all people. One posits that, with the Revolution, colonial elites transcended their well-entrenched identity as a dominant class, and even undermined their own influence, by wrenching their understanding of liberty from its longstanding symbiotic attachment to rank and privilege to espouse a radically new, universal meaning of freedom. The second postulates that revolutionary society rapidly moved on toward greater egalitarianism, while those in power stubbornly continued to cling to "reactionary" concepts of liberty.[1] Typically, both views share the premise that the arrival of the Revolution brought a new and wide-reaching meaning of liberty, essentially antagonistic to the old.

Such assumptions inevitably lead to a dilemma: what to do with what Jack P. Greene once called the "deep and abiding commitment of the revolutionary generation to inequality"?[2] Were they progressives or die-hard conservatives? Despite countless studies of class and social diversity in colonial America, the problem of an apparent contradiction implied by the coexistence of freedom and inequality at the birth of the nation is far from resolved. It remains the source of a lively academic debate as the pendulum swings back and forth between radical and conservative views of the Founders. By exploring the broader social, rather than legal, meanings of liberty in eighteenth-century American elite culture, especially those forged at the intersection of political idiom and identity, this essay offers a reassessment of some of the assumptions on which the history of the Revolution's ideological origins has often been based. It looks at the late colonial gentry (in the sense they used the term to describe themselves) neither as bearers of a "reactionary" liberty nor a "progressive" one, but rather as a group that essentially adhered to the inherited, privilege-based meanings of liberty and equality paramount in the British world during the century preceding 1764.

Liberty as Axiom

A good point of departure in reconstructing such meanings is the realization that linguistic formulations of liberty can only bear meanings allowed by the contemporary social and cultural market. This means that when we hold up such articulations for analysis, they first ought to be placed in the practical context of social relations. In other words, conceptualizations of liberty are not liberty. In 1776, as a few gentlemen were declaring in Philadelphia that all people are by nature created equal and endowed with unalienable rights, slaves, Indians, women, and the propertyless remained, and would long remain, untouched by the universalism of these formulations. Years later, heads rolled from the Paris guillotine on orders justified by the defense of liberty, fraternity, and equality. It is not the rhetorical or legal elegance of a given formulation of liberty but the uses to which it is put that tangibly affect lives and define its real meaning. Our question, therefore, is less whether liberty was verbally defined in this or that way, or whether it derived from this or that philosopher, but what was being communicated by the language of liberty about actual relations within society.

Any discussion of these relations must center on the socioeconomic elites who dominated the public scene in late colonial America, monopolized the educational capital and the production of political assumptions, and had a grand stake in preserving their station. In New England it was a combination of the clergy, powerful lawyers, and men of wealth, a ruling class that Abraham Bishop of Connecticut saw in 1800 as a form of continuing "aristocracy."[3] In the South it was a slaveholding, landed class, which in some colonies developed into a virtual oligarchy. In 1774 John Day, who had lived in British America for decades, identified a colonial gentry consisting of "the landed or moneyed interest," the "commercial men," "practicioners of the law," and the "clergy," a classification that does not much depart from the social composition of the fifty-five men who devised the Constitution.[4] While the existence of elites is not in dispute, historians have differed over the degree of their domination. Progressives divided them into conservatives and radicals. Charles Beard defined their elitism by their "economic interests," mostly ignoring their cultural identity.[5] Consensus historians shoved them under the carpet by emphasizing shared democratic values.[6] More recently, they have been presented as a dominant class that transformed itself with the Revolution, and created a modern, democratic ideological framework.[7] Newer studies by historians with a culturalist bent are uncovering a more complex colonial world in which relatively broad popular participation in political life upheld the domination of the gentry through webs of dependence within a still traditional and stratified society.[8]

Even a brief review of scholarship on colonial and revolutionary eras shows that the complexity of liberty's sociocultural ontology is rarely recognized. Instead, one often encounters a somewhat prosecutorial tone as inordinate attention is lavished on various "denials" of liberty, typically described in the language of "deprivations" and "strictures." Indeed, it is not too much to say that the current prevalence of race, class, and gender as analytical categories has deep roots in an axiomatic understanding of freedom, and has made much of American scholarship literally *a history of constraints on liberty.* It is time to reposition the debate and modify this reductionist interpretive model, which obscures the fundamentally relational nature of liberty and endows it with an abstract, teleological universalism. This model also engenders a propensity to uncover limitations and contradictions, instead of the much more important task of revealing the historically peculiar and rare convergences of circumstances that created freedom for certain groups of people.[9]

A few examples will suffice to illustrate the problem. A recent volume devoted to the origins of liberty in the new American republic opens by denouncing its "narrow and selfishly motivated beginnings," and portraying its evolution in the decades that followed as "constrained by old traditions and institutions hard to move," as if liberty were some timeless *Geist* outside of specific society, following its own logic and ready to shower its blessings on all, if only those who were most free did not want to *remain* more free than others.[10] Slavery is perhaps the most common argument for contradictions in the revolutionary elites' invocations to liberty. These invocations have been called a case of "amaurosis," a "truly wondrous argument,"[11] and an "obvious suggestion of hypocrisy."[12] On the same premise, Thomas Jefferson was labeled a "self-righteous hypocrite,"[13] John Locke accused of "inconsistency" in combining natural rights with an acceptance of slavery,[14] and the Founders branded insincere because they "spoke of the liberty and equality of citizens" while "the reality was different" as "promises were not fulfilled."[15] Elites have been reproached for wanting to remain elites and for holding on to existing social ranks; for being "unembarrassedly aristocratic" and seeking a "repudiation of equality";[16] for tolerating bondage as a "glaring contradiction in the Republicans' popular creed";[17] and for "partisan and aristocratic purposes that belied the . . . democratic language."[18] Jefferson's words on liberty were merely "glittering generalities" that defied "reality,"[19] and the authors of the Constitution made a "a colossal error of judgment" in not immediately expanding the rights of citizens.[20]

However noble the intent of these voices for equal freedom are, they represent two epistemological problems: they treat equal liberty as an axiom, and, consequently, they assume that there was one core meaning of liberty, widely shared among various social ranks and groups in eighteenth-century America. Such an approach deflects our attention from the process of changing tensions within metropolitan and colonial culture that continually modified the meanings of freedom. It shifts modern democracy backward in time. It takes the language of liberty out of social context, much like Louis Hartz did when he suggested that a cohesive, liberal "fragment" was extracted out of European culture and transferred to America, where—deprived of any "feudal" elements—it "had been established from the outset in colonial life."[21] It confuses abstract statements by the Founders with intentions to reengineer society by leveling its ranks. It makes them more modern than they knew, and portrays their commitment to cultural continuity in their adherence to pre-1764 meanings of liberty as an anomaly, a live dinosaur of sorts, surprisingly discovered beyond the time boundary that supposedly marked its extinction.

An important, though little-noticed, casualty of this approach has been the non-egalitarian origin of liberty at the roots of the new American nation. This elitist paternity has been routinely downplayed, if not denied, even though there is absolutely no reason why modern, democratic concepts *must* somehow originate from sources unblemished by inequality or injustice (for instance, an "idea" of universal liberty). On the contrary, they usually emerged incrementally from privilege, fabricated tradition, and the propaganda of power struggles. Unfreedom is not a historical anomaly. It is liberty that is exceptional, and unfreedom has overwhelmingly been the rule. Liberty has no separate ontology of its own. Like social class, economy, law, or political theory, it is not an autonomous category, but an abstraction taken out of a larger context of several interrelated systems functioning in a society. It was understood by eighteenth-century British elites not as an abstract public right but as a spectrum of enforceable privileges, with their fullest enjoyment exclusive to members of their own class. They tended to see those few liberties granted to the non-elites as passive rights, not implying full control over them by those who nominally held them. The great theorist of the English Revolution Henry Parker made such a distinction clear: "Liberty is the due birth-right, of every Englishman: but Liberty has its bounds, and rules. . . . By the laws of Liberty every man is to injoy, that which is his own: but since one man has far greater, and better things to injoy, than another, the liberties of one may extend further, than the Liberties of another."[22]

This is why early modern liberty cannot be studied in separation from the cultural world of those who had "better things to injoy" that legitimized such privilege. A gentleman's *private* cultural attributes were assumed to make him immune to licentiousness and interest, the main threats to liberty. "There is seldom an Instance of a man guilty of betraying his Country," noted Samuel Adams, "who had not before lost the feeling of moral Obligation in his private Connection."[23] As in England, the right to the fullest enjoyment of liberty became the heart of the colonial gentry's cultural self-definition. It was inseparable from a jealously guarded cult of personal independence that both validated their public authority and presumed to guard the public good contained in collective liberty. On the eve of the Revolution, the then still commonly made distinction between "the people" and "the better sort" did not signify an organic separation. On the contrary, the reigning assumption was that of a unified, "free," and "ordered" society resting on the premise that the elites would "naturally" be elected to power by the non-elites, and disinterestedly rule in everyone's name.

The Historical Ontology of Liberty

To understand the changes in post-1764 America, we need to take a closer look at three characteristics that defined the meaning of liberty up to then: its nature as a privilege, as a social relation, and as cultural property of the dominant class. The notion of liberty in early modern Britain grew directly out of noble privilege. Its main value for the elite lay in the fact that it protected them from the state. A government respecting liberty, said leader of the Long Parliament John Pym in 1641, is one whose goal is to "limit and restrain the excessive power and violence of *great* men."[24] From the time of the Glorious Revolution, British liberty became a well-established metaphor for a body of privileges enjoyed by free persons, designed to protect their personal freedom and property from the Crown (rather than to enable them to speak, publish, and so on). Property at this personal level was understood simultaneously as material possessions and a condition of personal independence, a cultural sine qua non of claiming fuller liberties. "Now, by enjoying Liberty," wrote a colonial gentleman in 1701, "I understand, the Liberty of their persons being free from Arbitrary, illegal imprisonments."[25] In their dispute with the British government after the Seven Years' War, it was this meaning that the colonial elites primarily had in mind. When Richard Henry Lee invoked "Liberty," it was in defense of "all the franchises privileges, and immunities of the free people," against "a lately adopted system of plantation government." He wished "to preserve in its greatest purity the excellent Constitution of England as settled at the Revolution."[26]

In other words, liberty was neither self-evident nor a timeless abstract but a man-made social reality, rooted in a selective exemption from the constrictions of state power, such as jurisdiction, taxation, or some other obligation (an exemption still traceable in the "Congress shall make no laws" language), rather than in a right to do things. This reality contained inequality in its very essence, for only some, but not others, were granted freedom from a particular constraint, or allowed some participation in government. To hold such freedoms *as privileges* required the existence of those who did not possess them. Liberty was not something one was entitled to, but something one was invested with, if certain conditions were met. The 1680 *General Laws and Liberties of the Province of New Hampshire* defined enfranchised freemen as those who had over "£20. rateable estate," and refers to them as "admitted to ye liberty of being freemen in this Province."[27] During the English Revolution, even the Levellers, with their radical program of democratizing the political system, clearly saw liberty as a privilege, and explicitly excluded the servants, the poor, and women from the franchise because they "depend on the will of other men."[28] The American Articles of Confederation of 1777 contained similar limitations. Its Article IV defines the "people" as "the free inhabitants of each of these states, paupers, vagabonds and fugitives from justice excepted" who are "entitled to all privileges and immunities of free citizens in the several states."[29] As privilege, eighteenth-century liberty was thus essentially a *social relation of difference*, existentially dependent on inequality. To Jack P. Greene's call, cited earlier, that we pay more attention to the revolutionary elite's commitment to inequality, one may therefore answer that inequality was not only not contradictory to their zeal for liberty, but—in a society still defined by oppositions between the free and the unfree, reason and passions, virtue and vulgarity, gentry and the common folk, independence and servility—it was one of its conditions.

A bridge that conjoined political privilege and the cultural identity of the privileged was property. Property, in people's minds, affirmed the relational meaning of liberty by demarcating divisions across society, and by assigning degrees of freedom. Property qualifications, in both the cultural and legal sense, were also liberty qualifications. Those with the greatest property claimed the fullest amount of liberty. And those who could claim property in liberty were the only ones who could properly own it. The unpropertied ranks could not do so, just as peasants in England were seen as culturally incapable of properly owning a library or portraits of ancestors, because they had no use for them. This cultural component of elite identity carried as much consequence for the realm of power as did the legal and political. If liberty was a gentry-made concept, so was the concept of the gentry itself (just as was the concept of "the poor"), and both should be examined as such, and not as neutral ideas devoid of normative baggage.[30] Ambitious provincial

American elites eagerly upheld these traditional notions because they contained desirable prescriptive assumptions about who qualified for authority and who did not. These prescriptions—all functioning as legitimizers of rank, power, and prestige—included material requirements (property), cultural requisites (education, virtue, taste), and generalizing categorizations of rank ("the better sort," "people of quality"). All were subtly but firmly interwoven within the cultural fabric. Property was an indispensable guarantor of the full enjoyment of liberty, and liberty from arbitrary power protected property and personal security. Property also provided independence, which, in turn, was a prerequisite of disinterestedness. Disinterestedness was deemed the foundation of public virtue, and thus a condition of occupying offices of influence. A culturally successful claim to be a member of the gentry class carried considerable social plausibility owing to the fact that habitual usage of these assumptions "naturalizes real differences, converting differences into nature."[31] In this process, both elites and non-elites participated actively; such assumptions were not merely imposed from above, they had to be internalized by both groups to function as "natural." Only then could elites come to be popularly perceived as intrinsic proprietors of certain attributes, and, by extension, carriers of liberty.

Virtue in the revolutionary era was not merely a "venerable abstraction" or a "schematic notion," as it is sometimes portrayed, but a preeminent cultural instrument of power, since only the virtuous could be trusted as bearers of full liberty.[32] On hearing of a setback for the Americans in 1770, Arthur Lee, future delegate to the Continental Congress, wrote that he was overwhelmed with anxiety that "there was not enough virtue in the country to sustain her liberties." There is little doubt that he understood liberty as an attribute only of those who were capable of being fully free. "Liberty," he noted, quoting Rousseau, "does not consist in any form of government, it exists in the heart of a free man; he bears it everywhere with him; a base man bears everywhere servitude."[33] According to Carter Braxton, signer of the Declaration of Independence, "Public virtue . . . means a disinterested attachment to the public good, exclusive and independent of all private and selfish interest, and which, though sometimes possessed by a few individuals, never characterized the mass of the people in any state." Such altruism was seen as a guarantee of political "equality on which the security of the government depends," because it was supposed to preclude "preferment."[34] An author writing in the *South Carolina Gazette* argued that only men with "great public virtue," that is, devoid of material and private interests, could be protectors of "liberty and the right in the people," and therefore "it must be on the virtues of such men only that freedom, justice, and security can ever rest."[35] Because culturally assigned rank itself signified such qualities, it could be effectively used as a metaphor for them. When in 1778 Gouverneur Morris rebuked Thomas Paine for questioning certain powers of the Congress, he pointed to Paine's low social origin, contemptuously calling him a "mere adventurer from England, without fortune, without family connections, ignorant even of grammar."[36]

The Revolution did not substantially change these notions; the patriot gentry saw itself as holding the cultural imprimatur for representing the people at large. This was well summed up by the Anti-Federalist "Farmer" who in 1788 observed in the *Maryland Gazette* that "the order of the gentry . . . is essential to perfect government, founded on representation. Every other model of introducing wealth into power, has proved vicious and abominable." Acknowledging that Americans were meritocratic and not "fixed and permanent" as in England, he postulated "an executive for life" as a countermeasure necessary for the survival of liberty in the new republic. When he mentioned "the people" as being free to govern themselves locally, he referred only to those who qualified, namely "landholders and consequently the most independent of mankind, mild by nature, moderate by manners, and persevering in every honest pursuit." In case this was not unambiguous enough, he clarified: "I mean not the lowest populace—I mean that class of citizens to whom the country belongs."[37] "Ownership" of the country was inseparable from "ownership" of liberty.

Colonial elites' ambition to excel in genteel attributes was not a question of simply reaffirming their identity. William Byrd II may have exuded confidence when he observed in 1735 that the Virginia landed gentry was financially and politically independent and lived "in health and plenty." Local government was firmly in their control since "our governor must first out wit us, before he can oppress us. And if ever he squeeze mony out of us he must first take care to deserve it."[38] But behind such assurances lurked uncertainty. The relatively recent social origin of the colonial gentry as elites, less distance between classes than in England, and an acute awareness of life on the peripheries of British culture all tended to increase—not diminish, as we have often been told—their motivations to pursue the genteel model. In addition, metropolitan contempt for their ambitions haunted them throughout the century.

This became painfully clear after the Seven Years' War in the context of sharp exchanges with Britain in which concerns about the dignity and ambitions of provincials suffused the language of law and constitutionalism. The colonial gentry had developed a solid sense of British patriotism based on a cult of liberty and proud exceptionalism. As George Mason, a fervent advocate of individual liberties and of a Bill of Rights in the Constitution, put it, "few men had stronger prejudices in favor of that form of government [British] under which I was born and bred, or a greater aversion to changing it . . . without an absolute necessity."[39] Meanwhile, British newspapers printed cartoons of semi-savage rebel leaders contrasted with refined and elegant British statesmen. The hurt pride of a colonial gentleman echoes in Benjamin Franklin's 1776 letter to Earl Howe, in which he refers to the metropolitan opinion of "our Ignorance, Baseness, and Insensibility."[40]

Despite popular tradition to the contrary, frequent late colonial and revolutionary denunciations of hereditary privileges, and of their corrupting effects on the British ruling class, should not be read as decrying the gentry model itself. Colonial elites had long detested them because it was precisely their shortage in America that was used by the metropolitans to deny them gentry status, and a consequent right to full privileges of liberty.[41] It was this entitlement that Samuel Johnson explicitly questioned in 1775 when he tied it to pedigree, a social criterion of exclusion. Referring to the revolutionary leaders, he pointed out with his trademark sarcasm that these "American lovers of liberty," being of low social descent, neither possessed "all the privileges of Englishmen" nor were entitled to "a vote in making laws."[42] In a similar reaction to colonial claims, James Macpherson ridiculed the Americans' "warm encomiums on the ancestors," noting that these forebears were poor and "could scarcely obtain credit." From this perspective, colonial anti-tax claims were really an "endeavor to establish into an inherent right what was actually an indulgence."[43] Public sentiment in England supported such views. In the words of one pro-American observer in London, "there was not a Cobbler in the Kingdom but considered the Americans as Indentured servants and Convicts."[44] If we consider that it was in this context that patriots like Richard Bland called for rights that would apply "without respect to the dignity of the persons concerned," we might be less inclined to ascribe to such calls a modern, broad meaning of "social equivalence," but rather to see them more narrowly, as an argument for more equality between colonial and metropolitan elites.[45]

Revolution and the Universal Language of Liberty

The broad universalism of the Founders' statements on freedom has always been at the center of debates over their radicalism or conservatism. It is often inferred that these formulations implied meanings dramatically wider in their social applicability than had been the case until then. The path to understanding these meanings does not lead through timeless "ideas of liberty" (these, alas, are often our own ideas "discovered" in the language of the Revolutionaries), but through gaining access to the subjective assumptions, deeply anchored in contemporary cultural context, of those who spoke for liberty. It is these prejudices that are elementary to our understanding of past experience because, even before a historical actor reflects on things, he operates "in a self-evident way in the family, society, and state" and thus "constitute[s] the historical reality of his being."[46] Culture for most people is a solid reality; it makes sense of their lives and creates order, but studying its values is pointless without rooting them in a specific time and place.

Universal formulations of liberty and rhetorical inclusion of all members of a society were not invented during the American Revolution. Not only did kings traditionally speak for all the people, but political writers, especially beginning with the English Revolution, increasingly used nominally universal language, drawing on its power to better legitimize their arguments. The great theorist of natural law John Selden best explained the subtle persuasiveness of using such idioms when he observed that calling liberty absolute was "just as a line is often extended indefinitely to demonstrate something in geometry."[47] Such abstractions were far from being denials of selective liberty. Invocations of the universal "liberties of the people" were routinely uttered by members of the gentry and aristocracy engaged in various strivings—*within the elite class*—for political influence. In 1754, English landowner Thomas Beckford became engaged in a blatant manipulation of elections through the corrupt system of "rotten boroughs" in an attempt to have *all four* of his brothers elected to Parliament. But in his letter to the Duke of Bedford, who controlled the boroughs, he not only invoked "the liberty of the country" as being at stake, but insisted that "there are not four men in the kingdom more zealously attached to . . . the liberties of the people."[48] The meaning of such claims derived not so much from a worldview based on the political primacy of the people, as from the assumption that only the elites could represent the entire population. This meaning was transplanted intact to colonial America. The tidewater planter elite in the South Carolina assembly contemptuously rejected (and suppressed) the Regulator's demands for a more equitable representation in the colony's government. But when in 1769 the Carolina assembly became involved in a protracted conflict with the Privy Council, great planters like Henry Laurens and Arthur Lee consistently described their own position in terms of the "Right of the People," and "Rights and Privileges of British subjects" and the "inalienable Birthright of English subjects."[49] Clearly, the assemblymen saw themselves and their decisions as a representative voice of all the "people." There was no irony in denying equal rights to frontiersmen; for the gentry, the meaning of those rights was still elitist in nature. Even a brief glance at a letter, written in 1775 to George Washington by Richard Henry Lee, Patrick Henry, and Thomas Jefferson, demonstrates the cultural continuity of this meaning. The authors asked for his "patronage and favor" in securing a prominent position for another member of the Virginian planter elite, Edmund Randolph. They commended Randolph for his "Gentlemans abilities," for his social origins in that he represented "our young gentry," for his "extensive connections," and for "his desire to serve his Country."[50] Gentility and public virtue continued as taken-for-granted, exclusive cultural qualifiers of representing the people.

The tendency to frame liberty in universal terms is inherent to revolutions and times of political conflict. Oliver Cromwell presided over the English Revolution under the banner of broad liberty, but was ruthless in preserving the power of the gentry and in eliminating the "levelling" radicals who would apply liberty to a wider social sphere.[51] Early modern British elites developed a sophisticated and abstract language of liberty to confirm their privileges whenever these were contested. One common method was to stress their antiquity; the Magna Carta, little talked of earlier, resurfaced as a useful precedent during the conflict with Stuart autocracy in the 1640s. A common strategy was to employ absolute concepts (nature, will of the people, laws of history) to legitimize new regimes, and to anchor elites in universals and unalienables that appeared to transcend the current power struggles. Such usage, however, rarely meant that these elites had suddenly freed themselves from the meanings of words of a year or two earlier, or from relational assumptions about who held the title to the full range of freedoms. Even references to "self-evident" truths, which included liberty, were most often meant in the narrow sense of evident only for those who had the ability to see them as such.[52] Leaders of the American Revolution needed universal points of reference to assure themselves and the public that the disruption of a system sanctioned by long history and deeply entrenched in social psychology was based on absolute foundations that transcended monarchy and patriotic loyalty to Britain. An intention to substantially reengineer relations within society was not a prime issue on their agenda. Leaders of the French Revolution used the concept of a "general will," derived from Jean-Jacques Rousseau's notion of popular sovereignty, in a similar manner. Since they assumed the mantle of representing such "general will," understood as a singular absolute, transcending specific political differences, all opposition to them could be, and was, portrayed as irrational and directed against the tide of history. This readily justified their authority (even when their acts plainly contradicted their words) and gave an almost cosmic sanction to repressions against opponents.[53] To point out this mechanism is simply to say that although the universal framing of ideas of liberty furthered in the long term the cause of freedom at the cultural level (even if effected by dictatorial regimes), what endowed those ideas with contemporary meaning was the way they were appropriated by those able to produce and promulgate such a meaning. Any given intellectual articulation of liberty is, as a rule, a product of the author's struggle with specific, current societal issues, constructed out of concepts taken from a cultural arsenal available at the time.[54]

This brings us to another reason for the shift to more absolute formulations of liberty in the late eighteenth century: the Enlightenment. Just as in mid-eighteenth-century America and Europe it was bad taste to wear an unpowdered wig, so was it no longer intellectually fashionable to exclude ordinary people from the vision of a future enlightened society. This vision supplied the elites with a new authority and a new role to play on the social stage. They were now to be providers of enlightened governance for all, taking responsibility for the improvement of the human condition. Instead of being, as before, privileged as an elite of betters (of birth, property, or position), they now became privileged anew as agents for the betterment of all, shepherds of the ignoble masses who could not *yet* speak for themselves. People should rest assured, wrote Jefferson, commenting on the "ignorance" of the Shaysites, that their interests would be properly represented by elected delegates to Congress, who would "mingle frequently with the mass of citizens."[55] The newly fashionable "mingling" should not be read as implying equality. In 1774 Gouverneur Morris could still warn the American "gentry" and "people of property" that the rising political conscience of the common folk might soon lead to "the domination of a riotous mob," but only a decade later such language would become "unchic" even in the salons.[56] Roy Porter has aptly called this phenomenon "nominal inclusion."[57] It helped defuse conflict and enhance the social stability needed to govern. It built on older traditions of public conversation and virtual representation and was thus closely attached to the established cultural identity of British elites. But its link with the vision of progress is what made it a genuinely exciting project for a Jefferson, a Madison, or an Adams, providing a transcendent affirmation of the pivotal role of their class in society and history. It was culturally so attractive because it continued to set them apart from non-elites, but also, symbolically, included them among the abstract and idealized "people," while making them missionaries of progress.

Instead of overtly distancing themselves from the common folk, the Founding elites now invoked inclusion and opportunity for all, while putting more emphasis on education, politeness, and good breeding as signs of social distinction (in effect applying another old gentry mechanism of separation from the non-elite). Brilliant Massachusetts lawyer Theophilus Parsons noted that any future "free permanent constitution" must harmoniously unite the opinion of the "bulk of the people," who do not have "the means of furnishing themselves with proper information," and of the "men of education and fortune," possessing virtues that "a liberal education aided by wealth can furnish," and capable of determining "what is the true interest of any state." From those who are not "gentlemen of leisure," the latter abilities "are not to be generally expected."[58] "Freemen should always acquire knowledge;" wrote Israel Evans, "this is a privilege . . . unknown to slaves; this creates a conscious dignity of his importance as a rational creature, and a free agent. . . . Where there is wisdom, virtue, and liberty, there mankind are men." "If America would flourish as a republick, she need only attend to the education of her youth," noted another author, because "in a republican government, learning ought to be universally diffused."[59] They all hoped that in a future ideal state, acquiring property and education would allow for more people from the general "bulk" to become enlightened enough to attain proper public virtues—a safely remote, idealized image that the gentry evidently devised by looking in the mirror.

One indication that it was a gentry-generated vision was that widespread stress was placed on the *future* education of the masses. After all, it was a long and well-entrenched tradition that a gentleman's education prepared him for public service rather than for a mere professional career. When the young Theodorick Bland, son of a prominent colonial family and future officer in Washington's army, was sent to Edinburgh in 1761 to study, he saw it above all as preparation for political office in Virginia, appropriate to his genteel rank. In a letter to his father, he wrote that "at four years, the farthest, by a diligent application, I shall be perfectly qualified to enter on that scene of action which I have been so long preparing for, and which . . . I hope will yield the proposed advantages, honour and happiness to myself, my parents, and country."[60] During the post-revolutionary decade, the future enlightenment of ordinary people became an important component of elite discourse on liberty and reflected the well-established genteel link between education and political participation. The Anti-Federalist "Farmer," who excluded the lowest populace from the current political scene, nevertheless declared that someday in the future they too would become educated in "the principles of free government," and "light would penetrate, where mental darkness now reigns."[61] Another gentry-made concept was that of future ownership of land making the masses more enlightened. Titled land tenure could give common folk a means of achieving personal independence. Since "very few Men, who have no property, have any Judgment of their own," noted John Adams, "the only possible way of preserving the Ballance of Power on the side of equal Liberty and Public Virtue, is to make the Acquisition of Land easy to every Member of Society . . . so that the Multitude may be possessed of landed Estates."[62] The views of Jefferson on this are too well-known to need elaboration. The central point is that, although there was to be no immediate change in the system in which the gentry remained the ruling elite as defined by wealth, virtue, and education, ordinary people were now told they were no longer excluded, since they too could become members by someday acquiring the *same* qualifying attributes as the gentry.

To dismiss the historical significance of such nominal inclusion as simply a strategy to preserve elite domination is to miss its progressive role in the expansion of liberty. It was progressive not *despite* the fact that the new inclusion of the people was symbolic, but precisely because it was so. Culture operates mostly through the symbolic sphere. The newly inclusive, elite-made language compensated symbolically for the socially unequal distribution of rights and liberties in practice. The gentry, seeing themselves as the only fully legitimate representatives of the country's interests, came to identify themselves with an abstraction called "the People," a social entity that they felt they personified. This act of symbolic communication provided them with as much real power over real people as heredity did for the English aristocracy. But the very same cultural mechanism that gave a forceful new legitimacy to the elite gave ordinary people a potent instrument to question the elite's monopoly of privileges. More importantly, invoking the People produced a fateful effect, unanticipated by the elites: it *created* the People, in the sense that they came to exist as a popular belief in the public mind. A new cultural matrix for thinking about liberty was born.

Therefore, when in the period from the Stamp Act to the constitutional debates the public sense of liberty began to change, the cause was less an intentional social and political universalism of elite pronouncements about freedom than the accelerated appropriation of this language of freedom by the non-elites. It was made possible by a gradual decline in the gentry's ability to arbitrate its meaning, and by an intensified communication process. Surprisingly little attention has been paid to the defensive reaction to this development from the elite, who clearly expected their dominance to continue in the new republic. There is little doubt that, during the Revolution, the stress republican gentlemen ideologues placed on the "natural" identity of interests among all social ranks routinely presupposed a virtual representation of all by the elite. This was not a conceptual novelty; it derived directly from the old, entrenched British notion of an organic society.[63] It was altogether consistent of the fifty-five or so gentlemen who wrote the Constitution to do it behind closed doors, without publicizing their debates or seeking public support. Revolutionary leaders and signers of the Constitution mostly represented moderate Enlightenment thought, and had little interest in government as an agent of social change. While it might be an agreeable thought today that they would vote themselves out of their heretofore solid local, and now national, power in the name of social leveling, their doing so would in reality be a spectacular historical anomaly. To abandon their claim to exclusive possession of the fullest liberty would be to saw off the branch on which they were sitting, for it would not only destroy their distinctive cultural identity, but also eliminate the cultural premises crucial for reproducing the relations of power.

Their target was to balance the interests of different classes, as opposed to moving toward an egalitarian society. The idea, in full accord with English tradition, was that "common people should have a part and share of influence," a set of liberties appropriate to their rank, but not encroaching on the liberties of the privileged. For instance, to "hold open to them the offices of senators, judges, and offices to fill which expensive education is required, cannot answer any valuable purposes for them; they are not in a situation to be brought forward and to fill these offices."[64] The president of Virginia's Committee on Safety, Edmund Pendleton, was unyielding in the belief that a "democracy, considered as *referring determinations*, either legislative or executive, TO THE PEOPLE AT LARGE, is the worst form imaginable. Of all others, I own, I prefer the true English constitution, which consists of a proper combination of the principles of honor, virtue, and fear." A New York author similarly asserted that "men of good education and deep reflection, only, are judges of the form of government," and expressed alarm that, in order to obtain the political support of non-elites, overly ambitious gentlemen would appeal to "the passions and prejudices of the less discerning classes of citizens and yeomanry," thus deceiving "unthinking people" into believing that their "liberty is invaded," and only leading to "anarchy and wild uproar."[65] It was not untypical to give the elite a religious sanction, as when Jonathan Edwards Jr. told potential voters that "of all forms of government a republic most essentially requires virtue," and therefore "by the same reasons by which you are obligated to choose the Lord for your God, you are obligated to seek out and by your suffrages to promote to legislative authority, such as are of the same character," that is, "to promote the wisest and the best."[66]

It is evident that in the decades after the Revolution the gentry fully expected to continue as a political elite, exclusively qualified as carriers of all the privileges of liberty. Unlike the language of constitutional issues, such as sovereignty, the argument in this case did not require major changes; it was still framed in the traditional, old-gentry vocabulary that attached merit to wealth and social rank. American republicanism was presented to the public as, by definition, a system that *required* elites, privileged by merit, as guarantors of freedom. Instead of pursuing coats of arms, as so many did before the Revolution to legitimize their rank on metropolitan terms, they were, subsequent to it, unimpeded in raising merit to the point of becoming the sole foundation of virtue. Pendleton insisted on a "firm" administration "to preserve that virtue which they [political philosophers] all declare to be the pillar on which the government, and liberty, its object, must stand." For him, plain pragmatism dictated that there was not a sufficient "aggregate fund of virtue" in society at large to base a government capable of suppressing "licentiousness" solely on "the American spirit."[67] The former provincial gentleman now assumed the mantle of a republican "aristocrat of merit," but the person wearing it was essentially the same.

The sense of entitlement to privilege was shared by the gentry across the new republic. A New York Anti-Federalist merchant in 1788 was as convinced as Virginia's Pendleton that in the new republic the elite would "naturally" continue to be elected to offices when he wrote that "this Government is so constituted that the representatives will generally be composed of the first class in the community, which I shall distinguish by the name of natural aristocracy." He noted that although America had "no legal or hereditary distinctions . . . every society naturally divides itself into classes," and that "birth, education, talents and wealth, create distinctions among men as visible and of as much influence as titles, stars and garters." The only danger was that "the populace" would create such pressures that "the considerate and good, who adorn private life, and such only can be safely trusted in public station, will never commit themselves to a situation where a conscientious discharge of duty may embitter the evening of life." Liberty would be threatened by any shift in the social status quo, for "there can be no fixed and permanent government that does not rest on the fixed and permanent orders and objects of mankind."[68] New England scholar and minister Elizur Goodrich saw the natural elite as the indispensable hub of the new nation: "Happy are the free and virtuous people, who pay strict attention to the natural aristocracy, which is the institution of heaven; it appears in every assembly of mankind. . . . Happy the people who have the wisdom to discern the true patriot of superiour abilities, in all his counsels ever manifesting a sincere regard to the public good, and never with a selfish view." As late as 1794, Noah Webster argued that the elite's "personal influence" was not the same as that of the old aristocracy, but that it was an "influence which men derive from offices, the merit of their services, age, talents, wealth, education, virtue," and he assumed as an axiom that "natural or customary aristocracy" exists "universally among men."[69] Benjamin Rush was well known for his revolutionary condemnation of the old, British-derived concept of the gentleman as a social parasite who did not work, and who lived "upon the public or his friends." Yet, years later, as he witnessed the social expansion of democracy, he expressed bitter disillusionment that politics, no longer controlled by men of quality, fell into the hands of "the young and ignorant and needy part of the community."[70]

Expectation among the revolutionary elite that "natural aristocracy" should hold more privileges than others is not usefully explained as "conservative."

They merely relied on the deeply entrenched assumption that "the nature of civil society requires, that there should be a subordination of order, or diversity of ranks and conditions in it; that certain men or orders of men be appointed to superintend and manage such affairs as concern the public safety and happiness." In "equal and free governments," where "the PEOPLE are the fountain of power and authority," these elite men were to be "the guardians of the public liberty," and the superiority of their order "entitle them . . . to the obedience and submission of the lower."[71] Making people the sovereign and invoking their will as the source of all power not only did not contradict this view, but strengthened it with a highly effective sanction.

The ubiquitous language of liberty in the revolutionary era was not in itself new, but its penetration of the public arena and its wide effect on public conversation were. This was occasioned by the pressing need of the political class to muster support for independence and war, to legitimize the new state, and to validate their authority. The impact of this intense, freedom-related communication process soon confronted the gentry's expectations of continuity as a dominant group with a monster they themselves helped create. Political debates, earlier limited to gentlemanly exchanges at closed sessions of legislatures and in polite journals, were now made accessible through newspapers, sermons, and tavern and coffeehouse talk, while the drama of events injected the discourse of rights and liberties into popular culture. The nominal inclusiveness of the new parlance, its symbolic elevation of people over power, the universalism of rights portrayed as anchored in nature, and the emphasis on the achievability of virtue through merit, created a genuine threat that the gentry would no longer be able to define the meaning, and therefore the social boundaries, of liberty. The lofty rhetoric of rights was effectively popularizing among the wider public the more abstract aspects of liberty, enlarging its signification beyond the gentry orbit, and putting it on a new social trajectory. The non-elite public arena, influenced by pioneer individualism, mobility, new means of disseminating information, denominational pluralism, and religious appeals to individual consciousness, was already a favorable environment for an adoption of such language for its own needs.[72]

What first started with the fight by the colonial political class for a redefinition of British liberty to protect their own vital interests soon moved on to a situation in which other groups invested their own, different interests in this concept, and made anti-elitist use of the elite-fashioned language of rights. These ranged from laborers who, during the Stamp Act riots in New

York, called Governor Cadwalader Colden a "Murderer of their Rights and Privileges," to Rhode Island statesman Stephen Hopkins, who in 1787 called the received meaning of liberty nothing but "contradiction and inconsistence" since it did not extend the supposedly unalienable rights to African slaves.[73] A realization that public discourse was beginning to revise the notion that private life and public service were inseparable spheres, thus shifting the meaning of liberty according to one's status to liberty as a more abstract quality of life, came as a surprise to many. When in 1783 Washington and other gentlemen were founding the exclusive Society of Cincinnati, they saw its elitist character as perfectly appropriate for their class. They felt they deserved membership by virtue of merit; after all, twenty-seven of them took part in the Constitutional Convention. They were startled by widespread outbursts against the Society's hereditary membership and aristocratic ceremonies. Many critics believed with William Ellery that "it is in reality and will turn out to be an hereditary peerage." By then, liberty talk had penetrated the culture deeply; public service, thus far strongly implying the virtue of disinterestedness, no longer exempted one from being attacked for excessive "private attachments." "It is a literal truth," noted one author, "that the democratic clubs . . . while running mad with the abhorrence of aristocratic influence, are attempting to establish precisely the same influence under a different name."[74]

It would be an understatement to say that the patriot gentry were concerned with non-elites making new claims to slices of the liberty cake, competing with the established, exclusive consumers and distorting the very recipe in the process. This culturally unauthorized but rampant rhetoric of liberty led Edward Rutledge to observe with dismay that "the people of this world are being made dupes of a word." Everywhere, he complained, "'Liberty' is the motto," and it is widely used to undermine the power of the established elite, for "every attempt to restrain licentiousness or give efficacy to Government is charged audaciously upon the real advocates of Freedom as an attack upon Liberty." Theophilus Parsons worried that liberty had been held up to such "dazzling colors" that many no longer understood that freedom also required "subordination." The *Anarchiad* caricatured the deception of common people by the likes of Mr. Wronghead who was daily "planning pop'lar schemes, and nightly rapt in democratic dreams," to please the "vulgar ears."[75] One of the most conspicuous indications of the elite's alarm at the cultural atrophy of the perception of the gentry as a uniform class, distinguished by the possession of public virtue, was the frequency of its attacks on the emergence of party and faction. These critiques were invariably framed in the old language of virtue and disinterestedness. Typical in the revolutionary and federal eras were condemnations of "the selfish spirit" in public officials as "unpardonable," threatening to "destroy all harmony of sentiment," and causing "public resolutions" to show "more the complexion of party-attachment, than the public good." Noah Webster noted bitterly that "it is on points of private local utility, or on those of doubtful tendency, that men split into parties . . . victory is the object and not public good."[76] This sentiment against party was not merely a response to emerging political factions as such, as it is usually depicted. It was a reaction to the fact that "party" contradicted impartiality (disinterestedness) as well as the entrenched idea of the gentry as a unified class of true carriers of liberty, and thus undermined the essence of gentry cultural identity. Objective relations of power tend to reproduce themselves as symbolic relations of power in the form of visions of the social world that promote those relations of power.[77] The old cultural image of the gentry was remarkably effective in producing in people's minds an awareness of social boundaries, distances, and inequalities. Unsurprisingly, its disruption was a cause for alarm in the ranks.

Interpreting Liberty

The post-1764 change in the meaning of liberty within American culture did not involve replacing the existing meaning with one antithetical to it. The process of broadening its social boundaries had begun, but it was not a radical, qualitative shift. Instead, it was the start of a long, painful, chaotic, and halting transformation, only much later to be marked with such highlights of modernity as the abolition of slavery, women's franchise, and civil rights legislation. Only very gradually were general freedoms extracted from the socially specific privileges of liberty. In each case, they were concessions, made in large part because changes in the cultural context that altered the meaning of liberty made them *conceivable*. It is therefore not very helpful to imagine that the revolutionary leaders threw the class-bound meaning of liberty, together with monarchy, into the dustbin of history and replaced it with its diametrical opposite in an abrupt episode where "overnight modern conceptions of public power replaced older archaic ideas."[78] A simple oppositional model does not fully explain the nature and dynamic of such shifts within the intertwined cultural and political processes. These involved tensions between the colonial ruling class, which had adopted the British gentry ethos, and the metropolitan arbiters who denied them legitimacy; between the gentry-bound concept of liberty, as both a privilege and a definer of dominant identity, and the need to propagate it more widely to gain internal support and external validation of political claims; between the public's gradual appropriation of the new discourse of liberty and the desire of the elites to preserve the existing relations of power. No simple dichotomy can explain such unexpected results of these tensions as, for instance, the case of backcountry North Carolina, where oaths of loyalty came to be required in 1778 and where some of the common folk opposed to swearing them used the patriot language of resistance to "arbitrary power" against the very patriot elite that demanded the oaths.[79]

A multidimensional rather than oppositional perspective might also help avoid interpretations based on an a priori assumption that admitting all social groups equally into the privileges of liberty was a culturally viable proposal in the 1770s and 1780s, had it not been resisted by a conservative ruling class. As one historian put it, the revolutionary leaders' rhetoric of freedom merely "masked the political exclusion of certain groups," and only much later, "when the rules and the reality [came] together [did] the Rule of Law become more than an apology or a masquerade."[80] We ought to take another look at the venerable concept of the "central paradox of American history," used as a framework to interpret the coexistence of a "dedication to liberty and dignity among the leaders of the American Revolution" with "a system of labor that denied human liberty and dignity," a model that inevitably leads to the question whether "the vision of a nation of equals [was] flawed at the source."[81] The anachronism of such a framework surfaces when we realize that the leaders' dedication was genuine and nonparadoxical, but it was a dedication to a pre-egalitarian, elite-made liberty. They no more deserve to be questioned why their point of departure was not a more modern meaning of freedom, than they should be caricatured because they "aped the style of the English country gentleman."[82] In both cases they drew on existing cultural legitimacies, well rooted in the past, not the present, as all legitimacies must be to be valid at all.

The temptation to use a dichotomous, oppositional standard of interpretation looms large even in the most sophisticated of studies. It is seductive because it helps to explain progress as a tidy trajectory "leading" to modernity, and neatly divides historical actors into progressives and reactionaries. For instance, in her analysis of the "paradox" of elitism and egalitarian democracy in the 1790s, Joyce Appleby juxtaposes two antagonistic concepts of liberty circulating in America. One, a "classical" concept held by the Federalists, assumed a society divided between the virtuous and the rest, and stressed such notions as the right of a corporate body to self-determination and local government, the idea of free and independent men participating in politics, and the right of "secure possession" of property. Its opposite, a "liberal concept of liberty," was based on assumptions that were "individualistic, egalitarian, abstract, and rational," and rejected classical beliefs in social rank and disinterestedness as foundations of civic virtue. That these contradictory "meanings of liberty" co-occurred after the Revolution is a wonder, considering their "fundamental incompatibility." "So at odds were these two liberties," writes the author, "that it is hard to understand how they could have coexisted together in the same political discourse. This is a puzzle yet to be solved."[83]

Recognizing the elitist paternity of revolutionary liberty and the persistence of the transplanted, restricted meaning of liberty in the age of the Revolution, as outlined above, offers a solution to this puzzle. It suggests that the classical and the liberal notions of liberty were not as different, or opposed, as they might seem, because they both derived from the same core meaning, historically shaped by the ethos and privileges of the British ruling classes, and because behind these notions stood one and the same social elite, albeit with differing views on government. For them, the core meaning of liberty involved a highly individualistic cult of personal independence based on property, a veneration for equality (but within the gentry class only), and an assumption that independence engendered disinterestedness, the foundation of public virtue and a legitimizer of rank and authority. The leaders who supposedly stood behind the two opposite camps, the Federalists and the Jeffersonians, were overwhelmingly members of the same ruling class, with similar interests in power and a similar identity as gentry. They were also far from being fundamentally divided on the question of authority. One can certainly point to significant differences among them in terms of distinction and dignity, even conflicts, such as the attacks of such ambitious men as Patrick Henry and Thomas Jefferson against the social hermeticism of the old tidewater oligarchy.[84] But these were rivalries for influence *within* the gentry class, and while old-style patronage may have been publicly criticized by Henry, he was by no means reluctant to seek it to advance himself.

As suggested above, gentility and republicanism not only were not at odds, but needed each other. When American leaders condemned "the worthless

Nobility and Gentry of England, who meanly creap into the Tyrants service," or when they expressed contempt for the local, "aristocrated gentry," they were far from rejecting the concept of the "true" gentry as a virtuous and meritorious class. They were emphasizing the contrast between the two, and signaling that they represented the latter group well.[85] What may appear to be an idea of a "classless society" was mostly an abstraction, a countercultural device directed against hereditary privilege, but not against rank and privilege as such. The difference between the two groups identified by Appleby was that one openly stressed the need for ranks, while the other promoted an idealized vision for an egalitarian *future.* However, as the correspondence between Jefferson and John Adams vividly demonstrates, both groups firmly believed that, in the meantime, they would continue as the dominant class, validated in its authority by "merit," a republican clone of the much earlier, gentry-made concept of "people of quality."[86] Finally, it is not likely that Jefferson, with his "liberal liberty," rejected disinterestedness as the basis of virtue. His passionate promotion of land ownership as the ideal foundation of future, yeoman-based, republican citizenship was deeply rooted in the old, landed gentry ethos of disinterestedness and independence achievable exclusively through landholding. Cultural assumptions do not change overnight.

In sum, we ignore the discriminating, elitist paternity of freedom at our peril. The meaning of modern American liberty grew less from a rejection of, and incompatibility with, the old, exclusivist one, than from a social expansion of the latter's various constituent privileges, such as protections, rights, and enfranchisement. The old liberty should not be looked upon—as it is in much of the current canonical literature—as merely an anti-model of modernity, waiting to be replaced with a new, "liberal" one. Rather, it should be studied as a shell within which the various future components of modern liberty were born, and from which they were over time extracted, in a piecemeal fashion, as socially broader rights. In other words, specific rights and freedoms first had to be invented and legitimized as such by some before they could be appropriated by others, something that tends to be obscured unless we step outside the box framed by the analytical categories of class antagonism and cultural hegemony. For instance, the poor in eighteenth-century Britain could not enjoy habeas corpus, even if it was widely referred to as a basic British liberty.[87] But habeas corpus had first to be invented (in this case negotiated and established in the public sphere as a privilege of the propertied class) in order to be subsequently available as a distinct, legitimate standard to those who had never before commanded such a right, but who would, at an opportune moment, claim it. Each such invention, however exclusive in its application, added to the existing batch of liberties recognized by the culture. It was thus, in its essence, progressive, a fact often obscured when we constrain our focus to its social delimitations.

In this light, the Revolution appears much less of a radical turning point, characterized by an abandonment of an old, aristocratic sense of liberty in favor of a modern one. When members of the revolutionary elite wrote and spoke about liberty, practically the whole relevant vocabulary used was supplied to them by the preceding century of British history. Assertions of rights anchored in nature and of a right to personal freedom, equality, happiness, habeas corpus, trial by jury, protection of property, parliamentary representation, and religious toleration were not only not new, but culturally crystallized and widely functioning under the rubric of liberty in public discourse at least since 1688.[88] It is implausible to assume that this vocabulary had suddenly discarded the inherent meanings of social relationships it had for so long carried. These meanings are lost if we use looking glasses that filter out their cultural context to extract only the sign but not its significance. Then, indeed, the revolutionaries may appear before us as leading "the greatest utopian movement in American history," trying to create a society based on abstract, ideal principles.[89] In reality the Founders were not primarily articulators of ideas, and even less so utopian dreamers. They owned land, exported commodities, employed people, loaned money, speculated, ran stores, governed, passed and executed laws, occupied offices, provided welfare, and created powerful kinship networks. They required legitimacy for all this, before and after the Revolution, and legitimacy cannot be invented—it must build on what is already culturally valid. This is why the song of liberty they wrote for the new republic was based on what they viewed as the best compositions of the preceding century. Future choirs would read the lyrics in new ways and use them to further their own ambitions, just as British ancestors provided the Founders with a usable vocabulary of liberty they then employed in their struggle against Britain. There is no reason why this liberty could not have been both conservative in its elitism and progressive in the way it embedded a set of affirmative standards in the culture and thus created new social space for inclusiveness.

The fragile and complex historical ontology of liberty cannot be reduced solely to power relations, legal formulations, or symbolic means of expression.

Early modern episodes in which its social realm expanded cannot be explained as events primarily powered by a supposedly widely shared idea of freedom. Nor did liberty grow by virtue of itself. It was, as a rule, a concession, a privilege made possible by a particular equilibrium of power, of which cultural sanction was a vital component. Freedoms for new categories of people were usually recovered and reconstituted from those secured earlier as privileges by other groups. Liberty's mode of existence was primarily that of a social relation, a wholly man-made phenomenon, rather than an abstract axiom. The history of American freedom after 1764 is not a story of an attack on the club of traditional liberty in order to destroy it and replace it with an entirely new one. Rather, it is ultimately a lengthy chronicle of various social groups—including, at one point, the revolutionary elite itself, unacknowledged as legitimate by the metropolis—consecutively storming the doors of the exclusive club of owners of liberty, and demanding membership with full privileges.

Notes

Introduction

1. Figures on colonial population growth are taken from Jack P. Greene, *Pursuits of Happiness: The Social Development of Early Modern British Colonies and the Formation of American Culture* (Chapel Hill, 1988), 178–179, and also from John J. McCusker and Russell R. Menard, *The Economy of British America, 1607–1789* (Chapel Hill, 1985), 211–235. The comparative figures for London (and Scotland) are from E. A. Wrigley, "A Simple Model of London's Importance in Changing English Society and Economy, 1650–1750," *Past and Present* 37 (1967): 44–70, and Michael Anderson, ed., *British Population History: From the Black Death to the Present Day* (Cambridge, 1996), 118–120, 210–211. In 1775, there were approximately 3 million people living in British-America, 7 million in England, 3.5 million in Ireland, 1.5 million in Scotland, and a half million in Wales.

2. See Richard Bushman, "American High-Style and Vernacular Cultures," in *Colonial British America: Essays on the New History of the Early Modern Era,* ed. Jack P. Greene and J. R. Pole (Baltimore, 1984), 345–383, and also Trevor G. Burnard, *Creole Gentlemen: The Maryland Elite, 1691–1776* (New York, 2002).

3. Statistics on immigration to the colonies are from Greene, *Pursuits of Happiness,* 7–8; Bernard Bailyn, *Voyagers to the West: A Passage in the Peopling of America on the Eve of the Revolution* (New York, 1986), 24–26; and David Eltis, *The Rise of African Slavery in the Americas* (Cambridge, 2000), 9.

4. Bernard Bailyn, *The Peopling of British North America: An Introduction* (New York, 1986).

5. See McCusker and Menard, *The Economy of British America,* 219–232.

6. On the contested construction of British identity in this period, see Linda Colley, *Britons: Forging the Nation, 1707–1837* (New Haven, 1992).

7. David Armitage, *Ideological Origins of the British Empire* (Cambridge, 2000), 11; Anthony Pagden, *Lords of All the World: Ideologies of Empire in Spain, Britain, and France, 1500–1800* (New Haven, 1995).

8. Jack P. Greene, "Empire and Identity from the Glorious Revolution to the American Revolution," in *The Oxford History of the British Empire,* ed. P. J. Marshall, 2:208–230 (Oxford, 1998).

9. See for example, James H. Merrell, *The Indians' New World: The Catawba and Their Neighbors from Encounter through the Era of Removal* (Chapel Hill, 1989).

10. Contrast Edward M. Cook, Jr., *Fathers of the Towns: Leadership and Community Structure in Eighteenth-Century New England* (Baltimore, 1976), with Barry Gaspar, *Bondmen and Rebels: A Study of Master-Slave Relations in Antigua* (Baltimore, 1985).

11. See Jack P. Greene and J. R. Pole, "Reconstructing British-American Colonial History: An Introduction," in Greene and Pole, eds., *Colonial British America,* 14–16; Greene, *Pursuits of Happiness,* 174. For an example from South America, see A. J. R. Russell-Wood, "Centers and Peripheries in the Luso-Brazilian World, 1500–1808," in *Negotiated Empires: Centers and Peripheries in the Americas, 1500–1820,* ed. Christine Daniels and Michael V. Kennedy, 115–116 (New York, 2002).

12. See for example Richard Waterhouse, *A New World Gentry: The Making of a Merchant and Planter Class in South Carolina, 1670–1770* (New York, 1989).

13. John M. Murrin, "Anglicizing an American Colony: The Transformation of Provincial Massachusetts" (PhD diss., Princeton University, 1966); Jack P. Greene, *Imperatives, Behaviors, and Identities: Essays in Early American Cultural History* (Charlottesville, 1992), 10–11, 53–57, 300–303.

14. This developmental model was first described in the introduction to Greene and Pole, eds., *Colonial British America,* 13–16. For Greene's later elaboration see *Pursuits of Happiness,* 170–206.

15. See, for example, James R. Perry, *The Formation of Society on Virginia's Eastern Shore, 1615–1655* (Chapel Hill, 1990).

16. Benjamin Franklin, *The Autobiography and Other Writings,* ed. Kenneth Silverman, Penguin Classic Edition (New York, 1986), 80.

17. See Carole Shammas, "The Domestic Environment in Early Modern England and America," *Journal of Social History* 14 (1980): 14–17.

ONE: The Nature of Slavery

The author thanks Fred Jaher, Harry Liebersohn, and members of the History Workshop at the University of Illinois for their comments on an earlier version of this essay.

1. William Bartram, *The Travels of William Bartram: Naturalist's Edition,* ed. Francis Harper (New Haven, 1958), 298–299; Laurens to John Bartram, 9 Aug. 1766, in *The Papers of Henry Laurens,* ed. Philip Hamer et al., 5:153–154 (Columbia, SC, 1968–2003); Bartram to William Bartram, 5 Apr. 1766, *The Correspondence of John Bartram, 1734–1777,* ed. Edmund Berkeley and Dorothy Smith Berkeley (Gainesville, 1992), 661.

2. Bartram, *Travels,* 298–299.

3. Thomas Cooper and David J. McCord, eds., *The Statutes at Large of South Carolina* (Columbia, SC, 1836–41), 7:352.

4. John Lawson, *A New Voyage to Carolina,* ed. Hugh T. Lefler (Chapel Hill, 1967), 32–33; Timothy Silver, *A New Face on the Countryside: Indians, Colonists, and Slaves in South Atlantic Forests, 1500–1800* (Cambridge, 1990), 26–28, 176–177.

5. Keith Thomas, *Man and the Natural World: A History of the Modern Sensibility* (London, 1983), 56.

6. H. Roy Merrens, ed., *The Colonial South Carolina Scene: Contemporary Views, 1697–1774* (Columbia, SC, 1977), 94.

7. Old Testament accounts of wild beasts attacking human communities and disrupting agriculture include Lev. 26:22 and Ps. 80:8–9, 80:13. On early modern views of the relationship between human sin and wild animals, see Thomas, *Natural World,* 156–157.

8. Agricola was Charles Pinckney's pseudonym. *South-Carolina Gazette,* 8 Oct. 1744 (hereafter *SCG*).

9. James Glen, *A Description of South Carolina . . .* (London, 1761), facs. reprint in Chapman J. Milling, ed., *Colonial South Carolina: Two Contemporary Descriptions* (Columbia, SC, 1951), 14; Merrens, ed., *Colonial South Carolina Scene,* 264.

10. *SCG,* 25 Aug. 1757; David S. Shields, *Oracles of Empire: Poetry, Politics, and Commerce in British America, 1690–1750* (Chicago, 1990), 71, 68–72.

11. George Ogilvie, "Carolina; or, the Planter" (1791), reprinted in *The Southern Literary Journal* 19 (1986): 46, 47, 48–50, 51–52.

12. *The Shaftesbury Papers and Other Records Relating to Carolina and the First Settlement on Ashley River Prior to the Year 1676* (1897; repr. Charleston, 2000), 308.

13. Johann Martin Bolzius, "Johann Martin Bolzius Answers a Questionnaire on Carolina and Georgia," ed. and trans. Klaus G. Loewald et al., *William and Mary Quarterly,* 3rd ser., 14 (1957): 230–231; [Alexander] Hewit, "An Historical Account of the Rise and Progress of the Colonies of South Carolina and Georgia" (1779), in *Historical Collections of South Carolina,* ed. B. R. Carroll, 1:79 (London, 1836).

14. J. H. Easterby, ed., *The Colonial Records of South Carolina: The Journal of the Commons House of Assembly, May 18, 1741–July 10, 1742* (Columbia, SC, 1953), 84; Hewit, "Historical Account," 1:416–18; John Guerard to Thomas Rock, 30 July 1753, John Guerard Letterbook, South Carolina Historical Society, Charleston (hereafter SCHS). On responses to this hurricane and other natural disasters, see Matthew Mulcahy, "'Melancholy and Fatal Calamities': Disaster and Society in Eighteenth-Century South Carolina," in *Money, Trade, and Power: The Evolution of South Carolina's Plantation Society,* ed. Jack P. Greene, Rosemary Brana-Shute, and Randy J. Sparks, 278–298 (Columbia, SC, 2001).

15. Eliza Lucas Pinckney to [Lady Carew], 7 Feb. 1757, *The Letterbook of Eliza Lucas Pinckney 1739–1762,* ed. Elise Pinckney (Chapel Hill, 1972), 88; Hewit, "Historical Account," 1:331–332; John Guerard to William Jolliff, 21 Oct. 1752, Guerard Letterbook; "sad havock": Josiah Smith, Jr., to George Austin, 31 Jan. 1771, Josiah Smith, Jr., Letterbook, Southern Historical Collection, University of North Carolina, Chapel Hill.

16. Peter H. Wood, *Black Majority: Negroes in Colonial South Carolina from 1670 through the Stono Rebellion* (New York, 1974), 117–119, 30–31; see also John Solomon Otto, "The Origins of Cattle-Ranching in Colonial South Carolina," *South Carolina Historical Magazine* 87 (1986): 121–122 (hereafter *SCHM*).

17. Judith A. Carney, *Black Rice: The African Origins of Rice Cultivation in the Americas* (Cambridge, MA, 2001), 46–49, 78–98.

18. Bolzius, "Questionnaire on Carolina," 259; Richard Hutson to Mrs. Rizpah Rivers, 19 May 1776, Richard Hutson Letterbook, SCHS; Philip D. Morgan, *Slave Counterpoint: Black Culture in the Eighteenth-Century Chesapeake and Lowcountry* (Chapel Hill, 1998), 187n, 141–142; Ira Berlin and Philip D. Morgan, eds., introduction to *Cultivation and Culture: Labor and the Shaping of Slave Life in the Americas* (Charlottesville, 1993), 30–31; Alexander Moore, "Daniel Axtell's Account Book and the Economy of Early South Carolina," *SCHM* 95 (1994): 284; Drayton, *A View of South Carolina As Respects her Natural and Civil Concerns* (Charleston, SC, 1802), 125.

19. Charles Ball, *Slavery in the United States: A Narrative of the Life and Adventures of Charles Ball, A Black Man* (New York, 1837), 324–325, 319, 262–263. See also 230, 223, 227, 166–167, 202–203.

20. Wood, *Black Majority,* 120; Charles Joyner, *Down by the Riverside: A South Carolina Slave Community* (Urbana, 1984), 148–149; Janet Schaw, *Journal of a Lady*

of Quality . . . , ed. Evangeline Walker Andrews and Charles McLean Andrews (New Haven, 1934), 176; Margaret Washington Creel, *"A Peculiar People": Slave Religion and Community-Culture Among the Gullahs* (New York, 1988), 153–156.

21. *SCG,* 4 Apr. 1756. On Sampson, see also Terry W. Lipscomb, ed., *The Colonial Records of South Carolina: The Journal of the Commons House of Assembly, November 21, 1752–September 6, 1754* (Columbia, SC, 1983), xxvii–xxviii, 334–335; John Bartram, "Diary of a Journey through the Carolinas, Georgia and Florida from July 1, 1765, to April 10, 1766," *Transactions of the American Philosophical Society* 33 (1942): 21–22.

22. Laurens to James Theodore Rossel, 8 Apr. 1776, in *Laurens Papers,* 5:99–100.

23. Robert Olwell, *Masters, Slaves, and Subjects: The Culture of Power in the South Carolina Low Country, 1740–1790* (Ithaca, 1998), 79–80; See also Eugene Genovese, *Roll, Jordan, Roll: The World the Slaves Made* (New York, 1974), 615–616.

24. Morgan, *Slave Counterpoint,* 151–154; Ball, *Slavery in the United States,* 388–389, 398–399, 483–484, 490, 411; S. Max Edelson, "Affiliation without Affinity: Skilled Slaves in Eighteenth-Century South Carolina," in Greene et al., eds., *Money, Trade, and Power,* 239–240.

25. *SCG,* 4 Aug. 1758; John Bartram to William Bartram, 9 Apr. 1766, *Bartram Correspondence,* 665; *Laurens Papers,* 5:54n.

26. Smith to George Austin, 31 Jan. 1774, 22 July 1774, Josiah Smith, Jr., Smith Letterbook; Glen, *Description of South Carolina,* 96.

27. Robert Raper to John Colleton, 23 Sept. 23, 1759, Robert Raper Letterbook, (photoduplicate of original in West Sussex Record Office), SCHS; Laurens to William Yate, 5 Feb. 1766, in *Laurens Papers,* 5:70; Kenneth E. Lewis, "Plantation Layout and Function in the South Carolina Lowcountry," in *The Archaeology of Slavery and Plantation Life,* ed. Theresa A. Singleton, 46, 59 (Orlando, 1985); J. W. Joseph, "Building to Grow: Agrarian Adaptations to South Carolina's Historical Landscapes," in *Carolina's Historical Landscapes: Archaeological Perspectives,* ed. Linda F. Stine et al., 46 (Knoxville, 1997). A British officer noted that throughout the well-settled plantation region between Edisto River and Charlestown, the woods had been "only clear'd about the Houses," Entry for 7 Mar. 1780, John Peebles Diary, South Caroliniana Library, University of South Carolina, Columbia. On location of slave housing see Bolzius, "Questionnaire on Carolina," 257; Bartram, "Diary of a Journey," 21.

28. On mortality in colonial South Carolina and the higher death rates of white versus black immigrants, see Peter A. Coclanis, *The Shadow of a Dream: Economic Life and Death in the South Carolina Low Country, 1670–1920* (New York, 1989), 38–47.

29. R. W. Kelsey, ed. and trans., "Swiss Settlers in South Carolina," *South Carolina Historical and Genealogical Magazine* 23 (1922): 89–90; see also Wood, *Black Majority,* 132 and ch. 5.

30. Louisa Susannah Wells, *The Journal of a Voyage from Charlestown, S.C., to London* . . . (New York, 1906), 77; Merrens, ed., *Colonial South Carolina Scene,* 230–231.

31. For a survey of early promotional writings, see Jack P. Greene, *Imperatives, Behaviors, and Identities: Essays in Early American Cultural History* (Charlottesville, 1992), ch. 4.

32. Merrens, ed., *Colonial South Carolina Scene,* 20–21; Bartram, "Diary of a Journey," 13; Records in the British Public Record Office Relating to South Carolina, South Carolina Department of Archives and History, Columbia, 6:287; Bolzius, "Question-

naire on Carolina," 238, 239; Merrens, ed., *Colonial South Carolina Scene,* 101, 102–103; Peter Collinson to John Bartram, 25 Dec. 1767, *Bartram Correspondence,* 694.

33. Hewit, "Historical Account," 1:88; Robert Allen, "Agriculture during the Industrial Revolution," in *The Economic History of Britain Since 1700,* ed. Roderick Floud and Donald McClosky, 113–114 (Cambridge, 1994); [George Milligen-Johnston], *Short Description of the Province of South Carolina, with an Account of the Air, Weather, and Diseases, at Charles-Town* (1763) in Milling, ed., *South Carolina: Contemporary Descriptions,* 138–139. See also *Laurens Papers,* 4:336.

34. Merrens, ed., *South Carolina Colonial Scene,* 14–15; Milligen-Johnston, *Short Description,* 124; *American Husbandry,* ed. Henry J. Carmen (1775; repr. New York, 1939), 261; Hewit, "Historical Account," 1:75; William Stephens, *The Journal of William Stephens, 1743–1745,* ed. E. Merton Coulter (Athens, GA, 1958–59), 1:251; Laurens to William Flower, 10 July 1747, in *Laurens Papers,* 1:23; Bolzius, "Questionnaire on Carolina," 239–240; Hewit, "Historical Account," 1:322, 50.

35. Alexis de Tocqueville, *Democracy in America,* trans. by George Lawrence, ed. J. P. Mayer (New York, 1988), 352, 352n. On Africans as a "biological elite" in West Indian plantation colonies and the cultural use Europeans made of these perceived "advantages" see Kenneth F. Kiple, *The Caribbean Slave: A Biological History* (Cambridge, 1984).

36. Quoted in Wood, *Black Majority,* 84, see also 84–85.

37. Quoted in Sylvia Frey, "Liberty, Equality, and Slavery: The Paradox of the American Revolution," in *The American Revolution: Its Character and Limits,* ed. Jack P. Greene, 241 (New York, 1987).

38. See Diane M. Sydenam, "Practitioner and Patient: The Practice of Medicine in Eighteenth-Century South Carolina," (PhD diss., The Johns Hopkins University, 1978), 1–39; see also Joyce E. Chaplin, *An Anxious Pursuit: Agricultural Innovation and Modernity in the Lower South, 1730–1815* (Chapel Hill, 1993), 117–122.

39. Hewit, "Historical Account," 1:110; quoted in Greene, *Imperatives, Behaviors, and Identities,* 281.

40. See Hewit, "Historical Account," 191, 47–48, 268; "high and haughty" quoted 268.

41. H. Roy Merrens, ed., "A View of Coastal South Carolina in 1778: The Journal of Ebenezer Hazard," *SCHM* 73 (1972): 190; Josiah Smith, Jr., to George Austin, 30 Jan. 1773, Smith Letterbook; Laurens to John Ettwien, 19 Mar. 1763, in *Laurens Papers,* 3:373; Josiah Smith, Jr., to James Caldwell, 24 Mar. 1776, Smith Letterbook.

42. Drayton, *View of South-Carolina,* 16–17; Milligen-Johnston, *Short Description,* 126; quoted in Robert Aldredge Croom, "Weather Observers at Charleston, South Carolina, 1670–1871" (MA thesis, College of Charleston, South Carolina, 1936), 39; William Gerhard De Brahm, *Philosophico-Historico-Hydrogreography of South Carolina, Georgia, and East Florida* (c. 1772), in *Documents Connected with the History of South Carolina,* ed. P. C. J. Weston, 179–181 (London, 1856); See also Bolzius, "Questionnaire on Carolina," 230, 231.

43. Russell R. Menard, "The Africanization of the Lowcountry Labor Force, 1670–1730," in *Race and Family in the Colonial South,* ed. Winthrop D. Jordan and Sheila L. Skemp, 81–108 (Jackson, MS, 1987).

44. Quoted in Greene, *Imperatives, Behaviors, and Identities,* 92.

45. Olwell, *Masters, Slaves, and Subjects,* 64–67; Cooper and McCord, eds., *Statues of South Carolina,* 7:352; Frank J. Klingberg, ed., *The Carolina Chronicle of Dr. Francis Le Jau, 1706–1717* (Berkeley, 1956), 55.

46. Cooper and McCord, eds., *Statutes of South Carolina,* 7:398–399, 404.

47. See Richard Ligon, *A True and Exact History of the Island of Barbados* . . . (London, 1657), 46, Early English Books Online. Chadwyk-Healey; http://eebo.chadwyck.com/search. See also Alex Bontemps, *The Punished Self: Surviving Slavery in the Colonial South* (Ithaca, 2001), 19–20, 59–60.

48. Edelson, "Affiliation without Affinity," 217–218; see also Bontemps, *The Punished Self,* ch. 5.

49. J. Channing to [Telfair], 10 Aug. 1786, Edward Telfair Papers, William R. Perkins Library, Special Collections, Duke University, Durham, NC; Robert Pringle to Edward and John Mayne & Co., 19 Sept. 1740, in *The Letterbook of Robert Pringle,* ed. Walter B. Edgar (Columbia, SC, 1972), 1:247; William Hyrne to Thomas Boone, 15 Mar. 1770, Raper Letterbook; quoted in Marcus W. Jernegan, "Slavery and the Beginnings of Industrialism in the American Colonies," in *The Other Slaves: Mechanics, Artisans, and Craftsmen,* ed. James E. Newton and Donald L. Lewis, 14 (Boston, 1978).

50. *SCG,* 9 Feb. 1738, 2 Jan. 1755, 16 Nov. 1769; Bolzius, "Questionnaire on Carolina," 255, 256.

51. Edelson, "Affiliation without Affinity," table 9.1, 222–223.

52. Quoted in Jernegan, "Slavery and Industrialism," 14; Edelson, "Affiliation without Affinity," 243.

53. See John K. Thornton, "African Dimensions of the Stono Rebellion," *American Historical Review* 96 (1991), 1101–1113; Daniel C. Littlefield, *Rice and Slaves: Ethnicity and the Slave Trade in Colonial South Carolina* (Baton Rouge, 1981), 8–21; Berlin and Morgan, eds., *Cultivation and Culture,* 11.

54. John Bartram to William Bartram, 5 Apr. 1766, in *Bartram Correspondence,* 661.

55. —— to Mr. Boone, 24 July 1720, Item 125, Vol. 32 (1720–21), 57–58, in *Calendar of State Papers, Colonial Series, America and West Indies, 1574–1739,* CD-ROM (London, 2000).

56. Cooper and McCord, eds., *Statutes of South Carolina,* 7:413.

57. Laurens to James Penman, 9 Feb. 1768, in *Laurens Papers,* 5:592.

58. The Assembly first instituted a duty on slave imports in 1703, which was revised and elaborated in 1716, 1719, and 1722. For a survey of this legislation see David D. Wallace, *The Life of Henry Laurens, With a Sketch of the Life of Lieutenant-Colonel John Laurens* (1915; repr. New York, 1967), 80–88 and 81n-85n.

59. Cooper and McCord, eds., *Statutes of South Carolina,* 3:556–557, 561–562. See also Darold D. Wax, "'The Great Risque We Run': The Aftermath of Slave Rebellion at Stono, South Carolina, 1739–1745," *Journal of Negro History* 67 (1982): 140–144.

60. The Duty Act expired after three years, but the economic crisis that accompanied King George's War (1739–48) extended its effect.

61. Glen, *A Description of South Carolina,* 45.

62. Walter Minchinton, "A Comment on 'The Slave Trade to Colonial South Carolina: A Profile,'" *SCHM* 95 (1994): 49.

63. Thomason to Isaac Harleston, [c. 1780], Isaac Child Harleston Letters, Robert Scott Small Library, Special Collections, College of Charleston, SC.

64. *SCG,* 17–24 Sept. 1772; Laurens to William Yate, 5 Feb. 1755, in *Laurens Papers,* 5:70; Laurens to Peter Horlbeck, 6 Apr. 1765, in *Laurens Papers,* 4:602. On the importance of judging character to the proceedings of local slave courts, see Olwell, *Masters, Slaves, and Subjects,* ch. 2.

65. On this point see the case of Thomas Jeremiah, a free black harbor pilot put to death by white authorities in 1775, Olwell, *Masters, Slaves, and Subjects,* 234–236.

66. Quincy, "Journal," 456; Morgan, *Slave Counterpoint,* 386; Gabriel Manigault to Mrs. Manigault, 5 Sept. 1775, Manigault Family Papers, box 1 (letter), South Caroliniana Library, University of South Carolina, Columbia, SC.

67. John Bartram to William Bartram, 5 Apr. 1766, *Bartram Correspondence,* 662. Such interest in slave character, however distorted the results, should qualify Alex Bontemps's assertion that mainland planters regarded slaves as "object[s] devoid of subjectivity" and never as "self-aware human beings," *The Punished Self,* 12, 22, and passim.

68. *SCG,* 16 July 1737.

69. On the concept of virtue in early America see Greene, *Imperatives, Behaviors, and Identities,* 208–235; see also J. G. A. Pocock, *The Machiavellian Moment: Florentine Political Thought in the Atlantic Republican Tradition* (Princeton, 1975).

70. Drayton, *View of South-Carolina,* 149, 146–147.

71. See Jacquelyn Dowd Hall, "'The Mind That Burns in Each Body': Women, Rape, and Racial Violence," in *Powers of Desire: The Politics of Sexuality,* ed. Ann Snitow, Christine Stansell, and Sharon Thompson, 328–349 (New York, 1983).

72. For examples of such scholarship, see Berlin and Morgan, eds., *Cultivation and Culture.*

TWO: "For Want of a Social Set"

1. Peter Dubois to Samuel Johnston, Feb. 1757; Peter Dubois to Samuel Johnston, 8 Feb. 1757, 5 Mar. 1757, Filmed portion, box 1, Johnston Series, Hayes Collection, Southern Historical Collection, Chapel Hill, NC.

2. Darret B. Rutman with Anita H. Rutman, *Small Worlds, Large Questions: Explorations in Early American Social History, 1600–1850* (Charlottesville, 1994), 292–295.

3. Lorena S. Walsh, "Community Networks in the Early Chesapeake," in *Colonial Chesapeake Society,* ed. Lois Green Carr, Philip D. Morgan, and Jean B. Russo, 219 (Chapel Hill, 1988). See also James R. Perry, *The Formation of A Society on Virginia's Eastern Shore, 1615–1655* (Chapel Hill, 1991).

4. This essay derives from a larger research project that focuses more specifically on processes related to regional development. See Bradford J. Wood, *This Remote Part of the World: Regional Formation in Lower Cape Fear, North Carolina, 1725–1775* (Columbia, SC, 2004). Many of the propositions advanced in this essay have been more fully demonstrated and explicated in the longer study, and *This Remote Part of the World* also contains a more comprehensive discussion of the sources and methodologies used in the following pages. In both studies the Lower Cape Fear region has been roughly defined as New Hanover County, NC, and, after the original county was divided in 1764, as New Hanover and Brunswick Counties, NC.

5. Kenneth A. Lockridge, *A New England Town: The First Hundred Years* (New York, 1970); Philip J. Greven, *Four Generations: Population, Land, and Family in Colonial Andover, Massachusetts* (Ithaca, 1970); John Demos, *A Little Commonwealth: Family Life in Plymouth Colony* (New York, 1970); Michael Zuckerman, *Peaceable Kingdoms: New England Towns in the Eighteenth Century* (New York, 1970).

6. See, for example, Jack P. Greene, "Autonomy and Stability: New England and the British Colonial Experience in Early Modern America," *Journal of Social History* 7

(1974): 171–194; Edward M. Cook, Jr., *The Fathers of the Towns: Leadership and Community Structure in Eighteenth-Century New England* (Baltimore, 1976), xi.

7. Rutman, *Small World, Large Questions,* 35–54; Richard R. Beeman, "The New Social History and the Search for 'Community' in Colonial America," *American Quarterly* 29 (1977): 422–443.

8. The best introduction to Rutman's ideas on these matters can be found in *Small Worlds, Large Questions,* 34–54, 287–304. See also Darret B. Rutman with Anita H. Rutman, *A Place in Time: Middlesex County, Virginia, 1650–1750* (New York, 1984), and *A Place in Time: Explicatus* (New York, 1984).

9. In this vein, see the review of Perry's book by Jean B. Russo, *William and Mary Quarterly,* 3rd ser., 49 (1992), 533–535, but for an example of the persistent tendency to define communities in narrow terms more appropriate to the northern colonies, see Helena M. Wall, *Fierce Communion: Family Life and Community in Early America* (Cambridge, MA, 1995).

10. For some recent exceptions that have devoted attention to local networks, see Christopher Morris, *Becoming Southern: The Evolution of a Way of Life, Warren County and Vicksburg, Mississippi, 1770–1860* (Oxford, 1995), 15–18, 89–90, 99–102, 193; Karin Wulf, *Not All Wives: Women of Colonial Philadelphia* (Ithaca, 2000), 119–151; Joan R. Gunderson, "Kith and Kin: Women's Networks in Colonial Virginia," in *The Devil's Lane: Sex and Race in the Early South,* ed. Catherine Clinton and Michelle Gillespie, 90–108 (Oxford, 1997).

11. For an exception, see George D. Terry, "'Champaign Country': A Social History of an Eighteenth-Century Lowcountry Parish in South Carolina, St. Johns, Berkeley County," (PhD diss., University of South Carolina, 1981).

12. Richard Hofstadter, *America at 1750: A Social Portrait* (New York, 1971), 3.

13. On a related process of adaptation in early South Carolina, see Joyce E. Chaplin, An Anxious Pursuit: Agricultural Innovation and Modernity in the Lower South, *1730–1815* (Chapel Hill, 1993), 93–109.

14. Edward Moseley's "A New and Correct Map of the Province of North Carolina" identified over forty Lower Cape Fear estates in 1733. In 1770, John Collet's "A Compleat Map of North Carolina" located a similar number of plantations. For reproductions of these maps, see William P. Cummings, *The Southeast in Early Maps with an Annotated Check List of Printer and Manuscript Regional and Local Maps of Southeastern North America during the Colonial Period* (Chapel Hill, 1958), plates 52 and 66. In the early twentieth century Alfred Moore Waddell constructed a map of Lower Cape Fear plantations before 1760 for *A History of New Hanover County and the Lower Cape Fear* (Wilmington, NC, 1909). Waddell's research provided names for almost seventy plantations and gave general locations for over two-thirds of them, though in some cases the empirical basis for Waddell's assertions remains questionable.

15. "Report of the Commissioners Sent from Barbadoes to Explore the River Cape Fear" [1663], William L. Saunders, ed., *The Colonial Records of North Carolina* (Raleigh, 1886–90), 1:69 (hereafter *Colonial Records*); William S. Powell, ed., *North Carolina Gazeteer: A Dictionary of Tar Heel Places* (Chapel Hill, 1968), 424.

16. "A New Voyage to Georgia," in *Collections of the Georgia Historical Society* (Savannah, 1840–1916), 2:68.

17. The sources used to identify landowners were: Margaret Hofmann, ed., *Province of North Carolina: Abstracts of Land Patents, 1773–1729* (Rocky Mount, NC,

1979); Hofmann, ed., *Colony of North Carolina: Abstracts of Land Patents, 1737–1852*, vols. 1–2 (Raleigh, 1982–84); New Hanover County Real Estate Conveyances, 1734–75, Brunswick County Real Estate Conveyances, 1764–75, North Carolina Department of Archives and History, Raleigh; Alexander Walker, ed., *New Hanover County Court Minutes, 1738–1785*, vols. 1–2 (Bethesda, MD, 1958–59); Waddell, *A History of New Hanover County;* Cummings, *The Southeast in Early Maps.*

18. Tax lists exist for the years 1755, 1762, and 1763 for both counties, for New Hanover County only in 1767, and for Brunswick County only in 1769 and 1772. An unidentified and incomplete list also exists for New Hanover County during this period, probably from 1765. All of these lists can be obtained in the North Carolina Department of Archives and History.

19. *Cape Fear Mercury,* 29 Dec. 1773.

20. "A New Voyage to Georgia," in *Collections of the Georgia Historical Society* (Savannah, 1840–1916), 2:59; William S. Powell, *The North Carolina Gazetteer: A Dictionary of Tar Heel Places* (Chapel Hill, 1968), 294; Lee, *Lower Cape Fear,* 201–202.

21. John MacDowell to the Society for the Propagation of the Gospel, 15 June 1762, *Colonial Records,* 7:730.

22. Cummings, *The Southeast in Early Maps.*

23. See notes 10 and 11, this chapter.

24. Powell, *North Carolina Gazetteer,* 295.

25. Janet Schaw, *The Journal of a Lady of Quality; Being the Narrative of a Journey from Scotland to the West Indies, North Carolina, and Portugal, in the Years 1774 to 1776,* ed. Evangeline W. Andrews and Charles M. Andrews (New Haven, 1923), 281.

26. Nicholas Christian to S.P.G., 27 Aug. 1774, *Colonial Records,* 9:1022; Laws, *Colonial Records,* 23:447; Walker, ed., *New Hanover County Court Minutes,* 1:6, 34.

27. Historians have found it difficult to recapture the range of interactions available to settlers anywhere in colonial America, and the limited source materials available for studying the Lower Cape Fear present a number of challenges. Innumerable conversations must have occurred every day, influenced the thoughts of the participants, and not been recorded in any retrievable way. Yet many interactions can be found in the surviving records of the Lower Cape Fear and, if it is difficult to assess the meanings of these interactions for contemporaries, it is possible to discern some very important and suggestive patterns. These interactions can best be culled from wills, powers of attorney, kinship connections, conveyances, legal actions, and various other pieces of information. These disparate pieces of information reveal little by themselves, but they can provide valuable information when linked together in a computer database. In this particular case, interactions were recorded in the computer and sorted by name, enabling the creation of another database with a set of surprisingly detailed biographical files for many Lower Cape Fear landowners and residents. To render analysis more manageable, this study focuses especially on patterns of interactions for individuals living in three Lower Cape Fear neighborhoods: Rocky Point, Lockwoods Folly, and Town Creek. For more details on the methodology used here, see Wood, *This Remote Part of the World.*

28. Because of a legal culture that vested property in heads of households and allowed little separate identity to married women and to children, many interactions that are recorded under the names of male heads of households probably concerned and involved the participation of other family members. Also, because existing sources

do impose limitations on any analysis of local interaction in the eighteenth-century Carolinas, data from neighborhoods have been considered in combination with more general evidence about social interaction in the Lower Cape Fear in an attempt to provide a more detailed description of social networks.

29. The correlation coefficient for the distances and ties mentioned in wills or material related to kinship or powers of attorney equaled −.84. The correlation coefficient for the ties related to business transactions such as land conveyances equaled −.89. Both of these coefficients indicate a strong relationship, where 0 indicates no relationship, −1 indicates a perfect negative correlation, and +1 indicates a perfect positive relationship.

30. The following discussion of the Moore family's kinship networks and genealogy relies heavily on Mabel L. Webber, comp., "The First Governor Moore and His Children," *South Carolina Historical and Genealogical Magazine* 37 (1936): 1–23.

31. These ten landowners were Roger Moore, Maurice Moore, Samuel Swann, James Hasell, Sr., George Burrington, John Porter, Jr., John Baptista Ashe, Edward Moseley, Arthur Dobbs, and Robert Halton.

32. The top ten slave owners, based on averages from available tax lists, were William Dry, George Moore, Sr., William Moore, William Ross, Sr., Frederick Gregg, Richard Quince, Jr., Maurice Moore, Jr., Richard Eagles, Jr., John Grange, Sr., and Samuel Swann, Sr.

33. The data on wills used in the next few pages has been derived from the following sources: New Hanover County Wills, 1734–80, Brunswick County Wills, 1764–80, and Secretary of State's Office Wills, North Carolina Department of Archives and History; Bryan J. Grimes, ed., *Abstracts of North Carolina Wills* (Raleigh, 1910); Grimes, ed., *North Carolina Wills and Inventories in the Office of the Secretary of State* (Raleigh, 1912); *Colonial Records,* vols. 1–10; Stephen E. Bradley, ed., *Early Records of North Carolina from the Secretary of State Papers* (Keysville, VA, 1992).

34. Lower Cape Fear testators appear to have adapted patriarchal inheritance patterns to compensate for patterns of demographic disruption, much as testators did in the South Carolina Lowcountry as described in John Crowley, "Family Relations and Inheritance in Early South Carolina," *Histoire sociale/Social History* 17 (1984): 35–57.

35. A "nuclear family" is defined here as a head of household, plus a spouse and at least one child.

36. Laws, *Colonial Records,* 23:790–801.

37. The same statistical techniques used to examine other kinds of interaction yielded no statistically significant results when applied to the relationship between New Hanover County civil suit interactions and the distance between the neighborhoods of Lockwoods Folly, Rocky Point, and Town Creek.

38. John Barnett to the S.P.G., 15 Sept. 1770, *Colonial Records,* 8:229.

THREE: "Almost an Englishman"

1. Paul Gilroy, *The Black Atlantic: Modernity and Double Consciousness* (Cambridge, MA, 1993), 1. Space limitations obliged omission of much of the theoretical framework that informed my original draft of this essay. I expect to publish an expanded version elsewhere.

2. See for example, Ira Berlin, "Time, Space, and the Evolution of Afro-American Society on British Mainland North America," *American Historical Review* 85 (1980), 44–78; Mechal Sobel, *Travelin' On: The Slave Journey to an Afro-Baptist Faith* (Westport, 1979) and *The World They Made Together: Black and White Values in Eighteenth-Century Virginia* (Princeton, 1987); Gary Nash, *Forging Freedom: The Formation of Philadelphia's Black Community, 1720–1840* (Cambridge, MA, 1988); Vincent Harding, *There Is a River: The Black Struggle for Freedom in America* (New York, 1981); Sterling Stuckey, *Slave Culture: Nationalist Theory and the Foundations of Black America* (New York, 1981), and Sterling Stuckey, "The Skies of Consciousness: African Dance at Pinkster in New York, 1750–1840," in *Going Through the Storm: The Influence of African American Art in History* (New York, 1994), 53–80.

3. See, for example, John Thornton, "African Dimensions of the Stono Rebellion," *American Historical Review* 96 (Oct. 1991), 1101–1113; and John Thornton, "Central African Names and African-American Naming Patterns," *William and Mary Quarterly*, 3rd ser., 50 (Oct. 1993), 727–742.

4. See Ira Berlin, "From Creole to African: Atlantic Creoles and the Origins of African-American Society in Mainland North America," *William and Mary Quarterly*, 3rd ser., 53 (Apr. 1996), 251–288; but also Ira Berlin, *Many Thousands Gone: The First Two Centuries of Slavery in North America* (Cambridge, MA, 1998), 1–215.

5. Thornton, *Africa and Africans*, 206; see also Thornton's discussion of Christianity in the Kingdom of Kongo and the way scholars have interpreted it in John Thornton, "The Development of an African Catholic Church in the Kingdom of Kongo, 1491–1750," *Journal of African History* 25 (1984), 147–167; and also John Thornton, *The Kingdom of Kongo: Civil War and Transition, 1641–1718* (Madison, 1983).

6. Sidney Mintz and Richard Price, *The Birth of African-American Culture: An Anthropological Perspective* (Boston, 1992).

7. For an illuminating explication of this process, see Robert Farris Thompson, *Flash of The Spirit: African and Afro-American Art and Philosophy* (New York, 1984).

8. Paul Edwards, ed., *Equiano's Travels: The Interesting Narrative of the Life of Olaudah Equiano or Gustavus Vassa the African* (New York, 1967), 25–26.

9. Ibid., 27.

10. Ibid., 31.

11. See the narrative of James Albert Ukawsaw Gronniosaw in Adam Potkay and Sandra Burr, eds., *Black Atlantic Writers of the Eighteenth Century: Living the New Exodus in England and the Americas* (New York, 1995), 34.

12. See S. E. Ogude, *Genius in Bondage: A Study of the Origins of African Literature in English* (Ile-Ife, Nigeria, 1983), 32–38.

13. Ogude, *Genius*, 33–35; and Henry Louis Gates, Jr., *The Signifying Monkey: A Theory of Afro-American Literary Criticism* (New York, 1988).

14. Potkay and Burr, *Black Atlantic Writers*, 31; and Gates, *Signifying Monkey*, 134.

15. David Dabydeen, "The Role of Black People in William Hogarth's Criticism of Eighteenth-Century English Culture and Society," in *Essays on the History of Blacks in Britain*, ed. Jagdish S. Gundara and Ian Duffield, 30–57 (Aldershot, UK, 1992); according to London's *Public Advertiser* (6 Jan. 1787), there was such sympathy for the black poor in London at the end of the century that white beggars commonly disguised themselves as blacks.

16. Edwards, *Equiano's Travels*, 43.

17. Ottobah Cugoano, *Thoughts and Sentiments on the Evil of Slavery* (London, 1769), 13.

18. Keith A. Sandiford, *Measuring the Moment: Strategies of Protest in Eighteenth-Century Afro-English Writing* (Selinsgrove, PA, 1988), 93.

19. John C. Shields, ed., *The Collected Works of Phillis Wheatley* (New York, 1988), 18; future quotations will be from this edition without further attribution.

20. For details of Philip Quaque's life, see F. L. Bartels, "Philip Quaque, 1741–1816," *Transactions of the Gold Coast and Togoland Historical Society* 5 (1955), 153–177; C. F. Pascoe, *Two Hundred Years of the S.P.G.: An Historical Account of the Society of the Propagation of the Gospel in Foreign Parts, 1701–1900* (London, 1901), 1:256–258; and Margaret Priestley, "Philip Quaque of Cape Coast" in *Africa Remembered: Narratives by West Africans from the Era of the Slave Trade,* ed. Philip D. Curtin, 99–139 (Madison, 1967).

21. The Society for the Propagation of the Gospel in Foreign Parts (SPG), which sponsored Quaque's education, was convinced that "the English tongue was the heaven-sent medium of religion and civilization;" Bartels, "Philip Quaque," 166–167.

22. See, for example, the letters written to the SPG from missionaries in South Carolina published, among other places, in Frank J. Klingberg, *An Appraisal of the Negro in Colonial South Carolina: A Study in Americanization* (Washington, 1941), passim.

23. See the biographical sketch of Newport Gardner in Edward A. Park, *Memoir of the Life and Character of Samuel Hopkins, D.D.* (Boston, 1854), 154–156, quotation 154n.

24. See William D. Piersen, *Black Yankees: The Development of an Afro-American Subculture in Eighteenth-Century New England* (Amherst, 1988), 117–140; Lorenzo J. Greene, *The Negro in Colonial New England* (1942; repr. New York, 1968), 249–255, 328; Joseph P. Reidy, "'Negro Election Day' and Black Community Life in New England, 1750–1860," *Marxist Perspectives* 1, no. 3 (fall 1978): 102–115.

25. Priestley, "Philip Quaque of Cape Coast," 131.

26. Paul Edwards and David Dabydeen, eds., *Black Writers in Britain, 1760–1890* (Edinburgh, 1991), 106.

27. Priestly, "Philip Quaque of Cape Coast," 137.

28. Vincent Carretta, ed., *Olaudah Equiano, The Interesting Narrative and Other Writings* (New York, 1995).

29. Priestley, "Philip Quaque of Cape Coast," 133.

30. Edwards and Dabydeen, *Black Writers,* 110.

31. Pascoe, *S.P.G.,* 1:257.

32. Edwards and Dabydeen, *Black Writers,* 102.

33. Priestley, "Philip Quaque of Cape Coast," 138–139.

34. Pascoe, *S.P.G.,* 1:258. Perhaps his sponsors were simply neglectful in sending his salary, rather than Quaque refusing to accept it, for he willed his stipendiary arrears to his descendants; see Bartels, "Phillip Quaque," 170.

35. Bartels, "Phillip Quaque," 257.

36. Carretta, *Equiano,* 135.

37. See, for example, John S. Mbiti, *African Religions and Philosophy* (Garden City, NY, 1969), and also Alma Gottlieb, "Le Relgioni in Africa / L'Africa Occidentale: Spiriti e Culti [Religion in Africa / West Africa: Spirits and Cults], in *Enciclopedia Italiana: Storia del secolo XX,* vol. 3 (Rome, forthcoming).

38. Potkay and Burr, *Black Atlantic Writers,* 43.

39. William H. Robinson, *Phillis Wheatley and Her Writings* (New York, 1984), 44–45.

40. Robinson, *Phillis Wheatley,* 337.

41. Ray A. Kea, "Modernity, African Narratives, and Social Identity in the Eighteenth-Century Atlantic World," unpublished paper presented at the African Studies Society Meeting, Chicago, Illinois, Fall 1998, 6; the English observer is quoted on p. 13; I thank both my colleague Ron Atkinson for bringing this paper to my attention and Professor Kea for sharing it with me; see also Ray A. Kea, *Settlements, Trade, and Politics in the Seventeenth-Century Gold Coast* (Baltimore, 1982); Philip Curtin claims that there were more free Africans in Europe in the eighteenth century than there were Europeans living in Africa, Curtin, *Africa Remembered,* 13.

42. James Walvin, *Black and White: The Negro and English Society, 1555–1945* (London, 1973), 85–86.

43. Paul Edwards and Polly Rewt, eds., *The Letters of Ignatius Sancho* (Edinburgh, 1994), 106.

44. Sandiford, *Measuring the Moment,* 75.

45. For figures on Britain's black population see, inter alia, Peter Fryer, *Staying Power: The History of Black People in Britain* (London, 1984), 68; and Gretchen Gerzina, *Black London: Life before Emancipation* (New Brunswick, NJ, 1995), 5.

46. The quotations are from Fryer, *Staying Power,* 70 and 81 respectively. For Black Britain, see Gerzina, *Black London,* 6 and 14; Folarin O. Shyllon, *Black Slaves in Britain* (London, 1974); Shyllon, *Black People in Britain* (London, 1977); and the essays contained in Gundara and Duffield, eds., *Essays on the History of Blacks in Britain.*

47. Carretta, *Equiano,* 69.

48. Vincent Carretta, ed., *Letters of the Late Ignatius Sancho, An African* (New York, 1998), ix–x; Carretta indicates (p. xii) that Sancho's marriage was one of only two all-Black marriages recorded during the century.

49. Edwards and Rewt, eds., *Letters of Ignatius Sancho,* 104–105n.

50. Ibid., 182.

51. Ibid., 205.

52. Ibid., 220, 227.

53. Ibid., respectively 62, 230, 35.

54. Ibid., 56–57.

55. Ibid., 72.

56. Ibid., 232.

57. Robinson, *Phillis Wheatley,* 286; Ogude, *Genius,* 63.

58. Ogude, *Genius,* 60–62; Julian D. Mason, Jr., ed., *The Poems of Phillis Wheatley* (Chapel Hill, 1966), 87n; for the controversy over Wheatley's birthplace, see M.A. Richmond, *Bid the Vassal Soar: Interpretive Essays on the Life and Poetry of Phillis Wheatley, (ca. 1753–1784) and George Moses Horton, (ca. 1797–1883)* (Washington, 1974), 12 and 70–71; Vincent Carretta, ed., *Phillis Wheatley: Complete Writings* (New York, 2001), xiii; Robinson, *Phillis Wheatley,* 3–8 and 286n; Julian D. Mason, Jr., ed., *The Poems of Phillis Wheatley: Revised and Enlarged Edition* (Chapel Hill, 1989), 37n.

59. Robinson, *Phillis Wheatley,* 327; Richmond, *Bid the Vassal Soar,* 21. Such prominent African-American personalities as the Massachusetts merchant Paul Cuffe and Maryland mathematician and surveyor Benjamin Banneker also preferred, or assumed they were expected, to eat apart from white people, indicating a developing

or prevailing social custom. This despite the fact that Cuffe built an integrated school for children in his community. See Lamont D. Thomas, *Rise to Be a People: A Biography of Paul Cuffe* (Urbana, 1986), 21, 27; Silvio A. Bedini, *The Life of Benjamin Banneker* (Rancho Cordova, CA, 1972), 128–129; and William B. Settle, "The Real Benjamin Banneker," *Negro History Bulletin* 16, no. 6, (Mar. 1953), 131.

60. Robinson, *Phillis Wheatley*, 340.

61. Richmond, *Bid the Vassal Soar*, 12 and 20–21; see Robinson, *Black New England Letters*, 30, for Wheatley's seating at Old South Church.

62. See inter alia, Richmond, *Bid the Vassal Soar*, 48–52.

63. Edwards and Dabydeen, *Black Writers*, 102.

64. James Clifford, *The Predicament of Culture: Twentieth-Century Ethnography, Literature and Art* (Cambridge, MA, 1988), 344; see also W. Jeffrey Bolster, *Black Jacks: African American Seamen in the Age of Sail* (Cambridge, MA, 1997), 35.

65. For the debate over the reliability of Equiano's autobiographical details, see Vincent Carretta, "Olaudah Equiano or Gustavus Vassa? New Light on an Eighteenth-Century Question of Identity," *Slavery and Abolition* 20 (Dec. 1999), 96–105; and Daniel C. Littlefield, *Rice and Slaves: Ethnicity and the Slave Trade in Colonial South Carolina* (Baton Rouge, 1981; repr. Urbana, 1991), 143–151; and also Daniel C. Littlefield, "'Abundance of Negroes of that Nation': The Significance of African Ethnicity in Colonial South Carolina," in *The Meaning of South Carolina History: Essays in Honor of George C. Rogers, Jr.*, ed. David R. Chesnutt and Clyde N. Wilson, 19–38 (Columbia, SC, 1991).

66. Edwards and Rewt, eds., *Letters of Ignatius Sancho*, respectively 8, 121, 134, and 142.

67. Ibid., 155, 103.

68. Ogude, *Genius*, 10, 16.

69. This story is related, among other places, in Paul Edwards and James Walvin, *Black Personalities in the Era of the Slave Trade* (Baton Rouge, 1983), 204–210; all the following quotations concerning Naimbanna are taken from this source.

FOUR: Conservation, Class, and Controversy in Early America

Many individuals deserve thanks for their assistance with this essay: most of all, Jack Greene for his superlative examples of how one should write history, and my wife Anne for enough research and secretarial help to make her really a coauthor. Allen Bushong, Peggy Clark, Charles Kovacik, Charles Lesser, and Michael Smith all made useful suggestions, while Jo Cottingham and the rest of the interlibrary loan staff of Thomas Cooper Library at the University of South Carolina worked wonders.

1. *A Journal of the Pilgrims at Plymouth: Mourt's Relation, A Relation or Journal of the English Plantation Settled at Plymouth in New England, by Certain English Adventurers Both Merchants and Others*, ed. Dwight B. Heath (New York, 1963), 30.

2. William Cronon, *Changes in the Land: Indians, Colonists, and the Ecology of New England* (New York, 1983), 170.

3. Many of Greene's works are relevant, but the quotation comes from *Pursuits of Happiness: The Social Development of Early Modern British Colonies and the Formation of American Culture* (Chapel Hill, 1988), 169; Cronon, *Changes in the Land;* Mart A. Stewart, "*What Nature Suffers to Groe*": *Life, Labor, and Landscape on the Georgia Coast,*

1680–1920 (Athens, 1996); Timothy Silver, *A New Face on the Countryside: Indians, Colonists, and Slaves in South Atlantic Forests, 1500–1800* (Cambridge, 1990); J. P. Kinney, *The Development of Forest Law in America Including Forest Legislation in America Prior to March 4, 1789* (New York, 1972), 361–401; Yasuhide Kawashima and Ruth Tone, "Environmental Policy in Early America: A Survey of Colonial Statutes," *Journal of Forest History* 27 (Oct. 1983): 168–179; Thomas A. Lund, *American Wildlife Law* (Berkeley, 1980).

4. William Cronon, "Modes of Prophecy and Production: Placing Nature in History," *Journal of American History* 76 (Mar. 1990): 1122–1131; E. P. Thompson, *Whigs and Hunters: The Origin of the Black Act* (New York, 1975); Douglas Hay, Peter Linebaugh, John G. Rule, E. P. Thompson, and Cal Winslow, *Albion's Fatal Tree: Crime and Society in Eighteenth-Century England* (New York, 1975); P. B. Munsche, *Gentlemen and Poachers: The English Game Laws, 1671–1831* (Cambridge, 1981).

5. Kathryn E. Holland Braund, *Deerskins and Duffels: The Creek Indian Trade with Anglo-America, 1685–1815* (Lincoln, NE, 1993); Cathy Matson, "'Damned Scoundrels' and 'Libertisme of Trade': Freedom and Regulation in Colonial New York's Fur and Grain Trades," *William and Mary Quarterly,* 3rd ser., 51 (July 1994): 389–418; John J. McCusker and Russell R. Menard, *The Economy of British America, 1607–1789* (Chapel Hill, 1985), 97–100, 173–174, 191–192.

6. Sir William Blackstone, *Commentaries on the Laws of England,* 9th ed. (1783; repr. New York, 1978), 1:223, 289, 290; 2:14–15, 403, 410; Joseph Chitty, *A Treatise on the Game Laws* (1812; repr. New York, 1979), 1:4; Munsche, *Gentlemen and Poachers,* 9.

7. "The Charter of the Forest, 1217," *English Historical Documents,* ed. Harry Rothwell et al. (New York, 1975), 3:337–340; Munsche, *Gentlemen and Poachers,* 10, 11.

8. Chitty, *Treatise on the Game Laws,* 1:446–447; Joyce Lee Malcolm, *To Keep and Bear Arms: The Origins of an Anglo-American Right* (Cambridge, MA, 1994), 72; 22 and 23 Car. 2. c. 9. s. 136, Danby Pickering, ed., *The Statutes at Large* (Cambridge, 1763), 8:347.

9. Chitty, *Treatise on the Game Laws,* 1:464; Thompson, *Whigs and Hunters,* 21–23, 63; Chester Kirby, "The English Game Law System," *American Historical Review* 38 (Jan. 1933): 240–262; Munsche, *Gentlemen and Poachers,* 6.

10. Chitty, *Treatise on the Game Laws,* 1:245, 272, 283, 299, 303–304.

11. Ibid., 1:470–471, 473, 499, 500.

12. Blackstone, *Commentaries on the Laws of England,* 2:411–412; Chitty, *Treatise on the Game Laws,* 1:446; Malcolm, *To Keep and Bear Arms,* 89, 103–106, 115; *English Historical Documents,* ed. Andrew Browning et al. (1966; repr. London, 1996), 6:123.

13. Munsche, *Gentlemen and Poachers,* 17; Douglas Hay, "Poaching and the Game Laws on Cannock Chase," in Hay et al., *Albion's Fatal Tree,* 246.

14. Blackstone, *Commentaries on the Laws of England,* 4:173, 415, 416; *The Gentleman's Magazine* (Mar. 1770), 122.

15. Robert G. Albion, *Forests and Sea Power: The Timber Problem of the Royal Navy, 1652–1862* (Cambridge, MA, 1926), 30, 97, 107, 117.

16. Quotes in Clarence J. Glacken, *Traces on the Rhodian Shore: Nature and Culture in Western Thought from Ancient Times to the End of the Eighteenth Century* (Berkeley, 1967), 485–486, 492–94; Simon Schama, *Landscape and Memory* (New York, 1995), 177–179; Paul W. Bamford, *Forests and French Sea Power, 1660–1789* (Toronto, 1956), 19–21, 29.

17. Keith Thomas, *Man and the Natural World: A History of the Modern Sensibility* (New York, 1983), 17–18; Glacken, *Traces on the Rhodian Shore*, 152–157, 162–166, 293, 480–481.

18. Silver, *A New Face on the Countryside*, 53–54; Robert M. Weir, *Colonial South Carolina: A History* (1983; repr. Columbia, SC, 1997), 12–13; Cronon, *Changes in the Land*, 37–38; Anthony Pagden, "The Struggle for Legitimacy and the Image of Empire in the Atlantic to c. 1700," in *The Oxford History of the British Empire*, ed. Nicholas Canny, 1:41–46 (Oxford, 1998).

19. Roderick Nash, *Wilderness and the American Mind*, 3rd ed. (New Haven, 1982), 23–43, 84 (quotation from Thoreau); *Bradford's History of Plymouth Plantation, 1606–1646*, ed. William T. Davis (New York, 1908), 96; Weir, *Colonial South Carolina*, 263; *The Debates in the Several Conventions on the Adoption of the Federal Constitution as Recommended by the General Convention at Philadelphia in 1787 Together with the Journal of the Federal Convention*, ed. Jonathan Elliot (Philadelphia, 1836), 4:285.

20. Gordon G. Whitney, *From Coastal Wilderness to Fruited Plain: A History of Environmental Change in Temperate North America, 1500 to the Present* (Cambridge, 1994), 55–56; Stewart, "*What Nature Suffers to Groe*," 9–10; *Peter Kalm's Travels in North America: The English Version of 1770*, ed. Adolph B. Benson (New York, 1937), 1:185, 289, 362, 369–370.

21. Quoted in David G. Allen, *In English Ways: The Movement of Societies and the Transferral of English Local Law and Custom to Massachusetts Bay in the Seventeenth Century* (Chapel Hill, 1981), 76–77, 217; Sumner C. Powell, *Puritan Village: The Formation of a New England Town* (Garden City, NY, 1965), 69; Jessica Kross, *The Evolution of an American Town: Newtown, New York, 1642–1775* (Philadelphia, 1983), 60; John Cox, Jr., ed., *Oyster Bay Town Records* (New York, 1916), 1 (1653–1690): 2, 223, 236.

22. "Concessions to the Province of Pennsylvania—1681," in *The Federal and State Constitutions[,] Colonial Charters and Other Organic Laws*, ed. Francis N. Thorpe, 5:3046 (Washington, DC, 1909); Weir, *Colonial South Carolina*, 44; Kinney, *The Development of Forest Law in America*, 361–365 and passim.

23. Joseph J. Malone, *Pine Trees and Politics: The Naval Stores and Forest Policy in Colonial New England, 1691–1775* (Seattle, 1964), 10, 27, 54, 140.

24. McCusker and Menard, *Economy of British America*, 318–321; Laurens to John McQueen, 10 Sept. 1785, *The Papers of Henry Laurens*, ed. Philip Hamer et al. (Columbia, SC, 1968–2003), 16:593; Virginia S. Wood, *Live Oaking: Southern Timber for Tall Ships* (Boston, 1981), 32, 48.

25. Kawashima and Tone, "Environmental Policy in Early America," 176; John Bakeless, *The Eyes of Discovery: The Pageant of North America as Seen by the First Explorers* (Philadelphia, 1950), 223; *Peter Kalm's Travels*, 1:154.

26. Thorpe, ed., *Federal and State Constitutions*, 5:3036, 3068; William Penn, "Conditions or Concessions to the First Purchasers," in *The Papers of William Penn*, ed. Richard S. and Mary Maples Dunn, 2:98–99, and 235, 363, 376n8, 377 (Philadelphia, 1982); *Minutes of the Provincial Council of Pennsylvania from the Organization to the Termination of the Proprietary Government* (Harrisburg, 1851–52), 4:18, 1:292, 3:269; *Pennsylvania Gazette*, 8 June 1732.

27. *Minutes of the Provincial Council of Pennsylvania*, 3:566–567, 4:17, 20, 24–25; *Pennsylvania Gazette*, 19 Mar. 1761.

28. *Minutes of the Provincial Council of Pennsylvania,* 4:284; Steven K. Vernon, "Fishing Around Philadelphia," *Pennsylvania Heritage* 18 (1990): 25–26; *Burnaby's Travels Through North America Reprinted From the Third Edition of 1798,* ed. Rufus R. Wilson (New York, 1904), 97–98; Nicholas B. Wainwright, *The Schuylkill Fishing Company of the State in Schuylkill, 1732–1982* (Philadelphia, 1982), 9, 12, 42.

29. *Pennsylvania Gazette,* 24 June 1762, 13 Mar. 1766, 11 Apr. 1771.

30. Ibid., 3 Apr. 1760, 19 Mar. 1761.

31. Ibid., 16 Apr. 1767, 4 Apr. 1771 (2), 8 Feb. 1786.

32. Ibid., 19 Mar., 2 Apr., and 26 Nov. 1761; 17 Aug. and 12 Oct. 1769.

33. *Minutes of the Provincial Council of Pennsylvania,* 9:730; *Pennsylvania Gazette,* 10 Aug. 1774, 15 Oct. 1783; *Minutes of the Supreme Executive Council of Pennsylvania, from its Organization to the Termination of the Revolution* (Harrisburg, 1853), 12:611.

34. *Pennsylvania Gazette,* 21 Dec. 1785 and 4 Jan., 11 Jan., 1 Feb., 8 Feb., 22 Feb., 15 Mar., 19 Apr., 31 May, 14 June, 5 July, and 26 July 1786.

35. Ibid., 22 Nov. 1786; 14 May 1788; 11 Nov. 1789; and 4 May, 23 Feb., and 27 Apr. 1791.

36. Thorpe, ed., *Federal and State Constitutions,* 5:3035–3044, 3068, 3075; Albert C. Myers, ed., *Narratives of Early Pennsylvania, West New Jersey, and Delaware, 1630–1707* (New York, 1912), 207; *Papers of William Penn,* ed. Dunn, 2:98–101, 571, 572. For manors, see George Wheeler, "Richard Penn's Manor of Andolhea," *Pennsylvania Magazine of History and Biography* 58 (1934): 194.

37. *The Statutes at Large of Pennsylvania in the Time of William Penn: Compiled Under the Authority of the Act of May 19, 1887, as Supplemented,* vol. 1 (1680–1700), comp. Gail M. Beckman (New York, 1976), 147, 173–174; *The Laws of the Province of Pennsylvania: Now in Force, Collected into One Volume,* 191–192 (Evans 3086); Robert J. Dinkin, *Voting in Provincial America: A Study of Elections in the Thirteen Colonies, 1689–1776* (Westport, CT, 1977), 35.

38. W. W. Hening, ed., *The Statutes at Large Being a Collection of all the Laws of Virginia* (Richmond, 1823), 3:328; Alexander Spotswood to the Council of Trade, 6 Mar. 1710 [1711], "The Official Letters of Alexander Spotswood, Lieutenant-Governor of the Colony of Virginia, 1710–1722," *Virginia Historical Society Collections* 1 and 2 (1882): 49–50.

39. *The Secret Diary of William Byrd of Westover, 1709–1712,* ed. Louis B. Wright and Marion Tinling (Richmond, 1941), xxiii, 128, 85, x, 400, 405; *The Writings of George Washington from the Original Manuscript Sources, 1745–1799,* ed. John C. Fitzpatrick (Washington, DC, 1931–44), 29:295–296.

40. *Pennsylvania Gazette,* 11 Mar. 1731, 25 Oct. 1733.

41. Chapters 323 and 383, *Statutes at Large of Pennsylvania, 1682–1801,* ed. J. T. Mitchell and Henry Flanders, 17 vols. (Harrisburg, 1896–1911); *Pennsylvania Gazette,* 17 Apr. 1760.

42. *Pennsylvania Gazette,* 17 Apr. 1760; *Minutes of the Provincial Council of Pennsylvania,* 8:451–454. For the context of these plans, see Fred Anderson, *Crucible of War: The Seven Years' War and the Fate of Empire in British North America* (New York, 2000), 384–388.

43. The *Pennsylvania Gazette,* 8 Mar. 1770, prints the Pennsylvania act; Thompson, *Whigs and Hunters,* app. I, 270–277, conveniently supplies the Waltham Black Act. For the Blacks, see Robert G. Crist, "Cumberland County," in *Beyond Philadelphia: The*

American Revolution in the Pennsylvania Hinterland, ed. John B. Frantz and William Pencak, 114 (University Park, PA, 1998).

44. *Pennsylvania Gazette,* 18 Sept. 1776 and 23 Oct. 1776 (2); Thorpe, ed., *Federal and State Constitutions,* 5:3081–3103.

45. Thorpe, ed., *Federal and State Constitutions,* 6:3760, 3770; Robert E. Shalhope, *Bennington and the Green Mountain Boys: The Emergence of Liberal Democracy in Vermont, 1760–1850* (Baltimore, 1996), 171; *Pennsylvania Gazette,* 14 Nov. 1787, 9 Jan. 1788.

46. *The Documentary History of the Ratification of the Constitution,* ed. Merrill Jensen et al. (Madison, 1976–), 2:597–598, 618, 624.

47. Lund, *American Wildlife Law,* 140n2; *The Papers of James Madison,* ed. Charles F. Hobson and Robert A. Rutland (Charlottesville, 1962–91), 12:58–59, 196–210, esp. 201. For a convenient introduction to the debate over the Second Amendment, see "Forum: Historians and Guns," *William and Mary Quarterly,* 3rd ser., 59 (Jan. 2002): 203–268; Carol T. Bogus, ed., "Symposium on the Second Amendment: Fresh Looks," *Chicago-Kent Law Review* 76, no. 1 (2000); and Malcolm, *To Keep and Bear Arms.*

48. *Pennsylvania Gazette,* 30 July 1788.

49. *Virginia Gazette* (P&D), 18 Dec. 1766; *William Elliott's Carolina Sports by Land and Water Including Incidents of Devil-Fishing, Wild-Cat, Deer and Bear Hunting, Etc.,* ed. Theodore Rosengarten (1846; repr. Columbia, SC, 1994), 260; Alexander Thomson, "News from America, 1774," in *Discoveries of America: Personal Accounts of British Emigrants to North America during the Revolutionary Era,* ed. Barbara DeWolfe (Cambridge, 1997), 118–119.

50. "Forum: Historians and Guns," 203–268; Elizabeth G. Brown, *British Statutes in American Law, 1776–1836* (Ann Arbor, 1964), 13 and passim; Thomas Cooper and David S. McCord, ed., *The Statutes at Large of South Carolina* (Columbia, SC, 1837–41), 2:401; *Pennsylvania Gazette,* 23 Jan. 1793, 30 Mar. 1796.

51. *Pennsylvania Gazette,* 19 Feb. 1761, 25 Jan. 1770; *Writings of George Washington,* 3:92, 96; Mary N. Stanard, *Colonial Virginia: Its People and Customs* (Philadelphia, 1917), 260.

52. *The Diary of Colonel Landon Carter of Sabine Hall, 1752–1778,* ed. Jack P. Greene (Charlottesville, 1965), 2:905; *William Elliott's Carolina Sports,* 258.

53. *Pennsylvania Gazette,* 25 Jan. and 8 Feb. 1770.

54. Durand Echeverria, *Mirage in the West: A History of the French Image of American Society to 1815,* ed. Gilbert Chinard (Princeton, 1957), 80.

55. *Pennsylvania Gazette,* 17 May 1786.

56. Ibid., 1 Feb. 1770; Gary Kulik, "Dams, Fish, and Farmers: Defense of Public Rights in Eighteenth-Century Rhode Island," in *The Countryside in the Age of Capitalist Transformation: Essays in the Social History of Rural America,* ed. Steven Hahn and Jonathan Prude, 25–50 (Chapel Hill, 1985).

57. Cooper, *The Pioneers, or the Sources of the Susquehanna, A Descriptive Tale,* ed. James F. Beard (Albany, 1980), 229; E. Arthur Robinson, "Conservation in Cooper's *The Pioneers,*" *Publications of the Modern Language Association of America* 82 (1967): 564.

58. Thomas P. Slaughter, *The Natures of John and William Bartram* (New York, 1996), 66; *Peter Kalm's Travels,* 1:270; Calvin Martin, *Keepers of the Game: Indian-Animal Relationships and the Fur Trade* (Berkeley, 1978).

59. *Sketches of Eighteenth Century America: More "Letters from an American Farmer" by St. John De Crevecoeur,* ed. Henri L. Bourdin, Ralph H. Gabriel, and Stanley T. Williams (New Haven, 1925), 118, 86; *Virginia Gazette* (P&D), 27 July 1769.

60. *The Complete Writings of Thomas Paine,* ed. Philip S. Foner (New York, 1945), 1:503; Charles A. Miller, *Jefferson and Nature: An Interpretation* (Baltimore, 1988), 223; Edwin M. Betts and Hazelhurst B. Perkins, *Thomas Jefferson's Flower Garden at Monticello* (Charlottesville, 1971), 4.

61. *Peter Kalm's Travels,* 1:93n3; Thomas, *Man and the Natural World,* 273; quoted in Miller, *Jefferson and Nature,* 51. See also, Glacken, *Traces on the Rhodian Shore,* 693.

62. *The Diary of Colonel Landon Carter,* 2:829.

FIVE: Beyond Declension

1. Bernard Bailyn, *The New England Merchants in the Seventeenth Century* (New York, 1955), 112. The declension model has its origins in Perry Miller, *The New England Mind: From Colony to Province* (Cambridge, MA, 1953). John McCusker and Rusell Menard note that "Perry Miller was often hostile and occasionally contemptuous of economic history." *The Economy of British America, 1607–1789* (Chapel Hill, 1985, 1991), 92n1. A team of social historians working in the 1970s collectively reinforced the declension model. Examples include Kenneth Lockridge, *A New England Town, the First Hundred Years: Dedham, Massachusetts, 1636–1736* (New York, 1970); Michael Zuckerman, *Peaceable Kingdoms: New England Towns in the Eighteenth Century* (New York, 1970); James Henretta, "Families and Farms: *Mentalité* in Pre-industrial America," *William and Mary Quarterly,* 3rd ser., 35 (1978): 3–32; Paul Boyer and Stephen Nissenbaum, *Salem Possessed: The Social Origins of Witchcraft* (Cambridge, MA, 1974); William Cronon, *Changes in the Land: Indians, Colonists, and the Ecology of New England* (New York, 1983); Christopher Clark, "The Household Economy, Market Exchange, and the Rise of Capitalism in the Connecticut Valley," *Journal of Social History* 13 (1979): 169–190.

2. Stephen Innes provides the most systematic appraisal of Weber in *Creating the Commonwealth: The Economic Culture of Puritan New England* (New York, 1995). His work owes a debt to Christine Leigh Heyrman, *Commerce and Culture: The Maritime Communities of Colonial Massachusetts, 1690–1750* (New York, 1984). The quotes are from Alan Taylor, *American Colonies* (New York, 2001), 159; and Joyce Appleby, "The Vexed Story of Capitalism Told by American Historians," *Journal of the Early Republic* 21 (2001): 9.

3. Appleby, "The Vexed Story of Capitalism," 4.

4. Jack P. Greene, *Pursuits of Happiness: The Social Development of Early Modern British Colonies and the Formation of American Culture* (Chapel Hill, 1988); Lois Green Carr, Russell R. Menard, and Lorena S. Walsh, eds., *Robert Cole's World: Agriculture and Society in Early Maryland* (Chapel Hill, 1991).

5. A selection of this scholarship includes Daniel Vickers, *Farmers and Fishermen: Two Centuries of Work in Essex County Massachusetts* (Chapel Hill, 1991); Vickers, "Working the Fields in a Developing Economy: Essex County, Massachusetts, 1630–1675," in *Work and Labor in Early America,* ed. Stephen Innes, 49–69 (Chapel Hill, 1988); Heyrman, *Commerce and Culture;* Gloria Main and Jackson T. Main, "Economic Growth and the Standard of Living in Southern New England," *Journal of Economic*

History 48 (1988): 27–46; John Frederick Martin, *Profits in the Wilderness: Entrepreneurship and the Founding of New England Towns in the Seventeenth Century* (Chapel Hill, 1991).

6. The general impact of this quest on colonial development is best summarized in John J. McCusker and Russell Menard, *The Economy of British America, 1607–1789* (Chapel Hill, 1984), 51–71.

7. Nathanial B. Shurtleff, ed., *Records of the Governor and Company of the Massachusetts Bay in New England* (Boston, 1853–54), 1:158 (2 Sept. 1635); 230 (8 June 1638); 257–258 (22 May 1639); 101 (7 Nov. 1632); "The Company's First Letter of Instruction to Endicott and His Council," (17 Apr. 1629), reprinted in Alexander Young, *Chronicles of the First Planters of the Colony of the Massachusetts Bay, From 1623–1636* (Boston, 1856), 163. Details on the early fishing trade are recounted in excellent detail in Vickers, *Farmers and Fishermen,* 85–116.

8. John Tinker to John Winthrop, *Winthrop Papers* IV, 207 (27 Feb. 1639); Thomas Dudley to the Lady Bridget, Countess of Lincoln, reprinted in Everett Emerson, ed., *Letters from New England: The Massachusetts Bay Colony, 1629–1638* (Amherst, 1976), 74 (12 and 28 Mar., 1630–31); John Davenport and Theophilus Eaton to the Massachusetts General Court, *Winthrop Papers* 4:19 (12 Mar. 1638); John Winthrop to Simon D'Ewes, *Winthrop Papers* 3:200 (20 July 1635).

9. For the contrast between the infrastructure prevailing in England and New England in the 1630s, see James E. McWilliams, "From the Ground Up: Internal Economic Development and Local Commercial Exchange in the Massachusetts Bay Region, 1630–1710" (PhD diss., The Johns Hopkins University, 2001), ch. 2.

10. All of these incidents were recorded in *The Journal of John Winthrop, 1630–1649,* 137 (24 Nov. 1634); 87 (17 Jan. 1633), and 129–130 (30 Sept. 1634).

11. *Journal of John Winthrop, 1630–1649,* 71 (July 1632), 124 (4 Aug. 1634), and 131 (20 Oct. 1634); John Winthrop to John Winthrop, Jr., *Winthrop Papers* 4:118 (May 1639).

12. This point, interestingly, would be obvious to any historian of the early nineteenth-century U.S. economy, a period when the country's domestic economy was coming to absorb more products than the export economy. Nevertheless, due in large part to the dominance of the staples theory of economic growth on colonial American economic history, historians almost never apply an analysis of infrastructural status to regional economies during this time period.

13. Information on cow keeping can be found throughout the town records. See Newtown Court Records, 23 (6 June 1636) and 28 (May 1636); Dorchester Town Records, 30 (19 Apr. 1637); and Salem Town Records, 85 (19 Apr. 1637).

14. Newtown Court Records, 22 (23 Apr. 1636) and 25 (5 Dec. 1636); Braintree Records, 3 (23 Feb. 1634) and 5 (2 Apr. 1635); and Dorchester Town Records, 23 (2 May 1636). A similar process prevailed in the Chesapeake, as is revealed in Lois Green Carr, Menard, and Walsh, eds., *Robert Cole's World,* ch. 2.

15. Salem Town Records, 68 (31 Mar. 1638); Dorchester Town Records, 24 (10 Sept. 1637); Boston Records, 40 (25 Mar. 1639).

16. Newtown Court Records, 22 (23 Apr. 1636) and 6 (2 Mar. 1633).

17. Salem Town Records, 9 (6 Apr. 1635) and 9 (12 Mar. 1634); Dorchester Town Records, 9 (3 Nov. 1634).

18. Dorchester Town Records, 11 (17 Apr. 1635), 17 (27 June 1636), and 22 (16 Jan. 1636); Boston Records, 12 (17 Nov. 1636).

19. Salem Town Records, 84 (25 Feb. 1635); Boston Records, 3 (12 Dec. 1634); Dorchester Town Records, 9 (29 Dec. 1634).

20. Several kinds of consumption prevailed at once in early New England. Settlers might harvest timber for local use, regional exchange, or exportation. In the 1630s, I argue elsewhere, local demand prevailed, and settlers cleared timber for themselves and their immediate neighbors. This kind of behavior has too often been portrayed as evidence of a preindustrial mentality that stood in sharp contrast to the impending profit-hungry exporters. In contrast, it seems more the reflection of settlers wisely choosing to meet infrastructural needs before trying to export their resources. New England, they knew, was more than a trading post—it was their new home. McWilliams, "From the Ground Up," ch. 2.

21. Boston Records, 4 (23 Mar. 1635); Newtown Town Records, 46 (8 Nov. 1642); Dorchester Town Records, 36 (14 Nov. 1637).

22. Information on fence viewers was gleaned from the following cases in the Boston Records (BR) and Dorchester Town Records (DTR): DTR, 6 (24 May 1634); DTR, 10 (10 Feb. 1634); DTR, 20 (16 Jan. 1636); DTR, 31 (18 Mar. 1637); DTR 33 (23 Apr. 1638); DTR, 37 (13 Feb. 1638); BR, 3 (9 Feb. 1634); BR, 4 (23 Mar. 1635); BR, 9 (21 Mar. 1636); BR, 33 (16 Apr. 1638); BR, 52 (30 Mar. 1639).

23. There is a chronological issue with these farmer account books that needs to be addressed. Few account books survive from the seventeenth century. Those that do usually document transactions from later in the century, as do the three surveyed here. While it would be ideal to cite account books kept in the 1640s and 1650s in order to demonstrate the earliest emergence of local trading patterns, such evidence does not exist. Fortunately, the habits of local exchange remained relatively steady throughout the century, so the use of accounts from the 1670s to 1700—while not ideal—still captures the flavor of the habits that New England traders were forming earlier in the century.

24. Harrison Ellery and Charles Pickering Bowditch, *The Pickering Genealogy*, vol. 1 (privately printed, 1897), 44–46.

25. John Pickering Account Book, John Hovey Acct., 96.

26. Ibid., Keefer Acct., 106.

27. Ibid., Harvey Acct., Marsten Acct., Neale Acct., Kempton Acct.

28. Ibid., Ingersoll Acct., Marsten Acct.

29. John Barnard Account Book, Francis Faulkner Acct.

30. Ibid., Francis Faulkner Acct.

31. Ibid., Tyler Acct. (22 June 1703); Lovejoy Acct. (1699).

32. Ibid., accts. with Nathanial Stevens, Joseph Parker, and William Andel.

33. Background on Burnham comes from "Deed from John Burnham Sr. to John Burnham Tertious," 1 Mar. 1693–94, Essex Deeds, Bk. 10, 23–25; Elizabeth Puckett Martin, *Deacon John Burnham of Ipswich and Ebenezer Martin of Rehobeth, Massachusetts and Some of their Descendants* (Baltimore, 1987); Roderick H. Martin, *The Burnham Family of Genealogical Records of the Descendants of the Four Emigrants of the Name Who Were Among the Early Settlers in America* (Boston, 1869); Thomas Franklin Waters, *Ipswich in the Massachusetts Bay Colony, 1633–1700* (Ipswich, 1905).

34. John Burnham Account Book, N. Perkins Acct. (28 Mar. 1700–11 Dec. 1704); Isaac Perkins Acct. (11 July 1698–5 May 1705).

35. John Burnham Account Book, 1704–5.

36. Ibid., Joseph Whipple Acct. (17 Nov. 1697, 11 June 1698); Nathanial Rust Acct. (10 Feb. 1703–27 Oct. 1705); Thomas Perrin Acct. (10 May 1693–9 May 1694); Isaac Littlehale Acct. (17 June 1692–15 May 1694).

37. Ibid.

38. George Corwin Account Book, 1651–56; located in the Philips Library, Peabody Essex Museum, Salem, Mass. Again, a note on chronology: Corwin's activity, as documented in these early accounts, precedes the economic activity of the commercial farmers discussed in the previous section. Nevertheless, as the commercial farming activity portrayed above was meant to reflect the tenor of commercial farming activity throughout the entire century, it is perfectly likely that the local activity with which Corwin interacted was quite similar.

39. David Hancock, "'A World of Business to Do': William Freeman and the Foundations of England's Commercial Empire, 1645–1707," *William and Mary Quarterly*, 3rd ser., 57 (2000): 4–30; Jacob Price, "What Did Merchants Do? Reflections on British Overseas Trade, 1660–1790," *The Journal of Economic History* 46 (1989): 267–284.

40. Bailyn, *New England Merchants*, 134–139; Clarence L. Ver Steeg, *The Formative Years, 1607–1763* (New York, 1964), 174; Jack P. Greene, *Pursuits of Happiness*, 76.

41. George Corwin Account Sample File, 1651–56; Benjamin Balch Acct. (Feb. 1652 to Jan. 1655), George Corwin Account Book, 30.

42. "Mr. Norrice" Acct. (Nov. 1653–Mar. 1655), George Corwin Account Book, 55.

43. John Leach Acct. (Mar. 1653–Nov. 1653), George Corwin Account Book, 31; Thomas Gordon Acct. (Feb. 1652–Sept. 1653), George Corwin Account Book, 32; John Beckett Acct. (Sept. 1655–Feb. 1655), George Corwin Account Book.

44. George Corwin Account Sample, 1653–56.

45. George Corwin Account Sample, 1653–56; George Corwin Account Books, 1651–53, Nathanial Pickman Acct. (Sept. 1655–Mar. 1656), #0; Joseph Jencks Acct. (Dec. 1652–Jan. 1653), 2; and Elias Stileman Acct., (Aug. 1653–July 1654), 62.

46. Darrett B. Rutman, "Governor Winthrop's Garden Crop: The Significance of Agriculture in the Early Commerce of Massachusetts Bay," *William and Mary Quarterly*, 3rd ser., 20 (1963): 396–397.

47. Jack P. Greene, *Pursuits of Happiness*, 8.

SIX: Paternalism and Profits

1. Influential statements of the opposing positions can be found in Eugene D. Genovese, *Roll, Jordan, Roll: The World the Slaves Made* (New York, 1974), and James Oakes, *The Ruling Race: A History of American Slaveholders* (New York, 1982). A synopsis of the debate can be found in Mark M. Smith, *Debating Slavery: Economy and Society in the Antebellum American South* (New York, 1998).

2. Allan Kulikoff, *From British Peasants to Colonial American Farmers* (Chapel Hill, 2000), 37. The literature on the capitalist transformation in early America is enormous. For a selection see Kulikoff, "The Transition to Capitalism in Rural America," *William and Mary Quarterly* (hereafter *WMQ*), 3rd ser., 46 (1989); Stephen Hahn and Jonathan Prude, eds., *The Countryside in the Age of Capitalist Transformation: Essays in the Social History of Rural America* (Chapel Hill, 1985). For a spirited critique of this literature, see Richard Bushman, "Markets and Composite Farms in Early America," *WMQ*, 3rd ser., 55 (1998): 351–374.

3. Genovese, *Roll, Jordan, Roll,* passim.

4. Ibid., 10–13.

5. Ibid., 7–25.

6. For Genovese's dating of the emergence of paternalism see ibid., 6.

7. See, Philip Morgan, "Three Planters and Their Slaves: Perspectives on Slavery in Virginia, South Carolina, and Jamaica, 1750–1790," in *Race and Family in the Colonial South,* ed. Winthrop D. Jordan and Sheila L. Skemp, 38, 42–54 (Jackson, MS, 1987).

8. Philip Morgan, *Slave Counterpoint: Black Culture in the Eighteenth-Century Chesapeake and Lowcountry* (Chapel Hill, 1998), 296–298, quote at 296; Ira Berlin, *Many Thousands Gone: The First Two Centuries of Slavery in North America* (Cambridge, MA, 1998), 152.

9. On the increase in tobacco output see Morgan, *Slave Counterpoint,* 164–165, quote at 164. On the demographic maturation of the slave population as cause for a spur in productivity, see Lorena S. Walsh, *From Calabar to Carter's Grove: A History of a Virginia Slave Community* (Charlottesville, 1997), 117.

10. On the greater productivity of the Piedmont, see Walsh, *From Calabar to Carter's Grove,* 209.

11. On the turn to wheat, the intensification of labor regimens that it entailed, and the conflicts that resulted, see Lois Green Carr and Lorena S. Walsh, "Economic Diversification and Labor Organization in the Chesapeake, 1650–1820," in *Work and Labor in Early America,* ed. Stephen Innes, 144–188 (Chapel Hill, 1988); and Walsh, "Work and Resistance in the New Republic: The Case of the Chesapeake," in *From Chattel Slaves to Wage Slaves: The Dynamics of Labour Bargaining in the Americas,* ed. Mary Turner, 105–107 (Kingston, Jamaica, 1995). On planters' sensitivity to market prompts, see Walsh, *From Calabar to Carter's Grove,* 120, 122–123.

12. On the gentry's reliance on metropolitan norms see, for example, Michal Rozbicki, *The Complete Colonial Gentleman: Cultural Legitimacy in Plantation America* (Charlottesville, 1998), 118–121. For other attempts to reconcile evidence of paternalism with planters' immersion in the international marketplace see Morgan, *Slave Counterpoint,* 244–245, 259, 316; Robert Olwell, *Masters, Slaves, and Subjects: The Culture of Power in the South Carolina Low Country, 1740–1790* (Ithaca, 1998), 187–211; and Jeffrey Robert Young, *Domesticating Slavery: The Master Class in Georgia and South Carolina, 1670–1837* (Chapel Hill, 1999).

13. For an iteration of these dynamics in Virginia see Morgan, *Slave Counterpoint,* 326–334. For examples from South Carolina, see Olwell, *Masters, Slaves, and Subjects,* 211–218. For the centrality of judicial and paternal metaphors to the self-conception of Virginia's great planters see Rhys Isaac, *The Transformation of Virginia: 1740–1790* (Chapel Hill, 1982), 344–350; Rhys Isaac, "Communication and Control: Authority Metaphors and Power Contests on Colonel Landon Carter's Virginia Plantation, 1752–1778," in *Rites of Power: Symbolism, Ritual, and Politics Since the Middle Ages,* ed. Sean Wilentz, 275–302 (Philadelphia, 1985).

14. Hunter D. Farish, ed., *Journal and Letters of Philip Vickers Fithian, 1773–1774: A Plantation Tutor in the Old Dominion* (Williamsburg, 1943), 129.

15. See James Baird, "Between Slavery and Independence: Power Relations between Dependent White Men and Their Superiors in Late Colonial and Early National Virginia With Particular Reference to the Overseer-Employer Relationship," (PhD diss., The Johns Hopkins University, 1999), 223–246.

16. 2 Jan. 1774, Robert Carter Daybook, Duke University Library, Durham, NC (hereafter DUL); see also 22 Sept. 1776 in the same source.

17. J. H. Norton to Battaile Muse, 30 June 1786, Battaile Muse Papers, DUL.

18. John Mercer to Battaile Muse, 6 Dec. 1778, Battaile Muse Papers, DUL.

19. Ibid., 18 May 1780.

20. Ibid.

21. J. H. Norton to Battaile Muse, 30 June 1786, Battaile Muse Papers, DUL.

22. Of course, a planter's slaves often did have something to gain from such interactions. Slaves often competed with their overseers for the use of the plantation's corn, for example.

23. Samuel Straughan to Robert Carter, 27 Sept. 1786, Carter Family Papers, Virginia Historical Society, Richmond, VA (hereafter VHS).

24. For other examples of conflicts between overseers and slaves over work regimens, see Morgan, *Slave Counterpoint,* 193; Berlin, *Many Thousands Gone,* 133–134; Walsh, *From Calabar to Carter's Grove,* 119. Also, in a nineteenth-century context, see William Dusinberre, *Them Dark Days: Slavery in the American Rice Swamps* (Athens, GA, 2000), 160.

25. Cited in Mechal Sobel, *The World They Made Together: Black and White Values in Eighteenth-Century Virginia* (Princeton, 1987), 236–237.

26. Battaile Muse to George William Fairfax, n.d. [after Sept. 1784], Battaile Muse Papers, DUL.

27. Simon Sallard to Richard Chapman, 25 Jan. 1736, Simon Sallard Letters, University of Virginia Library, Charlottesville, VA (hereafter UVA).

28. See also the example in Walsh "Work and Resistance in the New Republic," 110. For the same dynamic in a different context, see Dusinberre, *Them Dark Days,* 200–201. Kinship ties often provided the foundation for work resistance. See Walsh, *From Calabar to Carter's Grove,* 50.

29. Entry of 24 June 1757 in Jack P. Greene, ed., *The Diary of Colonel Landon Carter of Sabine Hall, 1752–1778* (Charlottesville, 1965), 1:160.

30. William Douglas to Francis Jerdone, 30 Aug. 1782, Jerdone Family Papers, College of William and Mary Library, Williamsburg, VA (hereafter CWM).

31. For the potential risks involved in choosing to inform on a current overseer see Dusinberre, *Them Dark Days,* 252, 257.

32. On the size of plantations, see Morgan, *Slave Counterpoint,* 35–42; Allan Kulikoff, *Tobacco and Slaves: The Development of Southern Cultures in the Chesapeake, 1680–1800* (Chapel Hill, 1986), 331, 338. On the size of work units see Carr and Walsh, "Economic Diversification and Labor Organization in the Chesapeake, 1650–1820," 162–165; Walsh, *From Calabar to Carter's Grove,* 289n26; Morgan, *Slave Counterpoint,* 187–191; Kulikoff, *Tobacco and Slaves,* 385–387. The addition of wheat to crops under cultivation greatly increased the number of individual tasks to be completed, and so resulted in smaller work units.

33. Based on a sample of seventeen from Lancaster County Suit Papers and Cumberland County Court Papers, 1750–85, Library of Virginia, Richmond, VA (hereafter LOV). Most common remunerative agreements called for planter-employers to pay overseers a share of what the labor force under the overseer's superintendence produced that year. The basic agreement, of which there were many variations, allowed the overseer one share of the tobacco crop, each full hand under his supervision being

counted as a share also. Thus, if an overseer managed five slaves, he would obtain one-sixth of the tobacco's return (after paying his share of the transport and inspection costs). The evidence of share payments allows us, then, to estimate the size of the average work force contracted out to an overseer (though only in a couple of instances in the sample deployed was this deduction needed—in the majority of cases the number of slave charges was stated). While the evidence of such payments is most abundant among plantation papers, those sources tend to be skewed toward the wealthiest planters. In order to arrive at a more balanced approximation, I have relied here upon court records under the premise that overseers' grievances (many of the suits are for nonpayment of back wages) were not related to the number of charges under their supervision; See Baird, "Between Slavery and Independence."

34. Tithe lists, compiled within each county, listed the names of all free men over the age of sixteen, and of all slaves, male and female, above sixteen years of age. They allow us to distinguish between householders and dependents.

35. The majority of such dependents were what I term nonfamilial dependents, having a different surname from the household head. In households with fewer slaves, while it was not uncommon for there to be a free dependent, only rarely did the likelihood of having such a dependent reach 50 percent. Moreover, below the aforesaid slaveholding thresholds it was far more likely that a free dependent shared the householder's surname, presumably being his son. It is highly likely, then, that given on the one hand the close association between a household's size of slaveholding and the likelihood that the household contained a free dependent, and on the other hand the much greater reliance of households with larger slaveholdings on nonfamilial dependents, that those free dependents listed in households falling above the threshold were overseers.

36. Harry J. Carman, ed., *American Husbandry* (1775; repr. New York, 1939), 188.

37. Thomas Anburey, *Travels Through the Interior Parts of America* (London, 1794), 2:328. Additionally, Landon Carter observed that "other gentlemen of Estates are more happy than I can be in substituting the care of others and confiding in it, whilst they enjoy the ease of not thinking about their affairs." Entry of 20 May 1772 in Greene, ed., *Diary of Landon Carter*, 2:688. Though the captious Carter is not the most objective of commentators, his impressions do suggest the need to differentiate between those deeply involved in the supervision of their plantations, such as Carter himself or George Washington (men whose commitments to their plantations were carefully recorded in diaries), and others who, though understanding the importance of close oversight, were content to contract those responsibilities out to third parties (and who left no diaries). It suggests, too, that the exponents of the paternalism evinced earlier in the paper might also have been attempting to distinguish themselves from their less conscientious neighbors.

38. I multiplied free tithables by four and slave tithables by two to arrive at a figure for the total county population and its free and slave components.

39. See Morgan, *Slave Counterpoint*, 39.

40. Henry Fitzhugh to Messrs. John Stewart and Campbell, 29 July 1766, cited in Morgan, *Slave Counterpoint*, 85.

41. On the expansion of slavery into the Piedmont, see Philip D. Morgan and Michael Nicholls, "Slaves in Piedmont Virginia," *WMQ*, 3rd ser., 46 (1989): 211–251; Morgan, "Slave Life in Piedmont Virginia, 1720–1800," in *Colonial Chesapeake Society*,

ed. Lois Green Carr, Philip D. Morgan, and Jean B. Russo, 433–484 (Chapel Hill, 1988); and Richard S. Dunn, "Black Society in the Chesapeake, 1776–1810," in *Slavery and Freedom in the Age of the American Revolution,* ed. Ira Berlin and Ronald Hoffman, 49–82 (Charlottesville, 1983).

42. These statistics are taken from Baird, "Between Slavery and Independence."

43. Ibid.

44. For the same dynamic in nineteenth-century South Carolina, see Dusinberre, *Them Dark Days,* 312.

45. Lorena Walsh finds that many overseers after 1790 were paid a salary rather than a share. See Walsh, "Plantation Management in the Chesapeake, 1620–1820," *Journal of Economic History* 49 (1989): 403n16. I have found no such shift.

46. William Dabney Ledger, Colonial Williamsburg Foundation Library, Williamsburg, VA; W. W. Abbot et al., eds., *The Papers of George Washington,* Colonial Series (Charlottesville, 1983), 6 (1759): 266; Randolph Tucker Papers, Brock Collection, Huntington Library, San Marino, CA.

47. Entry of 9 May 1772 in Greene, ed., *Diary of Landon Carter,* 2:678.

48. Anburey, *Travels Through the Interior Parts of America,* 2:329.

49. Moreau de St. Mery, *American Journey, 1793–1798,* trans. and ed. Kenneth Roberts and Anna M. Roberts (New York, 1947), 305. See also Walsh, *From Calabar to Carter's Grove,* 119.

50. Mercer to Bataille Muse, 1 May 1777, Battaile Muse Papers, DUL.

51. Thomas Fairfax to Battaile Muse, Dec. 1792, Battaile Muse Papers, DUL.

52. The otherwise paternalist Landon Carter, for example, lamented that overseers "tire as cornfields do," a sentiment echoed some years later by William Bolling who observed that overseers "all seem to wear out after a while and to require changing." 24 June 1757 in Greene, ed., *Diary of Landon Carter,* 1:302; Bolling cited in Morgan, *Slave Counterpoint,* 327. For the paternalism of Carter see Morgan, "Three Planters and Their Slaves," 42–54.

53. *Pridham v. Armistead,* 1759, Lancaster County Court Papers, LOV.

54. *Ross v. Mathews,* 1759, Cumberland County Suit Papers, LOV. It would appear that overseers needed to demonstrate that their dismissal was without cause. The plaintiffs in the two suits above seemed also to have felt it necessary to claim that following their dismissal their families had suffered deprivation. It is suggestive that in those cases where no such claims were made the suits were either dismissed or juries found for the defendant. See *Wheeler v. Hughes,* 1764, Cumberland Suit Papers, LOV; *Rock v. Carter,* 1762, and *Pinckard v. Tapscot,* 1767, Lancaster Court Papers, LOV.

55. Entry of 4 Dec. 1757 in Greene, ed., *Diary of Landon Carter,* 1:192.

56. Entry of 25 Apr. 1814, Philip Lightfoot Account Book, Alderman Library, UVA. Likewise, employers deducted periods of absence from their overseers' wages. See for example accounts submitted in *Fretwell v. Dunkley,* 1754, Cumberland Suit Papers, LOV.

57. *Rock v. Carter,* 1762, Lancaster County Court Papers, LOV.

58. Stephen Burdett to [?], 7 Mar. 1827, Elizabeth Barbour Ambler Papers, UVA.

59. Entry of 6 Oct. 1787, William Cabell Commonplace Book, VHS.

60. John Tayloe to Mr. Cannady, 17 June 1801, John Tayloe III Letterbook, Tayloe Family Papers, VHS. See also 12 Apr. 1770 and 15 May 1770 in Greene, ed., *Diary of Landon Carter,* 1:385, 410.

61. *Rutherford v. Ball* and *Ball v. Rutherford,* 1760, Lancaster County Court Papers, LOV.

62. *Hynds v. Bostick,* 1759, and *Bostick v. Hynds,* 1759, Cumberland Suit Papers, LOV.

63. Memo of an Agreement between William W. Smith and John Martin, 14 Sept. 1822, Pocket Plantation Papers, UVA.

64. Memorandum of Agreement between William Allason and Laurence Tompkins, 1779, William Allason Letterbook, LOV.

65. Articles of Agreement between Robert W. Carter and Hudson Lyle, Dec. 1828, Carter Papers, CWM. It is worthy of note that by the early nineteenth century most articles of agreement that included provisions for termination allowed the overseer compensation for the time he had completed.

66. Some employers preferred married overseers. The planter-lawyer John Mercer was not alone in his determination "never to trust to a Bachelor Overseer." John Mercer to Battaile Muse, 8 Aug. 1782, Battaile Muse Papers, DUL. George Washington, for example, intimated that a prospective overseer's "getting a wife will be no objection, as it will induce him from inclination, to do what he ought to be oblidged by articles, to agree to, that is, to be always at home." George Washington to Anthony Whiting, 29 Aug. 1791, in *The Writings of George Washington from the Original Manuscript Sources, 1745–1799,* ed. John Clement Fitzpatrick, 31:350 (Washington, DC, 1931). For more on married overseers see Baird, "Between Slavery and Independence," 114–115.

67. From the legal historian's perspective this is a key distinction between systems of free and unfree labor. See, for example, Christopher L. Tomlins, *Law, Labor, and Ideology in the Early American Republic* (New York, 1993) and Robert J. Steinfeld, *The Invention of Free Labor: The Employment Relation in English and American Law and Culture, 1350–1870* (Chapel Hill, 1991). However, in his most recent monograph Robert J. Steinfeld complicates the connection between distinct forms of labor and the legal remedies extended to the employer that were putatively associated with them. See Steinfeld, *Coercion, Contract, and Free Labor in the Nineteenth Century* (New York, 2001).

68. A conclusion based on my survey of admittedly fragmentary and incomplete suit papers from a number of Virginia counties. Perhaps employers rarely made use of the courts since the fact that an overseer's salary or share of the crop was only paid at the end of his term provided an inbuilt deterrent to an overseer departing early.

69. *Marr v. Davis,* 1751, Cumberland Suit Papers, LOV. Indeed, the escalation of the Marr-Davis dispute soon after suggests that the overseer's desertion was only incidental to the deeper conflict. Soon after the suit was initiated, Marr claimed that Davis was spreading the rumor that his employer had "fuck[ed] Judy [his] Negro wench." Not only had his good name been injured by this slander, Marr attested, but his "Wifes affections [were] also liable to be withdrawn from him & her former Good opinion of him and unity with him [had been] Turnd into Jealousy & Discord." See *Marr v. Davis,* Cumberland Suit Papers, 1757, LOV. In neither suit does it seem that Marr was successful, however. The former was dismissed and the latter ended in a nonsuit.

70. 10 Aug. 1783, Journal of Robert Wormeley Carter, Sabine Hall Collection, UVA.

71. 25 Apr. 1776 in Edward Riley, ed., *The Journal of John Harrower: An Indentured Servant in the Colony of Virginia, 1773–1776* (New York, 1963), 138.

72. Obviously, flight was not the prerogative of free laborers alone. As Michael Zuckerman has suggested, "running away was everywhere in early America the sovereign

remedy for the ills of the lower orders." See his "Toqueville, Turner, and Turds: Four Stories of Manners in Early America," *Journal of American History* 85 (1998): 39 and passim. We know, too, that even within slavery, though few outside of extraordinary circumstances fled their situation permanently, many more absconded temporarily, sometimes as a specific protest, sometimes to visit family "abroad." Nonetheless, the ability to leave an oppressive employer for good with limited legal consequences distinguished overseers from bound laborers in the most fundamental of ways.

73. On the link between distance from slavery and the tendency to sentimentalize the master-slave relationship, see Young, *Domesticating Slavery,* 75–76, and Berlin, *Many Thousands Gone,* 118. On the damage done to slave families by westward movement (and resistance to such displacement), see Walsh, *From Calabar to Carter's Grove,* 126, 131, 213; Morgan, *Slave Counterpoint,* 510, 521; Berlin, *Many Thousands Gone,* 122; and Walsh, "Plantation Management in the Chesapeake," 405.

74. On the diversity of new skills required on tidewater plantations, see Morgan, *Slave Counterpoint,* 209, and Walsh, *From Calabar to Carter's Grove,* 125, 131, 289n26. For Byrd, see Morgan, *Slave Counterpoint,* 244; for Mason, see Berlin, *Many Thousands Gone,* 117.

75. Thomas Jefferson to William Wirt, 5 Aug. 1815, in Albert Ellery Bergh, ed., *The Writings of Thomas Jefferson,* (Washington, DC, 1903), 14:337; and Barbour, James, Esq., President of the Agricultural Society of Albemarle at their meeting on the 8 Nov. 1825, Charlottesville, Va., Miscellaneous Papers, LOV.

76. John Mercer to Battaile Muse, 5 Oct. 1780, Battaile Muse Papers, DUL.

77. H. Washington to Battaile Muse, [no date] 1788, Battaile Muse Papers, DUL.

78. Quoted in Morgan, *Slave Counterpoint,* 329.

79. This discourse continued into the nineteenth century, see, for example, Dusinberre, *Them Dark Days,* 310.

80. On the emergence of wage labor and the erosion of traditional obligations in England see E. P. Thompson, *Customs in Common: Studies in Traditional Popular Culture* (New York, 1993), 9, 36–38, 43–46.

81. For the modernity of both forms of labor, see David Eltis, *The Rise of African Slavery in the Americas* (New York, 2000), 22. Eltis argues, however, that Europeans' reliance on African as opposed to potentially cheaper European slaves indicates that cultural considerations inhibited the quest for profit in plantation regimes. For a rebuttal, see Robin Blackburn, *The Making of New World Slavery: From the Baroque to the Modern, 1482–1800* (New York, 1997), 350–363.

SEVEN: "The Fewnesse of Handicraftsmen"

1. Michael G. Kammen, ed., "Maryland in 1699: A Letter from the Reverend Hugh Jones," *The Journal of Southern History* 29 (Aug. 1963): 371.

2. Richard Muir, *The English Village* (New York, 1980), 49.

3. Thomas Jefferson, *Notes on the State of Virginia,* ed. William C. Peden (Chapel Hill, 1954; repr. New York, 1972), 108–109.

4. John W. Reps, *Tidewater Towns: City Planning in Colonial Virginia and Maryland* (Williamsburg, VA, 1972), 58.

5. The legislature passed acts designating towns or ports of entry in 1668, 1669, and 1671; 1683, 1684, 1686, and 1688; and 1706, 1707, and 1708. The initial act specified locations where commissioners were to lay out streets and sell lots; successive acts

modified the sites in response to local objections and requests. See Reps, *Tidewater Towns*, 92–116, for a survey of the legislation.

6. William Hand Browne et al., eds., *Archives of Maryland* (Baltimore, 1883–1972), 7:609.

7. Jack P. Greene, review of *Of Consuming Interests: The Style of Life in the Eighteenth Century*, ed. Cary Carson, Ronald Hoffman, and Peter J. Albert, *William and Mary Quarterly*, 3rd ser., 53 (Jan. 1996): 185.

8. Taxables included all white males and all blacks and Indians, both male and female, over the age of fifteen, except those too ill or aged to labor. Population in 1706 estimated using the proportion of taxables to total population calculated for the 1704 census figures. See Jean B. Russo, *Free Workers in a Plantation Economy: Talbot County, Maryland, 1690–1759* (New York, 1989), 44–46, 67.

9. Midcentury population based on "The Population of Maryland, 1755," from *Gentleman's Magazine* 34 (1764), reprinted in Edward C. Papenfuse and Joseph M. Coale III, *The Hammond-Harwood House Atlas of Historical Maps of Maryland, 1608–1908* (Baltimore, 1982), 37. The 1783 tax assessment recorded 11,185 inhabitants, but listed no paupers for district 3. General Assembly (Tax Assessment), Talbot County, S1161-10-1, 3, 5, Maryland State Archives, Annapolis, MD. (All primary sources, unless otherwise noted, are at the Maryland State Archives.)

10. Jeremiah Banning, "Autobiography, 1733–1793," MS. 2433, Maryland Historical Society, 6.

11. Richard Campbell, in *The London Tradesman* (London, 1747; repr. London, 1969), identified approximately 170 in mid-eighteenth-century London.

12. A relatively simple, straight-sided cask, the hogshead demanded less skill from its maker than did most of the cooper's products. Planters wishing to introduce more self-sufficiency into their operations could reasonably begin by making hogsheads. A similar movement from independent craftsman to plantation workplace took place with shoemaking, which did not require a large investment in equipment or training to produce shoes suitable for bound laborers.

13. Land Office (Patents), FF 7/252; Talbot County Court (Land Records), RF 12/106, 264, 391; "Register," St. Peter's Parish, M295 (a long hiatus in births, between 1712 and 1723, might indicate the death of one wife and a remarriage); and Talbot County Court (Inventories), JB 2/69, 408 (debtors).

14. "A List of Taxables in Talbot County Anno Dom. 1733," Maryland State Papers, MdHR 19999–118/47.

15. Robert Goldsborough Ledgers, M1338, Maryland Historical Society, Baltimore, MD.

16. James B. Bordley, Jr., *The Hollyday and Related Families of the Eastern Shore of Maryland* (Baltimore, 1962), 127–139; Talbot County Court (Inventories), IB&IG 4/347; Talbot County Court (Judgments), FT 2/n.p., 6/1718 court; Talbot County Court (Inventories), JBG 4/33.

17. Prerogative Court (Wills), 25/345. Ruth Wilson, possibly a single woman or widow, and other women in a similar position may have utilized the second and third looms that weavers often owned (although these could also have been of different sizes, used for different types of cloth).

18. Only about sixty skilled servants or slaves can be identified in probate, court, or financial records; the majority were indentured servants. The forty owners of this

skilled labor possessed estates of above-average value and above-average numbers of bound or enslaved workers. These individuals were often merchants (ten) or innkeepers (six), whose businesses provided a steady flow of customers for the services of their skilled workers. Only three were artisans: tailor John Carslake owned a skilled tailor (status not specified), while the estates of blacksmiths William Dobson and John Oldham also included tailors (both indentured servants). Russo, *Free Workers,* 448–449.

19. Talbot County Court (Judgments), NTW/172, 8/1699 court.

20. St. Peter's Parish Vestry Minutes, M295, 8/1746–9/1753.

21. Edward C. Papenfuse, *In Pursuit of Profit: The Annapolis Merchants in the Era of the American Revolution, 1763–1805* (Baltimore, 1975), 8–10.

22. For the town's early development, see Nancy T. Baker, "Annapolis, Maryland 1695–1730," *Maryland Historical Magazine* 81 (Fall 1986): 191–209; Anthony D. Lindauer, *From Paths to Plats: The Development of Annapolis, 1651 to 1718,* Studies in Local History (Annapolis and Crownsville, MD, 1997); and Edward C. Papenfuse, *Doing Good to Posterity: The Move of the Capital of Maryland from St. Mary's County to Ann Arundell Towne, Now Called Annapolis,* Studies in Local History (Annapolis and Crownsville, MD, 1995).

23. Ebenezer Cook, "The Sotweed Factor," quoted in Aubrey C. Land, *Colonial Maryland: A History* (Millwood, NY, 1981), 135.

24. Papenfuse, *In Pursuit of Profit,* 10.

25. The Lords Baltimore lost administrative control of the colony with the overthrow of proprietary government in 1689, but retained ownership of the land and the right to collect quitrents or their equivalent. After the fifth Lord Baltimore converted to the Anglican faith, he regained control of the political and judicial systems. See Papenfuse, *In Pursuit of Profit,* esp. 10–12, for an analysis of the sources of growth.

26. Ebenezer Cook, "Sotweed Redivivus," quoted in Land, *Colonial Maryland,* 136.

27. Victor Hugh Paltsits, ed., *A Journal of Benjamin Mifflin on a Tour from Philadelphia to Delaware and Maryland, July 26–August 14, 1762,* reprinted in the *Bulletin of the New York Public Library* 39 (June 1935): 432.

28. J. F. D. Smyth, *A Tour in the United States of America* (London, 1784), 2:185.

29. Philip Padelford, ed., *Colonial Panorama, 1775: Dr. Robert Honyman's Journal for March and April* (San Marino, CA, 1959), 6.

30. Rev. Jonathan Boucher, *Reminiscences of an American Loyalist, 1738–1789* (Boston, 1925), 65.

31. It is not surprising, then, that one local middling family could afford over a twenty-year period to buy sets of six silver tablespoons from three different Annapolis silversmiths.

32. In the last two decades before the Revolution, the wealthiest segment of the city's population, with probated estates valued at £1,000 (deflated) or more, held a share of total wealth nine times greater than their proportionate share of total population. In rural Anne Arundel, by comparison, the same group's wealth was only three times their proportionate share of population (based on a study of all estates submitted for probate in Anne Arundel County between 1655 and 1777). See Jean B. Russo, "The Structure of the Anne Arundel County Economy," section 5, Final Project Report, NEH Grant RS-20199-81-1955, "Annapolis and Anne Arundel County, Maryland: A Study of Urban Development in a Tobacco Economy, 1649–1776," 4 and table V. Copy on deposit at the Maryland State Archives.

33. Although most of the county's woodworking artisans lived in rural parishes, woodworkers formed the largest group among artisans who lived in Annapolis.

34. See Nancy T. Baker, "The Manufacture of Ship Chandlery in Annapolis, Maryland, 1735–1770," *The Chronicle of the Early American Industries Association* 35 (Dec. 1982): 62–63, for a discussion of Annapolis's comparative advantages as a center for outfitting and repairing ships.

35. Context indicates that the occasional use of "seamstress" denoted a status rather than a skill. Russo, *Free Workers*, 114–118, examines paid domestic work of free white women. Mrs. Peter Redhead, who advertised sewing and millinery skills in the *Maryland Herald and Eastern Shore Intelligencer* in 1803 (25 Oct.), was the first woman to be identified by her craftwork.

36. *Maryland Gazette*, M1278, 27 Dec. 1749, 2 Aug. 1745, 1 Apr. 1746, 28 Oct. 1747, and 27 Mar. 1751.

37. Anne Arundel County Court (Judgment Record), IDB 1/296. The court referred Futier's suit to a single justice for settlement, who decided in her favor in Nov. 1765; Edmund Key, a prominent attorney, represented Futier. Few free blacks appear in eighteenth-century Annapolis records, but nineteenth-century census records list "laundress" as one of the most common occupations of free black women.

38. Chancery Court (Chancery Papers Exhibits), "Jesse Richardson Ledgers A, B, C, 1789–1794," MdHR 1550, Ledger B/77, and Talbot County Court (Indentures), 1794–1813.

39. Anne Arundel County Court (Judgment Record), IRB 1/32, 147.

40. Anne Arundel County Court (Judgment Record), IMB 2/310, Mar. 1767 court, and *Maryland Gazette*, M8, 27 May 1773 and 25 Feb. 1773.

41. *Maryland Gazette*, M7, 17 Jan. 1771; Anne Arundel County (Testamentary Papers), Box 4, folder 67; and *Maryland Gazette*, M1279, 6 Nov. 1755.

42. *Maryland Gazette*, M1280, 18 Nov. 1759, 4 Dec. 1760, and 25 Aug. 1763, and M1281, 5 Oct. 1769; Anne Arundel County Court (Judgment Record), IMB 1/700; and *Maryland Journal and Baltimore Daily Advertiser*, 9 Nov. 1778.

43. *Maryland Gazette*, M1279, 27 May 1756.

44. Ibid., M1281, 20 Mar. 1766.

45. The most notable examples of shop continuity in Talbot involved blacksmiths; the capital investment represented by a smithy undoubtedly ensured that whoever inherited the shop acquired the labor needed to continue its operation. See Russo, *Free Workers*, 260–262.

46. Roberts's first appearance in the records may have been as a "laborer" in 1719. Roberts did not die until 1788, when he would have been in his early 90s were he the person named in the court entry. Anne Arundel County Court (Judgments), 1718–1719 Mar., 326; Annapolis Mayor's Court, B/219, 7/19/1740; *Maryland Gazette*, M1278, 6 Sept. 1745 and 30 Aug. 1745; Commission Book 82: 111 (12/19/1744) and 113 (5/9/1745); and *Maryland Gazette*, M1278, 17 Mar. 1747, 6 July 1748, and 17 Jan. 1750; M1279, 5 Oct. 1752, 21 June 1753, 20 Aug. 1752, 13 Nov. 1755, 5 Jan. 1758, and 3 Feb. 1757; and M1280, 24 Jan. 1760.

47. *Maryland Gazette*, M1278, 6 Jan. 1747 and 8 July 1746.

48. Ibid., M1279, 24 Apr. 1755 and 23 Oct. 1755.

49. Ibid., M1281, 17 Aug. 1769.

50. Ibid., M1278, 13 Sept. 1745; M1279, 3 Aug. 1758; and M1280, 8 Mar. 1759, 3 Sept. 1761, and 11 Mar. 1762.

51. Ibid., M1278, 28 Dec. 1748, 14 June 1749, 30 May 1750, and 4 Dec. 1751; M1279, 16 July 1752 and 21 June 1753; and M1280, 5 Mar. 1761.

52. Ibid., M8, 19 Sept. 1773, 16 Dec. 1773, 17 Mar. 1774, 7 Apr. 1774, and 15 Dec. 1774; Prerogative Court (Inventories), 125/337; Nancy T. Baker, "An Overview of Masonry Crafts in Annapolis, Maryland, 1695–1776," Research Files, Historic Annapolis Foundation, appendices B-F and I; Marcia M. Miller, *Masters "in Theory and Practice": Artisans in Eighteenth-Century Annapolis,* Studies in Local History (Annapolis and Crownsville, MD, forthcoming); and Rosamond Randall Bierne and John Scarff, *William Buckland (1734–1774): Architect of Virginia and Maryland* (Baltimore, 1970), 1–11, 85.

53. See Nancy T. Baker, "Silversmiths in Colonial Annapolis," 17–25, in Jennifer Faulds Goldsborough, *Silver in Maryland* (Baltimore, 1983), for other diversified silversmiths; and Nancy T. Baker, "Annapolis, Maryland, 1695–1730," *Maryland Historical Magazine* 81 (fall 1986): 201–204, for examples drawn from other trades.

54. *Maryland Gazette,* M1278, 19 July 1749.

55. Ibid., M1280, 4 Oct. 1764; M1281, 22 June 1769; and M8, 30 Dec. 1773.

56. Russo, *Free Workers,* 167–171.

57. Robert Blair St. George, *The Wrought Covenant: Source Material for the Study of Craftsmen and Community in Southeastern New England, 1620–1700* (Brockton, MA, 1979), 14.

EIGHT: The Other "Susquahannah Traders"

Thanks to Michael McConnell and the Colonial History Workshop at the University of Minnesota for suggestions.

1. John W. Jordan, trans., "Bishop J. C. F. Cammerhoff's Narrative of a Journey to Shamokin, Penna., in the Winter of 1748," *Pennsylvania Magazine of History and Biography* (hereafter *PMHB*) 29 (1905): 161–172 (hereafter Cammerhoff); Shamokin Diary (hereafter SD), 6 Jan., 25 Feb., 2 Apr. 1748, Moravian Church Archives, Bethleham, PA: Records of the Moravian Mission Among the Indians of North America (microfilm, 40 reels), Reel 6, Box 121, Folder 4, Item 1 (hereafter MCA, reel/box/folder/item).

2. SD, 19 Sept. 1745; MCA, 28/217/12B/1; [Bernhard A. Grube,] "A Missionary's Tour to Shamokin and the West Branch of the Susquehanna, 1753," *PMHB* 39 (1915): 442–443 (hereafter Grube). Alison Duncan Hirsch, "'The Celebrated Madame Montour': 'Interpretess' Across Early American Frontiers," *Explorations in Early American Culture* 4 (2000): 97.

3. *Minutes of the Provincial Council of Pennsylvania* from the Organization to the Termination of the Propriatary Government, 16 vols. (Harrisburg, 1851–52) (hereafter *MPCP*), 1:397.

4. *MPCP,* 3:155. For the name, see *MPCP,* 3:45.

5. *Pennsylvania Archives,* 9 series, 138 vols. (Harrisburg and Philadelphia, 1852–1949), 1st ser., 1:231–232 (hereafter *PA*).

6. Logan to Cornish, 18 May 1732, Logan Letterbook, 1731–32 (hereafter LLB 1731–32), 59, Maria Dickinson Logan Papers, Historical Society of Pennsylvania, Philadelphia (hereafter HSP).

7. Frederick Jackson Turner, *The Character and Influence of the Indian Trade in Wisconsin: A Study of the Trading Post as an Institution* (1891; repr. Norman, 1977).

Among the recent work is Jennifer S. H. Brown, *Strangers in Blood: Fur Trade Company Families in Indian Country* (Vancouver, 1980); Sylvia Van Kirk, *Many Tender Ties: Women in Fur-Trade Society, 1670–1870* (Norman, 1980); Susan Sleeper-Smith, *Indian Women and French Men: Rethinking Cultural Encounter in the Western Great Lakes* (Amherst, MA, 2001). Covering similar ground, Alison Duncan Hirsch explores a topic akin to mine in her "Indian, *Métis*, and Euro-American Women on Multiple Frontiers," in *Friends and Enemies in Penn's Woods: Indians, Colonists, and the Racial Construction of Pennsylvania*, ed. William A. Pencak and Daniel K. Richter (University Park, PA, 2004).

8. Richard White, *The Middle Ground: Indians, Empires, and Republics in the Great Lakes Region, 1650–1815* (New York, 1991); Kathleen M. Brown, "Brave New Worlds: Women's and Gender History," *William and Mary Quarterly*, 3rd ser., 50 (1993): 317–323 (emphasis added); Kathleen M. Brown, "The Anglo-Algonquian Gender Frontier," in *Negotiators of Change: Historical Perspectives on Native American Women*, ed. Nancy Shoemaker, 26–48 (New York, 1995).

9. White, *Middle Ground*, 508 (and see 324); Kathleen M. Brown, *Good Wives, Nasty Wenches, and Anxious Patriarchs: Gender, Race, and Power in Colonial Virginia* (Chapel Hill, 1996), 67.

10. Peter C. Mancall, *Valley of Opportunity: Economic Culture Along the Upper Susquehanna, 1700–1800* (Ithaca, 1991), 50.

11. Evelyn A. Benson, "The Huguenot LeTorts: First Christian Family on the Conestoga," *Journal of the Lancaster County Historical Society* 65 (1961): 92–105 (hereafter Benson).

12. Gary B. Nash, "The Quest for the Susquehanna Valley: New York, Pennsylvania, and the Seventeenth-Century Fur Trade," *New York History* 48 (1967): 3–27; Francis Jennings, "The Indian Trade of the Susquehanna Valley," *Proceedings of the American Philosophical Society* 110 (1966): 406–424.

13. William A. Hunter, "Traders on the Ohio: 1730," *Western Pennsylvania Historical Magazine* 35 (1952): 89.

14. Cammerhoff, 164, 166–167, 169.

15. SD, 6 Jan. 1748, MCA, 6/121/4/1.

16. *MPCP*, 1:397 (Kyentarrah); Journal by Capt. Joseph Shippen, Fort Augusta, Shamokin, 1757–58 (hereafter JJS), Shippen Family Papers (hereafter SFP), HSP, entries of 18 and 21 Jan. 1758 (Chilloways).

17. James Le Tort, Account of Indian Debts, 1704, Logan Papers (hereafter LPHSP), Box 11, File 4, HSP (Loossemans Wife); Papers Relating to Indian Losses (hereafter PRIL), Indian Records Collection, HSP, 34 (Mohican John's Sister); Thomas Smallman's Account of Losses, 1765, George Croghan Papers (hereafter GCP), Box 5, Folder 7 (The Hatt's Grandaughter), HSP; Kenneth P. Bailey, ed., *The Ohio Company Papers, 1753–1817 . . .* (Arcata, CA, 1947), 130 (Opihelay's Old Wife and young Wife; hereafter *OCP*); Shamokin, Ledger B (hereafter SLB), 2 June–15 Dec. 1759, Gratz Collection (hereafter GC), Case 17, No. 16, 73, 74, 150 (John Hill's Mother), 135 (Woman with Hans Michael), HSP. (Thanks to Meghan Carey and Carrie Maylor for assistance with these ledgers.) I include names from accounts kept in the Ohio Valley; traders and tribes alike often operated in both regions.

Perhaps women simply preferred to remain anonymous; Susquehanna travelers remarked that native women could be shy. See John Bartram, *Observations on the*

Inhabitants, Climate, Soil, Rivers, Productions, Animals, and other Matters Worthy of Notice . . . (London, 1751), 59; Conrad Weiser, "Narrative of a Journey, made in the Year 1737 . . . ," *Collections of the Historical Society of Pennsylvania* 1 (1853): 14–15 (hereafter CW 1737).

18. SLB, 49, 50, 75, passim (A Woman); 50, 63, 64, 74, passim (Old Woman); Fort Augusta, Ledger A (hereafter FALA), 8 Apr.–24 Nov. 1762, GC, Case 17, No. 2, 14, 21, 22, 85 (Squaw).

19. FALA, 6, 7, 12, 64 (Peggy), 206, 225, 241, 251 (Cate), 17 (Jacob), 20 (Isaac); SLB, 63 (Poet), 81 (Woman Poet); *OCP*, 41 (Pockmarked Man), 56, 116 (Big Eard Fellow), 72 (One-Eyed Man, Big Woman), 132 (Mohickan Woman, Mohickon Moll), 142 (Nanteycook Will), 148 (Connay Man), 155 (Strong Woman); Indian Accounts, n.d., GCP, 6/30 (Flat-nosed woman).

20. PRIL, 38 (farting Womans family); *OCP*, 46 (Burnt Woman's Son), 120 (Bettys Bill); SLB, 97, 153 (Malley's Husband); Shamokin, Indian Commissioners Day Book, 15 Dec. 1759–30 May 1760, GC, Case 17, No. 31, 214 (Nance Sister's Husband); Shamokin, Indian Commissioners Day Book, 6 Nov. 1760–1 June 1761, GC, Case 17, No. 6, 251, 342 (Mingo Man with Peggey).

21. White, *Middle Ground*, 94.

22. James Logan, Account Book, 1712–20 (hereafter JLAB), 112, LPHSP; Weiser, "Memora[n]dum," 23 Aug. 1755, Penn Manuscripts, Indian Affairs, II, 26, doc. 100a, HSP.

23. Richard Peters, Account, 23 Jan. 1755, Penn MSS, Indian Affairs, IV, 9, HSP; *MPCP*, 3:337; William C. Reichel, *Memorials of the Moravian Church* (Philadelphia, 1870), 1:326, 330–331, 333, 350; *MPCP*, 7:671; "Account of Sums I paid to Indians," 22 7ber 1757, Penn MSS, Accounts, II, 35, doc. 109, HSP; Easton Account, 4–5 Aug. 1757, Philadelphia Yearly Meeting, Indian Committee Records, I, 387, Haverford College Library.

24. For women providing food, see *MPCP*, 6:665; Bartram, *Observations*, 59–62; John W. Jordan, ed., "Spangenberg's Notes of Travel to Onondaga in 1745," *PMHB* 3 (1879): 60, 61. For wampum, see Robert S. Grumet, ed., *Journey on the Forbidden Path: Chronicles of a Diplomatic Mission to the Allegheny Country, March–September, 1760*, Transactions of the American Philosophical Society, vol. 89, pt. 2 (Philadelphia, 1999), 89. Thanks to Daniel K. Richter for the wampum insight, and to Karim Tiro for the connection between food and diplomacy.

25. Account of Esther Hansen, 7 10 mo. 1734, Penn-Physick MSS (hereafter PPM), IX, 12, HSP. *MPCP*, 7:95; *PA*, 1st ser., 2:684–685, 3:87; Minutes of the Friendly Association, 1755–57, 17, 32, HSP; Account of Nich. Hitchcock, 27 Feb. 1735 [1733?], PPM, IX, 9.

26. "Witham Marshe's Journal of the Treaty held With the Six Nations . . . ," *Collections of the Massachusetts Historical Society* . . . , 1st ser., 7 (1801): 190; SD, 22 Oct. 1745, MCA, 28/217/12B/1.

27. Mancall, *Valley of Opportunity*, 48–54.

28. Martin Mack, Journey to Wyoming and Hallobank, 16 Apr. 1745, MCA, 28/217/12/3 (see also 12 and 19 Apr.); Grube, 442–443.

29. Mack, Journey, 12, 16 Apr. 1745, MCA, 28/217/12/3; Travel Diary (hereafter TD), 7–8 Oct. 1748, MCA, 30/225/2/1; SD, 29 May and 5 June 1748, MCA, 6/121/4/2.

30. William M. Beauchamp, ed., *Moravian Journals Relating to Central New York, 1745–1766* (Syracuse, 1916; hereafter *MJNY*), 16 (see also 25, 33–34); CW 1737, 14.

31. CW 1737, 6; *MPCP*, 6:153–154.

32. Albright G. Zimmerman, "The Indian Trade of Colonial Pennsylvania" (PhD diss., University of Delaware, 1966), 72; James Hendricks to Edward Shippen, 27 Oct. 1740, Burd-Shippen Papers, Letters (hereafter BSPL), American Philosophical Society, Philadelphia, PA (traders; hereafter APS); *MPCP,* 4:640–641 (corner), 7:33–35, 47, 57 (Harris's); Samuel Evans, "Lowrey Family," Lancaster County Historical Society, 42–43 (fireplace); *PA,* 1st ser., 2:318 (Weiser).

33. Nicholas Cresswell, *The Journal of Nicholas Cresswell, 1774–1777* (London, 1925), 103–104, 111; Evans, "Lowrey Family," 46.

34. SFP, vol. 27, Bills and Receipts, 1721–54, 26 (canoe); Weiser 1737, 14–15; SD, 21 Dec. 1754, MCA, 6/121/6/3 (ferrying); *OCP,* 137 (store goods); Cresswell, *Journal,* 105, 113 (horses).

35. White, *Middle Ground,* 60–75, 323–324, 333–334.

36. Cresswell, *Journal,* 103–122, quotations on 105–106, 113–114.

37. Bartram, *Observations,* 15.

38. *PA,* 1st ser., 3:437, 460; *MPCP,* 8:143, 147.

39. Bartram, *Observations,* 44 ("complimenting"), 56 ("infesting"), 67 ("occasional wife"); Cresswell, *Journal,* 122 (see also 108, 113–114).

40. Exceptions include occasional interpreting (see above) and bearing messages (see note 50 below).

41. *MPCP,* 4:633; Cammerhoff, 169; Richard Peters Letterbook, 1737–50, 381, Richard Peters Papers (hereafter RPP), HSP ("wench"); James Sullivan et al., eds., *The Papers of Sir William Johnson.* (Albany, 1921–65), 9:456; Larry L. Nelson, *A Man of Distinction among Them: Alexander McKee and the Ohio Country Frontier, 1754–1799* (Kent, OH, 1999), 27.

42. *MJNY,* 25, 26, 31, 62; JJS, 18, 21 Jan., 13 Feb. 1758; *PA,* 2nd ser., 2:626–627.

43. *MPCP,* 2:558 (emphasis added).

44. *PA,* 1st ser., 1:268–269; SD, 29 Apr., 7 May, 17 July, 5 Aug. 1755, MCA, 6/121/7/1.

45. *MPCP,* 2:248, 600.

46. Indian Commissioners Day Book, 1760–61, GC, Case 17, Compartment B, 214–220.

47. *PA,* 1st ser., 4:88–89; James Irvine to "Gentlemen," 13 July 1762, Deposition of Joseph Brown, July 1762, Deposition of Dennis McCormick, 17 July 1762, BSPL; Lt. C. Graydon to James Burd, 12 July 1762, and Joseph Shippen to James Burd, 20 July 1762, SFP, V.

48. *MPCP,* 3:48, 129, 406 (emphasis added), 8:144; SD, 31 Oct. 1745, MCA, 28/217/12B/1, 30 Jan., 24 Feb., 14–15 Mar. 1748, 6/121/4/1, 20 Mar. 1749, 6/121/5/1, 14 Sept. 1755, 6/121/7/1. See Peter C. Mancall, "Men, Women, and Alcohol in Indian Villages in the Great Lakes Region in the Early Republic," *Journal of the Early Republic* 15 (1995): 425–448.

49. Pennsylvania law allowed "wives of . . . men absent from the colony for long periods of time . . . [to] exercise all the legal rights necessary to engage in a business activity." Marylynn Salmon, "Equality or Submersion? Feme Covert Status in Early Pennsylvania," in *Women of America: A History,* ed. Carol Berkin and Mary Beth Norton (Boston, 1979), 110.

50. JLAB, 125, 133, 165, 169, 186, 212 (Anne Le Tort); JLAB, 119, and Logan, Ledger, 1720–27, 38 (Elizabeth Le Tort, Susanna Patterson); Logan to Samuel Blunston, 13 Nov. 1731, LLB, 1731–32, 19 (Martha Bailey). Leaving the capital, such women might also be

carrying letters or bearing provincial officials' greetings and a gift to Indians. Logan, Correspondence, 4:50, APS; Logan Letterbook, vol. 3 [1721–32] (hereafter LLB 3), 142, HSP; Logan to Blunston, 13 Nov. 1731, LLB 1731–32, 19; Benjamin Moore to Edward Shippen, 7 Oct. 1740, SFP, I, Correspondence.

51. Logan to Shippen, 3 Sept. 1730, LPHSP, 1/99; Logan to Blunston, 20 May 1740, Alverthorpe Letterbooks, C (hereafter ALC), 87, LPHSP.

52. Martha Bailey to Edward Shippen, 23 Feb. 1734/5, Lancaster County, Miscellaneous Papers, 1724–72, 17, HSP.

53. Logan to Shippen, 28 Oct. 1732[?], LPHSP, 2/34.

54. *MPCP*, 1:397, 435. For his journeys, see Benson, 97–100.

55. Bailey to Shippen, 23 Feb. 1734/5, Lancaster County, Miscellaneous Papers, 1724–72, 17, HSP.

56. Logan to Blunston, 25 4 mo. 1739, 24 Nov. 1740, ALC, 44, 111 (emphasis added).

57. John F. Watson, *Annals of Philadelphia and Pennsylvania, In the Olden Time . . .*, 2nd ed., 2 vols. (Philadelphia, 1845), 2:113–116; and see Charles A. Hanna, *The Wilderness Trail*, 2 vols. (New York, 1911), 1:176–177.

58. A possible exception—mention of "the White Women who make so much disturbance at Allegheny"—is in Peters to Weiser, 13 Apr. 1751, RPP, III, 35.

59. Gary T. Hawbaker, *Lancaster County, Pennsylvania: Quarter Sessions Abstracts*, Book 1 (Hershey, PA, 1986), 61–63; Logan to Blunston, 25 4 mo. 1739, ALC, 44.

60. *MPCP*, 2:554; 1:397, 435.

61. Chester County, Court of Quarter Sessions, Indictments, Feb. 1721/2, Chester County Archives, West Chester, PA (hereafter CCA).

62. Logan to Shippen, 18 Nov. 17—, LPHSP, 2/74.

63. Jennings, "Indian Trade of the Susquehanna Valley"; Zimmerman, "Indian Trade," chs. 4, 5, 7–9.

64. Logan to James Anderson, 5 Mar. 1730/1, Logan Letterbook, 1716–43, 229, LPHSP.

65. Logan to Andrew Galbraith, 5 Mar. 1733/4, Logan Letterbook, 1716–43, 386, LPHSP.

66. Logan to Blunston, 20 May 1740, ALC, 87. And see Logan to Galbraith, 18 Jan. 1739/40, ALC, 64.

67. Logan to John Wright, 23 Aug. 1727, LLB 3:109; Samuel Evans, "Some Early Indian Traders," *Papers Read before the Lancaster County Historical Society . . .* 9 (1905): 298 (Smith). Logan to Blunston, 11 Jan. 1735/6, Charles Francis Jenkins, Autograph Collection, Friends Historical Library, Swarthmore College; Zimmerman, "Indian Trade," 165–166; Patterson Will, 3 Oct. 1735, Will Book A-1-121, Lancaster County Archives (Patterson).

68. *MPCP*, 4:681 (demanded); Richard Peters to Richard Hockley, 2 Mar. 1753, Penn MSS, Additional Miscellaneous Letters, I, 80, HSP (any value); *PA*, 1st ser., 3:87 (Beggar); James Irvine to Governor, 13 July 1762, BSPL (Seeshocapee).

69. Leon deValinger, Jr., ed., *Court Records of Kent County, Delaware, 1680–1705*, American Legal Records, vol. 8 (Washington, DC, 1959), 121, 154; Zimmerman, "Indian Trade," 149–150.

70. *MPCP*, 2:554.

71. Chester County, Insolvent Debtors, May 1730, CCA.

72. "Copy of my Declaration to Jon Daven[port], 5 1 mo. 1733/4," LPHSP, 2/86; Logan to John Taylor, 6 May 1735, Taylor Papers, Corr. #3174, HSP; Logan to Blunston,

11 Jan. 1735/6, Jenkins Autograph Coll., Swarthmore College, Swarthmore, PA; Logan to Blunston, 29 May 1739, ALC, 41.

73. SD, 25 Feb. 1748, MCA, 6/121/4/1.

74. James E. Seaver, *A Narrative of the Life of Mrs. Mary Jemison*, ed. June Namias (1824; repr. Norman, 1992), 75–76.

75. Ibid., 77, 78, 79, 89.

76. Ibid., 75, 78–79, 81.

77. Ibid., 78, 80–81.

78. Ibid., xiii, 62–64, 69, 78–79, 85, 160.

79. *MPCP*, 7:284; 8:500.

80. *PA*, 2nd ser., 7:432, 436.

81. Grumet, ed., *Forbidden Path*, 108–109.

82. S. K. Stevens et al., eds., *The Papers of Col. Henry Bouquet*, 19 vols. (Harrisburg, 1940–43), serial 21649, pt. 1, 194, 196–197, 200 (hereafter *PCHB*); S. K. Stevens et al., eds., *The Papers of Henry Bouquet*, 6 vols. (Harrisburg, 1972–94), 6:274, 290–291 (hereafter *PHB*); James Irvine to the Commissioners, 30 June 1763, GC, Case 14, Box 10.

83. *PA*, 2nd ser., 7:459 ("suspicious"); Hunter to Col. James Burd, 7 June 1763, SFP, VI.

84. *PHB*, 6:274, 290–291; *PCHB*, ser. 21649, pt. 1, 194, 196–197, 200.

85. Irvine or Nathaniel Holland to the Commissioners, 5, 26 May; 12, 15, 26 ("Uneasiness"), 30 June; 15, 24 July, 3 Aug. 1763, GC, 14/10; Conference Held at Ft. Augusta, 19 July 1763, GC, 14/10; "Invoice of Sundry Goods and Merchandize brought Down here [Philadelphia] from The Trading House at Fort Augusta," 22 Aug. 1763, GC, 14/10; *PA*, 2nd ser., 7:462, 464–467.

86. *PCHB*, ser. 21649, pt. 1, 200; *PHB*, 6:291.

87. *MPCP*, 9:414; U. J. Jones, *History of the Early Settlement of the Juniata Valley* . . . (1855; repr. Harrisburg, 1940), 326; Harris to Burd, 12 Aug. 1768, BSPL.

88. Robert Greenhalgh Albion and Leonidas Dodson, eds., *Philip Vickers Fithian: Journal, 1775–1776* . . . (Princeton, 1934), 70–72. See also Mancall, *Valley of Opportunity*, ch. 4.

89. Jones, *Juniata Valley*, 124–125.

90. Jane T. Merritt, "Cultural Encounters along a Gender Frontier: Mahican, Delaware, and German Women in Eighteenth-Century Pennsylvania," *Pennsylvania History* 67 (2000): 509, 516, 519–520. See also Amy C. Schutt, "Female Relationships and Intercultural Bonds in Moravian Indian Missions," in Pencak and Richter, eds., *Friends and Enemies in Penn's Woods*.

NINE: A Death in the Morning

1. George French, *The History of Colonel Parke's Administration* (London, 1717), 1–2.

2. "The humble Addresse and Petition of the Under Subscribeing Members of the Assembly Gentlemen Freeholders Merchants and other Inhabitants of your Majestys Island of Antigua," in *Caribbeana*, 6 vols., ed. Vere Langford Oliver (London, 1909–19), 5:169–170.

3. Letter from Anne to Parke, 11 Feb. 1710, in Oliver, ed., *Caribbeana*, 5:170.

4. The negative depiction of the social and political development of England's West Indian colonies dates back to eighteenth-century commentators, such as Charles

Leslie and Ned Ward, and was central to James Anthony Froude's historiographical vision in *The English in the West Indies, or the Bow of Ulysses* (London, 1888). In the early 1970s, the nearly simultaneous appearance of Richard S. Dunn's *Sugar and Slaves: The Rise of the Planter Class in the English West Indies, 1624–1713* (Chapel Hill, 1973) and Carl and Roberta Bridenbaugh's *No Peace Beyond the Line: The English in the Caribbean, 1624–1690* (New York, 1972) revived Froude's condemnatory view of the English islands as social failures, a line which has been followed by Hilary McD. Beckles, Orlando Patterson, and, most recently, by Andrew J. O'Shaughnessy, *An Empire Divided: The American Revolution and the British Caribbean* (Philadelphia, 2000).

5. Jack P. Greene, "Changing Identity in the British Caribbean: Barbados as a Case Study," in Nicholas Canny and Anthony Pagden, eds., *Colonial Identity in the Atlantic World, 1500–1800* (Princeton, 1987); Gary A. Puckrein, *Little England: Plantation Society and Anglo-Barbadian Politics, 1627–1700* (New York, 1984).

6. Jack P. Greene, *Peripheries and Center: Constitutional Development in the Extended Polities of the British Empire and the United States, 1607–1788* (New York, 1990), 31.

7. Trevor Burnard, "Ethnicity in Colonial American Historiography: A New Organizing Principle," *Australasian Journal of American Studies* 10 (1992): 10.

8. "The humble Addresse and Petition," in Oliver, ed., *Caribbeana*, 5:169–170.

9. Cecil A. Kelsick, "The Constitutional History of the Leeward Islands," *Caribbean Quarterly* 6 (1960): 181.

10. Kelsick, "Constitutional History," 183.

11. Ibid., "Constitutional History," 181.

12. See Natalie A. Zacek, "Dangerous Tenants: Conflict and Community in a Colonial British American World, 1670–1770" (PhD diss., The Johns Hopkins University, 2000), passim, esp. ch. 5.

13. See Wylie A. Sypher, "The West Indian as a 'Character' in the Eighteenth Century," *North Carolina Studies in Philology* 1 (1939): 503–521, and Michal J. Rozbicki, "The Curse of Provincialism: Negative Perceptions of Colonial American Plantation Society," *Journal of Southern History* 63 (1997): 727–752.

14. Erin S. Mackie, "The Colorful Case of the Caribbean Creole," in *The Clothes That Wear Us: Essays on Dressing and Transgressing in Eighteenth-Century Culture*, ed. Jessica Munns and Penny Richards, 250–270 (Newark, DE, 1999). On credit and reputation, see Toby L. Ditz, "Shipwrecked: Imperiled Masculinity and the Representation of Business Failures among Philadelphia's Eighteenth-Century Merchants," *Journal of American History* 81 (1994): 51–80.

15. Robert Robertson, *A Detection of the State and Situation of the Present Sugar Planters of Barbadoes and the Leeward Islands* (London, 1732), 30.

16. For a discussion of sexually transgressive behavior and its threat to individual honor, see Natalie Zacek, "Sex, Sexuality, and Social Control in the Eighteenth-Century Leeward Islands," in *Sex and Sexuality in Early America*, ed. Merril D. Smith, 190–214 (New York, 1998).

17. See Joanne Freeman, "Dueling as Politics: Reinterpreting the Burr-Hamilton Duel," *William and Mary Quarterly*, 3rd ser. 53 (1996): 296.

18. An example of Leeward society's feelings about challenges to legal authority appears in the legislative records of St. Kitts in 1707, with respect to the "Complaint of the Constable of Basseterre; of one Boyde, That he should *presume to Abuse, and Contemn the Authority of this Island.*" The governor and council ordered that Boyde

should receive thirty-nine lashes, but "he comeing on his Knees before this board, and acknowledged his fault, his punishment was remitted" (C[olonial]. O[ffice]. 241/1: Minutes of Council, St. Kitts, 1704–27, Public Record Office of Great Britain and Ireland, Kew, London; emphasis mine). In this instance, the governing authority was challenged by a subject, and the only way by which the challenger could avoid a painful and humiliating punishment was to restitute symbolically the authority he had attacked by engaging in a semi-public ritual of self-abasement.

19. Kelsick, "Constitutional History," 181.

20. Jack P. Greene, *The Foundations of America: Political Life in Eighteenth-Century Virginia* (Williamsburg, VA, 1986), 31.

21. Dalby Thomas, *An Historical Account of the Rise and Growth of the West-India Collonies* (London, 1690), 42.

22. Anonymous, "Standing up for the Liberties of my Fellow Subjects," *The Barbadoes Packet* (London, 1720), 3 verso.

23. Helen Hill Miller, *Colonel Parke of Virginia* (Chapel Hill, 1989), xvi.

24. James Blair, quoted in Parke Rouse, Jr., *James Blair of Virginia* (Chapel Hill, 1971), 105.

25. Ibid., 106.

26. Miller, *Colonel Parke,* 83–84.

27. Parke was elected to the Commons as a member for Whitechurch, Hampshire, where he owned an estate, but was soon expelled on a charge of bribery; see Vere Langford Oliver, ed., *The History of Antigua,* 3 vols. (London, 1894–99), 1:2.

28. Dunn, *Sugar,* 144.

29. Codrington senior had been governor of the Leewards from 1689 to 1698, his son from 1699 to 1704.

30. C. S. S. Higham, "The General Assembly of the Leeward Islands," Part I, *English Historical Review* 41 (1926): 199–200, 203.

31. Noel Deerr, *The History of Sugar,* 2 vols. (London, 1949), 1:172.

32. Patricia U. Bonomi, *The Lord Cornbury Scandal: The Politics of Reputation in British America* (Chapel Hill, 1998), 109–111.

33. Stephen Saunders Webb, *The Governors-General: The English Army and the Definition of the Empire* (Chapel Hill, 1979), 486.

34. Quoted in Dunn, *Sugar,* 144. Parke claimed that "the Duke promised me the Government of Virginia at the Battle of Blenheim, but for some Reasons of State that was given to my Lord Orkney"; see Oliver, ed., *Antigua,* 1:lxxviii.

35. William Laws, *Distinction, Death, and Disgrace: Governorship in the Leeward Islands in the Early Eighteenth Century* (Kingston, Jamaica, 1976), 10.

36. Algernon E. Aspinall, "The Fate of Governor Parke," in Aspinall, *West Indian Tales of Old* (New York, 1969), 25; Higham, "General Assembly," 206.

37. Aspinall, "Fate," 34; Dunn, *Sugar,* 145.

38. Oliver, ed., *Antigua,* 1:169.

39. Charles Royster, *The Fabulous History of the Dismal Swamp Company* (New York, 1999), 17.

40. F[rederick]. G. Spurdle, *Early West Indian Government* (Palmerston, N.Z., n.d.), 39; Oliver, ed., *Antigua,* 1:lxxvi.

41. William Douglass, M.D., *A Summary, Historical and Political, of the First Planting, Progressive Improvements, and Present State of the British Settlements in North-America,*

2 vols. (London, 1755), 1:137; Bryan Edwards, *The History, Civil and Commercial, of the British Colonies in the West Indies,* 2 vols. (London, 1801), 1:477–478.

42. Dunn, *Sugar,* 145.

43. Bonomi, *Lord Cornbury,* 262.

44. Spurdle, *Government,* 11.

45. Ibid., 74, 187.

46. Aspinall, "Fate," 36.

47. Ibid., 34. Parke claimed that "the people of Nevis complain that I took from them some gunns and armes they did not want, and carryed them to St. Johns where they were wanted. I think 'tis my duty not to suffer the Queens stores to ly useless in one island when they are very much wanted in another" (Ibid., 28).

48. Oliver, ed., *Antigua,* 1:lxxxiii.

49. French, *Administration,* 94, 101, 155.

50. Ibid., 91.

51. Ibid., 132, 102.

52. Ibid., 163.

53. Ibid., 164.

54. Aspinall, "Fate," 38; Oliver, ed., *Antigua,* 1:lxxix.

55. Oliver, ed. *Antigua,* 1:lxxix, lxxx.

56. Ibid., 1:lxxxi; Bonomi, *Cornbury,* 186.

57. Elsa V. Goveia, *Slave Society in the British Leeward Islands at the End of the Eighteenth Century* (New Haven, 1965), 23.

58. Aspinall, "Fate," 40; Oliver, *Antigua,* 1:lxxxi; Oliver, *Caribbeana,* 5:170.

59. Aspinall, "Fate," 40.

60. Ibid., 42.

61. Ibid., 44.

62. Oliver, ed., *Antigua,* 1:lxxxi.

63. Aspinall, "Fate," 45–46.

64. Quoted in Dunn, *Sugar,* 146; French, *Administration,* 63.

65. Edward, *History,* 1:482.

66. Clymer, "Cromwell's Head and Milton's Hair: Corpse Theory in Spectacular Bodies of the Interregnum," *The Eighteenth Century* 40 (1999): 97. For an exploration of the political meanings of corpses, see Katherine Verdery, *The Political Lives of Dead Bodies: Reburial and Postsocialist Change* (New York, 1999).

67. French, *Administration,* 1, 86–87.

68. Dunn, *Sugar,* 118.

69. Ibid., 340.

TEN: Enjoying and Defending Charter Privileges

Epigraph: Samuel Greene Arnold, *History of the State of Rhode Island* (New York, 1860), 2:192.

1. The main modern works are David S. Lovejoy, *Rhode Island Politics and the American Revolution* (Providence, 1958); Sydney V. James, *Colonial Rhode Island: A History* (New York, 1975); and Sydney V. James, *The Colonial Metamorphoses in Rhode Island,* ed. Sheila L. Skemp and Bruce C. Daniels (Hanover, NH, 2000). I began to

work out my own interpretation in Edward M. Cook, Jr., "Rhode Island Voters in a Era of Partisan Realignment, 1760–1800," American Historical Association Convention, 1973; and Edward M. Cook, Jr., "Voting Participation in Early National Rhode Island: In Social and Ideological Perspective," Organization of American Historians Convention, 1986.

2. The outlines can be traced in Irwin Polishook, *Rhode Island and the Union, 1774–1795* (Evanston, 1969); and Patrick T. Conley, *Democracy in Decline: Rhode Island's Constitutional Development, 1776–1795* (Providence, 1977).

3. Mack E. Thompson, "The Hopkins-Ward Controversy and the American Revolution in Rhode Island: An Interpretation," *William and Mary Quarterly,* 3rd ser., 16 (1959): 363–375.

4. James, *Colonial Metamorphoses.*

5. John Russell Bartlett, ed., *Records of the Colony of Rhode Island and Providence Plantations* (Providence, 1856–65; hereafter *RICR*), 2:5–21.

6. Cf. Donald S. Lutz, *The Origins of American Constitutionalism* (Baton Rouge, 1988), 34–38.

7. Paul D. Halliday, *Dismembering the Body Politic: Partisan Politics in England's Towns, 1650–1730,* esp. 29–55. See also the classic work, Martin Weinbaum, *The Incorporation of Boroughs* (Manchester, 1937).

8. Halliday, *Dismembering,* 30–33, 41; Weinbaum, *Incorporation of Boroughs,* 9, 18–19, 97–108.

9. Ibid., 149–188.

10. Ibid., 189–212.

11. Ibid., 168. Although broad threats to void charters had been made during earlier periods of charter revision, only two forfeitures were pursued to conclusion from 1610 to 1683.

12. Jack P. Greene, *Peripheries and Center: Constitutional Development in the Extended Polities of the British Empire and the United States, 1607–1788* (Athens, GA, 1986), which may stand for a vast literature on constitutional change.

13. See, for example, Sydney James's comments on the paucity of reflective sources on such matters in *Colonial Rhode Island,* 155.

14. Edmund S. Morgan, *Puritan Dilemma: The Story of John Winthrop* (Boston, 1958), 193–195; T. H. Breen, *The Character of a Good Ruler: Puritan Political Ideas in New England, 1630–1730* (New Haven, 1970), 89–92; Bernard Bailyn, *The New England Merchants in the Seventeenth Century* (Cambridge, MA, 1955), 112–167; Richard Johnson, *Adjustment to Empire: The New England Colonies, 1675–1725* (New Brunswick, NJ, 1981), 34, 41, 96–98.

15. William Pencak, *War, Politics and Revolution in Provincial Massachusetts* (Boston, 1981), 75–81; Richard L. Bushman, *King and People in Provincial Massachusetts* (Chapel Hill, 1985), 77–78.

16. The steps may be traced in *RICR,* vol. 3; see also, James, *Metamorphoses,* 58–61; and James, *Colonial Rhode Island,* 110–127.

17. If they had any doubt that their religious system was an exceptional privilege, they had Lord Bellomont to remind them by obtusely citing the failure to set up an orthodox, established church as a violation of the laws of England, and hence of the charter; *RICR,* 3:385.

18. James, *Metamorphoses,* 40–56.

19. Ibid., 53–63.

20. *RICR*, 3:186–196; James, *Colonial Rhode Island*, 106–109; James, *Metamorphoses*, 56–58.

21. *RICR*, 3:257–260.

22. The 1690 governor, Henry Bull, was the last survivor of the original group of Rhode Island Antinomians, and represented a partial grounding of provisional government in principles independent of charter authority. Cf. Johnson, *Adjustment to Empire*, 299–300, where this sequence of events is interpreted straightforwardly as evidence of "internal weakness." A close reading of the exact sequence combined with Clarke's subsequent maneuvering inclines me to share James's view that there was an element of strategy in these decisions.

23. *RICR*, 3:285–300; James, *Colonial Rhode Island*, 106–109; James, *Metamorphoses*, 56–58.

24. *RICR*, 3:329–330.

25. Ibid., 3:331, 340, 385–401; James, *Colonial Rhode Island*, 124–127.

26. *RICR*, 3:390, 394.

27. Sydney V. James, "Rhode Island: From Classical Democracy to British Province," *Rhode Island History* 43 (1984): 132–133.

28. *RICR*, 4:16; James, *Colonial Rhode Island*, 131–155.

29. Sheila Skemp, "A Social and Cultural History of Newport, Rhode Island, 1720–1775" (PhD diss., University of Iowa, 1974); James, *Colonial Rhode Island*, 156–185.

30. James, *Colonial Rhode Island*, 135–155.

31. Elisha R. Potter [Jr.] and Sidney S. Rider, "Some Account of the Bills of Credit or Paper Money of Rhode Island from the First Issue in 1710, to the Final Issue, 1786," *Rhode Island Historical Tracts*, no. 8 (Providence, 1880), 1–25; James, *Metamorphoses*, 122–125.

32. James Cunningham, "Rhode Island and the Money Supply of Colonial New England," seminar paper presented at the Economic History Workshop, University of Chicago, Jan. 1985; James, *Colonial Rhode Island*, 171–176. The virtual refusal of the mainland towns to pay taxes to the central government can be traced in nearly every legislative session (*RICR*, vols. 3 and 4) from the late 1690s to 1715.

33. *RICR*, 4:393.

34. Not to be confused with the Grand Committee of the Council and assembly sitting in joint session that will be discussed below.

35. Cunningham, "Money Supply," 6, citing John MacGinnis, "Rhode Island Bills of Credit, 1710–1755" (PhD diss., Brown University, 1952) to the effect that the Grand Committee had collected 90 percent of the interest by 1740 and 61 percent of the principal by 1738. James, *Metamorphoses*, cites only the latter figure.

36. James, *Metamorphoses*, 117; John Hutchins Cady, *Rhode Island Boundaries, 1636–1936* (Providence, 1936), 10–19. The colony was divided into three counties in 1729, and two more were added at midcentury.

37. *RICR*, 2:1–21; James, *Metamorphoses*, 49–53; Sidney S. Rider, "The Origin, Meaning, and Duration of Existence in Rhode Island of the Political Word Prox," *Book Notes* 25 (1908): 201–204.

38. *RICR*, 2:6, 112–113; Lawrence Lowther, "Rhode Island Colonial Government, 1732" (PhD diss., University of Washington, 1964), 19–39; Lovejoy, *Rhode Island Politics*, 15–18.

39. Quoted in Edward Peterson, *History of Rhode Island and Newport* (New York, 1853), 146; *RICR*, 4:259–260.

40. Lowther, "Rhode Island Colonial Government," 35; Rider and Potter, "Some Account of the Bills of Credit," 25–35. Jenckes later claimed to have seen what was coming and to have given notice that he would not serve past his 1731 term. *RICR*, 4:459.

41. *RICR*, 4:454–461. The quotations are from 456, 458, 461.

42. James, *Colonial Rhode Island*, 176.

43. Lowther, "Rhode Island Colonial Government," 35; annual election results in *RICR*. In later periods of organized factionalism, the partisans would avoid overlapping nominations of deputies and assistants, so as to maximize numbers in each house and especially in the all-powerful Grand Committee. Deputies promoted after arriving in Newport could not be replaced before the Grand Committee sat.

44. Rhode Island, General Assembly, House of Deputies Journal, Early State Records Microfilm Series, 1734, 1735, 1736, 1737. For several of the years the tallies distinguish between proxes collected in the towns and "votes" delivered in person at General Election in Newport. Newport voters apparently did not prox, but routinely attended in person.

		Proxes	Votes
1736	For Governor	1520	656
1737	For Fifth Assistant (the highest recorded)	1516	359

The 1737 tallies record "votes" only for six assistant races and for General Treasurer. The numbers drop off for later offices, especially on the losing side as voters accepted the predictability of the outcomes.

45. Lowther, "Rhode Island Colonial Government," 37. He assumed that freemen would live forty years after admission, a very high figure, and he seems to have made no adjustment for out-migration. The bias is reduced by the fact that so many freemen had actually been admitted in the previous few years.

46. William Wanton to Gentlemen, 14 Aug. 1733, Manuscripts American, John Carter Brown Library, Providence, RI; William B. Weeden, *Early Rhode Island: A Social History* (New York, 1910), 224; Westerly file in files on Colonial Elections, Rhode Island State Archives, Providence, RI (hereafter RISA).

47. *RICR*, 5:81–246.

48. Hopkins had served as Speaker of the lower house as early as 1738–39, in the time of John Wanton; Jenckes was Speaker in 1747, during Gideon Wanton's second term. The balance between Newport and the country towns was shifting noticeably during these years. Greene himself was the first governor since the 1690s to live outside Newport. When Richard Ward wrote to him in 1742 to inform Greene that Ward had "declined Setting up for Gov'r," one of the inducements to run he offered Greene was that the Ward faction had recruited a Newport candidate for deputy governor, so that there will be no need of your moving to Rhode Island if you obtain the post." Richard Ward to William Greene, 5 Feb. 1742, Ward Papers, Rhode Island Historical Society, Providence, RI (hereafter RIHS).

49. The 1750 issue provoked a clandestine petition to the king from seventy-one alleged Rhode Islanders for a forced repeal of the paper money legislation. When rumors spread that the petition asked for the seizure of the charter, the assembly launched an investigation of the petitioners and instituted a flood of letters and memorials about their "valuable liberties and privileges." The tempest blew over when it became clear that the petition had not been directed at the charter and that the authorities at home were satisfied with banning paper money issues. *RICR,* 5:311–313, 315, 318, 330, 334, 359; Gertrude S. Kimball, *The Correspondence of the Colonial Governors of Rhode Island, 1723–1775* (Boston, 1902–3), 1:116–128, 130–132.

50. Examples of flashy but superficial plays on the issue in the mid-1750s were the Hopkins partisans' appointment of Gideon Wanton to the Grand Committee, and a series of rather pointless transfers of currency between the Grand Committee and the colony Treasury. *RICR,* 5:429, 562. See also James, *Colonial Rhode Island,* 281–282, 291–292.

51. Lovejoy, *Rhode Island Politics;* Thompson, "The Hopkins-Ward Controversy."

52. Richard P. McCormick, "New Perspective on Jacksonian Politics," *American Historical Review* 65 (1960): 288–301.

53. Based on an extensive compilation of voting data from the Brown Papers at Brown University; the Moses Brown Papers and Samuel Eddy Papers at RIHS, the State Archives, the Providence Gazette, and the respective Town Records. Cf. Lovejoy, *Rhode Island Politics,* 16–17, who forms different conclusions on less complete data.

54. Lovejoy, *Rhode Island Politics,* summarized the evidence fully.

55. For example, "A Lover of Liberty," "To the free-holders of the Town of Newport," 19 Apr. 1757, Ward Papers, Box 1, RIHS.

56. Brown Papers, L&P, 58–70, RIP, Subscriptions, 1765, now at Brown University Library. Also analyzed in Lovejoy, *Rhode Island Politics,* 83–84.

57. Brown Papers, L&P, 58–70, RIP.

58. Unanimity in Providence stemmed from the success of Ward's deputy governor, Elisha Brown, in engineering the secession and incorporation into the new town of North Providence of voters who favored Ward. By doing so, he hoped to influence the election of deputies in his and Ward's interest. *RICR,* 4:438; Lovejoy, *Rhode Island Politics,* 151–152.

59. Lovejoy, *Rhode Island Politics,* 86–90, summarizes the sources, although he interprets them differently.

60. 1761: Samuel Ward to Assembly, Miscellaneous Letters, RISA; Stephen Hopkins to Assembly, Ward Papers, RIHS. 1762: Samuel Ward to Assembly, Ward Papers, 26 Feb.; Stephen Hopkins to Samuel Ward, Letters from the Governor, 27 Feb., RISA. 1764: Stephen Hopkins to Samuel Ward, 28 Feb.; Samuel Ward to Assembly, 28 Feb.; Samuel Ward to Stephen Hopkins, 29 Feb.; Samuel Ward to James Honeyman, 2 Mar., all in Moses Brown Papers, Hopkins-Ward folder, RIHS. 1765: Negotiations, 28 Feb., Moses Brown Papers, Hopkins-Ward folder, RIHS. 1766: Daniel Jenckes to Samuel Ward, 1 Mar., Moses Brown Papers, Hopkins-Ward folder, RIHS. 1767: Negotiations, 28 Feb. to 27 Mar., Moses Brown Papers, Hopkins-Ward folder, RIHS; Analysis of E. Brown's Proposal, 13 Mar., Brown Papers, P-P6, Brown University. 1768: Negotiations, 5 Mar. to 24 Mar., Moses Brown Papers, Hopkins-Ward folder, RIHS; Moses Brown to Browns, 3 Mar., Miscellaneous, Brown Papers; 1 Apr. 1768 and 11 Apr. 1768, Brown Papers, P-P6; Negotiations, 1 Apr., John Brown Papers, RIHS; Elisha Brown to Samuel Ward, 18 Apr., Ward Papers, RIHS.

61. Lovejoy, *Rhode Island Politics*, 49–51, 82–83, 100–102; "ZY," *Newport Mercury*, 23 Apr. 1764; "OZ," *Newport Mercury*, 11 Mar. 1765 and 18 Mar. 1765.

62. *RICR*, 7:333

ELEVEN: Native Americans, the Plan of 1764, and a British Empire That Never Was

1. The text of the Plan of 1764 is printed in E. B. O'Callaghan and B. Fernow, eds., *Documents Relative to the Colonial History of the State of New York*, 15 vols. (Albany, 1853–87) (hereafter cited as *NYCD*), 7:637–641. Preliminary versions of this paper were presented at a University of Western Ontario History Department Seminar, 9 Nov. 2001; the Charles M. Andrews Symposium at Johns Hopkins University, 28 Sept. 2002; and the University of Minnesota Early American History Workshop, 8 May 2003. The author thanks the participants in those discussions and especially Brendan McConville, Andrew Miller, and Jean O'Brien for their comments.

2. The heading "An Uneasy Connection" is used with thanks to Jack P. Greene, "An Uneasy Connection: An Analysis of the Preconditions of the American Revolution," in *Essays on the American Revolution*, ed. Stephen G. Kurtz and James H. Hutson, 32–80 (Chapel Hill, 1973). William Johnson's quote is from *NYCD*, 8:84.

3. E. B. O'Callaghan, ed., *The Documentary History of the State of New-York*, vol. 2 (Albany, 1850), 454–455 (hereafter cited as *NYDH*).

4. William L. McDowell, Jr., ed., *Documents Relating to Indian Affairs, 1754–1765* (Columbia, SC, 1970), 357 (quotation); Kathryn E. Holland Braund, *Deerskins and Duffels: Creek Indian Trade with Anglo-America, 1685–1815* (Lincoln, NE, 1993), 103–108; J. Russell Snapp, *John Stuart and the Struggle for Empire on the Southern Frontier* (Baton Rouge, 1996), 54–67.

5. *NYDH*, 455.

6. Gregory Evans Dowd, *War under Heaven: Pontiac, the Indian Nations, and the British Empire* (Baltimore, 2002), while taking a more critical perspective on British policy than that offered here, agrees that basic structural questions concerning the British Empire were at the heart of this conflict (quotation from p. 1.)

7. [Robert Navarre?], *Journal of Pontiac's Conspiracy*, ed. M. Agnes Burton, trans. R. C. Ford (Detroit, [1912]), 28–30; Gregory Evans Dowd, *A Spirited Resistance: The North American Indian Struggle for Unity, 1745–1815* (Baltimore, 1992), 23–46.

8. Samuel Hazard, ed., *Minutes of the Provincial Council of Pennsylvania, from the Organization to the Termination of the Proprietary Government* (Harrisburg and Philadelphia, 1838–52), 7:269, 766–767; John W. Jordan, ed., "Journal of James Kenny, 1761–1763," *Pennsylvania Magazine of History and Biography* 37 (1913): 12–13; James Sullivan et al., eds., *The Papers of Sir William Johnson* (Albany, 1921–65), 4:95 (quotation) (hereafter cited as *JP*).

9. Anthony F. C. Wallace, *King of the Delawares: Teedyuscung, 1700–1763* (Philadelphia, 1949), 258–266; Ian K. Steele, *Warpaths: Invasions of North America* (New York, 1994), 234–242; Woody Holton, *Forced Founders: Indians, Debtors, Slaves, and the Making of the American Revolution in Virginia* (Chapel Hill, 1999), 138–139; Howard H. Peckham, *Pontiac and the Indian Uprising* (Princeton, 1947), 130–220. Circumstantial evidence suggests that the arsonists worked for the Connecticut-based Susquehanna Company, which, in defiance of Pennsylvania and the Crown, asserted a claim to land in the area. Within two weeks of the crime, settlers sponsored by the company had

taken up residence at Wyoming (Daniel K. Richter, *Facing East from Indian Country: A Native History of Early America* [Cambridge, MA, 2001], 191–201).

10. [Navarre?], *Journal of Pontiac's Conspiracy,* 38.

11. *JP,* 3:529–535.

12. Ibid., 3:515 (quotation), 597–598.

13. Michael N. McConnell, *A Country Between: The Upper Ohio Valley and Its Peoples, 1724–1774* (Lincoln, NE, 1992), 161–163; Richard White, *The Middle Ground: Indians, Empires, and Republics in the Great Lakes Region, 1650–1815* (Cambridge, 1991), 256–268.

14. *JP,* 3:515.

15. Ibid., 10:634 (quotation), 648–649; McConnell, *Country Between,* 159–181.

16. Fred Anderson, *Crucible of War: The Seven Years' War and the Fate of Empire in British North America, 1754–1766* (New York, 2000), 534; Jane T. Merritt, *At the Crossroads: Indians and Empires on a Mid-Atlantic Frontier, 1700–1763* (Chapel Hill, 2003), 176–180.

17. White, *Middle Ground,* 142–185; Patricia Galloway, "'The Chief Who Is Your Father': Choctaw and French Views of the Diplomatic Relation," in *Powhatan's Mantle: Indians in the Colonial Southeast,* ed. Peter H. Wood, Gregory A. Waselkov, and M. Thomas Hatley (Lincoln, NE, 1989), 254–255.

18. Alexander Henry, *Travels and Adventures in Canada and the Indian Territories between the Years 1760 and 1776,* ed. James Bain (New York, 1901), 43–45 (quotation); Bruce M. White, "'Give Us a Little Milk': The Social and Cultural Meanings of Gift Giving in the Lake Superior Fur Trade," *Minnesota History* 48 (1982): 65.

19. *JP,* 4:62.

20. Ibid., 3:721–722.

21. Ibid., 4:134.

22. *NYDH,* 447–448.

23. For examples, see *NYDH,* 459–460; *JP,* 5:490–491; and *NYCD,* 7:868–870.

24. *JP,* 5:762.

25. John Shy, *Toward Lexington: The Role of the British Army in the Coming of the American Revolution* (Princeton, 1965), 122–135, 192–204, quotations from p. 122.

26. See, for just one example, the plan outlined to Johnson by John Christopher Hartwick in Jan. 1756, *NYCD,* 4:294–295.

27. On 1 July 1763, Johnson wrote to the Board of Trade about the attacks on British posts in the Great Lakes and Ohio countries. His message was evidently received in mid- to late September and acknowledged in a return letter of 29 Sept. (*NYCD,* 7:567). The Proclamation, issued on 7 Oct., arrived in New York City on 30 Nov. (*JP,* 4:255–266).

28. *JP,* 10:977–984, quotation from p. 977.

29. *JP,* 10:982–983 (quotations); R. A. Humphreys, "Lord Shelburne and the Proclamation of 1763," *English Historical Review* 49 (1934): 246–247, 259–260.

30. *JP,* 5:547–548, 737; *NYDH,* 517–518.

31. Holton, *Forced Founders,* 3–38.

32. *NYCD,* 7:881.

33. Ibid., 7:836; *JP,* 5:375, 737; William A. Russ, Jr., *How Pennsylvania Acquired Its Present Boundaries,* Pennsylvania Historical Studies, no. 8 (University Park, PA, 1966), 12–26; David L. Preston, "Squatters, Indians, Proprietary Government, and Land in the

Susquehanna Valley," in *Friends and Enemies in Penn's Woods: Indians, Colonists, and the Racial Construction of Pennsylvania,* ed. William A. Pencak and Daniel K. Richter (University Park, PA, 2004), 199.

34. Francis Jennings, *Empire of Fortune: Crowns, Colonies, and Tribes in the Seven Years War in America* (New York, 1988), 101–108.

35. *NYCD,* 7:849–850, 891–892; Sung Bok Kim, *Landlord and Tenant in Colonial New York: Manorial Society, 1664–1775* (Chapel Hill, 1978), 281–415.

36. *NYCD,* 7:930–941,

37. Ibid., 7:671–674; Georgianna C. Nammack, *Fraud, Politics, and the Dispossession of the Indians: The Iroquois Land Frontier in the Colonial Period* (Norman, OK, 1969).

38. *NYCD,* 7:873–874.

39. Marjoleine Kars, *Breaking Loose Together: The Regulator Rebellion in Pre-Revolutionary North Carolina* (Chapel Hill, 2002), 27–54; Merritt, *At the Crossroads,* 19–49, 171–172; Preston, "Squatters, Indians, Proprietary Government, and Land," 180–200.

40. Daniel K. Richter, *The Ordeal of the Longhouse: The Peoples of the Iroquois League in the Era of European Colonization* (Chapel Hill, 1992), 137–138, 250–254, 263–265.

41. Verner W. Crane, *The Southern Frontier, 1670–1732* (1928; repr. New York, 1981), 120–154; Braund, *Deerskins and Duffels,* 81–100.

42. For examples see McDowell, ed., *Documents Relating to Indian Affairs,* 566–569, 576–579.

43. W. J. Eccles, *France in America* (New York, 1972), 119–120; Eccles, "The Fur Trade and Western Imperialism," *William and Mary Quarterly,* 3rd ser., 40 (1983): 341–362; White, *Middle Ground,* 108–119.

44. *JP,* 4:443–444.

45. Ibid., 10:983–984; Braund, *Deerskins and Duffles,* 100–102.

46. McConnell, *Country Between,* 43–45, 148–150, 161–163. Particularly under legislation passed in 1722, Pennsylvania attempted to license traders in a way similar to South Carolina's system. But a lack of enforcement mechanisms, along with an explicit exemption that allowed any Euro-American to trade with Indians from his own house, made the effort a virtual dead letter. See Albright G. Zimmerman, "The Indian Trade of Colonial Pennsylvania" (PhD diss., University of Delaware, 1966), 179–204.

47. *NYCD,* 7:560–561, 674.

48. McDowell, ed., *Documents Relating to Indian Affairs,* 481; John Smolenski, "The Death of Sawantaeny and the Problem of Justice on the Frontier," and Louis Waddell, "Justice, Retribution and the Case of John Toby," in Pencak and Richter, eds., *Friends and Enemies,* 104–143.

49. G. S. Rowe, "The Frederick Stump Affair, 1768, and Its Challenge to Legal Historians of Early Pennsylvania," *Pennsylvania History* 49 (1982): 259–288; Alden T. Vaughan, "Frontier Banditti and the Indians: The Paxton Boys' Legacy, 1763–1775," *Pennsylvania History* 51 (1984): 19–22; Linda A. Ries, "'The Rage of Opposing Government': The Stump Affair of 1768," *Cumberland County History,* 1, no. 1 (Summer 1984): 21–45.

50. *JP,* 5:201.

51. *NYCD,* 7:877.

52. Ibid., 7:842.

53. *JP,* 4:79; *NYCD,* 7:661–666, 976.

54. *NYCD,* 7:968.

55. Ibid., 7:668.

56. *JP,* 5:319–320, 336; *NYCD,* 8:30.

57. *NYCD,* 7:634–635.

58. Ibid., 7:637–638.

59. Ibid., 7:638–639.

60. To my knowledge, no systematic comparison of British policies in South Asia and North America in the 1760s has ever been undertaken, but for an introduction to the issues involved on the subcontinent see Rajat Kanta Ray, "Indian Society and the Establishment of British Supremacy, 1765–1818," in *The Oxford History of the British Empire,* ed. P. J. Marshall, 2:508–529 (Oxford, 1998).

61. *NYCD,* 7:640–641.

62. Ibid., 7:637, 639–641.

63. Ibid., 7:638, 641.

64. Ibid., 7:661–666, quotation from p. 663.

65. Clarence E. Carter, ed., "Observations of Superintendent John Stuart and Governor James Grant of East Florida on the Proposed Plan of 1764 for the Future Management of Indian Affairs," *American Historical Review* 20 (1915): 817–827, quotations from pp. 817, 820.

66. Snapp, *John Stuart and the Struggle for Empire,* 68–107.

67. Dorothy V. Jones, *License for Empire: Colonialism by Treaty in Early America* (Chicago, 1982), 42–52.

68. *JP,* 4:466–481, 485–488, 503–508, 526–533, 547–549, 579–583; *NYCD,* 7:652–653, 750–758; McConnell, *A Country Between,* 196–206; Anderson, *Crucible of War,* 617–637.

69. *NYCD,* 7:746–747.

70. Ibid., 7:838.

71. *JP,* 4:339, 396.

72. *NYCD,* 7:747–748, 842 (first quotation); *JP,* 5:1–5, 566–567 (second quotation); Sosin, *Whitehall and the Wilderness,* 73–98, 128–169.

73. *NYCD,* 7:880–882.

74. Ibid., 7:877–878, 915 (quotation).

75. Edmund S. and Helen M. Morgan, *The Stamp Act Crisis: Prologue to Revolution,* rev. paperback ed. (New York, 1963), 217–230; Kars, *Breaking Loose Together,* 46.

76. *NYCD,* 7:914.

77. Ibid., 7:881.

78. *JP,* 6:61.

79. *NYCD,* 7:981–983, quotation from p. 981; 8:7.

80. Ibid., 8:19–31, 57–58, quotations from pp. 22–23.

81. Ibid., 8:24–25, 31

82. Ibid., 7:637. If it had been passed, this provision of the Plan of 1764 would have been a major constitutional innovation, in overturning laws that had long since been approved by the Crown and in its assertion of a Parliamentary, rather than Crown, veto power. The Currency Act of 1764, by comparison, only banned *future* provincial emissions of paper money, and did nothing to call into question legislation that had previously passed without veto (Danby Pickering, ed., *Statutes at Large* [Cambridge, 1762–1869], 26:103–105).

83. Moncure Daniel Conway, ed., *The Writings of Thomas Paine* (New York, 1894), 1:100 (quotation); Edward Countryman, "Indians, The Colonial Order, and the Social

Significance of the American Revolution," *William and Mary Quarterly*, 3rd ser., 53 (1996): 342–362; Holton, *Forced Founders*, 35–38.

TWELVE: Between Private and Public Spheres

I wish to express my gratitude to the Virginia Historical Society for a fellowship, and to Saint Louis University for a Mellon grant, to research this essay.

1. Gordon S. Wood, *The Creation of the American Republic, 1776–1787* (New York, 1969), 59.
2. Jack P. Greene, *All Men Are Created Equal: Some Reflections on the Character of the American Revolution*, (Oxford, 1976), reprinted in *Imperatives, Behaviors, and Identities: Essays in Early American Cultural History* (Charlottesville, 1992), 238.
3. Christopher Grasso, *A Speaking Aristocracy: Transforming Public Discourse in Eighteenth-Century Connecticut* (Chapel Hill, 1999), 14. See also Edward M. Cook, *The Fathers of the Towns: Leadership and Community Structure in Eighteenth-Century New England* (Baltimore, 1976).
4. Quoted in Jack P. Greene, "Social Structure and Political Behavior in Revolutionary America: An Analysis of John Day's *Remarks on American Affairs*," in *Understanding the American Revolution: Issues and Actors* (Charlottesville, 1995), 122.
5. Charles Beard, *An Economic Interpretation of the Constitution of the United States* (New York, 1913), 17.
6. Louis Hartz, "A Theory of the Development of New Societies," in *The Founding of New Societies: Studies in the History of the United States, Latin America, South Africa, Canada, and Australia*, ed. Louis Hartz (New York, 1964).
7. Gordon S. Wood, *The Radicalism of the American Revolution* (New York, 1991).
8. Michal J. Rozbicki, *The Complete Colonial Gentleman: Cultural Legitimacy in Plantation America* (Charlottesville, 1998), 28–75. See also John Gilman Kolp, *Gentlemen and Freeholders: Electoral Politics in Colonial Virginia* (Baltimore, 1998).
9. On this and the following pages I rely on a number of insights from Zygmunt Bauman's theory of the sociogenesis of freedom. See Zygmunt Bauman, *Freedom* (Minneapolis, 1988).
10. R. W. Davis, "Series Foreword," in *Devising Liberty: Preserving and Creating Freedom in the New American Republic*, ed. David T. Konig, vi (Stanford, 1995).
11. John Phillip Reid, *The Concept of Liberty in the Age of the American Revolution* (Chicago, 1988), 45.
12. J. William Harris, *Plain Folk and Gentry in a Slave Society: White Liberty and Black Slavery in Augusta's Hinterlands* (Middletown, CT, 1985), 10.
13. Howard R. Temperley, "Jefferson and Slavery: A Study in Moral Perplexity," in *Reason and Republicanism: Thomas Jefferson's Legacy of Liberty*, ed. Gary L. McDowell and Sharon L. Noble, 85 (Lanham, MD, 1997).
14. Wylie Sypher, "Hutcheson and the 'Classical' Theory of Slavery," *Journal of Negro History* 24 (1939): 271.
15. Peter C. Hoffer, *Law and People in Colonial America* (Baltimore, 1992), 115.
16. Michael Zuckerman, "Rhetoric, Reality, and the Revolution: The Genteel Radicalism of Gordon Wood," *William and Mary Quarterly*, 3rd ser., 51 (1994): 698.
17. Joyce Appleby, *Capitalism and a New Social Order: The Republican Vision of the 1790s* (New York, 1984), 102.

18. Wood, *Creation,* 615.

19. Leonard Levy, *Jefferson and Civil Liberties: The Darker Side* (Cambridge, MA, 1963; repr. Chicago, 1989), 171.

20. Leonard Levy, *Origins of the Bill of Rights* (New Haven, 1999), 5.

21. Hartz, "A Theory of the Development of New Societies," 73.

22. Henry Parker, *An Answer to a Paper* (1651), quoted in Richard Tuck, *Natural Rights Theories: Their Origin and Development* (Cambridge, 1979), 151. On passive rights, see Tuck, *Natural Rights Theories,* 5–6.

23. Samuel Adams to James Warren, 4 Nov. 1775, in *Letters of Delegates to Congress: 1774–1789,* ed. Paul H. Smith, 2:299 (Washington, DC, 1976).

24. John Pym, "The Speech or Declaration of John Pym," in *The Struggle for Sovereignty: Seventeenth-Century English Political Tracts,* ed. Joyce L. Malcolm, 39 (Indianapolis, 1999).

25. *An Essay upon the Government of the English Plantations on the Continent of America* (1701), ed. Louis B. Wright (San Marino, CA, 1945), 21.

26. Richard Henry Lee's draft "Address to the People of Great Britain and Ireland," 11–18 Oct. 1774, in Smith, *Letters of Delegates,* 1:174; and his "Draft Address to the King," *Letters of Delegates,* 1:226.

27. "General Laws and Liberties of New Hampshire," in *Colonial Origins of the American Constitution: A Documentary History,* ed. Donald S. Lutz, 18–19 (Indianapolis, 1998).

28. Quoted in Perez Zagorin, *A History of Political Thought in the English Revolution* (London, 1954), 37.

29. Lutz, *Colonial Origins,* 377.

30. On the class origin of such concepts, see E. P. Thompson, *Customs in Common: Studies in Traditional Popular Culture* (New York, 1993), 17.

31. Pierre Bourdieu, *Distinction: A Social Critique of the Judgment of Taste,* trans. Edward Nice (Cambridge, MA, 1984), 68.

32. Bernard Bailyn, *The Ideological Origins of the American Revolution,* enlarged ed. (Cambridge, MA, 1992), 378. On the link between property and liberty, see Reid, *Concept of Liberty,* 68–73.

33. Arthur Lee to Dr. Theodorick Bland, 21 Aug. 1770, Bland Family MSS, Virginia Historical Society, Richmond, VA.

34. [Carter Braxton], "An Address to the Convention of the Colony and Ancient Dominion of Virginia" (1776), in *American Political Writing during the Founding Era, 1760–1805,* ed. Charles S. Hyneman and Donald S. Lutz, 1:334 (Indianapolis, 1983). On preferment see also Samuel West, "On the Right to Rebel against Governors," (Boston, 1776), in Hyneman and Lutz,1:443.

35. "The Tribune," *South Carolina Gazette* (6 Oct. 1776), in Hyneman and Lutz, *American Political Writing,* 1:95.

36. John Keane, *Tom Paine: A Political Life* (Boston, 1995), 178–179.

37. In J. R. Pole, ed., *The American Constitution: For and Against: The Federalist and Anti-Federalist Papers* (New York, 1987), 86, 93. The author is thought to be the framer and non-signer of the Constitution, John Francis Mercer.

38. William Byrd II to Peter Beckford, 6 Dec. 1735, in *The Correspondence of the Three William Byrds of Westover, Virginia, 1684–1776,* ed. Marion Tinling, 2:464 (Charlottesville,1977).

39. George Mason to George Mercer, 2 Oct. 1778, *The Virginia Historical Register* 1 (1848): 30.

40. Lester C. Olson, *Emblems of American Community in the Revolutionary Era: A Study in Rhetorical Iconology* (Washington, DC, 1991), 247, 72–123; Benjamin Franklin to Richard Howe, 20 July 1776, Cooper MSS, The Huntington Library, San Marino, CA.

41. Michal J. Rozbicki, "The Curse of Provincialism: Negative Perceptions of Colonial American Plantation Gentry," *Journal of Southern History* 63 (1997): 737–743.

42. Samuel Johnson, "Taxation No Tyranny," in *The Yale Edition of the Works of Samuel Johnson*, ed. Donald J. Greene, 10:413–454 (New Haven and London, 1958–90).

43. [James Macpherson], *The Rights of Great Britain Asserted against the Claims of America: Being an Answer to the Declaration of the General Congress* (London, 1776), 11.

44. Edmund Jenings to Robert Beverley, 9 Apr. 1766, Edmund Jenings MSS, Virginia Historical Society.

45. Bailyn, *Ideological Origins*, 307.

46. Hans Georg Gadamer, *Truth and Method*, trans. William Glen-Doepel (London, 1979), 245.

47. John Selden, *De Jure Naturali et Gentium* (1640), quoted in Tuck, *Natural Rights Theories*, 91.

48. May 1754, *The Letters of Horace Walpole, Earl of Orford* (London, 1840), 2:5.

49. Quoted in Jack P. Greene, ed., *The Nature of Colony Constitutions: Two Pamphlets on the Wilkes Fund Controversy in South Carolina* (Columbia, SC, 1970), 19 (Laurens), 186 (Lee).

50. To George Washington, 26 July 1775, in Smith, *Letters of Delegates*, 1:669.

51. Christopher Hill, *God's Englishman: Oliver Cromwell and the English Revolution* (New York, 1970), 262–265.

52. J. R. Pole, *The Pursuit of Equality in American History* (Berkeley, 1978), 52.

53. François Furet, *Interpreting the French Revolution*, trans. Elborg Forster (Cambridge, 1981), 54.

54. Bauman, *Freedom*, 29.

55. Jefferson to William Smith, 13 Nov. 1787, in *The Writings of Thomas Jefferson*, ed. Paul L. Ford, 4:466 (New York, 1894).

56. Gouverneur Morris to John Penn, 20 May 1774, in *American Archives: Consisting of a Collection of Authentick Records, State Papers, Debates, and Letters and Other Notices of Publick Affairs* . . . , ed. Peter Force, 1:342–343 (Washington, DC, 1837–46).

57. Roy Porter, "The Enlightenment in England," in *The Enlightenment in National Context*, ed. Roy Porter and Mikulas Teich, 11 (New York, 1981).

58. Theophilus Parsons, "The Essex Result" (Newbury, MA, 1778), in Hyneman and Lutz, *American Political Writing*, 1:490–491.

59. Israel Evans, "A Sermon Delivered at Concord" (1791), in *Political Sermons of the American Founding Era, 1730–1805*, ed. Ellis Sandoz, 2:1071 (Indianapolis, 1998); *The Worcester Speculator, Worcester Magazine* (Oct. 1787), in Hyneman and Lutz, *American Political Writing*, 1:700.

60. Theodorick Bland to Theodorick Bland, Sr., n.d., *The Bland Papers: Being a Selection from the Manuscripts of Colonel Theodorick Bland, Jr.*, ed. Charles Campbell, 1:17 (Petersburg, VA, 1840–42).

61. "The Farmer," 2 Mar. 1788, in Pole, *American Constitution*, 93, 95.

62. John Adams to John Sullivan, 26 May 1776, in Smith, *Letters of Delegates*, 4:74.

63. Wood, *Creation*, 59, 179.

64. "The Federal Farmer," 12 Oct. 1787, in Pole, *American Constitution*, 32.

65. Pendleton to Carter Braxton, 12 May 1776, *The Letters and Papers of Edmund Pendleton, 1734–1803*, ed. David J. Mays (Charlottesville, 1967), 177; *Daily Advertiser* (New York, 17 Oct. 1787), in *Friends of the Constitution: Writings of the "Other" Federalists, 1787–1788*, ed. Colleen A. Sheehan and Gary L. McDowell, 323 (Indianapolis, 1998).

66. Jonathan Edwards, "The Necessity of the Belief of Christianity," (Hartford, 1794), in Sandoz, *Political Sermons*, 2:1215–1216.

67. Edmund Pendleton, "Address to the Virginia Ratification Convention," in Mays, *Letters and Papers of Edmund Pendleton*, 520–521. See also Reid, *Concept of Liberty*, 116–117.

68. Melancton Smith, "Speech at the New York Ratifying Convention" (1788), in Pole, *American Constitution*, 102, 84–85.

69. Elizur Goodrich, "A Sermon Preached Before His Excellency Samuel Huntington" (Hartford, 1778), in Sandoz, *Political Sermons*, 1:920; Noah Webster, "The Revolution in France" (New York, 1794), in *Political Sermons*, 2:1289.

70. Quoted in Wood, *Radicalism*, 282, 366.

71. The Preceptor, "Social Duties of the Political Kind," *Massachusetts Spy*, Boston (21 May 1772), in Hyneman and Lutz, *American Political Writing*, 1:179, 181.

72. On how the meaning of the revolutionary abstractions of liberty "thickened" during the early nineteenth century, see the excellent study by Joyce Appleby, *Inheriting the Revolution: The First Generation of Americans* (Cambridge, MA, 2000).

73. Quoted in Gary B. Nash, *The Urban Crucible: The Northern Seaports and the Origin of the American Revolution* (Cambridge, MA, 1986), 101; essay by "Crito," *Providence Gazette and Country Journal*, 6 Oct. 1787, in Sheehan and McDowell, *Friends of the Constitution*, 446–447. For a superb discussion of the legal and constitutional side of the republican experimentation with rights, see Jack N. Rakove, "Parchment Barriers and the Politics of Rights," in *A Culture of Rights: The Bill of Rights in Philosophy, Politics, and Law, 1791 and 1991*, ed. Michael J. Lacey and Knud Haakonssen, 98–143 (Cambridge, 1991).

74. William Ellery to Francis Dana, 3 Dec. 1783, in Smith, *Letters of Delegates*, 2:178; David Osgood, "The Wonderful Works of God," in Sandoz, *Political Sermons*, 2:1233. See also Pole, *Pursuit of Equality*, 58.

75. Rutledge and Parsons quoted in Reid, *Concept of Liberty*, 121; David Humphreys et al., *The Anarchiad: A New England Poem*, ed. Luther G. Riggs (Gainesville, FL, 1967), 29–30.

76. Goodrich in Sandoz, *Political Sermons*, 1:927; Webster in Sandoz, *Political Sermons*, 2:1233.

77. Pierre Bourdieu, *Language and Symbolic Power*, ed. John B. Thompson, trans. Gino Raymond and Matthew Adamson (Cambridge, MA, 1991), 238. See also Wood, *Creation*, 471–518.

78. Wood, *Radicalism*, 187.

79. Paul D. Escott and Jeffrey J. Crow, "The Social Order and Violent Disorder: An Analysis of North Carolina in the Revolution and the Civil War," *Journal of Southern History* 52 (1986): 385.

80. Hoffer, *Law and People,* 123.

81. Edmund S. Morgan, *American Slavery, American Freedom: The Ordeal of Colonial Virginia* (New York, 1975), 4, 387.

82. Morgan, *American Slavery,* 368.

83. Appleby, *Capitalism,* 21, 17–19, 22, 21.

84. See Wood, *Creation,* 486–487.

85. Richard Henry Lee to Landon Carter[?], 19 Aug. 1777, in Smith, *Letters of Delegates,* 7:514; Nathaniel Peabody to Josiah Bartlett, 17 Aug. 1779, in Smith, *Letters of Delegates,* 13:384.

86. See, for instance, Jefferson to Adams, 28 Oct. 1813, in *The Adams-Jefferson Letters: The Complete Correspondence between Thomas Jefferson and Abigail and John Adams,* ed. Lester J. Cappon, 2:338–339 (Chapel Hill, 1959).

87. On eighteenth-century British understanding of the rights of the poor, see Michal Rozbicki, "To Save Them from Themselves: Proposals to Enslave the British Poor, 1698–1755," *Slavery and Abolition* 22, (2001): 27–50.

88. Porter, "The Enlightenment in England," 8–9.

89. Wood, *Radicalism,* 230.

Contributors

James M. Baird (Ph.D., The Johns Hopkins University, 1999) is an independent scholar. He is the author of "Between Slavery and Independence: Power Relations between Dependent White Men and Their Superiors in Late Colonial and Early National Virginia, with Particular Reference to the Overseer-Employer Relationship" (Ph.D. dissertation, The Johns Hopkins University, 1999).

Edward M. Cook, Jr. (Ph.D., The Johns Hopkins University, 1972) is a member of the History department at the University of Chicago. He is the author of *The Fathers of the Towns: Leadership and Community Structure in Eighteenth-Century New England.*

S. Max Edelson (Ph.D., The Johns Hopkins University, 1998) is Assistant Professor of History at the University of Illinois at Urbana–Champaign. A former director of the Carolina Lowcountry and the Atlantic World Program at the College of Charleston, he has written several essays on the history and culture of the Lower South in an Atlantic context. His forthcoming book examines planters, environment, and the development of South Carolina's plantation landscape.

Daniel C. Littlefield (Ph.D., The Johns Hopkins University, 1977) is Carolina Professor of History at the University of South Carolina. He is the author of *Revolutionary Citizens: African Americans, 1776–1804* and *Rice and Slaves: Ethnicity and the Slave Trade in Colonial South Carolina.*

James E. McWilliams (Ph.D., The Johns Hopkins University, 2001) is Assistant Professor of History at Texas State University, San Marcos. He is the author of *A Revolution in Eating: How the Quest for Food Shaped America* and *Puritan Pioneers: The Persistence of Economic Behavior in Seventeenth-Century Massachusetts,* both forthcoming. His work has appeared in the *New England Quarterly* and the *Journal of Interdisciplinary History.*

James H. Merrell (Ph.D., The Johns Hopkins University, 1982) is the Lucy Maynard Salmon Professor of History at Vassar College. He is the author of *The Indians' New World: Catawbas and Their Neighbors from European Contact through the Era of Removal* and *Into the American Woods: Negotiators on the Pennsylvania Frontier.*

Robert Olwell (Ph.D., The Johns Hopkins University, 1991) is Associate Professor of History at the University of Texas, Austin. He is the author of *Masters, Slaves, and Subjects: The Cultures of Power in the South Carolina Low Country, 1740–1790,* and is currently at work on a study of British colonial enterprise and imperial imagination in Florida, 1763–1783.

Daniel K. Richter (Ph.D., Columbia University, 1984) is the Richard S. Dunn Director of the McNeil Center for Early American Studies and Professor of History at the University of Pennsylvania. He is author of *The Ordeal of the Longhouse: The Peoples of the Iroquois League in the Era of European Colonization* and *Facing East from Indian Country: A Native History of Early America.*

Michal Jan Rozbicki (Ph.D., University of Warsaw, 1984) is Associate Professor of History at Saint Louis University. His most recent book is *The Complete Colonial Gentleman: Cultural Legitimacy in Plantation America.*

Jean B. Russo (Ph.D., The Johns Hopkins University, 1983) is associate general editor of the *Archives of Maryland Online* for the Maryland State Archives and historian for the Historic Annapolis Foundation. She is the editor, with Mark B. Letzer, of *The Diary of William Faris: The Daily Life of an Annapolis Silversmith.*

Alan Tully (Ph.D., The Johns Hopkins University, 1973) is Professor of History and Department Chair at the University of Texas, Austin. He is the author of *Forming American Politics: Ideals, Interests, and Institutions in Colonial New York and Pennsylvania* and "Colonial Politics" in Daniel Vickers, ed., *A Companion to Colonial America.*

Robert M. Weir (Ph.D., Case Western Reserve University, 1966) is Professor Emeritus of History at the University of South Carolina. His publications include *Colonial South Carolina: A History* and *"The Last of American Freeman": Studies in the Political Culture of the Colonial and Revolutionary South,* as well as other essays.

Bradford J. Wood (Ph.D., The Johns Hopkins University, 1999) teaches at Eastern Kentucky University. He is the author of *This Remote Part of the World: Regional Formation in Lower Cape Fear, North Carolina, 1725–1775*, which won the Hines Prize from the Carolina Lowcountry and the Atlantic World Program. He has also published several articles on the Carolinas during the eighteenth century.

Natalie Zacek (Ph.D., The Johns Hopkins University, 2000) is Lecturer in History and American Studies at the University of Manchester. She has published several articles on the history of the English colonies in the West Indies, and has just completed a monograph entitled *In the Kingdom of I: Conflict and Community in a British American World, 1670–1770* (forthcoming).

Index